Essays on Classical Rhetoric and Modern Discourse

Edited by
Robert J. Connors,
Lisa S. Ede, and
Andrea A. Lunsford

Southern Illinois University Press
Carbondale and Edwardsville

Library of Congress Cataloging in Publication Data

Main entry under title:

Essays on classical rhetoric and modern discourse.

   Bibliography: p.
   1. Rhetoric, Ancient—Addresses, essays, lectures. 2. English
language—Rhetoric—Addresses, essays, lectures. I. Connors,
Robert J., 1951–   . II. Ede, Lisa S., 1947–   .
III. Lunsford, Andrea A., 1942–   .
PN175.E84   1984   808   82–14718
ISBN 0–8093–1133–X
ISBN 0–8093–1134–8 (pbk.)

87 86 85 84   4 3 2 1

Frontispiece: Edward P. J. Corbett
(Photograph by Charles B. Wheeler)

Contents

Preface

The last thirty years have seen an evolution in the teaching of written discourse so profound as almost to deserve the title of a revolution. From being, as I. A. Richards said in 1936, the dreariest part of a college education, rhetoric has become one of the most vital and exciting areas of study within departments of English. Each year brings new insights and better methods to the study and teaching of writing, and it now seems certain that rhetorical studies will be at the heart of the English curriculum of the future. We seem, indeed, to be witnessing the rebirth of rhetoric in departments of English.

One of the primary elements in this rebirth is the rediscovery by composition scholars of the tradition of classical rhetoric. This classical tradition, over twenty-five hundred years old and composed of theorists as divergent as Plato and Quintilian, had been nurtured in departments of speech after English departments rejected rhetoric in the early part of this century and only relatively recently has classical rhetoric come again to be an informing principle for the study of written—as opposed to oral—discourse. It was English departments' misfortune that classical doctrines were lost to them for so long, as we are learning now. Scholars investigating written discourse and teachers of writing are being aided immeasurably by the classical rhetorical tradition, which as the most completely developed body of rhetorical theory provides a touchstone against which all other theory and practice can be measured.

There are several scholars in the last thirty years who might without irony be called Promethean figures, men who are responsible for the reintroduction of classical theory into the rhetoric of written discourse:

Richard Weaver, P. Albert Duhamel, Wayne C. Booth. It was Edward P. J. Corbett, though, whose scholarly essays on classical rhetoric most clearly established the connections between rhetoric and writing, and whose seminal textbook *Classical Rhetoric for the Modern Student* gave teachers of composition methods grounded in classical theory that had been lost to them for decades. More than any other single figure, Mr. Corbett made classical rhetoric accessible and important to a whole generation of scholars and teachers, and for that reason we wished to honor him with this collection of essays.

There are some in academic life who compel respect by the sheer force of their achievements. Deeply involved in scholarship, these academic giants contribute in essential ways to the life of their disciplines, but they sometimes have difficulty reaching beyond the theories and analyses to the human context that must give all our knowledge meaning. A few great scholars, however, combine great professional achievement with a humanity so modest and simple that it touches and inspires every person who comes into contact with them. They are the teachers who show by example as well as by precept, who give their students lessons in decency and humility along with the classroom facts and methods. They are the scholars who inspire others by their generosity and support as well as by their insights. Edward P. J. Corbett is one of these rare people.

In our professional lives we hear a great deal said about "respecting people's work" and not so much said about respecting people. As the profession grows and the work becomes more specialized, we sometimes lose sight of the person behind the words, of the personal context behind the process. So it is with great happiness that we can present these essays to Edward P. J. Corbett, not merely as fugitive pieces from "colleagues" and "acquaintances," but as a specially written tribute from his friends. Genius may compel respect and achievement admiration. Nothing can compel love. In these essays we hope that Mr. Corbett will see both the respect his achievements compel and the love that his friends feel for a man who truly exemplifies Quintilian's definition of a rhetorician: *vir bonus dicendi peritus* —"a good man, skilled in speaking."

Notes on Contributors

ANNETTE NORRIS BRADFORD is currently employed by IBM Corporation, Kingston, New York, where she works in Information Development writing tutorials for IBM products. She received her B.A. and M.A. in English from Auburn University and her Ph.D. from Rensselaer Polytechnic Institute in 1982. She has published on a variety of subjects including: cognitive immaturity and basic writers, self-regulating speech, the teaching of technical writing, rhetoric, and photo-illustration and communication graphics.

ROBERT J. CONNORS is Assistant Professor and Director of the English Writing Laboratory at Louisiana State University, Baton Rouge. He has published articles in *College English, College Composition and Communication, Rhetoric Society Quarterly, Freshman English News, Journal of Technical Writing and Communication,* and *Rhetoric Review.* He is interested in the history and sociology of composition and rhetoric.

FRANK J. D'ANGELO is Professor of English at Arizona State University and the Director of the Ph.D. emphasis in rhetoric and composition. His publications include *A Conceptual Theory of Rhetoric* (1975), *Process and Thought in Composition* (1977), and articles in *College Composition and Communication, Style, Quarterly Journal of Speech, Language and Style, Pre/Text, Journal of Popular Culture, Rhetoric Review, CEA Critic,* and *ADE Bulletin.* He is currently working on a book of theoretical essays that he is coediting with Richard Larson and others. He is also beginning work on a theoretical book tentatively titled "Rhetoric and Cognition: Toward a Metatheory of Discourse."

LISA S. EDE is Coordinator of Composition and Director of the Communication Skills Center at Oregon State University. She has published articles on composition and rhetoric in a number of journals, including *College Composition and Communication, Central States Speech Journal, Rhetoric Review,* and *Freshman English News.*

JOHN T. GAGE is Associate Professor of English and Director of Composition at the University of Oregon. His rhetorical study of modern poetics, *In the Arresting Eye: The Rhetoric of Imagism,* was published in 1981 and his essays on composition and literature have appeared in *College English, Philosophy and Rhetoric, Style, Rhetoric Review, Journal of Advanced Composition, Pacific Coast Philology, Alaska Quarterly Review, Thalia,* and other journals.

SARA GARNES is Assistant Professor of English and Director of the Section of Basic English at Ohio State University. She received an M.A. from the University of Iowa and a Ph.D. in Linguistics from Ohio State. She was the first Director of Ohio State's Writing Workshop, the remedial writing program based on the pioneering research of Andrea Lunsford. She has published articles on basic writing and is involved in research in discourse analysis and speech perception.

JAMES L. GOLDEN is Professor of Communication and Chairman of the Department of Communication at Ohio State University. He is co-author of *The Rhetoric of Blair, Campbell, and Whately* (1968), *The Rhetoric of Black Americans* (1971), and *The Rhetoric of Western Thought* (1976), and has published articles in *Quarterly Journal of Speech, Communication Monographs, Southern Communication Journal,* and *Communication Education.*

RICHARD L. GRAVES is Professor of English Education at Auburn University, and Director of the Sun Belt Writing Project, which is an affiliate of the National Writing Project. He is the editor of *Rhetoric and Composition: A Sourcebook for Teachers* (1976), and has published articles on the teaching of writing in *College Composition and Communication, English Journal, English Education, Phi Delta Kappan,* and other journals. He is interested in rhetorical theory, especially as it relates to the growth and development of writing ability; in the relationship between cognitive processes and writing; and in identifying techniques and strategies for effectively teaching written communication.

S. MICHAEL HALLORAN is Associate Professor of Communication at Rensselaer Polytechnic Institute, where he was awarded the Ph.D. in 1973. His publications have appeared in such journals as *Centennial Review, Central States Speech Journal, College Composition and Communication, College English, Personalist, Philosophy and Rhetoric, Journal of Technical Writing and Communication,* and *Quarterly Journal of Speech.* He is currently working on a history of the rhetorical tradition in America.

NAN JOHNSON is Assistant Professor of English at the University of British Columbia. Her recent publications include "Nineteenth Century Rhetoricians: the Humanist Alternative to Rhetoric as Skills Management," in *The Rhetorical Tradition and Modern Writing,* ed. James J. Murphy (1982). Current research is on the historical and contemporary relationship between rhetorical theory, poetics, and criticism.

JAMES L. KINNEAVY is Professor of English at the University of Texas at Austin. He is the author of *A Theory of Discourse* (1971) and *Aims and Audiences in Writing* (1976). He has published essays in *College English, College Composition and Communication, Rhetoric Society Quarterly,* and *Philosophy and Rhetoric,* and in numerous collections.

RICHARD L. LARSON is Professor of English and Director of the Institute for the Study of Literacy at Herbert Lehman College, CUNY. He is currently editor of *College Composition and Communication.* Professor Larson has published essays in *College English, Rhetoric Society Quarterly, English Leaflet, College Composition and Communication,* and in numerous collections.

JANICE M. LAUER is currently Professor of English and Director of the graduate program in rhetoric and composition at Purdue University; a co-author of *Four Worlds of Writing* (1980); author of articles on invention; member of the Board of Directors of the Rhetoric Society of America; director of an annual national Rhetoric Seminar: Current Theories of Teaching Composition.

ANDREA A. LUNSFORD is Associate Professor of English at the University of British Columbia, where she is also Coordinator of Composition. She is co-author of *Four Worlds of Writing* (1980). He articles have appeared in *College English, College Composition and Communication, Rhetoric Review, McGill Journal of Education,* and other journals.

JAMES C. RAYMOND is Director of Freshman English and an Assistant Dean of the Graduate School at the University of Alabama. His recent publications include *Clear Understandings: A Guide to Legal Writing,* with Ronald L. Goldfarb (1983); *Literacy as a Human Problem,* ed. (1982); *Writing (Is an Unnatural Act)* (1980); and articles in *College English* and *College Composition and Communication.* He is currently working on two additional textbooks and other essays on rhetoric and composition.

DONALD C. STEWART is Professor of English at Kansas State University. His current research interest—nineteenth century American rhetoric—is reflected in several of his recent publications: "Rediscovering Fred Newton Scott, *College English,* January 1979; "Some Facts Worth Knowing About the Origin of Composition Programs," *CEA Critic* , May 1982; "The Nineteenth Century," in *Historical Rhetoric: An Annotated Bibliography of Selected Sources in English,* ed. Winifred Horner (1980); and "The Present State of Scholarship in Nineteenth Century Rhetoric," in *The Present State of Scholarship in Rhetoric,* ed. Winifred Horner (1983).

PATRICIA SULLIVAN received her M.A. in English Literature from St. Louis University in 1975, was an instructor at the University of Wyoming from 1975 to 1980, and is a Ph.D. candidate in Rhetoric at Carnegie-Mellon University. She has published in seventeenth century British rhetoric and in technical writing. Currently, she is assessing the usefulness of empirical methods in the study of rhetorical invention.

LYNN QUITMAN TROYKA is Professor of Writing at Queensborough Community College of the City University of New York. She is also a Research Associate with the CUNY Office of Academic Affairs. She is co-author of *Steps in Composition* (1972) and *Taking Action* (1975), and she is author of *Structured Reading* (1978) and various essays in collections and in professional journals including *College Composition and Communication.* Her present research interests include the assessment of large-scale essay testing and psycholinguistically based relationships between reading and writing.

MERRILL D. WHITBURN is Chairman of the Department of Language, Literature, and Communication at Rensselaer Polytechnic Institute. In 1982–83 he was recipient of a Mina Shaughnessy Scholars Award from the Fund for the Improvement of Postsecondary Education to write a book on academic-industry relations in the field of technical communication. His article "The Plain Style in Scientific and Technical Writing" received a 1981 NCTE Technical and Scientific Writing Award. His other publications include "Ciceronian Rhetoric and the Rise of Science: The Plain Style Reconsidered" (with S. Michael Halloran), "The Conservation of Valued Experience," "A New Direction for English: Synthesis," and "Personality in Scientific and Technical Writing."

GEORGE E. YOOS is Professor of Philosophy at Saint Cloud State University and editor of *Rhetoric Society Quarterly*. He has published essays in *Philosophy and Rhetoric,* the *Quarterly Journal of Speech, College Composition and Communication,* and in several collections.

RICHARD YOUNG is Professor of English and Rhetoric and Head of the English Department at Carnegie-Mellon University, where he has been developing graduate programs in rhetorical studies. He received his Ph.D. in English Language and Literature from the University of Michigan in 1964. From 1964 to 1978 he was a member of the Department of Humanities at Michigan and, for five years, Chairman of the Department. While at Michigan he was also a Research Associate in the Center for Research on Language and Language Behavior, working on problems in rhetoric—particularly on problems associated with discourse structures larger than the sentence and with modern theories of rhetorical invention.

CHARLES ZAROBILA is a Graduate Teaching Associate and Doctoral Candidate in the English Department at Ohio State University. He received his M.A. from Syracuse University and has taught at John Carroll University. His dissertation is on the style of Herman Melville, and he has published in the *Walt Whitman Review* and the *Ohio Journal.*

Essays on Classical Rhetoric and Modern Discourse

1

The Revival of Rhetoric in America

Robert J. Connors, Lisa S. Ede, and
Andrea A. Lunsford

The earliest rhetorical instruction and theory in America were not classical in nature; they were informed not by Aristotle, Cicero, or Quintilian, but by Peter Ramus and Omer Talon. The work of these two curricular reformers, who assigned invention and arrangement to logic and left rhetoric to the study of style and delivery, formed the core of rhetorical instruction at Harvard, the first American university (founded in 1636), whose laws indicated that the primary purpose of rhetoric was to perpetuate the study of Latin and that its primary parts were *elocutio* and *pronunciatio*. Not until well into the eighteenth century did the works of Cicero and Quintilian become widely available—and influential—in colleges.[1] So the first "revival" of classical rhetoric actually took place in eighteenth-century America and can perhaps best be associated with John Ward's *A System of Oratory* (London, 1759), which Warren Guthrie views as the most pervasive synthesis of Greek and Roman theory then available.[2] Ward's book went beyond style and delivery to discuss invention and arrangement as well, hence reuniting the "offices" of classical rhetoric. *A System of Oratory* was widely used until the late eighteenth century, along with the Port Royal *Art of Speaking* (1696), which also demonstrated a more complete classical understanding of the nature and purpose of rhetoric.

We wish to give special thanks to Gary Tate, John Gerber, and Michael Halloran for providing many helpful suggestions and criticisms during the writing of this chapter.

Accompanying this rediscovery of the classical tradition was the growing influence of rhetoric in American colleges. College or university presidents frequently delivered the lectures on rhetoric; in fact, the first American "rhetoric" was written by the president of Princeton, John Witherspoon. And the first Boylston Professor of Rhetoric at Harvard (1806)[3] was John Quincy Adams, future president of the United States, whose *Lectures on Rhetoric and Oratory* (1810) thoroughly restated the classical doctrine.[4]

By the end of the eighteenth century, rhetoric was in full bloom. In a college curriculum which lacked rigid boundaries between subjects, rhetoric fulfilled its classical function as the art of communication, one which synthesized material from a wide variety of fields. The relatively small student bodies allowed the principles of rhetoric and dialectic to come into play in the classroom and in student tutorials. Furthermore, the increasing popularity of student debate societies, the use of oral examinations and recitations, and the public disputations associated with commencement at most colleges enhanced the position of rhetoric, which was essentially classical in its aim to produce good citizens skilled in speaking. As Michael Halloran demonstrates in "Rhetoric in the American College Curriculum," at this time "rhetoric in American colleges was the classical art . . . of public discourse [that] stood very near if not precisely at the center of pedagogical concerns."[5]

The Decline of Rhetoric

What, then, caused the decline of rhetoric after this first "revival"? The answers to this question lie in the progress of rhetoric in the late eighteenth and the nineteenth centuries, a progress for which we as yet have no authoritative history. Although we cannot offer any definitive answers in this brief chapter, it now seems probable that the decline of rhetoric in the nineteenth century is closely related to three major trends.

The first involves the association of rhetoric with belles-lettres, an association manifested in the lectures of both Adam Smith and Hugh Blair. Blair's *Lectures* (1783), the enormously popular and dominant text in American universities until around 1825, did not present a classical treatment of rhetoric. Instead, Blair devoted most attention to style, viewing invention as beyond the scope of rhetoric. Blair also emphasized the importance of developing "taste" in reading literary works, particularly poetry. Hence, the province of rhetoric was both truncated (to a focus on style) and diffused (to emphasize the aesthetic appreciation of literature rather than the active production of public discourse). The belles-lettres movement was by no means entirely negative; it was, after all, part of the long war waged on behalf of the vernacular in higher education. The journals of the time are full of intense and often bitter debate over whether classical language study should give way to "English" studies. By stressing the importance of instruction in the appreciation of literary works, the belles-lettres movement helped support the argument that the study of literature in English was a legitimate pursuit in colleges. Despite this positive effect, however, the belles-lettres movement also contributed to a major shift away from a focus on classical rhetoric as the productive art of public discourse.

The belles-lettres movement is inextricably linked to another major trend in nineteenth-century colleges and universities: increased specialization of disciplines and the concomitant rise of English departments.[6] Rhetoric is perhaps less suited than any other subject to specialization. Its major function in the classical period was as a synthetic art which brought together knowledge in various fields with audiences of various kinds; its goal was the discovery and sharing of knowledge. The specialization of knowledge which took place in nineteenth-century universities is most often associated with American scholars' discovery of the German system and its subsequent influence on the American curriculum. But an equally important contributor to departmentalization was the pressing and practical matter of how to deal with the rapid expansion of scientific knowledge and with enrollments that actually doubled in the last quarter of the century. Teachers had to contend not with a small group of students, whose progress they could closely guide and monitor through four years of study, but with large and increasingly unwieldy classes.

By the 1890s, departments of instruction had become vitally important to the bureaucratic organization of colleges. The trend toward specialization, steadily growing enrollments, and the continuing influence of belles-lettres led to what we now view as a permanent institution: the department of English. The first professors in the discipline fought hard to include the study of English literature in the curriculum. The figure who epitomizes their triumph is James Francis Child, Harvard's fourth Boylston Professor of Rhetoric (1851–76). In 1876, in a bid to keep him from moving to Johns Hopkins, Harvard created a new Chair of English Literature for Child, who then resigned the Chair of Rhetoric. In his new capacity, Child built a powerful academic department, one based almost exclusively on literary scholarship. It was this Harvard model which predominated in American higher education, in spite of attempts by teachers such as Fred Newton Scott of the University of Michigan to hold to a more classical rhetorical model.[7]

The triumph of the belles-lettres movement and the trend toward specialization were not solely responsible for the decline of rhetoric in the nineteenth century. Ironic as it may seem, the growing emphasis on writing in colleges, particularly the shift from oral to written evaluation of students, also played an important role. The early colleges had nothing resembling our present written examinations and set themes, preferring instead to test students' skills in oral discourse. But large classes demanded that teachers find ways to save time and standardize procedures; hence the rise of written examinations and essays. These examinations, and the set themes students wrote, took up less time than class debates or end-of-the-year disputations. Moreover, they lent themselves to systematic, standardized evaluation. Consequently, as Warren Guthrie points out, by 1850 most college curricula advertised "Rhetoric and Belles-Lettres" or "Rhetoric and Composition" rather than "Rhetoric and Oratory." The resulting emphasis on written discourse, with the inevitable loss of the powerful concept of oral *public* discourse, further weakened the ties between the new English discipline and the classical tradition.

Given our current understanding of the relationship between writing and learning, we might be tempted to view the increased emphasis on writing in nineteenth-century colleges as a boon. Unfortunately, the focus on writing—and the concomitant stream of books on "composition" —reinforced the narrow view of rhetoric as concerned only with style.[8] Alexander Bain's nineteenth-century texts on grammar and rhetoric, which were very influential in America, devote primary attention to elements of style in an attempt to increase students' powers of analysis and criticism.[9] Continuing reliance on Bain's 1866 text (rather than on his enlarged and radically revised 1889 edition), the simplistic codification of Bain's dicta in other texts, the emphasis on rigid rules for usage and arrangement on the parts of a discourse, and the focus on writing demanded by large classes— all these factors helped create a kind of assembly-line English curriculum. And accompanying the growing volume of student writing produced on the assembly line was the need to evaluate this writing in some standardized way. All these factors led to a preoccupation with standards of usage that grew, by the end of the century, into a cult of correctness.

This particular tendency was further exacerbated by the debate over college entrance examinations and the furor over the "illiteracy" of secondary school graduates. In 1880, Richard White charged that the public school system was a total failure; Adams Sherman Hill, the fifth Boylston

Professor of Rhetoric, complained of "a tedious mediocrity [in writing] everywhere"; and in 1889 C. C. Thach announced that "it is difficult to believe, at times, that many of the writers of college entrance papers are English-speaking boys."[10] The journals of this period, in fact, present many of the same charges made in recent years concerning the "literacy crisis."

The debate over standardizing entrance requirements was, of course, predictable, given the rise of specialization and the growth in enrollments. In this debate, Michigan and Harvard again took opposing points of view. The Michigan model, developed by Fred Newton Scott, called for university representatives to visit the public schools and examine faculty, curricula, and students. Scott defended his plan as "organic," noting that it brought the two levels of education face to face in working out standards and requirements. In his model we can easily see the influence of classical rhetoric, with its emphasis on dialectic and enthymematic reasoning as means of discovering knowledge. The Harvard model, on the other hand, was based on the Oxford-Cambridge tradition of using a set of arbitrary requirements for admission. To these, Harvard added a written examination for all applicants in 1874. Scott condemned these examinations, which were built around a required reading list, claiming that the rigid exams defied both the principles of learning and common sense and elicited "the merest fluff and ravelings of the adolescent mind, revealing neither the students' independent thought, nor command of English."[11] Again, however, the Harvard model—with its emphasis on uniform and standardized entrance examinations and its thinly veiled contempt for the public schools—prevailed, contributing directly to the rage for correctness which so undermined the traditional goals and functions of classical rhetoric.

Disciplinary Fragmentation and Stasis

Rhetoric, which had rediscovered its classical roots and flowered briefly in the eighteenth century as the art of communication in the conduct of human affairs, had withered by the end of the nineteenth. Departments of Rhetoric in American colleges increasingly became Departments of English Literature and Rhetoric, or simply Departments of English.[12] Belletristic scholarship came more and more to dominate the activities of these departments, and the first two decades of the twentieth century saw the institutionalization of the present two-tier literature/composition system in most English departments. Throughout this period, scholars of rhetoric and speech increasingly found themselves unwelcome strangers in the halls they had once ruled. With the standardization of the two-tier English department, the commitment of English to reading and writing rather than to speaking became obvious.

Scholars of oral rhetoric had to choose: they could remain within established English departments and be ignored to death, or they could strike out on their own. In 1914, they chose the latter option, and the National Association of Academic Teachers of Public Speaking (now the Speech Communication Association) seceded from the National Council of Teachers of English.[13] Led by such scholars as James Winans of Cornell and James M. O'Neill of Dartmouth, the NAATPS campaigned for separate departments of rhetoric and public speaking, and many such departments were created between 1915 and 1920. The always uneasy detente between literary scholars and rhetoricians had been shattered, and bitterness at the shabby treatment that had forced their secession from English was an element in the attitude of rhetorical scholars for many years.[14] Rhetoric, under which the arts of speaking and writing had been united, now saw these vital intellectual activities relegated to different, and often hostile, disciplines.

The period 1900–1920 marked a low point for the study of classical rhetorical theory. During this time rhetoric was left almost completely in the hands of the conservators of classical texts, most of whose work was done in Europe. In the able hands of such notable scholars as W. Rhys Roberts and S. H. Butcher, the great tradition of classical study was carried on in England as the establishment and annotation of texts continued. Germany also produced much rigorous work on classical rhetoric. Translations from classical languages continued apace, the Loeb Classical Library was active in issuing rhetorical classics in inexpensive editions, and European scholarship burgeoned. But like all things classical, ancient rhetoric was coming to be seen less and less as a living tradition and more and more as "cultural heritage," locked away in footnotes and museums. This trend was especially evident in America.

Written discourse pedagogy during this period was uninformed by classical tenets; its roots, as we have seen, were far shallower. Those few authors of composition texts who associated rhetoric with its classical emphasis on orality were drawn away from English between 1910 and 1920, leaving composition destitute of any link to classicism. Even in the new departments of speech there was relatively little scholarship done in classical theory during this period. The public speaking movement, which had been the motivating force behind the founding of the

NAATPS, was caught up for years with organizational concerns, with the founding of a journal as the group's organ (*The Quarterly Journal of Public Speaking*—now *QJS*), and with issues of the contemporary nature of speech education. The early issues of *QJS* published only a few articles on classical theory, and those which did appear were general and went into little depth. Prior to C. S. Baldwin's *Ancient Rhetoric and Poetic* of 1924, little new or original scholarship in classical rhetoric was undertaken in America. Indeed, it might be said that Baldwin initiated a new era in rhetorical scholarship when he published his *Ancient Rhetoric.*

Charles Sears Baldwin's scholarly career is almost a mirror of the problems we have been discussing. He began teaching during the late 1890s at the Department of Rhetoric at Yale, which was at that time a department of English in all but name. Assigned to teach freshman English, the young teacher soon began to write and publish composition textbooks in a standard style-centered vein. His *A College Manual of Rhetoric* of 1902 and *Composition: Oral and Written* of 1909 quite successfully synthesized the developing trends that were to make up what we now call "current-traditional rhetoric." In 1911 Baldwin was wooed away from Yale by the Department of Rhetoric at Columbia, which did not require a heavy load of freshman teaching, thus freeing him to devote more time to scholarship. At Columbia, Baldwin's interests began to shift away from the nineteenth-century rhetoric of composition and toward classical ideas, and from its beginnings in philosophy and composition, Baldwin's scholarly career thus took a sharp turn toward poetic and rhetoric. After 1917 he did no more work in pedagogy or written discourse, concentrating instead on his new interests. His *Ancient Rhetoric and Poetic* appeared in 1924; *Medieval Rhetoric and Poetic* in 1928. Baldwin obviously found rhetorical scholarship more challenging than the production of composition textbooks, and he began a tradition of renewed critical scholarship in classical rhetoric that has lasted to the present day. [15]

Throughout the mid- and late 1920s and into the 1930s, scholarship in classical rhetoric began in earnest in speech departments. Especially important to this movement were such disciples of James Winans as Wilbur Samuel Howell, Everett Lee Hunt, and Hoyt Hudson. Cornell continued to be a center of this renewal of scholarship on discourse, as were Dartmouth and the University of Pittsburgh. [16] Lane Cooper's critical translation and gloss of Aristotle's *Rhetoric* appeared in 1932, and suddenly the active scholarly voices discussing the great Roman rhetoricians were joined by a fresh chorus of Aristotle scholars. Departments of speech had come into their own, and after 1925 they carried on classical scholarship at high levels of excellence.

In English departments, however, very little of this renascence was felt. Each year drew composition teachers further from the vitality of traditional rhetorical theory; each year saw style-centered or current-traditional rhetoric strengthen its hold. Having rejected oral discourse prior to 1914, composition teachers could not take advantage of the scholarly revival taking place after 1924, and the discipline of composition became as a result an isolated backwater, cut off from all that might have nourished it. By 1936, composition pedagogy was so hidebound and sterile that it merited I. A. Richards' famous condemnatory judgment that rhetoric was "the dreariest and least profitable part of the waste the unfortunate travel through in freshman English."[17]

The Second Revival of Classical Rhetoric

Not until the late 1930s and the early 1940s did the first signs of a second revival of rhetoric begin to emerge. This rebirth of interest in rhetoric in English came from two sources: the "communications movement" and the growing discipline of literary criticism. The communications movement in American education began in 1944, when the first communications courses were taught at the State University of Iowa and at Michigan State University. These courses, designed and staffed by faculty members from both speech departments and English departments, combined elements of both disciplines. They emphasized all four of the communicative skills—speaking, writing, listening, and reading—and hence were the first important reintroduction of basic rhetorical principles into composition classrooms. The communications movement became increasingly important after World War Two, and in 1949 the growing interest in a rhetorical approach to communication skills resulted in the formation of the Conference on College Composition and Communication. This organization has, of course, proven to be an indispensable supporter of all further rhetorical developments in composition studies.[18]

If the communications movement and the rise of general interest in rhetoric provided a practical background for the revival of classical rhetoric, literary criticism helped it regain a theoretical foothold. The emergence of the New Critics in the late 1920s had an energizing effect upon criticism in general, and although New Criticism itself tended to be arhetorical (and even hostile to rhetoric insofar as rhetoric demands a context for discourse), it brought forth such important counterbalancing critical voices as those of Kenneth Burke and the Chicago Neo-Aristotelians. As early as his *Counter-Statement* of 1931, it was obvious that Burke's critical viewpoint was essentially rhetorical. He says in *Counter-Statement* that "effective literature could be nothing else but rhetoric,"[19] and this view became the guiding principle behind *A Grammar of Motives* and *A Rhetoric of Motives*. The latter, in particular, is indebted to Aristotle, but Burke drew classical rhetorical theory in general into his discussion.

Burke was always an independent, never attached to any critical "school" for very long. More important to the discipline as a whole was the work carried out at the University of Chicago by a group that would come to be called the Chicago Formalists or the Chicago Neo-Aristotelians. Under the intellectual leadership of Richard McKeon and Ronald S. Crane, this group used ancient poetic theory, in particular Aristotle's *Poetics,* to launch formalist attacks on the arhetorical, a prioristic work of the New Critics. As Cornell had been a center for speech education in the teens and twenties, the University of Chicago became a center for rhetorical and formalist criticism during the 1940s.

Indeed, many scholars responsible for the reintroduction of classical rhetorical theory to written discourse were attached to the University of Chicago in some capacity during the period 1945–55.[20] Richard McKeon's influence was widely felt, and the reputation he and Crane had established attracted such younger scholars as Richard Weaver, P. Albert Duhamel, Edward P. J. Corbett, and Wayne C. Booth. During the late 1940s both Weaver and Duhamel began to break away from the purely critical activities surrounding the McKeon/Crane circle and to publish essays concerned with the epistemological bases of classical rhetoric *as rhetoric.*[21] Though both men had been trained in literary scholarship, they found their interests gravitating more and more toward rhetorical problems.

Through the efforts of such people as Weaver and Duhamel, classical tenets of pedagogy began to reappear in writing courses in the College of the University of Chicago. Weaver's leadership was particularly important at this time; in essays like "Looking for an Argument" (1953) and in his distinctive textbook *Composition* (1957), he reintroduced to writing pedagogy such classical elements as the enthymeme and the *topoi*. In 1957 also, Donald Leman Clark, who had been a student of C. S. Baldwin at

Columbia, produced his *Rhetoric in Greco-Roman Education,* the first treatise to give a scholarly and well-rounded view of the pedagogy attached to classical rhetorical theory.

In spite of these harbingers of change, teachers of composition, content in their isolation, continued to emphasize grammatical and stylistic problems rather than rhetorical concerns. Most composition teachers knew of Weaver only through his text, and few were aware of Clark. When Daniel Fogarty's *Roots for a New Rhetoric,* which stressed Aristotle's contributions to contemporary rhetoric, was published in 1959 and lauded in speech departments, only scant attention was paid to it in English. Thus another important contribution to the revitalization of classical rhetoric passed by unheeded. This situation did not last long, however, because by 1960 composition was on the verge of a genuine revolution.

The rediscovery of classical rhetoric in its application to writing pedagogy began in 1962, when P. Albert Duhamel and his colleague Richard E. Hughes published *Rhetoric: Principles and Usage.* This was the first truly popular writing textbook to use classical theory as the informing principle of large sections of its discussion. Hughes and Duhamel said in their preface, "Perhaps the most significant difference between our book and those currently used in composition and rhetoric courses is our attempt to introduce the art of rhetoric as a systematic body of knowledge."[22] For the first time average writing teachers were trying out topical invention and classical argumentative forms—and were finding them effective and useful pedagogical aids. In the previous year, Wayne Booth had published his now-famous *The Rhetoric of Fiction,* and suddenly the very word *rhetoric* began to have a new magic to it. The rhetorical revival had begun in earnest.

The impact of this rhetorical revival on composition studies was confirmed by the 1963 CCCC, the conference that most historians of rhetoric point to as the first gathering of the "modern" profession of composition studies. During that year's meeting, Wayne Booth gave his paper on "The Rhetorical Stance," Francis Christensen delivered his "Generative Rhetoric of the Sentence," and, most important for classical studies, Edward P. J. Corbett spoke on "The Usefulness of Classical Rhetoric." All who attended that convention felt the galvanic charge in the air, the exciting sense of intellectual rebirth. Within the next five years the spirit which had been born at that convention began to transform the teaching of writing.

Corbett's essay on the use of classical theory in the writing classroom, published in *CCC* in October, was but the first of a whole series of articles he would write on the application of classical rhetoric to writing. Corbett's work culminated in his important textbook, *Classical Rhetoric for the Modern Student,* which appeared in 1965, and to which every scholar working in composition since owes a debt. *Classical Rhetoric for the Modern Student* was the most rigorous use of classical rhetoric attempted in modern education. As Corbett says in his Preface:

> The subject matter of this book would not seem to be revolutionary, for the methods of learning how to write have not changed very much since the Sophists first set up their schools of rhetoric in fifth-century Athens. In a sense, however, it is a new approach that is presented here, for the kind of rhetoric set forth in this book has been absent from American classrooms for about a century and has been replaced by other systems of teaching whatever is teachable about composition. In writing this book, the author believes that the elaborate system of the ancients . . . is still useful and effective—perhaps more useful and effective than the various courses of study that replaced it.[23]

After 1965 it is difficult to catalog all the different applications that have been found for classical rhetorical theory. Classical rhetoric was widely discussed and even began to be attacked in the literature, most notably by the Michigan tagmemic theorists Richard Young and Alton Becker—a sure sign that it was again a vital intellectual force. Throughout the post-1965 period, the suspicion and hostility that had for so long characterized the relations between English and speech departments began to dissolve as rhetorical study was pursued on both sides of the street. Writing teachers admitted that they had much to learn from their oral-discourse brethren, and rhetoric scholars showed themselves willing to work with their enthusiastic new colleagues. Classical rhetoric became an important element of this new cooperation.[24] Spearheading the move toward renewed cooperation among disciplines was the Rhetoric Society of America. The society's first newsletter, dated December 1968, lists as members of its founding board of directors Edward P. J. Corbett, Wayne Booth, John Rycenga, William Irmscher, Ross Winterowd, Henry Johnstone, Richard Larson, Robert Gorrell, Joseph Schwartz, Richard Hughes, Harry Crosby, Owen Thomas, and Donald C. Bryant. This group represents a true interdisciplinary mix, including departments of English, philosophy, speech, and linguistics. Moreover, this list includes the names of many of those who have been responsible for our renewed acquaintance with classical rhetoric.

Studies and textbooks based on classical theory have proliferated during the past fifteen years: particularly fruitful work has been done in the areas of invention, where topical systems have gained new popularity; arrangement, where classical *dispositio* has provided a touchstone against which other systems are measured; and style, where the classical concept of imitation promises gains in syntactic maturity for students. In addition, English scholars are once again becoming interested in classical rhetoric as a system, investigating its theoretical aspects and using it as an instrument with which to analyze both literary and nonliterary discourse. In short, classical rhetoric, after having been lost to writing instruction since the nineteenth century, is once again available to composition teachers in all of its theoretical and practical richness.

Rhetoric Today: Challenges and Opportunities

Up to this point, we have been speaking in broad historical terms about what *has* happened. And the general direction is clear: after a century of neglect a major revival of rhetoric—stimulated largely by a reawakening of interest in classical rhetoric—is under way. At present, scholars in speech communication and composition in America have perhaps their clearest understanding of rhetoric's scope and significance since the mid-1700s. We have been less successful, however, in applying this understanding to effect changes in our curricula. The following collection of essays is, perhaps more than anything else, concerned with this important next stage in the revival of rhetoric.

A brief review of the present status of rhetorical studies in American colleges and universities might help clarify the nature of the challenges and opportunities awaiting those in this field. Until very recently, one could summarize current research efforts quite succinctly: rhetorical scholars in speech communication emphasized theoretical and historical studies, while those in composition focused on pedagogy. Except in a few instances, there was little substantive interaction between the two disciplines.

In his 1978 review of recent research on rhetorical theory, Michael Leff comments on the negative implications of this split between theory and practice for those in speech: "In fact, then, our meta-rhetorical speculation is autotelic. It does not have an outlet for application, and as a result, our theoretical literature stutters at the level of pure abstraction. Ironically, however, this same literature keeps insisting that rhetoric is a practical discipline, that it operates mainly in the context of concrete problems, and that it calls for decisions leading to action."[25] The irony of this situation is only compounded when we note that one of the central characteristics of classical rhetoric was a unity of theory and practice.

Until recently the situation in composition was, of course, just the reverse. Composition had no scholarly journals equivalent to the *Quarterly Journal of Speech* or *Speech Monographs,* both of which published historical and theoretical articles as well as numerous reports of empirical studies (which also constitute a major interest in that field). With a few notable exceptions, most composition research was fundamentally pedagogical. This focus on pedagogy was by no means entirely negative. Michael Leff remarks, for example, on the sense of "common purpose" among those in composition: "Almost everyone in the discipline centers his inquiry on the problem of how to teach students to write good English prose."[26] But too often this inquiry occurred in an historical and theoretical vacuum, resulting in—at worst—ineffective pedagogical practices and—at best—a fruitless "reinventing of the wheel," a term used by Gary Tate in a 1976 CCCC talk to describe the majority of the articles he received as editor of *Freshman English News.*[27]

Perhaps the central reason for the dearth of theoretical and historical research in composition was the absence of graduate programs in the field. As those in English know, until very recently one could not take a Ph.D. with an emphasis in composition and rhetoric.[28] The teaching of writing simply was not an acceptable concern of "serious" scholars. We do not wish to discuss this situation, which has received significant attention recently,[29] except to make one observation: the establishment of graduate programs in composition and rhetoric was a major precondition to other positive developments in rhetorical studies. Such programs not only provide essential scholarly training to those interested in the teaching of writing; they also help to make composition, and its necessary theoretical background in rhetoric, acceptable to departments of English. A particularly promising trend has been the development of interdisciplinary rhetoric programs, programs which include scholars in speech and, on occasion, classics, linguistics, or cognitive psychology, in departments of English.[30] Such programs, for which the Rhetoric Society of America and its journal the *Rhetoric Society Quarterly* have consistently provided an important model, lead the way in efforts to increase involvement among those faculties once united in the study of rhetoric.

As a result of these efforts, the last ten years have seen a startling increase in the number and sophistication of theoretical and historical studies in the field of composition. Not only do journals such as *College*

English, College Composition and Communication, and the *Rhetoric Society Quarterly* reguarly publish contributions in these areas, but a number of other journals, such as *Pre/Text, Rhetorica, Philosophy and Rhetoric,* and *Rhetoric Review,* also encourage new directions in rhetorical research. Of particular importance is the interdisciplinary nature of these journals, many of which include representatives from both speech communication and English—and often from philosophy, classics, and linguistics—on their editorial boards.

Despite these signs of progress, many challenges remain. These challenges represent difficulties, but they offer important opportunities as well. Perhaps the major challenge is to continue the trend toward interdisciplinary efforts among scholars in composition, speech, philosophy, linguistics, and literature. Such efforts are never easy. The organization of our colleges and universities by its very nature most encourages and rewards disciplinary endeavors, and in times of financial difficulty, such as American colleges and universities now face, interdisciplinary activities become all the more problematical. But if rhetoric is once again to play a synthesizing, generative role in higher education, we must make interdisciplinary cooperation a major goal.

Such cooperation would allow us better to address a second major challenge: the need to continue working to bridge the gap between theory and practice in rhetorical studies. This gap is reflected not merely in the traditional contrasting research foci of speech and composition noted earlier. It also exists within the field of composition, in the division between those instructors who teach the majority of composition classes (and whose course load makes research of any kind a luxury they can seldom afford) and the relatively few teachers of writing who are able to become involved in rhetorical research. Once again, current conditions increase the difficulty of this challenge. They do not, however, lessen its importance.

The essays in this volume provide an indication of the richness and diversity of the resources we bring to meet these challenges. They also suggest a number of potentially fruitful research strategies and directions, providing in effect a preliminary map of the work that lies ahead of us. Chapters 2 through 6 constitute a new look at the past and remind us that we have much to learn about our rhetorical heritage. These essentially theoretical studies underscore the need for continued historical and theoretical research, a need also demonstrated by this chapter. Chapters 7 through 14 represent applications for the present and bring lessons learned from classical rhetoric to bear on contemporary issues in composition, thus providing a bridge between theory and practice. In chapters 15 through 17, which are questions for the future, we present essays which ask some very hard questions, such as whether writing is really necessary to learning and intellectual growth. These questions lead us into largely uncharted territory and suggest exciting possibilities for future research. Common to the varied approaches and viewpoints expressed in this volume is one central theme. The twentieth-century revival of rhetoric entails a recovery of the classical tradition, with its marriage of a rich and fully articulated theory with an equally efficacious practice.

2
Plato Revisited: A Theory of Discourse for All Seasons
James L. Golden

In 1965, Edward P. J. Corbett, Jr., attracted national attention with the publication of his influential book *Classical Rhetoric for the Modern Student*. In this volume, which was applauded by students of English and speech communication, Corbett successfully demonstrated that the essential elements of ancient rhetorical theory have an enduring relevance. In particular, he argued that the teachings of Aristotle, with their stress on the canons of rhetoric, may be utilized with profit in basic courses in composition and in oral communication. Of special importance to the modern student is the fact that Corbett achieved his goal without yielding to the tendency to become an uncritical disciple of classical doctrines. Instead he let these theories interact with modern ideas and practices in such a way that our understanding of human discourse was enhanced.

In keeping with the model established by Corbett, the burden of this essay is to revisit Plato for the purpose of examining his views on rhetoric and dialectic in light of developing trends in contemporary communication theory. These current trends, as my colleagues and I pointed out in 1976 and 1978, may be summarized under the following headings: rhetoric as meaning, rhetoric as value, rhetoric as motive, and rhetoric as a way of knowing.[1] To test Plato's ideas against these prevailing trends a series of five propositions will be presented.[2] We hope we will then be able to answer the question: What does Plato have to say to the present day student interested in the field of human communication?

Plato, first of all, was a highly significant thinker who recognized the centrality of discourse in its myriad forms, not only in the doing of philosophy but in the conducting of human affairs. Numerous accolades have been used to describe Plato's eminent position in western thought. He has been called "the divine Plato,"[3] "the prince of Greek wisdom,"[4] "an eminent master and teacher both of style and of thought,"[5] "the first of all writers or speakers,"[6] "the greatest of dialecticians,"[7] and the most influential philosopher in history.[8] Summarizing Plato's enormous impact, Giambattista Vico said, "A Plato . . . among the ancients was the equivalent of an entire university of studies of our day, all harmonized in one system."[9]

But while Plato's work as a philosopher has been fully seen and appreciated for almost twenty-four hundred years, some scholars vigorously maintain that he should be placed outside of the rhetorical tradition on the grounds that he was a lifelong enemy of rhetoric.[10] To buttress this claim, the ensuing representative arguments generally are used. 1) Plato did not permit rhetoric and poetry to be included in the *Republic,* 2) he upheld the validity of absolutism, thereby scorning the legitimacy of probability and its counterpart opinion, 3) he equated rhetoric with cookery and gratification of pleasure, and 4) he set the requirements for a true rhetoric on such a high level that these ends could never be fulfilled.

That some evidence can be used in support of each of the above claims there can be little doubt. Quite clearly Plato in his major rhetorical dialogues, *Gorgias* and *Phaedrus,* did express grave concerns about the way rhetoric was practiced in his day. Similarly he tells us in the *Republic* that rhetoric and poetry are to be banned from his utopian state. At the same time, however, there is a considerable body of data to suggest that Plato was dedicated to the idea that human communication was an indispensable aspect of one's existence. In all of his dialogues, we are able to find either tributes to the power and appeal of speech or scattered references to the rhetorical theory he espouses. In the *Timaeus* he notes, "but the river of speech, which flows out of a man and ministers to the intelligence, is the fairest and noblest of all streams."[11] And in the *Sophist* he observes, "To rob us of discourse would be to rob us of philosophy."[12]

This recognition of the significance of discourse doubtless was influenced by Plato's admiration of and appreciation for Socrates. As a result, in the dialogue *Euthyphro* he puts these words in the mouth of his master teacher: "I have a benevolent habit of pouring out myself to everybody, and would even pay for a listener, and I am afraid that the Athenians may think me too talkative."[13]

When examining Plato's commitment to the value of discourse, it is incumbent on us to appreciate the broad scope which his theory of rhetoric entails. Rhetoric, he held, embraces any form of discourse designed to win the soul. This includes the intrapersonal dimension, public speaking or oratory, and dialectic and related interpersonal communication forms. The fact that we have not always shown an awareness of the wide range of rhetoric envisioned by Plato is due, in part, to our excessive preoccupation with the *Phaedrus* and *Gorgias,* and our natural tendency to slight his other works. Illustrative of this point is our persistent failure to see Plato's stress on thinking as a fundamental aspect of rhetorical discourse.[14] In the *Theaetetus* and the *Sophist,* for example, we are told that the soul is capable of carrying on a dialogue with itself, "that to form an opinion is to speak," and that thinking and discourse are essentially the same process.[15] It is evident, therefore, that Plato, like Kenneth Burke and Chaim Perelman in the modern era, saw the need to place the intrapersonal communication pattern within the sphere of rhetoric.

Not surprisingly Plato, in keeping with the views held by his contemporaries, predictably highlighted public speaking or oratory as an important communication form. Notwithstanding his numerous attacks on the sophistic orators he had come to know, and his observations regarding the limitations of oratory in the doing of philosophy, he nevertheless recognized its essential role in governmental, legal, and private affairs. One must be gifted in the art of public speaking and in the art of rhetorical criticism of public address, Plato argued, if he is to be an effective statesman or lawyer; for it is the task of the leader to deliver orations for the purpose of arousing the soul, and pointing the way toward justice.[16]

Further proof of Plato's willingness to regard public communication, despite its partiality for an uninterruped flow of discourse, as a legitimate and vital part of rhetoric, is his occasional practice of constructing orations as integral parts of his dialogues. Not the least among these are Socrates' speech in the *Apology,* the three addresses on love in the *Phaedrus,* the funeral oration in the *Menexenus,* and the speech in praise of the god of love, Eros, in the *Symposium.* A careful reading of these speeches clearly suggests that Plato understood when and how an oration should be constructed and delivered.

A third rhetorical form, dialectic, will be treated at length in a later claim. Suffice it to say at this time that the fact that Plato put conversational discourse, whether utilizing the philosophical mode or informal interpersonal dialogue, in the larger category of rhetoric. Thus we read in the *Phaedrus,* "Taken as a whole, is not Rhetoric the art of winning the soul by discourse, which means not merely argument in the courts of justice, and all other sorts of public councils, but in private conference as well?"[17]

Not to be overlooked in an analysis of Plato's commitment to the significance of discourse in all of its forms was his own rhetorical practice in developing his dialogues. From beginning to end the dialogues are impressive specimens of rhetoric epitomizing excellence in the canons of *inventio, dispositio,* and *elocutio.* The arguments contain strong ethical, logical, and pathetic appeals consistent with Aristotle's recommendations for artistic proof;[18] the organizational patterns adhere to a well delineated method based on the combining of analysis and synthesis;[19] and the style is characterized by clarity, vividness, and appropriateness. These virtues in content, organization, and language control won the praise of such luminaries as Cicero, Quintilian, Longinus, and Demetrius, all of whom regarded Plato's writings as a model of rhetorical effectiveness worthy of imitation.[20] In sum, a close analysis of all of Plato's dialogues reveals, as Quintilian correctly observed, that rhetoric is "a genuine and honourable thing" which is crucial to the task of conducting our public and private affairs.[21]

A second important aspect of Plato's theory of discourse is an abiding belief in the premise that a major function of rhetoric is to generate, create, and discover knowledge. Before developing this claim it is necessary for us to focus on Plato's celebrated conception of knowledge and truth and his views on recollection. The subject of knowledge, which is integrally tied in with Plato's world view, has as starting and finishing points ideal forms situated in the mind of God. The forms represent true ideas, and, consequently, are eternal and unchanging concepts which remain for all people at all times the ultimate truth to be sought.

On a lower plane is the level of particular knowledge that stems from the world of sense. It is that type of knowledge related to physical objects which, when perceived, have the capacity to stimulate our senses. By the very nature of things, however, such knowledge is at best only an imperfect approximation of the original ideas located in heaven. To put it another way, particular knowledge emanating from our sensory perceptions is to be equated with appearance, opinion, and "semi-reality," while universal knowledge, the wellspring of all that is true, is to be identified with genuine reality.[22]

Plato illustrates his famous theory of ideas with a vivid example of three types of beds depicted by Socrates in Book X of the *Republic.* Herein is articulated a hierarchy of knowledge containing three categories placed in a descending order. Bed One stands for the perfect idea of a bed existing in God's mind, Bed Two represents the physical object constructed by the carpenter, and Bed Three is the artist's imitation of Bed Two.[23] Thus categories two and three, in deriving their impetus from imitation, are far removed from the idea of an authentic bed.

At first glance it would appear that Plato's notion of true forms, along with his explanatory example of the hierarchical order of beds, lends credence to the oft-repeated contention that Plato is little more than an absolutist who rejects outright all probabilistic claims. Such a conclusion, however, is not warranted. Commenting on Plato's theory of forms, Kenneth Burke observed that Plato's scheme is of considerable rhetorical value because of "its possible analogue in linguistic theory."[24] He explains by stating that

> if you consider any individual man as abstracted from the kinds of contexts in which alone a living man is possible, he has become, from the linguistic point of view, a sign or manifestation or imperfect exemplar of the "universal" word for his type or class of entity (the universal in this sense being "prior" to any particular entity that is included under this general head.)[25]

Similarly important in coming to an understanding of Plato's belief in the epistemic function of rhetoric was his tendency to associate knowledge with recollection. The following excerpts drawn from the dialogue *Meno* highlight this point of view:

> *Meno*: But what do you mean when you say that we don't learn anything, but that what we call learning is recollection? Can you teach me that it is so? . . . . *Socrates*: This knowledge will not come from teaching, but from questioning. He will recover it for himself. . . . And the spontaneous recovery of knowledge that is in him is recollection.[26]

If recollection consists of recalling that which earlier was known and is now forgotten, the question which then arises is: Under what circumstances and in what state did one have knowledge of the ideal forms and the true universals? Plato answers this query in the *Phaedo* by suggesting that "our souls must have existed somewhere else before they were confined in the body."[27] This "previous ideal existence" which subsequently was not remembered or only "dimly recalled" must be discovered anew through the process of recollection.[28]

Because of his conviction that learning and recollection are interrelated, Plato had little patience for those with poor memories. At one juncture in the dialogue *Critias,* he indicated that the central argument being advanced relied almost exclusively on the power of memory.[29]

Moreover, he asserted in the *Republic* that a soul who possesses a genuine philosophical nature must "have a good memory."[30]

It is against this background of Plato's theory of ideas and forms and his belief in the relationship between knowledge and recollection that we can trace the role rhetoric plays in the creation and discovery of knowledge. A major purpose in a rhetorical situation is to enable the participants through the means of dialogue to go beyond sensory experiences of the observable physical world and glimpse those universals that adhere to an ideal form. This movement from particulars to universals, or from the concrete to the abstract, gives us a "vision of the truth"[31] by setting into motion a recollection process involving the stimulation of our memory. Of significance here is the fact that none of the participants begin the dialogue with a knowledge of the answers to the questions or problems that are to be raised. Repeatedly Socrates, who usually functions as an interlocutor and as a surrogate for Plato, finds it necessary to remind the other rhetors in a given dialogue that he does not yet have the answers which he hopes are to be generated through a joint inquiry. With considerable frequency he makes such statements as these.

> Whereas the fact is that I am inquiring with you into the truth of that which is advanced from time to time, just because I do not know.[32]
>
> Was I not telling you just now—but you have forgotten—that I knew nothing, and was I not proposing to share the inquiry with you?[33]
>
> It isn't that, knowing the answers myself, I perplex other people. The truth is rather that I infect them also with the perplexity I feel myself. So with virtue now. I don't know what it is. You may have known before you came into contact with me, but now you look as if you don't. Nevertheless I am ready to carry out, together with you, a joint investigation and inquiry into what it is.[34]

These quotations clearly suggest that Plato was committed to an argument-centered theory of rhetoric. Freely he held that a communicator must be guided by good reasons—especially those grounded in first principles. Thus a premise which cannot be supported by a rational explanation fails to qualify as knowledge. Since reason is "the king of heaven and earth,"[35] the person who uses it well not only wins our respect but places upon us a moral obligation to agree with his conclusions. If, on the other hand, one does not have compelling reasons on his side it is necessary for us who do to "instruct him";[36] and, in turn, it is essential for him to modify his original position. Only in this way can knowledge and understanding be generated.

A third claim pertaining to Plato's theory of discourse is that rhetoric sets for itself the goal of promoting values. Even a casual reader of the dialogues can come to an awareness of the fact that the philosophy of Plato is a philosophy of values. The dominant concern expressed in most of the writings is with such ethical themes as "What is Virtue?" "What is Piety?" "What is Courage?" "What is Temperance?" "What is Friendship?" and "What is Justice?" Even when the subjects of rhetoric, love, and laws are discussed, the underlying emphasis deals with ethical intent, moral impact, and higher truths. At the heart of this concern with ethics or values is the concept of the "good," which is defined as follows in the *Republic*: "Now, that which imparts truth to the known and the power of knowing to the knower is what I would have you term the idea of the good."[37] This perspective led Plato to urge all people to follow the "supreme rule" challenging us to aspire "to be genuinely good";[38] and to advise rhetoricians to "make the good instead of the evil to seem just to the states."[39]

An important facet of Plato's notion of values is his treatment of the four primary cardinal virtues upheld by the Greeks—courage, temperance, wisdom, and justice. Although these virtues share a commonality because of their integral connection to the good life, they are sufficiently distinct to warrant a separate listing. Notwithstanding the fact that courage on one occasion is described as "a kind of salvation,"[40] it is relegated to a low level in the hierarchy of values on the grounds that "brutes," as well as humans, have a similar capacity to exemplify this partially instinctive virtue.[41]

Despite the above reservation, Plato carefully demonstrates the need for a communicator to display courage in articulating his arguments and convictions. This is especially true of the judge who, in fulfilling the role of rhetor, is ready to pronounce a verdict. The decision he is to announce and justify must be derived from first principles and be corroborated by reasonable explanations, and, consequently, not be influenced by the biases of the audience. To allow the audience to control or unduly influence a decision is to reduce the quality of the judge's reasons and to run counter to the process of education. In a similar manner, it will result in a corruption of taste on the part of the audience. "The judge," argues Plato, "takes his seat not to learn from the audience, but to teach them, and to set himself against performers who give an audience pleasure in wrong and improper ways."[42]

Courage comes into play in those situations in which the rhetor is called upon to select arguments that may appeal to the "one" on the one hand, and to the "many" on the other. This choice from Plato's standpoint generally should come down on the side of the one rather than in support of the multitude.

The virtue of temperance, like that of courage, is another vital dimension of the good. This value, when practiced properly, brings our desires and pleasures under control and promotes worthy actions. A temperate person avoids emotional excesses, maintains an attitude of moderation even when confronted with difficult situations, and, when the occasion demands it, errs in the direction of caution rather than of daring. As a result, temperance often comes into conflict with courage. Pitted against each other, therefore, may be reticence versus recklessness, or calmness versus fury. Yet these apparent opposites must be blended and woven together in a society and, indeed, in the same soul in order to provide a proper balance of mutually restraining forces. To accomplish this task, as Plato suggests in his dialogue the *Statesman,* is the duty of the communicator who holds a leadership position.[43]

We are now ready to turn to the two higher virtues, wisdom and justice. As noted in our earlier discussion on the epistemic nature of rhetoric, Plato viewed wisdom as an ultimate goal in life. In ranking the nine levels of souls in the *Phaedrus,* for example, he gave the preeminent position to the philosopher who by training and insight is the supreme lover of wisdom.[44] He further held that the person who achieves knowledge or wisdom experiences the true meaning of what it is to be good; and it is he alone who rids himself of false opinions, becomes an expert in a chosen field, enjoys full happiness, and comes into the presence of the gods.[45]

Thus far we have seen that communicators are expected to reveal the traits of courage, temperance, and wisdom. Yet to be discussed is what Plato perceived to be the noblest of all virtues—justice. Observe how, in the *Republic,* he interpreted justice as the great integrating virtue:

> I think that this [justice] is the only virtue which remains in the State when the other virtues of temperance and courage and wisdom are abstracted; and, that this is the ultimate cause and condition of the existence of all of them, and while remaining in them is also their preservative; and we were saying that if the three were discovered by us, justice would be the fourth or remaining one.[46]

Justice, according to Plato's view, occupies the first position; and it, in turn, is the catalytic force which embraces the other three.

Plato's belief in the value dimension of rhetoric contributed signifi-

cantly to his attitude toward ethos and criticism. A speaker is not prepared to engage in discourse, he asserted, unless he possesses the qualities
of "intelligence, good will, and candor."[47] He should at all times be
thoughtful in his subject matter, willing to speak to himself as well as to
the auditors, and interested in becoming an exemplar of the cardinal
virtues in his daily and professional life. As Socrates put it, "I compare the
man and his words, and note the harmony and correspondence of
them."[48]

This practice of comparing one's actions with the verbal symbols he
uses led Plato to apply rigid critical standards in his assessment of the
speaking performances of the sophists. With cutting sarcasm he described them as purveyors of apparent knowledge, "wizards" who imitated reality by using a "shadow play of words," artful deceivers who
relied on "the superfluity of their wits," and rhetorical tricksters who
were content to deliver "fawning speeches" designed to titillate the
fancy.[49] Similarly he taunted them for promising their students instruction in virtue, and then criticizing them for flagrant injustices because of
their refusal to pay their fees. "Now what can be more illogical than such
a story?" queries Socrates. "When the disciples have become good men
and just, freed from all injustice by the master, how could they, now
possessed of justice, do an injury to their master with what they don't
possess?"[50]

Plato, as noted earlier, had a world view that gave primacy to reason
as the principle motivating force to help us grasp the meaning of ideal
forms. From this perspective he never wavered at any stage in his life. But
we also have observed that equally important to him was his commitment
to ethics and values, and to the notion that all individuals should strive to
fulfill their potential consonant with their better selves. Out of this
conviction came another perspective on communication which acknowledged the legitimate role of persuasion in the rhetorical process. *As a
fourth claim, therefore, we can say that Plato, despite disclaimers to the contrary
in portions of the "Gorgias," was fully devoted to the idea of rhetoric as action.*
This conclusion regarding the efficacy and desirability of persuasion was
influenced by Plato's beliefs on the nature of man. Not only is man a
cognitive being concerned with rationality, he argued, but also a person
motivated by emotions or passions that sometimes cause irrational behavior. Often one is buffeted by such inherent traits as feelings of "pleasure, pain, and desire." Anticipating George Campbell, he noted that
"pains and pleasures exist side by side; opposite as they are, we experience
them simultaneously."[51]

Of all the emotions, the one which receives the greatest attention from Plato is love—a theme "immortalized" in "his Dialogues."[52] When he speaks of the virtues of wisdom and honor or the evil of gain, or the vision of truth in the *Republic,* he is inclined to preface these terms and phrases with the words "lovers of." Thus what matters is not these concepts in isolation, but whether or not a person is a lover of wisdom, honor, truth, or gain.[53] The subject of love is also the major thesis set forth in the *Symposium.* For our purposes, however, it is the treatment of love in the *Phaedrus* which has the most relevance. So well known is this dialogue to students of rhetoric that an extensive analysis here is not needed. Nevertheless it is useful to recall the three speeches on love which constitute the first half of this dialogue, for these presentations graphically depict the natural conflict that exists between reason and emotion or between logos and pathos. Recall, for instance, how the speech of Lysias and the first address of Socrates denigrated *eros* or love. This emotion, it was argued, has a deleterious effect on all those who experience it because it promotes strong feelings of envy, malice, jealousy, self-gratification, guilt, and uncontrolled desire. Love, moreover, may adversely affect our health, and render us disagreeable, contentious, and unproductive.

Following the delivery and analysis of the first two speeches, Socrates suddenly recanted and then presented a discourse elevating love to a lofty position. Love, he said, is a form of madness which releases the lover from "present ills," makes him more creative, and provides a degree of inspiration which helps one see the future. He then added that the lover in seeing beauty here below remembers the ideal beauty that is in the mind of God. In such a state of unity with God, there is not room for petty jealousies, spite, or trivialities.[54]

It is further instructive to observe what Socrates did following the conclusion of his second speech. As Grassi reminds us, Socrates next placed philosophy "under the sign of the Muses," and eloquently portrayed the myth of the "cicadae."[55] This blending of reasoning and emotions in the *Phaedrus* prompted Grassi further to say, "Plato sees true rhetoric as psychology which can fulfill its truly 'moving' function only if it masters original images (*eide*)."[56]

Since man is both a logical and a psychological being, and since reason and values come together, Plato found his rationale for supporting a form of persuasion that was moral/philosophical in nature. Persuasion, he came to believe, was necessary for the successful leadership of the state. A statesman, he asserted, must be capable of carrying out three functions: administer justice, perform as a general, and produce persuasion through oratory and public speaking.[57] Among the duties of the statesman is to know when, where, and in what manner persuasion is to be selected as the mode of influence to be employed in a situation. One of the areas requiring its use is in the creation and upholding of laws. As a result of persuasion we learn to recite the laws, experience conversion, and become effective citizens.[58]

Nor is persuasion limited to assisting us in serving the government. It has a similar task in helping us be better persons. "Gentle persuasion" should be used to set the soul free, to convey knowledge to the listeners, and to improve one's character.[59] As Socrates stated in the *Gorgias,* the persuader should be concerned with "how justice may be planted in the spirits of his fellow citizens, how injustice may be rooted up, and self-control engendered, self-indulgence extirpated—in a word, how every virtue may arise, all evil disappear."[60] Persuasion, in short, has as one of its principal goals to activate our emotions to the point that the listener will yearn to live a good life consistent with the cardinal virtues.

Grassi puts Plato's views of rhetoric as action in perspective by alluding to the three types of speech which often are made, two of which are wholly unacceptable. The first is the "external" or "rhetorical speech" which is dominated by emotion and opinion. Such discourse was vigorously attacked by Socrates in the *Gorgias* as a communication form based on self-gratification and excessive emotionalism. The second is an almost exclusively "rational" approach that stresses scientific demonstration and semantic purity while ignoring any semblance of pathetic proof. The "true rhetorical speech," which constitutes the only desirable type, combines appeals to the mind and the heart in a manner that "leads, guides, and attracts."[61]

A final consideration with respect to Plato's ideas on motives and persuasion are his useful suggestions in the area of audience analysis and adaptation. What a rhetor should know if he is to win the soul by discourse is a question that is raised throughout the dialogues. Plato deals with this recurring theme by emphasizing the need to understand the different personality and character traits that give uniqueness to a particular soul. Is the soul simple or complex?, he asks in the *Phaedrus.*[62] If it is multiform or pluralistic, then each aspect should be listed and described. He also tells us in the *Statesman* that people with certain kinds of dispositions feel akin to those who possess similar feelings and tendencies, but look with disfavor on those who have opposite traits.[63] In the *Republic,* he advises us to be aware of the fact that men may be separated into three groups according to their value commitments. Those interested in the ideal forms and cardinal virtues are "lovers of wisdom" and "lovers of honour"; others who are motivated by a desire for worldly possessions are "lovers of gain."[64]

Plato's insightful analysis of the different types of souls led him to urge potential rhetors to ask the following question: "What is its [the soul's] natural capacity of acting upon something, or of being acted on by something?"[65] This ability of the soul to initiate an action or to respond to a call for action was later related to knowledge and reality, as well as to the very essence of being, in the *Sophist*.[66] Where a particular listener or soul fits on an imaginary action scale, both as a potential initiator and respondent, determines, in part, the type of argument a speaker utilizes.

In addition to having a knowledge of the general characteristics associated with a soul, a persuader should also take into consideration such elements as age, sex, occupation, and locale; for each in its own way influences the attitudes, beliefs, and values. Although Plato here only gives us general hints, rather than a systematized plan for audience analysis and adaptation, these suggestions are informative and provocative. A speaker should take special care when addressing young people because their immaturity and lack of experience causes them to confuse the allegorical with the literal, and appearances with reality,[67] and makes them pay too much attention "to what the world will think."[68]

The old, on the other hand, should be able to cope with any type of argument. Through practical experience and the natural accumulation of knowledge that comes with age, they have developed the talent to distinguish reality from illusion; thus they are not easily duped by the false persuader.[69] By virtue of their status in the state, the elderly also have earned the right to be revered. Consequently the young should yield to their leadership role, remain silent when the old are speaking, extend special privileges to them in a social gathering, and honor their advice and admonitions.[70]

Plato was somewhat advanced beyond his contemporaries in his analysis of sex differences and the part they would play in rhetorical situations. Although he shared the prevailing view that men were somewhat superior to women in degree, he saw no differences in kind. In describing the ideal state, he said, "There is no special faculty of administration in a state which a woman has because she is a woman, or which a man has by virtue of his sex, but the gifts of nature are alike diffused in both; all the pursuits of men are the pursuits of women."[71] It follows, therefore, that similar appeals could be made to each group.

What Plato says about occupations and their influence on the soul is also compelling. Indeed he even relates one's choice of an occupation to the quality of his soul. Of the nine souls discussed in Socrates' second speech in the *Phaedrus,* the following rank order, ranging from high to low, was used: 1) philosopher or lover of wisdom, 2) king or ruler, 3) statesman or merchant, 4) athlete or trainer, 5) diviner, 6) poet and other imitators, 7) artisan or farmer, 8) sophist or demagogue, and 9) tyrant.[72] A person's nature, therefore, dictates the type of employment that is to be pursued.[73]

Not only did Plato pinpoint such factors as age, sex, and occupation, he likewise was one of the first writers in the ancient world to recognize the relationship between locale and the rhetorical process. Where one lives, he held, conditions his outlook on life. A quest for knowledge, he stated with an attitude of condescension, "is the special characteristic of our part of the world." By contrast, however, the people of Phoenicia and of Egypt are motivated primarily by a "love of money."[74] But if men are conditioned in different ways by the location in which they live, they share a universal pride in their hometown and country. In developing this point, Plato observed: "Had the orator to praise Athenians among Peloponnesians, or Peloponnesians among Athenians, he must be a good rhetorician who could succeed and gain credit. But there is no difficulty in a man's winning applause when he is contending for fame among the persons whom he is praising."[75]

Plato summarizes his recommendations for adapting to an individual soul by listing a four-step procedure which must be followed in every detail if successful action is to be achieved. First, a description of the soul, including a reference to its simple or pluralistic form, is required. Secondly, it should be determined to what extent the soul is capable of acting on something or being acted on by something. This should be viewed in accordance with the subject at hand. Thirdly, from the available means of persuasion, arguments and proofs should be selected that are suitable to the soul's personality, disposition, and character, and to the conditioning forces that have molded him. Finally, a proper style or language control should be used in order to produce the intended meaning.[76]

Yet to be considered in Plato's ideas on audience analysis and adaptation is his call for prudence and judgment on the part of the speaker regarding the possible length of a speech, methods for conciliating an audience in the introduction, and means for relating delivery patterns to the content of the message. As might be expected, Plato set no specific limit on the time span of a speech, recommending instead that the theme must be adequately covered before a conclusion is reached. The subject matter and nature of the argument, and not listener expectations or pleasure, therefore, should be the determining factor. Plato was impatient with those who complained either about the length or the brevity of a message or argument unless they could present convincing proof that more or less time was needed to complete the discussion.[77]

The speaker should also use sound judgment in knowing what type of proem to use for a particular topic or occasion. To illustrate this point, he remarked that for controversial subjects, such as the presentation of laws, a friendly, docile manner and common ground appeals are necessary.[78]

Additionally, Plato felt that a speaker's gestural and vocal patterns should be adapted to the needs of a rhetorical situation and to man's natural proclivity to respond to imitation as an instructional and persuasive strategy. This was essential, he believed, for the generation of meaning. Unlike his student Aristotle, who downgraded delivery by making it a subordinate part of style, Plato gave these suggestions for adapting one's gestures and voice control to the essential quality of the thing being described:

> We should imitate the nature of the thing; the elevation of our hands to heaven would mean lightness and upwardness; heaviness and downwardness would be expressed by letting them drop to the ground; if we were describing the running of a horse, or any other animal, we should make our bodies and their gestures as like as we could to them. . . . For by bodily imitation only can the body ever express anything. . . . And when we want to express ourselves, either with the voice, or tongue, or mouth, the expression is simply their imitation of that which we want to express.[79]

On the basis of this analysis of Claim Four, it would appear that Plato held firmly to the view that one of the primary functions of rhetoric is to persuade the listener to adopt specific courses of action and, when necessary, to modify his beliefs and attitudes in accordance with ideal forms and societal values. Seen from this perspective, rhetoric is aligned with moral reformation of life. To produce this type of persuasive result, a rhetor has no recourse but to adapt his appeals to the specific requirements of an audience, the subject, and the occasion.

The preceding four claims have identified Plato's interest in all types of discourse, and his recognition of the threefold function of rhetoric: to create knowledge, to promote values, and to produce action. Implicit in each of these functions is the role that discourse plays in the generation of meaning. The final question to be analyzed is this: What kind of philosophical-rhetorical method is needed in order to actualize the functions outlined by Plato? The answer to this problem may be stated as Claim Five.

The single most useful and effective communication method is the dialogue form which Plato invented and called dialectic. Dialectic as described by Plato "is the copingstone of the sciences"—a science which is set above all other sciences.[80] Using metaphorical language, he further said that dialectic is the guide that directs us "on the voyage of discourse."[81] Plato is careful to make the point that it is more than regular conversation that so often is content to deal with such a mundane theme as "persons." What makes dialectic so appealing to Plato is the fact that it fastens its attention on noble abstract "things" such as "knowledge and being."[82] Dialectic, in sum, takes the special form of philosophical conversation—a true rhetoric in "which the philosopher persuades and ennobles the soul of his beloved."[83]

One of the reasons for its inclusion in the realm of science is the predictable structure and methodology that is used. Dialectic when practiced in a proper manner adheres to a clearly organized pattern which moves in a chronological sequence beginning with a definition of terms and ending with a vision of the ideal as seen in universals. Since all reasoning should proceed from definition, each particular that is introduced must be defined. In one of the dialogues Socrates reminded Gorgias that both of them had frequently witnessed the failure of a discussion because vital definitions were not forthcoming.[84]

Division and integration or unification, consisting of analysis and synthesis, is a second step in the dialectical process. Each subject must be divided according to the kinds or species represented, and then the parts must be related to the whole. To divide a species at a point other than the appropriate joints is to perform like "a clumsy butcher."[85] This separation of a species into units that are differentiated from each other must be repeated until no further division is possible.[86]

Once the dividing has been completed, analysis is replaced by synthesis. Here the units or parts are combined in an ascending order, moving from the lowest to the highest species or from particulars to first principles. This progression from the concrete to the abstract or universal enables the participants to move from a hypothesis as starting point to a vision of the ideal form.[87]

In addition to the two major components noted above, dialectic makes use of several rhetorical strategies presented in a sequential pattern. The initial strategy consists of the phrasing of thoughtful questions which demand a fitting response. These interrogations must be relevant, provocative, and fair; and they must focus on worthwhile and significant themes. Moreover, they should be sufficiently broad and general in scope so as to provide a wide latitude of responses in the early stages of the discussion.

After an interlocutor raises a question, the respondent should develop an answer which sets forth hypotheses and demonstrates them through reasoning supported by examples, analogies, and parallel cases.[88] But if examples and analogies constitute a desirable means for demonstrating a point, the same is not true for the practice of piling up quotations or testimony from a wide variety of witnesses. The quality of the testimony of a well informed single witness is far more persuasive than the statements of large numbers of people—a practice so often sought in courts of law—who have no conception of ideal forms or universals.[89]

As soon as a response is given to a question, the interlocutor proceeds to the third step which includes refutation and cross-examination. Both Socrates and Plato saw refutation as a purifying process. Thus in the *Sophist,* we read these lines: "For all these reasons, Theaetetus, we must admit that refutation is the greatest and chiefest of purifications, and he who has not been refuted, though he be the Great King himself, is in an awful state of impurity."[90] The participant in a dialectical discussion does not meet his responsibility if he lets an untrue or inexact statement go unchallenged. One who falls into this error through neglect or lack of courage deceives both himself and the other speakers taking part in the dialogue. In all, the purpose of refutation or cross-examination is not to make fun of a respondent or to show one's versatility and skill in tripping up an opponent, but to test the validity of an argument. Effective and responsible refutation, therefore, will win the respect of those whose answers are rebutted fairly.[91]

Following the refutation and cross-examination, a fourth and final step is instituted consisting of a modification of the original position. This alteration of view results, one hopes, in a conclusion shared by each participant. The agreement that is eventually reached is the natural outcome of the dialectical procedure, and is rooted in the ideal of moral obligation.

When analyzing the four rhetorical strategies included in the dialectical method of discourse, it is useful to observe the alternating roles of the participants in a discussion. Each, in turn, has an opportunity to question, to cross-examine, to respond, and to refute. Consequently all of those who take part are on the same level. Michel Meyer explains the process:

> As each participant, in turn, . . . becomes the questioner, his interlocutor, inversely, takes on the role of answerer. It is for this reason that dialectic—as discourse composed of questions and answers—makes the interlocutors absolutely equal, and makes it impossible for them to take on a position of authority with respect to the other.[92]

The elements of dialectic, as discussed in the preceding section, are summarized in the diagram. When examined in detail, the diagram shows that Plato's theory of dialectic draws upon science for its definition and structure, upon philosophy for its subject matter, and upon rhetoric for its strategies. Dialectic, in sum, is a means for bringing science, philosophy, and communication together for the purpose of generating knowledge and producing moral persuasion.

Dialectic

Definitions
1. "The copingstone of the sciences"
2. "The guide on the voyage of discourse

Subject Matter
1. Things
2. Knowledge
3. Being

Purposes
1. To generate understanding concerning ideal forms
2. To stimulate recollection
3. To evaluate the soul

Structure
1. Definition of terms
2. Analysis
   (a) Dividing forms into particulars
   (b) Dividing particulars until no further separation is possible
3. Synthesis
   (a) Moving upward from the concrete to the abstract
   (b) Combining particulars so as to form universals

Rhetorical Strategies
1. Questioning
2. Answering and justifying
3. Cross-examining and refuting
4. Modifying original view until agreement is reached on the problem

One additional point is worth noting here if we are to have a full understanding of Plato's perspectives on dialectic. Plato's unusual emphasis on the nature and quality of one's answers represents an important departure from the practice of Socrates, who gave to questioning the highest rank among the four steps inherent in dialectic.[93] To illustrate this contention, let us examine the three metaphors that were used to describe the stances assumed by Socrates in a typical dialogue.

The first metaphor was that of a "gadfly." In the *Apology,* Socrates boasted that he was God's gift to the state—a sort of "gadfly" whose task was to question the beliefs, attitudes, and values of leaders and other citizens.[94] Thus he asked probing questions of anyone who would listen, and then followed up their responses with other questions.

The second metaphor was drawn from the sea animal called a sting ray. When Meno attempted to define virtue only to have Socrates question his answers, Meno impatiently observed: "I think that not only in outward appearances but in other respects as well you [Socrates] are exactly like the first sting ray that one meets in the sea. Whenever anyone comes into contact with it, it numbs him, and this is the sort of thing that you seem to be doing to me now."[95] Meno proceeded to say that he thought he knew what virtue was, having lectured on this subject on numerous occasions; but now, he confessed, total confusion and doubt have set in. Socrates' comment at this point was instructive. "As for myself," he said, "if the sting ray paralyzes others only through being paralyzed itself, then the comparison is just, but not otherwise."[96] He then admitted that he himself did not have the answers to the questions he raised.

Perhaps the most meaningful metaphor was the one which Socrates used to describe his strong partiality for questions. He proudly referred to his designated role as a midwife whose aim was to help a dialogue participant give birth to ideas. In describing this function, Socrates pushed aside those criticisms which pictured him as an interrogator who did not know the answer to his own questions. While admitting the validity of this charge, he offered the following defense: "God compels me to be a midwife, but does not allow me to bring forth."[97] This high priority position given to questioning by Socrates is brought into clear focus in these words:

> You forget . . . that I [Socrates] neither know, nor profess to know, anything of these matters; you are the person who is in labour, I am the barren midwife. . . . And I hope that I may at last help to bring your own opinion into the light of day: when this has been accomplished, then we will determine whether what you have brought forth is only a wind-egg or a real and genuine birth.[98]

It is evident, as the foregoing discussion suggests, that questioning occupied a key role in dialectic as seen from the perspective of Socrates. But as Meyer perceptively argues this emphasis is not shared by Plato—especially in the middle and late dialogues. Gradually questioning, though still necessary, began to be deemphasized; at the same time an increased stress was placed on the process of answering. Commenting on this fact, Meyer noted, "Plato will ascribe a diminishing role to questioning in the acquisition of knowledge by focusing more and more on the answer regardless of the question to which it refers."[99]

The above conclusion is of immense importance in assessing the relevance and thrust of Plato's theory of rhetoric for modern students. As answers take precedence over questions or problems, the notion of justification in argument becomes a vital rhetorical necessity. Moreover, the scene is set for elevating the concept of probability and for preparing the way for the introduction of what Aristotle was to call the rhetorical syllogism.[100]

The five claims discussed in this essay have been singled out for the purpose of glimpsing the primary elements in Plato's theory of discourse. In order to see them come together in summary form, let us briefly examine the approach used in the *Symposium* which, along with the *Republic,* is generally regarded as Plato's greatest dialogue.[101]

Taking place in a banquet setting featuring social communion and drink, this influential dialogue includes all of the major types of communication—informal conversation, speeches, and dialectical discourse. The underlying thesis of these presentations was the subject of love as it emanates from the god called Eros. The five speeches devoted to this theme had as their primary focus the generation of understanding, the promotion of values, and the producing of action. Consider, in particular, the celebrated address of Agathon. This well-structured and moving speech began with an explanatory introduction containing a set of rules and guidelines for delivering a speech of praise. This was followed by a tribute to Eros who, according to Agathon, exemplified not only the virtues of tenderness and gracefulness but the four cardinal virtues of courage, temperance, wisdom, and justice. In the development of these values, the speaker utilized logical and emotional appeals, reinforced by examples, analogies, and quotations expressed in vivid language. As Agathon concluded his oration and the guests gave their approval by applauding his eloquent effort, Socrates calmly but forcefully asked a series of questions designed to put the speech into clearer focus.

At this point the emphasis shifted from the discussion of Agathon's speech to a recreation of a reported dialogue on love which presumably took place between Socrates and a woman named Diotima who was reputed to be an expert on love. All of the principal elements of Plato's dialectical method were evident in this discussion. Definition of terms, the blending of analysis and synthesis, refutation and response, and shared answers unfolded as the disputants, relying on the process of recollection, moved in a hierarchical progression from an understanding of physical beauty to that of the eternal beauty or form in the mind of God.

Symposium then drew to a close with a speech from Alcibiades eulogizing Socrates for his lifelong devotion to truth, his personification of love, and the rigor of his dialectical procedure. *Symposium,* in short, is a testimonial both to Plato's well-conceived and executed theory of rhetoric and his ability to put his own high rhetorical ideals into practice.

What, we may ask in conclusion, can we say about the impact of Plato's theory of discourse on his contemporaries and on subsequent theorists? Our response to this question must, of necessity, place Plato in a favorable light. Notwithstanding the fact that he occasionally was overly idealistic and sometimes inconsistant in articulating his theories, he is to be commended for his imaginative insights. With virtually no guidelines to serve as a precedent and no models to imitate, he molded a theory of discourse which has had an enormous evolutionary thrust. It was a theory that provided the basic structure and inspiration for Aristotle's *Rhetoric,* and for many of the ideas later developed in the writings of Cicero and Quintilian. Similarly the Platonic standards for a true rhetoric doubtless influenced such British and Continental scholars as Vico, Blair, and Campbell.

Even more remarkable, I feel, is Plato's relevance for contemporary students of rhetoric. His conviction that human discourse is central to man's existence; that rhetoric at its highest seeks to create knowledge, promote values, and produce action; and that dialectic, with its reliance on argument, represents the ideal rhetorical method place him squarely in the tradition of modern thought.

From the claims advanced in this study, three conclusions may be drawn which one hopes will have special significance for those teachers of English and speech who see a close relationship between classical theories of discourse and current communication needs of college and university students. First, Plato, contrary to much of the opinion associated with his perceived legacy, developed a complete system of rhetoric that embraced all of the elements of a communication model—the source, message, channel, and receiver—and included an appropriate stress on each of the standard five canons—invention, disposition, style, memory, and delivery. Moreover, it was a system that takes into consideration most of the specialized communication forms. Intrapersonal, interpersonal, and public communication commanded his attention; so, too, did speaking, writing, and criticism.[102]

Secondly, Plato's strong preference for an ethics-centered theory of discourse gave to his ideas a permanent relevance. In developing these moral views, he taught us that effectiveness alone is an inadequate criterion for measuring the genuine worth of a rhetorical transaction. To this aspect of evaluation must be added the concept of a sense of responsibility and the requirement of adapting rhetorical appeals to our better natures. This value-laden approach contributed importantly to the shaping of Richard Weaver's philosophy on the sermonic nature of language and to Chaim Perelman's assertion that the major function of discourse is to gain adherence of the minds of the audience concerning the ethical precepts that bind a society.

Finally, the rhetorical teachings of Plato, while emphasizing the various forms of communication, highlight in an impressive way the potential influence of dialectic as an innovative and powerful instructional device. By stressing abstract ideas and generative universal principles, the analysis and synthesis of both simple and complex concepts, and a dialogical method of constructing arguments and counter arguments, dialectic constitutes an ideal approach for producing knowledge.

In sum, to revisit Plato is to come to an appreciation of the appealing notion that he was "a man for all seasons." At the same time it reminds us again of the wisdom of Edward P. J. Corbett in recommending that we turn to the past in order to learn more about the present and the future.

3

On Distinctions between Classical and Modern Rhetoric

Andrea A. Lunsford and Lisa S. Ede

The tentative emergence of a modern or a "new" rhetoric has been characterized by the attempt both to recover and reexamine the concepts of classical rhetoric and to define itself *against* that classical tradition. The works of Richard Weaver, Richard McKeon, Kenneth Burke, Donald Bryant and, later, Albert Duhamel, Chaim Perelman, and Edward P. J. Corbett helped draw attention to major tenets and values of the classical system. Daniel Fogarty's important *Roots for a New Rhetoric* (1959) stands at a metaphorical crossroads, affirming the continuing need for a viable rhetoric and sketching in the broad outlines of a "new" rhetoric that would meet that need:

> [The new rhetoric] will need to broaden its aim until it no longer confines itself to teaching the art of formal persuasion but includes formation in every kind of symbol-using . . . ; it will need to adjust itself to the recent studies in the psychology and sociology of communication; and, finally, it will need to make considerable provision for a new kind of speaker-listener situation.[1]

The years since 1959 have witnessed numerous attempts to define modern rhetoric more fully—attempts that consistently have rested on distinctions drawn between classical rhetoric and an emerging "new" system.[2] We believe that focusing primarily on distinctions between the "old" and the "new" rhetoric has led to unfortunate oversimplifications and distortions. Consequently, our purpose in this essay is to survey the distinctions typically drawn between classical and modern rhetoric, to suggest why these distinctions are inaccurate and, most importantly, to note the compelling similarities between classical and modern rhetoric. These similarities, we believe, can help clarify the features essential to any dynamic theory of rhetoric.

Although stated in widely varying terms, the distinctions persistently drawn between classical and modern or "new" rhetoric fall under four related heads. Images of man and of society provide one area frequently cited as distinguishing the two rhetorical periods. According to many definers of new rhetoric, the classical tradition, and especially Aristotle, defined man as a "rational animal" who dealt with problems of the world primarily through logic or reason and who lived during a time characterized by stable values, social cohesion, and a unified cultural ideal.[3] In contrast, modern rhetoric defines man as essentially a "rhetorical" or "symbol-using" or "communal" animal who constitutes the world through shared and private symbols.[4] And this modern man is said to live not in a simple, cohesive society but in an aleatoric universe in which generally agreed upon values and unifying norms are scarce or nonexistent.[5] In such a universe, it is argued, the bases of classical rhetoric are simply inadequate.

The second distinction often drawn between classical and contemporary rhetoric—that classical rhetoric emphasizes logical proofs while modern rhetoric stresses emotional (or psychological) proofs—is closely related to the first. Young, Becker, and Pike argue, for example, that Aristotle's image of man as a rational animal had a direct influence on his rhetoric: "Underlying the classical tradition is the notion that although men are often swayed by passions, their basic and distinguishing characteristic is their ability to reason . . . . [Thus for classical rhetoricians] logical argument . . . was the heart of persuasive discourse."[6] According to Douglas Ehninger, this preference for logical proof is also evident in classical invention, which focuses on the analysis of subject matter at the expense of a concern for "the basic laws of human understanding." As a result, Ehninger notes, a successful classical orator has to be "an expert logician," while the modern speaker or writer needs, in contrast, to be "a keen student of practical psychology."[7]

A third often-cited distinction between the two periods concerns the rhetor-audience relationship, a relationship said to be characterized in the classical period by manipulative, antagonistic, one-way or unidirectional communication.[8] The new rhetoric is conversely said to posit not an antagonistic but a cooperative relationship between rhetor and audience, one based upon empathy, understanding, mutual trust, and two-way or "dialogic" communication.[9] *In Rhetoric: Discovery and Change,* for instance, Young, Becker, and Pike reject what they see as the classical model of "skillful verbal coercion" and introduce instead a "Rogerian rhetoric" of "enlightened cooperation."[10] In his 1967 and 1968 essays describing systems of rhetoric, Douglas Ehninger labels the new rhetoric "social" or "sociological" and argues that it is an "instrument for understanding."[11]

The final distinction often drawn between the two periods is inextricably related to the rhetor-audience relationship just described. This distinction results from identifying the goal of classical rhetoric as persuasion, while the goal of the new rhetoric is identified as communication. In his widely influential 1936 study, *The Philosophy of Rhetoric,* I. A. Richards articulates this view:

> Among the general themes of the old Rhetoric [which he associates with Aristotle] is one which is especially pertinent to our inquiry. The old Rhetoric was an offspring of dispute; it developed as the rationale of pleadings and persuadings; it was the theory of the battle of words and has always been itself dominated by the combative impulse.[12]

Wilbur Samuel Howell, whose works on sixteenth-, seventeenth-, and eighteenth-century rhetoric have become standard texts, also identifies persuasion as the goal of classical rhetoric and specifically argues that the "new" eighteenth-century rhetoric explicitly embraced exposition and communication as goals.[13] Recent articles by Otis Walter, Richard Ohmann, Herbert Simons, Douglas Ehninger, Richard Young, and Paul Bator describe classical (and often specifically Aristotelian) rhetoric as emphasizing success or winning above all else, often depicting rhetors as attempting to coerce or impose their will on others.[14] In Ohmann's words, classical rhetoric is "concerned, fundamentally, with *persuasion.* The practical rhetorician—the orator—seeks to impel his audience from apathy to action or from old opinion to new, by appealing to will, emotion, and reason. And the novice . . . learns the tricks."[15] Most of these writers claim that the new rhetoric, on the other hand, stresses not coercive persuasion but communication, understanding, and reduction of threat through dialogue.

Table 1 summarizes the four distinctions which are persistently drawn between classical and modern rhetoric. Of the many points which could be made about these distinctions, one seems particularly crucial: they resolve to two contradictory claims about the nature of classical rhetoric. The first two distinctions, which view the classical image of man as a rational being and the logical proofs as supreme, discount

Table 1: Major Distinctions Typically Drawn between Classical and Modern Rhetoric

Classical Rhetoric	Modern Rhetoric
1. Man is a rational animal living in a society marked by social cohesion and agreed-upon values.	1. Man is a symbol-using animal living in a fragmented society.
2. Emphasis is on logical (or rational) proofs.	2. Emphasis is on emotional (or psychological) proofs.
3. Rhetor-audience relationship is antagonistic, characterized by manipulative one-way communication.	3. Rhetor-audience relationship is cooperative, characterized by emphatic, two-way communication.
4. Goal is *persuasion*.	4. Goal is *communication*.

classical rhetoric as too rationalistic.[16] The latter two, which present the rhetor-audience relationship in classical rhetoric as antagonistic and uni-directional and its goal as persuasion (in the narrowest, most limited sense), discount classical rhetoric as too dependent upon emotional man-ipulation and coercion.

This disconcerting contradiction is perhaps the strongest evidence that the conventional understanding of classical rhetoric, as embodied in the above distinctions, is seriously flawed. The resulting confusion has led not only to major distortions and misrepresentations of classical rhetoric, but to critical misunderstandings of our own potential system as well. Although we believe a strong argument can be made that these distinctions distort classical rhetoric in general, space restrictions do not permit us to make such a case here.[17] Instead, we have chosen to use Aristotle as the locus of our discussion because the Aristotelian theory is the most complete of all classical rhetorics and, more importantly, be-cause many current misconceptions grow out of a limited reading of Aristotle's *Rhetoric*. In particular, we wish to argue that the distinctions we have outlined reflect two major problems: 1) a failure to relate Aristo-tle's *Rhetoric* to the rest of his philosophy; and 2) serious, persistent misunderstandings about the nature and function of the *pisteis* and of the *enthymeme* in Aristotelian rhetoric.

One of the most essential characteristics of Aristotle's philosophical system is its integration. It is no accident, for example, that Aristotle begins his work on rhetoric by carefully noting its relationship with dialectic. As William M. A. Grimaldi observes in his *Studies in the Philosophy of Aristotle's Rhetoric,* Aristotle in this work "insists from the outset upon showing the relation of his comments to his work on dialectic, epistemology, ethics, and even metaphysics. . . . Throughout the analysis his constant explicit and implicit reference to his own philosophical work clearly reveals that he was working with his own philosophical system in mind."[18]

A recent article by Christopher Lyle Johnstone on "An Aristotelian Trilogy: Ethics, Rhetoric, Politics, and the Search for Moral Truth" demonstrates how the failure to relate Aristotle's analysis of rhetoric to his discussion of ethics and politics has resulted in critical misinterpretations of Aristotle's intent.[19] As an example, Johnstone cites the often-quoted passage in the *Rhetoric* in which Aristotle emphasizes the necessity of "putting the judge in 'a certain' or 'the right' frame of mind," a statement often used as evidence that Aristotle advocates crass emotional manipulation (p. 9). What commentators have failed to recognize is that in the *Nicomachean Ethics* Aristotle consistently uses the same phrase to mean "the *morally* right condition, the state in which emotion is amenable to rational guidance" (p. 9). This emphasis on rational guidance should not, however, be interpreted as support for the view that Aristotle advocates an exclusively rational rhetoric since the end of rhetoric, as Aristotle clearly indicates, is *krisis* (judgment), "an activity of the practical intellect, and thus one directed by *logos* and *pathos* functioning in a complementary relationship. As a result 'the right frame of mind' can only be taken to refer to that emotional state that, when joined by reason in the process of judging or deciding, makes intelligent and responsible choice possible" (pp. 9–10).[20]

This example is symptomatic of the misunderstandings that can occur when commentators ignore the fundamental connections among Aristotle's writings. Lawrence Rosenfield makes a similar point in "Rhetorical Criticism and an Aristotelian Notion of Process," which explores the relationship between Aristotle's concept of process, or "the way in which an object acquires characteristics or properties," and his concept of animism.[21] Basic to Rosenfield's argument is his assertion that "the essential contribution of the concept of animism to Aristotle's notion of process is that of dynamic interaction between an agent and an object undergoing change" (p. 4). As a result, Rosenfield questions whether in Aristotelian rhetoric "the figure which best captures the communicator's role . . . is not that of a puppeteer, who manipulates his audience according to his skill at persuasion, but that of a mid-wife who focuses and directs energies inherent in the listener himself" (p. 8). In fact, Aristotle's metaphysics intrinsically rejects exploitive or "monologic" communication from speaker to listener (p. 15).

As even this brief discussion should suggest, investigations of the relationship between Aristotle's rhetorical and philosophical writings can help us locate alternatives to previous interpretations of the *Rhetoric* which have, simplistically, tended to characterize that work as exclusively committed either to rational or emotional appeals. In order fully to resolve the reductive dilemma posed by these contradictory interpretations, however, we must finally turn to the *Rhetoric* itself, particularly to the *pisteis* and the *enthymeme*. For much of the confusion surrounding the *Rhetoric* can be traced, finally, to an inadequate understanding of the nature of and interrelationships among Aristotle's methods of proof.

As William Grimaldi observes, the traditional conception of the nature and role of the *pisteis* is that they are "three independent modes of rhetorical demonstration: non-logical (or quasi-logical) demonstration by the use of *ethos* and *pathos,* and logical demonstration by means of the *enthymeme,* the syllogism of rhetoric" (*Studies,* p. 65).[22] Such a view encourages the conflict between the role of reason and emotion in the *Rhetoric* which has complicated interpretations of that work and led to the contradiction noted above. For if the *pisteis* are viewed as discrete, separable elements of discourse, then *logos* and its tool the *enthymeme* may be isolated and crowned supreme (as some commentators have done). Or *pathos* may hold sway instead, resulting in a view of rhetoric as overly emotional and manipulative. The solution to this dilemma must be to replace an oversimplified notion of the *pisteis* as elements that can be added to discourse—rather like ingredients in a recipe—with a more complex understanding of the inseparable strands that link people engaged in discourse.

In his *Studies in the Philosophy of Aristotle's Rhetoric* and *Aristotle, Rhetoric I: A Commentary,* William Grimaldi articulates such an enriched, corrective perspective.[23] His complex argument cannot be fully described here, but particularly central to his discussion are: 1) his analyses of the multiple uses of the words *pistis* and *pisteis* in the original text[24] and of the pre-Aristotelian history of the word *enthymeme*; and 2) his discussion of the relationship of the *eide* and *koinoi topoi* to the *pisteis* (*logos, ethos,* and *pathos*) and of these *pisteis* to *enthymeme* and *paradeigma* (example). The resulting analysis represents a powerful alternative explication of the basic method of rhetorical discourse as outlined in the *Rhetoric.* In this method, the *enthymeme* is not a mere tool of *logos,* nor do the three *pisteis* of *logos, ethos,* and *pathos* function independently of one another. Rather, they interact in the *enthymeme* and *paradeigma,* the two central methods of rhetorical demonstration—the former deductive, the latter inductive.

Thus Grimaldi clarifies our understanding of the *enthymeme*, broadening its generally accepted definition as the limited tool of *logos* to one of the two modes of inference through which rhetor and audience together move toward *krisis*.

Grimaldi's analysis thus dissolves the apparent contradiction between reason and emotion in the *Rhetoric* and demonstrates that the contradictory interpretations of classical rhetoric we described earlier represent a false dichotomy. Aristotle's *Rhetoric* is neither an abstract theoretical treatise in praise of *logos* nor a handbook of manipulative emotional tricks. Rather, through the *enthymeme*, which (along with *paradeigma*) integrates and organizes the *pisteis* of *logos, ethos,* and *pathos,* Aristotle develops a system of language use whereby individuals unite all their resources—intellect, will, and emotion—in communicating with one another. The *Rhetoric,* then, acknowledges that we are moved to *krisis* not just by knowledge but by emotion as well: "In rhetorical discourse the audience must be brought not only to knowledge of the subject but knowledge as relevant and significant for they are either indifferent, opposed, or in partial agreement. . . . If the whole person acts then it is the whole person to whom discourse in rhetoric must be directed" (*Studies,* pp. 146–47).

An understanding of how Aristotle's *Rhetoric* relates to his entire philosophical system and of how the *enthymeme* and the *pisteis* function in the *Rhetoric* suggests that the characterization of classical rhetoric summarized in Table 1 is inadequate and misleading. The first distinction, which posits classical man as solely a rational being living in a stable society seems particularly oversimplistic. As our discussion of the *enthymeme* indicates, the rational man of Aristotle's rhetoric is not a logic-chopping automaton but a language-using animal who unites reason and emotion in discourse with others. Aristotle (and indeed, Plato and Isocrates as well) studied the power of the mind to gain meaning from the world and to share that meaning with others.[25] And far from being a highly stable society marked by agreement on all values, Aristotle's Greece was one of upheaval: old beliefs in the gods were increasingly challenged, the political structure of the Greek city state system was under attack, and the educational system was embroiled in deep controversy.[26]

Equally inadequate is the second distinction, held by those who argue that classical rhetoric privileges logical proofs. As we have seen, such a view oversimplifies Aristotle's own complex analysis of the nature of reason, ignoring his careful discrimination of the speculative and practical intellect. In addition, this distinction misrepresents the nature and function of the *enthymeme* and the *pisteis*.

If *logos, ethos,* and *pathos* are dynamically related in the *enthymeme,* the third traditional distinction, which characterizes the rhetor-audience relationship in classical rhetoric as antagonistic and unidirectional, is equally unacceptable. Further support to this position is given by Lawrence Rosenfield's discussion of Aristotle's concept of process and by Lloyd Bitzer's analysis of the *enthymeme* in "Aristotle's Enthymeme Revisited," which argues that since "enthymemes occur only when speaker and audience jointly produce them . . . [they] intimately unite speaker and audience and provide the strongest possible proofs."[27] Far from being "one-way," "manipulative," or "monological," Aristotle's rhetoric provides a complete description of the dynamic interaction between rhetor and audience, an interaction mediated by language. Seen in the light of Aristotle's entire system of thought, the rhetorical elements of rhetor, audience, and subject matter are dynamic, interlocking forces.

Finally, if the relationship between the rhetor and the audience in Aristotle's system is indeed dynamic and interdependent, then the goal of Aristotelian rhetoric can hardly be persuasion in the narrow or pejorative sense in which it is used by those who equate persuasion with manipulation and coercion. We suggest that a much more accurate way to describe Aristotle's concept of the goal of rhetoric is as an interactive means of discovering meaning through language.[28] It is, as Richard Hughes notes in "The Contemporaneity of Classical Rhetoric," "a generative process," one in which the rhetor "is both investigator and communicator."[29] As Grimaldi observes, rhetoric was for Aristotle "the heart of the process by which man tried to interpret and make meaningful for himself and others the world of the real" (*Studies,* p. 54). This process may be termed "persuasion," only in the broad sense that all language is inherently persuasive. In his discussion of the function of rhetoric, Kenneth Burke says that "there is no chance of our keeping apart the meanings of persuasion, identification ('consubstantiality') and communication." We have thus, Burke notes, "come to the point at which Aristotle begins his treatise on rhetoric."[30]

In spite of the large body of scholarship which should have kept us from drawing misleading distinctions, the view of classical rhetoric as manipulative, monologic, and rationalistic persists. We believe that we, therefore, must also come back to Aristotle, to a richer understanding of how his theory can enrich and illuminate our own. Indeed, major distinctions between Aristotelian and contemporary rhetoric do exist, but these distinctions are more fundamental than those traditionally cited. While we shall note these distinctions, we wish to stress what we believe are compelling similarities between the two rhetorics, similarities which draw contemporary rhetoric closer to the classical system rather than further away from it. Our understanding of these similarities and of the profound distinctions which must accompany them, as outlined in Table 2, will help us identify those qualities which must characterize any vital theory of rhetoric.

Table 2: Similarities and Qualifying Distinctions between Classical and Modern Rhetoric

1. Both classical and modern rhetoric view man as a language-using animal who unites reason and emotion in discourse with another.
   Qualifying distinction:
   Aristotle addresses himself primarily to the oral use of language; ours is primarily an age of print.
2. In both periods rhetoric provides a dynamic methodology whereby rhetor and audience may jointly have access to knowledge.
   Qualifying distinction:
   According to Aristotle, rhetor and audience come into a state of knowing which places them in a clearly defined relationship with the world and with each other, mediated by their language. The prevailing modernist world view compels rhetoric to operate without any such clearly articulated theory of the knower and the known.
3. In both periods rhetoric has the potential to clarify and inform activities in numerous related fields.
   Qualifying distinction:
   Aristotle's theory establishes rhetoric as an art and relates it clearly to all fields of knowledge. Despite the efforts of modern rhetoricians, we lack any systematic, generally accepted theory to inform current practice.

One similarity between classical and modern rhetoric is their shared *concept of man as a language-using animal who unites reason and emotion in discourse with another.* Central to this concept is the role of language in the creation of knowledge or belief and its relationship to the knowing mind. We have already demonstrated the ways in which Aristotle's *Rhetoric* unites reason and emotion. In addition, Aristotle's works on logic, ethics, and epistemology as well as the *Rhetoric* demonstrate that Aristotle recognized the powerful dynamism of the creating human mind. These works further indicate that Aristotle was aware of man's ability to use symbols and that he viewed language as the medium through which judgments about the world are communicated.

Modern theories, of course, also posit language as the ground of rhetoric. This view is articulated in Burke's famous statement that rhetoric "is rooted in an essential function of language itself, a function that is wholly realistic, and is continually born anew; the use of language as a symbolic means of inducing cooperation in beings that by nature respond to symbols."[31] Theorists as dissimilar as I. A. Richards, Chaim Perelman, and Wayne Booth hold parallel views on the relation between language and rhetoric.

As expected in rhetorics removed by twenty-three hundred years, however, Aristotle's system of language use differs from ours. The resultant distinction between the two periods is potentially profound: Aristotle addressed himself primarily to oral discourse; modern rhetorics have addressed themselves primarily to written discourse. Our understanding of the historical and methodological ramifications of the speaking/writing distinction has been hampered by the twentieth-century split among speech, linguistics, philosophy, and English departments. Despite the work of scholars such as Walter Ong, Kenneth Burke, and Jacques Derrida, many questions about the relationship of speech and writing remain unanswered and, in some cases, unexplored.[32]

The second major similarity we find between Aristotelian and modern rhetoric is the view of rhetoric as a *techne or dynamic methodology through which rhetor and audience, a self and an other, may jointly have access to knowledge.*[33] We have already examined Aristotle's concept of the *enthymeme* and the ways in which it united speaker and audience, *logos, ethos,* and *pathos,* in the pursuit of knowledge leading to action. In modern theory, particularly the work of Kenneth Burke, rhetoric provides the means through which we may both achieve identification with an other and understand that identification through the attribution of motives. Similarly, Chaim Perelman's rhetorical system posits rhetoric as the process through which rhetor and audience gain access to knowledge.

We believe that such a view of rhetoric as creative or epistemic must characterize any viable, dynamic rhetoric and, indeed, any other view reduces the role of rhetoric to a "naming of parts" or to stylistic embellishment, reductions characteristic of many rhetorical theories. But this basic similarity should not mask an equally important distinction between classical and modern rhetoric. As we have seen, this distinction concerns not the notion of man, the nature of proof, the speaker-audience relationship, nor the goal of rhetoric. Instead, this distinction concerns the nature and status of knowledge.[34]

In Aristotle's system, knowledge may be either of the necessary or the contingent. Knowledge of the necessary or universal, *episteme*, operates in the realm of the theoretical or scientific. Breaking with Plato, Aristotle admits of another kind of knowledge, that of the contingent. Such knowledge, *doxa*, is the way of knowing contingent reality (that is, the world around us that is both characterized and limited by change). Rhetoric's realm is limited to the contingent, and the connections among language, thought, and that reality are grounded in an epistemology which posits reality independent of the knower. In short, rhetoric uses thought and language to lead to judgment (*krisis*) as the basis of action in matters of this world. And for Aristotle, that world of contingent reality, though itself in a state of flux, could be understood by systematic application of the intellect because that reality was itself thought to be informed by stable first principles.

Modern rhetorical theory rests on no such fully confident epistemology, nor does knowledge enjoy such a clearly defined status. In fact, we are in radical disagreement over what "knowledge" may be, though we generally agree on man's ability to communicate that disagreement. Hence, for the modern period, connections among thought, language, and reality are thought to be grounded not in an independent, chartable reality but in the nature of the knower instead, and reality is not so much discovered or discoverable as it is constituted by the interplay of thought and language. Though we lack a fully articulated theory, Kenneth Burke, Richard Weaver, and Wayne Booth offer intensive investigations into the rhetoric of this interplay; and works in disciplines as diverse as anthropology, language philosophy, literary criticism, philosophy, psychology, and the physical sciences suggest that, as Michael Polanyi says in the opening of *Personal Knowledge,* "We must inevitably see the universe from a centre lying within ourselves and speak about it in terms of a human language shaped by the exigencies of human intercourse. Any attempt rigorously to eliminate our human perspective from our pictures of the world must lead to absurdity."[35]

Rhetoric's grounding in language and its potential ability to join rhetor and audience in the discovery of shared (communicable) knowledge suggests a third compelling similarity between classical and modern rhetoric: *in both periods rhetoric has the potential to clarify and inform activities in numerous related fields.* By establishing rhetoric as the *antistrophos* or corollary of dialectic,[36] Aristotle immediately places rhetoric in relation to other fields of knowledge, and these relationships are painstakingly worked out in the *Organon.* Rhetoric, poetics, and ethics all involve *doxa,* knowledge of contingent, shifting reality. Hence, rhetoric is necessarily useful in addressing complex human problems in any field where certainty is unachievable.

In addition, Aristotle's *Rhetoric* provided a theory that was intimately related to practice. For the Greeks, and indeed for the Romans who followed them, rhetoric was a practical art of discourse which played a central role in education and in the daily affairs of citizens. Aristotle's work established a theoretical relationship among belief, language, and action; Isocrates, Cicero, and Quintilian all adapted and acted out that theory, Quintilian using it as a basis for a rhetoric which would serve as a way of knowing and a guide to action throughout a person's life.

From the time of Quintilian, the history of rhetoric has been haunted by a whittling away of domain, a compartmentalization of its offices, and a frequent dramatic separation of theory and practice. The most obvious instance of rhetoric's diminution is Ramus' assignment of *inventio* and *dispositio* to logic, thus leaving rhetoric with a concern only for style. Even George Campbell and Alexander Bain, both of whom attempted to ground rhetoric in a full psychology, did not fully admit invention into the province of rhetoric. Not until philosophers began to recapture the crucial conception of language as a meaning-making activity, an essential element in the social construction of reality, has rhetoric had the opportunity to regain some of its lost status and scope, to inform both education and ordinary behavior and thus clarify a number of related fields.

Why, thus far at least, has this opportunity not been realized? A partial answer to this question must lie in what we see as a final qualifying distinction between classical and modern rhetorics. Aristotle's theory is revolutionary in that it establishes rhetoric as an art and relates it clearly to all fields of knowledge. Despite the efforts of modern rhetoricians, we lack any such systematic theory to inform current practice. In fact, our age has witnessed a curious divorce between rhetorical theory and practice and an extreme fragmentation of our discipline. Earlier in this essay, we alluded to the large body of rhetorical "theory" which argues that modern rhetoric is characterized by understanding, mutual sharing, and two-way communication. Yet how well does such theory account for or describe twentieth-century rhetorical practice, which has surely reached new heights (or depths) of manipulative use of language?

The position of rhetorical theory and practice in education is equally fragmented. While theorists in speech departments consider the theoretical concept of "dialogic communication," their counterparts in English departments struggle over abstruse questions of intentionality in literary texts, and scholars in linguistics departments strive to describe the abstract grammar of a sentence. Meanwhile, instruction in rhetorical practice—speaking, writing, and reading—is usually relegated to graduate students and part-time instructors and looked upon as menial "service." As a result, most of our textbooks offer compendia of "how-to" tips but fail to ground that advice in a theoretical framework that would relate language, action, and belief.[37]

Such a situation is a far cry from Aristotle's elegant theory, from Cicero's powerful statesmanship, or from Quintilian's masterful pedagogy. But if our failure to articulate a systematic theory which informs current practice is great, our need is even greater. We believe that the work of such theorists as Kenneth Burke, Chaim Perelman, Wolfgang Iser, Richard Weaver, and Wayne Booth offers a modern ground for the reunion of rhetorical theory and practice. But such a reunion demands that we attempt to reinstate rhetoric at or near the center of our curriculum, as the art of using language in the creation—and sharing—of knowledge and belief.

One way to begin this task is by eschewing the false distinctions that have been drawn persistently between classical and modern rhetoric and by building instead on their powerful similarities. If we see Aristotle's *Rhetoric* as a work which unites rhetor and audience, language and action, theory and practice, then we have a model for our own *antistrophos*. If rhetoric is to reach its full potential in the twentieth century as an informing framework for long-divorced disciplines and for instruction and conduct in reading, writing, and speaking, then we must define ourselves not in opposition to but in consonance with the classical model.

4

The Evolution of the Analytic *Topoi*: A Speculative Inquiry

Frank J. D'Angelo

In his article "Invention: A Topographical Essay," Richard Young asserts that teachers of writing need to know more about the history of invention. "Understanding invention," he writes, "requires, among other things, that we understand the history of invention."[1]

> One reason for this is that some of the most significant work in the 2500-year life of the discipline was done at its inception. Plato and Aristotle, and later Cicero and Quintilian, defined what are still by and large the basic issues, at least in Western rhetoric. We cannot understand what is happening unless we understand what happened. Furthermore, without a knowledge of history, we have no way of knowing what is genuinely new, what is redundant, what is promising, what has been tried before and found wanting. But perhaps more important than enabling us to understand and assess present developments, a knowledge of the history of invention provides us with conceptual systems which we can work within, or modify, or react against—an intellectually stimulating situation and probably necessary if the discipline is to grow.[2]

These are all excellent reasons for pursuing the study of invention. But as Richard Young laments, "histories of invention are rare."[3] In addition, the subject is so broad. Classical invention, for example, included much more than what many teachers of writing think of when they think about invention. It included the two kinds of proof that Aristotle discusses in the *Rhetoric*: inartistic and artistic. Artistic invention in turn consisted of three kinds of appeals: ethical, emotional, and logical. The logical appeal included two kinds of reasoning about a subject: deduction (based on the syllogism and the enthymeme) and

50

induction (based on the argument from example). Classical invention also placed great importance on the concept of *stasis* (the main point at issue in an argument) and on the *topoi*, and it is with the *topoi* that I will be chiefly concerned in this paper.

For a number of years, I have been trying to trace the historical development of the analytic *topoi*. In the process, I have discovered that I could better understand the *topoi* to the extent that I could see them emerging in stages of increasing abstraction and to the extent that I was able to view them within a developmental perspective. In an article that appeared in the *Quarterly Journal of Speech,* I had theorized that the series of stages through which the composing process passes recapitulates a sequence of stages in the evolution of consciousness. "In this view, the composing process is analogous to universal evolutionary processes in which an original, amorphous, undifferentiated whole gradually evolves into a more complex, differentiated one."[4]

In this essay, I would like to make a related point—that the evolutionary development of the analytic *topoi* recapitulates these same generalized stages. More specifically, the analytic *topoi* begin in an undifferentiated state in oral poetic narrative where they are embedded in the narrative continuum, and they emerge historically in stages of increasing abstraction, differentiation, and hierarchic integration. The evolution of the analytic *topoi* seems to follow a basic principle of developmental psychology: that "whenever development occurs, it proceeds from a state of relative lack of differentiation, to a state of increasing differentiation, articulation, and hierarchic integration."[5]

These stages, as I shall present them, are to some extent arbitrary and idealized, without clear transitions from one stage to another. I present them, however, as a working hypothesis to be modified in the light of better evidence. My primary purpose in presenting them is to provide a conceptual framework for a better understanding of invention and the composing process.

Global Stage

The first stage in the evolution of the analytic *topoi* is the global stage. Of this stage we have scanty evidence, since we must assume the ontogeny of invention in terms of spoken language long before the individual is capable of anything like written language. But some hints of how logical invention might have developed can be found in the work of Eric Havelock. In his *Preface to Plato,* Havelock, in recapitulating the educational experience of the Homeric and post-Homeric Greek, comments that the psychology of the Homeric Greek is characterized by a high degree of automatism.

> He is required as a civilised being to become acquainted with the history, the social organisation, the technical competence and the moral imperatives of his group. This in turn is able to function only as a fragment of the total Hellenic world. It shares a consciousness in which he is keenly aware that he, as a Hellene, partakes. This over-all body of experience (we shall avoid the word "knowledge") is incorporated in a rhythmic narrative or set of narratives which he memorises and which is subject to recall in his memory. Such is poetic tradition, essentially something he accepts uncritically, or else it fails to survive in his living memory. Its acceptance and retention are made psychologically possible by a mechanism of self-surrender to the poetic performance and of self-identification with the situations and the stories related in the performance. . . . His receptivity to the tradition has thus, from the standpoint of inner psychology, a degree of automatism which however is counter-balanced by a direct and unfettered capacity for action in accordance with the paradigms he has absorbed.[6]

Preliterate man was apparently unable to think logically. He acted, or as Julian Jaynes, in *The Origin of Consciousness in the Breakdown of the Bicameral Mind,* puts it, "reacted" to external events. "There is in general," writes Jaynes, "no consciousness in the Iliad . . . and in general therefore, no words for consciousness or mental acts."[7] There was, in other words, no subjective consciousness in Iliadic man. His actions were not rooted in conscious plans or in reasoning. We can only speculate, then, based on the evidence given by Havelock and Jaynes that logical invention, at least in any kind of sophisticated form, could not take place until the breakdown of the bicameral mind, with the invention of writing. If ancient peoples were unable to introspect, then we must assume that the analytic *topoi* were a discovery of literate man. Eric Havelock, however, warns that the picture he gives of Homeric and post-Homeric man is oversimplified and that there are signs of a latent mentality in the Greek mind. But in general, Homeric man was more concerned to go along with the tradition than to make individual judgments.

For Iliadic man to be able to think, he must think about something. To do this, states Havelock, he had to be able to revolt against the habit of self-identification with the epic poem. But identification with the poem at this time in history was necessary psychologically (identification was necessary for memorization) and culturally (the epic poem preserved the laws, history, tradition, mores, and social imperatives of the group). To make the poem an object of knowledge, writes Havelock, the contents, which appear in the epic story implicitly as acts or events that are carried out by important people, must be abstracted from the narrative flux. "Thus the autonomous subject who no longer recalls and feels, but knows, can now be confronted with a thousand abstract laws, principles, topics, and formulas which become the objects of his knowledge."[8]

The analytic *topoi*, then, were implicit in oral poetic discourse. They were "experienced" in the patterns of epic narrative, but once they are abstracted they can become objects of thought as well as of experience. As Eric Havelock puts it,

> If we view them [these abstractions] in relation to the epic narrative from which, as a matter of historical fact, they all emerged they can all be regarded as in one way or another classifications of an experience which was previously "felt" in an unclassified medley. This was as true of justice as of motion, of goodness as of body or space, of beauty as of weight or dimension. These categories turn into linguistic counters, and become used as a matter of course to relate one phenomenon to another in a non-epic, non-poetic, non-concrete idiom.[9]

The invention of the alphabet made it easier to report experience in a non-epic idiom. But it might be a simplification to suppose that the advent of alphabetic technology was the only influence on the emergence of logical thinking and the analytic topics, although perhaps it was the major influence. Havelock contends that the first "proto-thinkers" of Greece were the poets who at first used rhythm and oral formulas to attempt to arrange experience in categories, rather than in narrative events. He mentions in particular that it was Hesiod who first parts company with the narrative in the *Theogony* and *Works and Days*. In *Works and Days,* Hesiod uses a cataloging technique, consisting of proverbs, aphorisms, wise sayings, exhortations, and parables, intermingled with stories. But this effect of cataloging that goes "beyond the plot of a story in order to impose a rough logic of topics . . . presumes that Hesiod is operating with the help of the written word."[10]

The kind of material found in the catalogs of Hesiod was more like the cumulative commonplace material of the Renaissance than the abstract topics that we are familiar with today. Walter Ong notes that "the oral performer, poet or orator needed a stock of material to keep him going. The doctrine of the commonplaces is, from one point of view, the codification of ways of assuring and managing this stock."[11] We already know what some of the material was like: stock epithets, figures of speech, exempla, proverbs, sententiae, quotations, praises or censures of people and things, and brief treatises on virtues and vices. By the time we get to the invention of printing, there are vast collections of this commonplace material, so vast, relates Ong, that scholars could probably never survey it all. Ong goes on to observe that

> print gave the drive to collect and classify such excerpts a potential previously undreamed of. . . . the ranging of items side by side on a page once achieved, could be multiplied as never before. Moreover, printed collections of such commonplace excerpts could be handily indexed; it was worthwhile spending days or months working up an index because the results of one's labors showed fully in thousands of copies.[12]

To summarize, then, in oral cultures rhetorical invention was bound up with oral performance. At this stage, both the cumulative topics and the analytic topics were implicit in epic narrative. Then the cumulative commonplaces begin to appear, separated out by a cataloging technique from poetic narrative, in sources such as the *Theogony* and *Works and Days*. Eric Havelock points out that in Hesiod, the catalog "has been isolated or abstracted . . . out of a thousand contexts in the rich reservoir of oral tradition. . . . A general world view is emerging in isolated or 'abstracted' form."[13] Apparently, what we are witnessing is the emergence of logical thinking. Julian Jaynes describes the kind of thought to be found in the *Works and Days* as "preconscious hypostases." Certain lines in Hesiod, he maintains, exhibit "some kind of bicameral struggle."[14]

The first stage, then, of rhetorical invention is that in which the analytic *topoi* are embedded in oral performance in the form of commonplace material as "relationships" in an undifferentiated matrix. Oral cultures preserve this knowledge by constantly repeating the fixed sayings and formulae. Mnemonic patterns, patterns of repetition, are not added to the thought of oral cultures. They are what the thought consists of.

Analytic Stage

The second stage is characterized by increasing complexity and differentiation. Naturally there is much overlapping between stages. The first stage I have arbitrarily ended about 700 B.C., around the time of

Hesiod. I begin the second stage with the pre-Socratic philosophers around 624 B.C., although one might easily argue that the analytic stage begins with the conceptualization of rhetoric in the latter part of the fifth century B.C.

Based on Julian Jaynes' comment that certain lines in Hesiod exhibit "some kind of bicameral struggle," I am tempted to suggest that the first *topoi* emerged out of some kind of binary opposition. Robert Ornstein maintains that the lateral specialization of the brain is related to the evolution of language as well as to two modes of consciousness. The left hemisphere is related to linear, sequential thought, whereas the right hemisphere is related to holistic, intuitive thinking. These dominant modes suggest that primitive thinking might have been based on some kind of polarity.[15]

It would be a simplification to suggest that pre-Socratic Greek thought was characterized exclusively by polar thinking. Nevertheless, G. E. R. Lloyd, in his book *Polarity and Analogy: Two Types of Argumentation in Early Greek Thought,* does suggest that polarity and analogy were the dominant types of argument and methods of explanation in early Greek thought. In this study, Lloyd traces the development of logic and of the scientific method from Anaximander, Heraclitus, Parmenides, Zeno, and Anaxagoras through Democritus, the Pythagoreans, the Sophists, Gorgias, Plato and Aristotle. And he concludes that until we get to Plato and Aristotle, Greek thinkers failed "to distinguish sufficiently between similarity and identity, or between those modes of opposites that form mutually exclusive and exhaustive alternatives, and those that do not."[16] In other words, pre-Socratic philosophers tended to think in broad categories in a rough order of topics, rather than in the more differentiated kinds of categories that we find in Aristotle.

According to Mario Untersteiner, Protagoras was the first to devise the notion of the *topoi*. Protagoras discovered that two "logoi" of opposition were inherent in all reality, and he explained "the art of finding the *pro* and *contra* on all questions which could be put forward in a speech."[17] Lloyd, however, does not attribute the discovery of the *topoi* to Protagoras, but sees instead a long line of evolutionary development from Anaximander to Aristotle. "Cosmological, physiological and pathological theories based on opposites are extremely common both in the Presocratic philosophers and in the Hippocratic writers,"[18] he says, supporting this generalization with numerous examples from pre-Socratic writers. For example, Anaximander (c. 610–545 B.C.), in his theory of the formation of the world from the Boundless, speculates that "the first things that appear seem to have been a pair of opposed substances, whether 'the hot' and 'the cold' or 'flame' and 'air' or 'mist'."[19] Parmenides (c. 540–470 B.C.) postulates a pair of opposite primary substances, light and night, to account for the origin of the universe. Anaxagoras (499–427 B. C.) describes "an original mixture of all things which contains pairs of opposites"—wet and dry, hot and cold, bright and dark, and so forth.[20] Lloyd provides too much material for accurate summary, but he himself summarizes the main types of arguments involving opposites in the pre-Platonic period later on in the book.

> First, there is the putting of a choice between opposite alternatives in order to force an admission (as, for example, in Parmenides and Melissus); second the proof of a thesis by refuting the opposite (usually contrary) thesis (as notably in Zeno and Melissus); third the refutation of a thesis by showing that opposite (again usually contrary) consequences follow from it (Zeno); and fourth the refutation of a thesis by first stating certain alternatives one of which must be true if the thesis is true and then disproving each of these alternatives in turn (Gorgias).[21]

Lloyd then goes on to criticize the arguments from opposites that he had previously considered. The terms used in these arguments were equivocal, and those used to refer to opposites were not strictly defined. The relationships between opposites were often oversimplified or mis-defined. For example, there were no clear-cut distinctions between con-traries and contradictories that we later find in Aristotle. Nor were there "explicit" general distinctions drawn between different types of oppo-sites.[22]

Plato himself, Lloyd says, "was responsible for drawing certain important distinctions between different types of opposites, for clarifying the problem of contradiction, and, in particular, for showing that appar-ently contradictory statements in which a thing is asserted to be (in some sense) and not to be (in some other sense) are not contradictions at all."[23] Plato developed many of these distinctions in several of his dialogues through his method of Division. In practice, the form that Plato's method takes is a dichotomy—a genus is divided into a species or into a pair of contraries. But even in Plato, Lloyd contends, the alternatives vary a great deal. When Plato puts a choice between a pair of opposites, the choices are not always exhaustive ones.[24] Aristotle gives the most detailed and systematic treatment of the modes of opposition. He distinguishes between contraries and subcontraries, contraries and contradictories, cor-relatives, and so forth. Aristotle makes important distinctions between opposites that none of his predecessors had made.[25]

Just as the pre-Socratic philosophers tended to use polar thinking in their methods of argument to explain cosmological theories, so also they tended to use analogy in their speculative thinking to suggest that if two things resemble each other in one or more respects, they resemble each other in other respects. "Comparisons have a specially important and fruitful role in early Greek thought," writes Lloyd, "as the source of theories concerning phenomena which could not, in the nature of things, be investigated directly."[26] But just as the use of opposites in arguments by pre-Socratic thinkers was not always exact, neither was their use of analogies. Some of the analogies were farfetched. Some did not take into account negative instances.

Plato made certain important contributions to the logic of analogy, but it was Aristotle who gives the fullest description of analogy in his discussion of the paradigm. Aristotle divides paradigms into three groups: historical parallels, examples drawn from other fields, and fables. He classifies the paradigm as a rhetorical argument based on analogy, but since Aristotle is interested in the attainment of certainty in reasoning, he rejects all forms of induction except "the complete enumeration of particulars."[27]

What this brief look at polarity and analogy in early Greek thinking suggests is that by the time we get to Aristotle, the commonplace material which began to emerge around the time of Hesiod is well on its way to becoming the analytic *topoi*. Walter Ong summarizes this movement succinctly.

> Oral culture had generated the commonplace as part of its formulary apparatus for accumulating and retrieving knowledge. Script gave further play to the formulary drive, making it possible to assemble and classify the commonplaces by fixing them in one way or another on the surface of a written page. The result was first the theoretical codifications of "analytic" commonplaces (that is, the lists of headings or *loci*) by the Sophists, by Aristotle in his *Topics* and by Cicero, Quintilian, and others.[28]

The analytic commonplaces, then, emerged from the cumulative commonplaces as "relationships," on a scale of increasing abstraction from their origin in experience, to their gradually being detached from thousands of contexts in oral performance and epic narrative in the form of commonplace material. How was this done? The link between the cumulative commonplaces and the analytic *topoi* might possibly be found in the Aristotelian notion of the *topoi* as material from which enthymemes are formed. Prior to Aristotle, the *topoi* were used for particular speeches. As Friedrich Solmsen points out in his article "The Aristotelian Tradition in Ancient Rhetoric," "the *topoi* had before Aristotle been ready-made arguments or commonplaces 'into which they expected the speeches of both parties to fall most frequently.' "[29] But in Aristotle, the common topics are independent of particular subject matter.

In his discussion of the general topics in Book II of the *Rhetoric,* Aristotle lists twenty-eight *topoi* or "lines of arguments."[30]

1. opposites	15. inward thoughts/outward show
2. inflections	16. proportional results
3. correlative terms	17. identical results
4. more and less	18. altered choices
5. time	19. attributed motives
6. opponent's utterance	20. incentives and deterrents
7. definition	21. incredible occurrences
8. ambiguous terms	22. conflicting facts
9. division	23. how to meet slander
10. induction	24. cause to effect
11. existing decisions	25. course of action
12. parts to whole	26. actions compared
13. simple consequences	27. previous mistakes
14. criss-cross consequences	28. meaning of names

But these *topoi* were not the kind of abstract, analytic topics as we are accustomed to view them today. Scholars such as William Grimaldi contend that

> the rather truncated form in which the topics have come to us have been rather unfortunate since there has been lost along the way the far richer method of discourse on the human problems they provide. Seen as mere static, stock "commonplaces," stylized sources for discussion on all kinds of subject matter, they have lost the vital, dynamic character given to them by Aristotle, a character extremely fruitful for intelligent, mature discussion of the innumerable significant problems which face man. These *topoi* are "the primary, indivisible and inherent components from which enthymemes are to be constructed."[31]

For example, the first of the Aristotelian *topoi* is that of "opposites." (This *topos* is eminently suggestive of a kind of opposition in early Greek polar arguments.) A typical enthymeme that could be constructed using this topos would be: Temperance is good/Intemperance is bad. In other words, the *topoi* in Aristotle were used to construct propositions. They were embedded in these propositions as "relationships," and as Donovan Ochs suggests, in his article "Aristotle's Concept of the Formal Topics," these enthymemes could then easily be translated into syllogistic arguments. For purposes of discussion, Ochs puts the enthymemes that fall under the topic of opposites into a convenient scheme that looks like the following:[32]

Example A:
Premise one: Temperance is good
Premise two: Intemperance is bad

Example B:
Premise one: [If] war is cause of present evils
Premise two: [Then] peace is remedy

What is striking about this scheme is that it suggests the manner in which the *topoi* may have been abstracted from the narrative context or from cosmological arguments in early Greek thought. The *topoi* as unselfconscious rhetorical devices had been in existence before the conceptualization of rhetoric. But they were implicit and understood. Gradually, someone recognizes that a series of narrative statements or propositions which had been merely juxtaposed could be linked together in an explicit way. In other words, logical thinking may reside in a statement without the form of that statement expressing explicit logical coherence. This is the method of *mythos,* rather than *logos.* Finally, the Greeks develop the logic that is inherent in speech and in oral poetic narrative and give names to the relationships that exist between the propositions in an enthymeme. As Donovan Ochs' scheme suggests, the relationship between the two propositions in Examples A and B is that of opposition. Thus, opposition becomes the categorical name for this Aristotelian *topos.*[33]

What is also striking about this enthymemic material is its close relationship to commonplace material such as maxims, proverbs, sententiae, treatises on virtues and vices, and so forth. A look at almost any collection of maxims or proverbs will reveal how easily they can be used as premises for enthymemes. In the *Rhetoric,* Aristotle indicates that maxims come under the head of enthymemes. He says that a maxim is a sentiment or a general statement, not about one particular thing, but about anything. If the syllogistic form is taken away from the enthymeme, what remains is the premise or the conclusion, either of which can be a maxim.

What we seem to be seeing is a transition from the commonplace material which began to emerge around the time of Hesiod to the enthymemic material of Aristotle. This enthymemic material in turn becomes more abstract in form, reduced to categories such as opposites, cause and effect, definition, division, and so forth. The notion of the commonplaces as subject matter did not disappear with the emergence of the analytic topics. The cumulative commonplaces existed in countless numbers in commonplace books and in print, alongside the analytic topics. In Aristotle alone, according to some scholars, 200 or more *topoi* can be found. Erasmus' collection of commonplace material in the *Adages, Apothegms,* and *Colloquies* numbers in the thousands. But it is apparent that in addition to increasing in size and complexity, the topics are also developing in terms of increasing abstraction. By the time we get to Cicero, the topics are well on their way to becoming abstracted lists, consisting of categories such as definition, partition, etymology, conjugates, genus, species, analogy, difference, contraries, adjuncts, antecedents, consequents, contradictions, cause, effect, and comparison.[34]

Classical invention evidently reaches its peak with Cicero and then declines in the medieval and Renaissance periods. It would appear that at this point we have a fairly good generalized picture of the evolutionary development of the *topoi*. But our view becomes more complicated when we begin to look at the idea of invention as it appears in the English stylistic rhetorics of 1600 to 1800. During this time, there seems to be a shift from invention to style in the rhetoric of that period, especially in the work of those rhetoricians known as figurists. However, in her book, *Shakespeare's Use of the Arts of Language,* Sister Miriam Joseph has shown that the figurists were not wholly concerned with style, that in fact they "covered practically the same ground as the combined works on logic and rhetoric, whether traditionalist or Ramist."[35] To show this close fit between the figures of style and the topics of invention, Sister Miriam Joseph reorganizes the figures by relating them first to grammar and then to the three rhetorical appeals.[36]

Grammar: schemes of words: of construction
the vices of language
figures of repetition
Logos: the figures related to
(a) logical topics: testimony, definition, division, genus, species, adjunct, contrary, contradictory, similarity, dissimilarity, comparison, cause, effect, antecedent, consequent, notation, conjugates
Pathos: the figures of affection and vehemence
Ethos: the figures revealing courtesy, gratitude, commendation, forgiveness of injury

She develops this scheme in more detail in part three of her book by aligning specific schemes or tropes to particular topics and logical forms. For example, irony is a figure of style which she relates to contraries. Figures of degree, such as greater, equal, and less, she relates to the topic of comparison. Metaphor is related to the topic of similarity.

In his article "Invention in English 'Stylistic' Rhetorics: 1600–1800," J. Donald Ragsdale supports Sister Miriam Joseph's point of view about the figures of speech. The impression one gets, he says, when looking at what theorists have to say about the so-called figures of ornament or figures of ostentation "is that style is somehow unrelated to invention; that it is either embroidered onto invention or crafted to stand alone. Yet, a close examination of English 'stylistic' rhetorics published between 1600 and 1800 reveals an intimate, organic relationship obtaining between the figures of speech and invention."[37] Like Sister Miriam Joseph, Ragsdale attempts to align the figures of speech to one of the three classical divisions of the inventional appeals.

Like the *topoi,* the schemes and tropes have a long antiquity. Both Gorgias and Isocrates discuss the figures. Aristotle discusses them briefly in the *Rhetoric.* Cicero gives a detailed account of them in *De Oratore.* Quintilian, in the *Institutio Oratoria,* gives an even more extended treatment. In the Renaissance, the figurists list hundreds of figures of style. The sheer number of *topoi* and figures found in the works of rhetoricians such as Cicero, Quintilian, Longinus, Erasmus, Sherry, Peacham, Puttenham, and Day is overwhelming. Truly the period dating approximately from the Sophists to about the seventeenth or eighteenth century can be described as the stage of differentiation in the evolution of the analytic *topoi.*

Stage of Synthesis

The third stage in the evolutionary development of the analytic *topoi,* the stage of synthesis and hierarchic integration, has its roots in the seventeenth and eighteenth centuries, but it begins to blossom in the late nineteenth and twentieth centuries. It coincides with the shift in rhetoric from tradition to theory.

In his article "Tradition and Theory in Rhetoric," S. M. Halloran draws a distinction between tradition and theory by commenting that the rhetorical tradition that flourished in Greece and Rome was built on the cultural ideal of the orator, the good man skilled in speaking who embodied the wisdom and knowledge of the culture. Modern rhetoric, he contends,

> is characterized by a level of theoretical vigor unknown to the classical tradition. For Longinus or Augustine, it was sufficient to record what the respected practitioners of rhetoric did, and perhaps to speculate on how they might have done better. The modern rhetorician "builds" or "constructs" a theory . . . and the resulting conceptual structure must withstand minute critical appraisal. The goal of the classical rhetorician was to prepare others to speak in conformity with the established rhetorical conventions. The goal of the modern theorist is to achieve an abstract understanding of the rhetorical process, and thereby to be able to predict the outcome(s) of a given rhetorical transaction. [38]

Because modern theorists are trying to achieve an abstract understanding of the rhetorical process, their paradigms are likely to be inclusive (drawing from a wide variety of other theories and disciplines) and eclectic in both methodology and epistemology.

With Halloran's remarks as preface, what do we find when we begin to look at the theory and practice of rhetoric and composition in the nineteenth and twentieth centuries? We find that scholars are beginning to assimilate and integrate a large body of materials for their specific purposes. In the medieval and Renaissance periods, classical concepts were preserved piecemeal, scattered in manuals on letter writing, books of logic, grammars, and so forth. There were taxonomies of a kind, but no one attempted to achieve the kind of abstract understanding of rhetorical processes that Halloran talks about. Francis Bacon supposedly began the process of understanding, and according to some scholars, much of the theory and practice of rhetoric and composition can be viewed as an extension of some basic ideas laid down by Bacon. Some also point to the achievements of belletristic writers such as Joseph Addison, Edmund Burke, or Hugh Blair, or to the Elocutionists in the eighteenth century. But whatever may have been the contributions of these scholars, it appears that the empiricists such as John Locke, David Hartley, and David Hume were to have an important influence on composition theorists such as Alexander Bain and William Cairns in the nineteenth century.

I said earlier that rhetorical invention begins to decline in the Renaissance and continues to decline in subsequent periods as more and more emphasis is put on style, or logic, or taste, or genius. In the nineteenth century, rhetorical invention, and the analytic *topoi,* seem to disappear, except for purposes of formal debate. But a close look at nineteenth-century composition textbooks reveals that the *topoi* did not disappear. Because they took a different form, they went unnoticed. They are there, in composition textbooks, under the guise of the methods of developing paragraphs.

When one looks closely at the methods suggested for developing paragraphs, and later longer stretches of discourse, one finds categories such as definition, comparison, contrast, exemplification, and cause and effect that are remarkably like the classical *topoi*. They are, in fact, the *topoi* which have become displaced as inventional strategies and later appear as organizational principles. Later these categories reappear in the twentieth century in textbooks as "patterns" of development.

Like the classical *topoi,* the figures of speech did not disappear in the nineteenth century. In many composition textbooks, they appear in much the same format as they had in earlier periods. But textbook writers and scholars at this time are attempting to assimilate the figures to some larger pattern. That pattern is to be found in the laws of association of associationist psychology. For example, in *The Principles of Written Discourse,* Theodore Hunt maintains that figurative language is founded on the laws of association that include figures of resemblance, figures of contrast, and figures of contiguity. Figures of resemblance include simile, metaphor, and allegory. Figures of contrast include antithesis, epigram, and irony.[39] Figures of contiguity include metonymy and synecdoche. Similar lists of figures related to the laws of association can be found in James de Mille's *The Elements of Rhetoric* and David Hill's *The Science of Rhetoric.*[40]

This systematization of a large body of experience and knowledge that we see taking place in the nineteenth century begins to increase in the twentieth century. The topical systems of a number of contemporary rhetoricians and theorists reveal a movement toward increasing abstraction and synthesis. For example, William F. Nelson, in his article "Topoi: Evidence of Human Conceptual Behavior," points out that the topical system set forth in John F. Wilson and Arnold C. Carroll's *Public Speaking as a Liberal Art* resembles the categories found in the classification of ideas in *Roget's International Thesaurus.* Wilson and Arnold's topics include the categories of existence, degree, time, causality, correlation, genus-species, similarity, dissimilarity, spatial attributes, form, motion, substance, and so forth.[41] These categories in turn resemble the *topoi* of classical rhetoric. More specifically, the topics enumerated by Boethius and transmitted by Peter of Spain in the late medieval period are similar to the categories of Wilson, Carroll, and Roget. These categories include:

definition, description, genus, quantity, mode, time, place, species, cause, effect, similars, opposites, and contradictory.[42]

Nelson takes it as an axiom that "a kind of categorizing behavior (contiguity transfer) is intrinsic with man."[43] He then goes on to present evidence to validate this axiom, as well as several others, and he concludes that:

1. Meaning tends to cluster according to language categories, and the superordinates of these language categories are identifiable.

2. Cognitive activity tends to cluster according to categories, and semantic representations of the superordinates of cognitive categories are identifiable.

3. Rhetorical arguments cluster according to categories, and the superordinates of these categories are identifiable.

4. Philosophical inquiry tends to cluster according to categories, and semantic representations of the superordinates classificatory of philosophical ideas are identifiable.

5. The observable semantic representations emanating from each of these areas share common elements.

6. Variance in the superordinates of categories is minimal and relatively unaffected by time, space, and cultural influence.[44]

Nelson views these categories as reflecting "patterns of human conceptual behavior." It is possible also to interpret them as reflecting a necessary stage in the evolution of consciousness. They seem to fit the general pattern of what Pierre Teilhard de Chardin, in *The Phenomenon of Man,* calls the "law of increasing complexity-consciousness." As these categories relate to the evolution of rhetorical invention, the multiplication, scattering, and divergence of the *topoi* in previous eras leads to the exploration and modification of the forms of many of the categories. At a critical point, certain clusters of these categories begin to converge. Convergence leads to the union of elements and to the emergence and formation of newer and higher levels. Yet in none of these new configurations is the integrity of the individual category lost. No real synthesis ever occurs that does not differentiate.

Kenneth Burke's theoretical work shows this same tendency toward synthesis. In my article "Notes Toward a Semantic Theory of Rhetoric Within a Case Grammar Framework," I have attempted to show that the terms of Kenneth Burke's pentad (*act, scene, agent, agency, purpose*) constitute a kind of superordinate set of rhetorical topics within which can be subsumed the deep structure categories of case grammar. These in turn can provide the user with a powerful set of *topoi* that can be used to probe any subject whatsoever. Typical of the categories used by case grammarians, together with the kinds of questions that each category suggests, are the following: *verb* (What was done?), *agent* (Who did it?), *instrument* (By what means?), *manner* (In what manner?), *reason* (Why?), *locative* (Where?), and *temporal* (When?). The reader will recognize in these categories resemblances not only to the inflectional case categories of Latin grammar, but also to the classical *topoi*. [45]

In his article "The Grammar of Coherence," W. Ross Winterowd provides a set of coherence categories that he claims will specify the relationships that obtain in any stretch of discourse. These are seven in number: 1) coordinate, 2) obversative, 3) causative, 4) conclusive, 5) alternative, 6) inclusive, and 7) sequential. Winterowd sees these categories as providing a "form-oriented set of topics." What these linguistic and rhetorical studies suggest is that new theories in linguistics are converging with theories of rhetoric and composition to provide a new synthesis. [46]

Characteristic of this tendency of modern theorists to draw ideas from a wide variety of theories and disciplines is the tagmemic-based theory of invention of Richard Young, Alton Becker, and Kenneth Pike. Tagmemic invention is based on tagmemic theory in linguistics, but it takes its controlling metaphor from field theory in physics. According to tagmemic theory, the individual perceives the world from three different perspectives—as if it were static, as if it were a continuum, and as if it were a network of relationships. What we know of the world is a function of the relationship of these modes to each other. As Kenneth Pike explains it in "Language as Particle, Wave and Field":

> Language, seen as made of particles, may be viewed as if it were *static*— permanent bricks juxtaposed in a permanent structure, or as separate "frames" in a moving-picture film. The view of language made up of waves sees language as *dynamic*—waves of behavioral movement merging one into another in intricate, overlapping, complex systems. The view of language as *functional* sees language as a system with parts and classes of parts so interrelated that no parts occur apart from their function in the total whole, which in turn occurs only as the product of these parts in functional relation to a meaningful social environment. [47]

In *Rhetoric: Discovery and Change,* the topics of invention are presented as a series of superordinate categories, arranged in a chart in the form of a grid, consisting of nine slots: three across the top, three in the middle, and three across the bottom. The horizontal categories from left to right are labeled contrast, variation, and distribution. The vertical categories are particle, wave, and field. Within each slot in a series of questions designed to help the investigator probe for ideas.[48] What is interesting about these categories is that they subsume the more traditional rhetorical categories. For example, a static view of an idea or object yields such topics as description and definition. A wave view yields the topics of process and cause and effect. A field view of reality suggests the topics of comparison and contrast and classification. Not only does this heuristic procedure present a currently scientifically valid way of looking at experience, but it is also more economical than, for instance, a system such as classical rhetoric in which the user might have to assimilate twenty-eight *topoi* or more. The value of tagmemic theory is partly in its generality, in its ability to assimilate a large number of specific categories to its general purpose.

It should be apparent at this point in our discussion that no theory of rhetoric or of invention is a unique creation. Theories of invention evolve from other theories or emerge from older patterns. This is one reason why teachers of writing need to know more about the history of rhetoric and the history of rhetorical invention. In my own theoretical work, I have been extremely self-conscious about that history and about the extent to which theoretical systems are elaborated through a series of stages or levels, and in attempting to articulate that self-consciousness, I have taken ideas from a variety of sources.

In trying to trace the historical development of the analytic *topoi*, I noticed that the *topoi* seem to disappear in the nineteenth century except for purposes of formal debate. They become displaced as inventional strategies and reappear in nineteenth-century British and American textbooks as methods of developing paragraphs. In the twentieth century, they appear in textbooks as "patterns of organization." I also noticed that the classical tropes were related to the methods of development and to the *topoi* in significant ways. These observations led me to conclude that the *topoi*, the modes, and the tropes are merely convenient names that rhetoricians have given to processes that are structurally related. In other words, the *topoi*, the modes, and the tropes have a psychogenetic basis in the stages of cognitive development.[49]

In order to relate these ideas to one another, I theorized that the composing process is a movement from an undifferentiated whole to differentiated whole and that it repeats in microcosm the history or the evolution of consciousness. In this view, the composing process is holistic and organic. Invention, arrangement, and style, rather than being separate processes, are organically related to each other and to underlying thought processes in important ways.[50]

In order to organize the *topoi,* the modes, and the tropes, I appropriated the terms "static," "progressive," and "repetitive" from Kenneth Burke's discussion of form in *Counterstatement* and used them as superordinate categories, similar to Young, Becker, and Pike's concepts of particle, wave, and field, Kenneth Burke's Pentad, and Kinneavy's modes.[51]

In order to depict how the *topoi* become displaced as inventional strategies and embedded in discourse as methods of organizing ideas, I borrowed from Claude Levi-Strauss the concept of the paradigm. As I use the term, the paradigmatic structure of an essay constitutes a kind of "latent" structure of the essay. Like Levi-Strauss' paradigms, these paradigms are idealizations that represent rhetorical competence. They are also schematic; that is, they are models or patterns that are abstract and general. They are global patterns—undetailed general plans. They are also very much like rhetorical enthymemes, except that they are more abstract and general. And like rhetorical enthymemes, they are constructed from the *topoi.* In brief, paradigms are structural counterparts of the *topoi.*[52]

It should be obvious that in attempting to trace the evolutionary development of invention through these idealized stages I have neglected the work of a number of important rhetorical theorists. Nor did I do justice to the complexities of the theories of the scholars I have mentioned. But I chose certain theorists because their work enabled me to make the kinds of connections I needed to make. The reader can determine for himself or herself the degree to which other theories fit the general pattern. Despite these omissions and the gaps in the pattern I have presented, I feel confident that the broader picture will prove to be correct. Finally, I am not attempting to present the reader with an historical sketch. I present this essay as a speculative, conceptual framework that may have heuristic value.

There are, then, good reasons for looking at the evolution of the analytic *topoi* within the kind of developmental framework that I have suggested. One reason is that it may afford us a greater understanding of changing ideas about the nature of invention. For example, it helps to explain what happened to the *topoi* and to invention in the nineteenth century. The "methods of developing paragraphs" is the specific form that the classical "lines of reasoning" about a subject took in the nineteenth century. In this view, invention did not disappear. It merely took a different form, with the heuristic burden being put on structural patterns. Another reason for looking at the evolution of the analytic *topoi* within a developmental framework is that it may give us a greater insight into human conceptual development. The evidence presented by scholars such as Eric Havelock and G. E. R. Lloyd about preliterate Greek thinking suggests that the singer of tales and the pre-Socratic Greek thinkers thought differently about the world than we do. A third reason for viewing the evolution of the analytic *topoi* within a developmental framework is that it may hold out the hope that rhetorical invention, like evolution in general, is progressing toward a goal whose end is nothing less than universal convergence.

5

Translating Theory into Practice in Teaching Composition: A Historical View and a Contemporary View

James L. Kinneavy

At the present time a debate which was particularly acute in antiquity has been revived—though with some significant variations, both in the content of the issue and in the motivations which occasion the dispute. The core controversy in the entire educational history of classical *paideia* occurred between 390 and 323 B.C. The argument moved back and forth from the Sophists, to Plato, next to Isocrates, back to Plato, and then to Aristotle. Historically, the decisive winner was Isocrates—but it will be interesting to unravel the layers of the debate over whether theory or practice and how much of each should govern the rhetorical schooling given the young Athenians (and later the entire Mediterranean world).

In many respects the same issue is being fought today in two different terrains. Within English departments, those knowledgeable in rhetorical theory and criticism suddenly find themselves in a position somewhat similar to the situation of new critics in the early forties—in possession of a new body of exciting knowledge and able to influence in a massive way the teaching of English in college and high school circles. How much of this new (and old) theory should be injected into classroom practice is a question being asked across the entire country. And in other areas, especially in existentialism, anthropology, and political theory, the question of theoretical versus practical knowledge is again being waged—and the roots of the debate are replanted from the seeds of the controversy of the fourth century B.C., because the sources of the existentialists and the Marxists are Isocrates, Aristotle, and Cicero.

69

I would like to sketch in some detail this curious reincarnation and attempt to see its relevance to the typical English department of the 1980s. I will first outline the controversy in antiquity and then sketch the long classical tradition of education which it engendered. Finally, I will look at the current contest between *theoria* and *praxis* within and without the English departments.

The Polemic in Antiquity and the Classical Rhetorical Tradition

I have placed the classical debate in the fourth century B.C., but its roots extend back into the fifth with the invention of rhetorical prose by the Sophists. Sequential prose itself, particularly as practiced by historians and philosophers, was the result of a conscious revolt against the inability of poetry to perform these tasks. In the middle of the sixth century B.C., a number of philosophers (Anaximander of Miletus, Pherecydes of Syros, Anaximenes of Miletus) initiated the art of prose and advocated a simple unadorned prose.[1] Anaximander is also called by Bury the first writer of "scientific" prose.[2] Hecataeus, often called the father of history, and his successors, writing in the early half of the fifth century, maintained the same emphasis.

The Sophists of the fifth century, however, were not interested in factual reporting nor in philosophical speculation as such. They trained their students to succeed in law courts and in politics. Rhetoric was born in the courtrooms of Sicily and the assemblies of Greek city-states, and simple, unadorned prose is not the most effective weapon before juries or political assemblies. Consequently, the Sophists introduced into prose the poetic techniques of emotional appeal, of figures of speech, and of rhythmic and rhymic structures which the historians had earlier repudiated. This interesting move from poetry to metaphysics and history and thence to rhetoric has been brilliantly chronicled by Ernst Cassirer in his major works and summarized in his short masterpiece *An Essay on Man.*[3]

It is not inaccurate to represent the movement from philosophic and scientific prose to rhetorical prose as a move from *theoria* to *praxis,* for the Sophists generally did not accept the epistemological basis of *theoria,* a level of certainty in knowledge, and opted instead for a degree of probability as the best that man could attain in his political and legal activities. This, in fact, became the major issue in the fourth-century debate. Plato and the early Aristotle took over the philosophers' position in the full-flowered debate that ensued and Isocrates and the late Aristotle took over the Sophists' position.

Plato: The Dominance of *Theoria*

Plato, following Parmenides, insisted on a certainty in his politics, his ethics, and his rhetoric (both in the earlier *Gorgias* and the later *Phaedrus*); in taking this position he was opposing the relativism and probabilities which the Sophists had advocated. In fact, Plato's epistemology dominated his entire corpus. The locus classicus of the Platonic position can be seen in the *Republic,* where Plato lines up the levels of certainty and probability. In the famous parable of the cave in *Republic* VI, 511D–E, Plato has listed science, thought, belief, and probability as the descending graded relations to truth. And those who live in the cave, chained, with their backs to the light of the fire and who see only shadows created by the light of the fire are those who live by belief and probability. The same hierarchy is outlined in several different places in Plato.

How is this epistemology carried over into Plato's pedagogy? The answer is clear in the *Phaedrus,* a late work in the Platonic corpus, but a work consistent with the middle period epistemology of the *Republic.* Plato still demeans those who live by belief and probability; in discourse such thinking results in rhetoric. A true rhetoric—which he does not see as yet existing—would strive for the certainties of science (*theoria*), the highest level of thinking outlined in the *Republic.* In effect, such a rhetoric would be equivalent to dialectic which would attain truth.

Plato's pedagogical technique in teaching this doctrine can be seen in the organization of the *Phaedrus.* In that dialogue, Socrates and Phaedrus successively examine and discuss three speeches, one by Lysias (allegedly) and two by Socrates. The principles of a Platonic rhetoric are systematically erected by a careful analysis of each of the speeches in turn (each speech, incidentally, representing a level of the epistemological ladder). This fundamentally inductive technique of deriving general principles by examining particular instances thus arrives at the Platonic theory of rhetoric. The truth must be known, the type of audience which is addressed must be known, the nature of the soul-types of the audience must be matched to the type of argument used, and so forth.

The capstone of the Platonic rhetorical system, however, was the notion of *kairos,* the concept of timeliness. Unlike the first component of his rhetorical system, the epistemological level of certainty, this second component of the *kairos*-doctrine, as it has been called, was accepted by most of the Sophists, most notably by Gorgias as well as by Isocrates, by Alcidamas, and by Aristotle.

Let us look at Plato's statement of the doctrine. It occurs close to the end of the dialogue in a section in which Socrates is explaining to Phaedrus how a "writer must go about the business if one intends to be as scientific a writer as possible." Having explained that different arguments must be used with different kinds of audiences, Socrates continues:

> Very well. When a student has attained an adequate grasp of these facts *intellectually*, he must go on to see with his own eyes that they occur in the world of affairs and are operative *in practice*; he must acquire the capacity to confirm their existence through the sharp use of his senses. If he does not do this, no part of the *theoretical* knowledge he acquired as a student is as yet of any help to him. But it is only when he can state adequately what sort of man is persuaded by what sort of speech, when he has the capacity to declare to himself with complete perception in the presence of another, that *here* is the man and *here* the nature that was discussed *theoretically* at school—*here, now, present* to him in *actuality*—to which he must apply this kind of speech in this sort of manner in order to obtain persuasion for this kind of activity—it is only when he can do all of this and when he has, in addition, grasped the concept of *propriety of time* [*kairos*]—when to speak and when to hold his tongue, and when to use and when not to use brachylogy, piteous language, hyperbole for horrific effect, and, in a word, each of the specific devices of discourse he may have studied—it is only *then,* and not *until then* that the finishing and perfecting touches will have been given to his science.[4] (my italics)

Unfortunately, this capstone of the Platonic rhetoric has never received the attention it deserves, possibly because it seems to be at variance with the general direction of Plato's thinking.[5] Indeed even in antiquity, no one seems to have analyzed the notion of *kairos* very carefully, as Dionysius of Halicarnassus remarked.[6] This is probably true, despite the fact that Gorgias built his entire system of thought from sense perception through ethics to aesthetics on *kairos* and despite the attention given the concept in medicine.

Summarily, if we were to attempt a graphic representation of Plato's pedagogy of rhetoric incorporating his epistemology, we might represent it as an inductive technique of arriving at theory, which theory is then applied to a given subject matter at the right time and to the right audience. The subject matter is known with a measure of certainty, arrived at by dialectic. The speech might have to be discussed and re-written—and the *Phaedrus* itself exemplifies this technique admirably.

I have attempted to incorporate these major facets in the first circle of the figure "Three classical pedagogies for teaching composition."

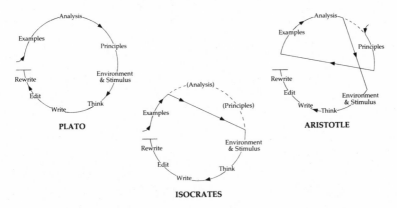

Three classical pedagogies for teaching composition

Isocrates: The Dominance of *Praxis*

On the issue of epistemology Isocrates directly opposed Plato. Like the Sophists, Isocrates was convinced that absolute rules of science, promising certainty, were not a human possibility. In speech after speech he inveighed against the type of theory and science represented by Parmenides and Plato. In particular he used the lessons of the contemporary political scene to warn Athenians against such an absolutism. Twenty-three years of war with Greek states fighting domination by Persia, twenty-seven years with other Greek states fighting Athenian domination, seventeen years of war with Athens and Thebes and other Greek states fighting Spartan domination, and seven years of opposition to Theban domination, with each dominating agency attempting to impose absolutes on the others, have taught Athenians a hard-earned lesson: some compromise was necessary. The issues were not pure falsehood versus pure truth. Opinion, conjecture, and belief were more practically reliable than absolutes, certainty, and science. In his speech to the Assembly "On the Peace" between Athens and her former allies against Persia (Sparta and Thebes), in 355 B.C., he repeatedly pointed to attempts on the part of one or the other of the allies to impose absolute standards on the rest and of the persistent failures of these moves. Early in the speech he told the Athenians that "they ought not to think that they have exact knowledge of what the result will be, but to be minded toward these contingencies as men who indeed exercise their best judgment, but are not sure what the future may hold in store."[7]

In a later speech, he generalizes to all knowledge:

> For since it is not in the nature of man to attain a science by the possession of which we can know positively what we should do or what we should say, in the next resort I hold that man to be wise who is able by his powers of conjecture to arrive generally at the best course, and I hold that man to be a philosopher who occupies himself with the studies from which he will most quickly gain that kind of insight. [8]

When Isocrates applied his epistemology to rhetoric, some interesting corollaries followed. He adopted a trilogy common enough at the time and made it the fundamental structure of his pedagogy of teaching, a structure which has endured till our time. There are, he says, three factors which have to be taken into consideration in learning how to write: natural talent, theory, and practice. Of the three, he thinks that talent is by far the most important and that practice is of second importance; theory (or rules or study) is of third rank. This trilogy can be seen throughout the history of rhetoric. In Latin, it was referred to as *natura, studium, exercitatio*. Ben Jonson repeats the formula as a given, as do Sidney, Milton, and other Renaissance figures.[9]

His method of practice was to give the student a model of a specific kind of writing and have him imitate it, almost slavishly. The different kinds of writing were compared to the different kinds of gymnastic exercises. In practice, this double methodology (kinds of discourse and imitation) was embodied in the *progymnasmata,* the set of preparatory exercises which the student imitated in his training getting him ready to go into the college equivalent of the time, the *ephebia,* which nearly always was held in the city gymnasium, whence the name *progymnasmata*. The institution of the *ephebia* continued the rhetorical education of the young man and was the central educational experience of all of the city-states of the Mediterranean area for almost seven hundred years (from 300 B.C. to 400 A.D.). It was a required experience for the future citizen of the city-states (some 350 in the Mediterranean area), and the academic core of the experience was further intensive training in rhetoric taught by the Isocratean method.

Cicero and Quintilian refer to these exercises, and some of them have survived from later periods. The sequence was usually the following: fables, tales, edifying stories, proverbs expanded, refutations, confirmations, factual narratives, encomiums, comparisons, impersonations, descriptions, theses, legislations.[10]

The kinds of discourse emphasized in the *ephebia* itself were found in the types of speeches—political, legal, or ceremonial—or in the issues embodied in the speeches—the matters of fact, or definition, or value. It was through these "kinds" of discourse, learned by an almost mechanical imitation, that most of the writers of western civilization in antiquity, the Middle Ages, and the Renaissance learned to write. Isocrates, in this sense, is the father of western humanism.[11]

The imitation method of Isocrates is graphically represented in the middle circle in the Figure. He exemplified his methodology in the *Antidosis,* using his own speeches for examples, and following them by discussions. We know that he advocated and practiced heavy editing and rewriting. But there was considerably less theory than in Plato, with the consequent dominance of practice. And *practice* in Isocrates meant both the epistemological level of probability (rather than certainty) and the pedagogical level of exercising. In both senses, *praxis* was opposed to *theoria.*

Aristotle: The Synthesis of *Theoria* and *Praxis*

In his youth Aristotle had probably studied rheotric under Isocrates, but he had transferred to Plato's school, and there he taught rhetoric. In this period of Aristotle's development he wholeheartedly adopted the Platonic basis of *theoria* (scientifically certain axioms) for his theology, his ethics, his politics, and his rhetoric. We know this from the masterly studies of his development by Jaeger, Düring, and Nuyens.[12] Chroust's studies, in particular, support this position for Aristotle's early rhetorical work.[13]

Consequently, we can assume that he followed Plato's emphasis on *theoria,* in contrast to talent and practice. Plato had repeated the same trilogy that Isocrates used, but where Isocrates placed *theoria* last in importance, Plato considered it most important, as *Phaedrus* 269 D–E clearly shows.

Later, however, probably as the result of Isocrates' repeated emphasis on the uncertain character of all thinking in the areas of the human sciences,[14] Aristotle reverted to the Sophistic and Isocratean position that in these disciplines only a measure of probability or belief was possible. He retained a belief in the certainty of theory in some sciences (such as theology, astronomy, metaphysics, and mathematics). But in the human sciences, which more and more occupied his attention, Aristotle settled for the probable. And these were the areas of *praxis* (practical thinking) and *poiesis* (making artifacts).

His treatise on *Rhetoric* thus belongs with his important works in ethics and politics—the human sciences which involve the contingent, the variable, the changeable, *and therefore the free.* The sciences in *theoria,* on the contrary, involve the eternal, the unchangeable, the necessary, and the predetermined. Politics, ethics, rhetoric, and poetics enable us to change some aspect of our life and therefore we can deliberate about the ways we may choose to effect the change. These areas of life more and more preoccupied the mature Aristotle.

Aristotle's *Rhetoric,* therefore, sides with Isocrates in the epistemological debate with Plato. But, like Plato, Aristotle still held on to the importance of rhetorical and psychological principles (though not at a level of certainty) for teaching students the political, legal, and ceremonial types of speeches. Like Plato and Isocrates, Aristotle adopted the notion of training students to a limited number of kinds of discourse. Aristotle's pedagogy of rhetoric, consequently, is a compromise between Plato and Isocrates in pedagogical technique, but an epistemological siding with Isocrates.

In practice, Aristotle assumes that the principles of rhetoric have already been arrived at (by Plato, or Isocrates, or himself), and he teaches by first stating the principles, illustrating them by examples, and then having the students apply them to the subject matter at hand in the right environment. Examples in Aristotle, therefore, are not data for generalizations (as they are in Plato), but illustrations of principles. Aristotle's method is distinctly deductive. And, although Aristotle also believed in the importance of *kairos,* he does not give this notion the central position it had occupied in Plato. In this one sense, he is more theoretical than Plato.

The pedagogical methodology of Aristotle is graphically presented in the third circle in the figure. It attempts to embody the technique of teaching embodied in Aristotle's *Rhetoric.* Thus the *Phaedrus,* the *Antidosis,* and the *Rhetoric* exemplify different epistemologies and different pedagogical corollaries.[15]

Some Current Concerns with Theory and Practice

The debate among Plato, Isocrates, and Aristotle thus centered around several critical notions: an epistemological controversy between science and probability (*episteme* and *pistis*), the relative importance of environmental situation (*kairos*), and the pedagogical corollaries to be drawn from these positions. Now, I believe that the same basic issues confront contemporary rhetoric. There are two major emphases in the contemporary scene which reincarnate the two concerns of antiquity: a sense of situational context or *kairos,* and a "practical" epistemology that incorporates probabilistic thinking.

In fact, I have recently been progressively tantalized by, impressed with, excited by, and inspired with the realization that important scholars in such diverse areas as philosophy, semiotics, anthropology, theology, and logic exhibit these two important and central tendencies. First, they insist, often shrilly, on the overwhelming importance of situational (and cultural) context in the study of discourse. Secondly, they also insist, despite the impressive advances of symbolic logic, statistics, and computer study in this century, on the distinctive character of the logic of actual discourse.

Situational Context

Some of these scholars take a very comprehensive look at the necessity of some context for interpreting discourse. Others have limited their concerns to more narrow areas. Let us look at some representatives of each tendency.

Certainly one of the most thoroughgoing of the views of the necessity of some context to interpreting anything is that of modern hermeneuticists stemming from the work of Martin Heidegger. Heidegger enlarged the earlier concerns of biblical, legal, and literary hermeneuticists into a position usually called "philosophic hermeneutics." Heidegger's main work, *Being and Time,* poses the hermeneutic problem in its largest dimension: all understanding is a matter of interpretation.[16] Consequently hermeneutics is *the* basic epistemological issue. And in *any* interpretation, man brings to the process a prestructure which incorporates a *preholding* of the totality of the being to be interpreted, a *preview* of its unity, and a *preconception* of the structural complexity of the object. The German words are *Vorhabe, Vorsicht,* and *Vorbegriff,* and they are repeated at many critical junctures in *Being and Time*. [17] Such a prestructure to interpretation is obviously the result of one's cultural and situational context, within which the interpretation is to take place.

For this reason Heidegger emphasizes the unique nature of the interpretive act. Hans-Georg Gadamer, one of Heidegger's contemporaries, has carried this insistence even further. In his many books and articles he continually insists on the necessity of *prejudices* (the German word is *Vorurteil,* prejudgement, but Gadamer prefers the connotations of the English word *prejudice* in the translation precisely because it emphasizes the situational bias). [18]

An important literary and rhetorical critic who takes an equally comprehensive view of the importance of situational context is Kenneth Burke. His pentad—act, agent, agency, purpose, scene—is an attempt to reduce the elements of a situational context to a system. All interpretation must take account of these elements of the dramatistic situation, he insists. [19] In addition, the second critical dimension of Burke's system, the pervasive Hegelian dialectic, is a persistent reminder, throughout the entire Burkean canon, of the noncertainty of any scientific logic in the discourse of the symbolic animal. To use his favorite figure of speech, the synecdoche, Burke can be said to be representative of the entire movement which I am here sketching.

Heidegger's most famous theological disciple was undoubtedly Rudolf Bultmann, possibly the greatest theologian of this century. Bultmann probably takes as comprehensive a view of the importance of prestructure as does Heidegger, but his application of the principle has been mainly in biblical hermeneutics. First, and most dramatically, he contests that the message of the Bible was embodied in the cultural myths of the contemporaries of the biblical authors—this was necessary so that the message could be interpreted at that time. But each age has to separate the essential messages of the Bible from these mythical contexts and not take the myths for the truths of the Bible. To get the message, each age must bring its own cultural and historical prestructures to the interpretation of the Bible. [20] Secondly, Bultmann insists that the genres of the books of the New Testament were also culturally grounded in the life situation (*Sitz im Leben*) of the people of the time. [21] He carried on an intense sociological analysis of these genres, a study which others continue today.

A somewhat less comprehensive, though still far-reaching epistemological principle, also grounded on the importance of situational context, can be seen in the work of some ethnomethodologists. Their basic assumption is that the methodology to be used in describing and analyzing a culture is the methodology which that group itself uses in its internal interactions to accomplish its own goals.[22] One of the major motivations for the technique was the realization on the part of these analysts that much research in the social sciences used the categories of an external science to gauge the actions of a group which was not at all attempting to "do" that kind of science at all. In other words, to understand the "practical reasoning" of the subculture, it was unfair to assess it by the standards of western scientific reasoning.[23]

Consequently, ethnomethodology in one stroke asserts the two approaches we have seen in the other movements—the insistence on situational or cultural context and the difference between much practical reasoning and scientific logic as we usually conceive it.

A very similar position to that of the ethnomethodologists, though with quite different motivations, is that advocated by some Marxists attempting to elaborate on the Aristotelian distinction between *theoria* and *praxis*, a distinction revived by a group of young left Hegelians in the 1840s in order to emphasize the kind of knowledge which leads to action and to change, not just to sterile speculation. This emphasis on *praxis* became a persistent theme throughout the entire Marxist corpus. Neglected for some time, it has recently been reemphasized by some important contemporary Marxists. And in Marx, as well as in these modern disciples, the difference between *theoria* and *praxis* lies in the taking into account of the actual context in any political action. Sartre, Marcuse, Habermas, Bourdieu, Bernstein, and others all take this direction in analyzing *praxis*.[24]

In the field of rhetorical analysis, a position potentially as comprehensive as that of Heidegger or Burke has been taken by Lloyd Bitzer. His important article on rhetorical situation in *Philosophy and Rhetoric* certainly has been influential in several areas.[25] Even its attackers have acknowledged its impact, particularly in the field of rhetorical analysis.[26]

Logic and Epistemology

It is clear that many of the stances outlined in the previous section have distinct epistemological implications. In some cases, the relation of rhetoric to logic and epistemology has been pointed out. But there are additional voices in this matter which are not so closely allied to an insistence on situational context, theorists to whom the question of *theoria* versus *praxis* is still of vital importance.

In historical and theoretical books which have massive epistemological implications, Ernesto Grassi and Samuel Ijselling have attempted to reintegrate the history of rhetorical thought into that of philosophical thought. Both emphasize important names in the rhetorical tradition which are frequently dismissed as philosophically unimportant by most contemporary professionals in that area—names like those of Isocrates, Cicero, Quintilian, and Vico. Both emphasize the practical basis of rhetorical thought for real-world philosophical applications.[27]

In a somewhat narrower spectrum, some other influential movements ought to be mentioned. Some concern deduction rather in an isolated manner, some deal almost exclusively with inductive generalizations. A few involve both.

In deduction, particularly in the field of ethics, Kurt Baier's moral system, based, as he says, on good reasons, not necessarily on the best reasons, eschews deductive rigorous certainty in its decision inferences. Ethics operates at the level of belief and probability, not at the level of deductive certainty, he maintains—a position remarkably similar to that of Isocrates and of the late Aristotle, as we have seen. Baier's position has been influential in both ethical and rhetorical circles.[28]

Chaim Perelman and L. Olbrechts-Tyteca, analyzing legal and political documents, take a somewhat similar stand. They recognize the probable nature of much deductive reasoning in these fields. Secondly, they also insist on the different types of axioms or premises which different types of audiences will allow for deductive inferences in legal, political, and religious thought.[29]

Some of the philosophers and political scientists mentioned above in connection with situational context also address themselves specifically to the question of scientific logic. Thus Heidegger has attacked the priority of scientific reasoning and the quantifiability of some types of issues.[30] Pollock,[31] Adorno,[32] and Horkheimer[33] have also raised the question of the quantifiability of certain political concepts. Mehan, an ethnomethodologist, has made frontal assaults on some empirical sociological research. He asks why many invalid interviews on the intimacies of divorce relations are any more valid than one such interview: "To think that these 'problems' can be resolved by adding this one woman's responses to thousands of others and transforming them all from 'sloppy' conversation into numerals seems not so much hopeless as absurd."[34]

It is abundantly clear from even this brief sketch that there are tendencies in modern thought which parallel two of the major motifs in classical rhetoric. These concerns, evident in many varied fields, are too insistent and too frequent to be ignored. And some of them, acknowledged in rhetorical theory, have not yet been carried over into composition practice and rhetorical analysis.

In epistemological assumptions, we may well yet be too Platonic: we teach the logic of certainty borrowed from traditional and modern logic. We have yet to learn from the modern disciples of Isocrates and the later Aristotle. In matters of situational context, we may well not be Platonic enough: we still do not place composition practice and rhetorical analysis into the situational context of the student and modern society. We have much to learn from the modern disciples of the author of the *Phaedrus* in this matter.

6

Rational Appeal and the Ethics of Advocacy

George E. Yoos

Although I wish to set my analysis of the ethics of advocacy initially in the work of Aristotle, comparing and contrasting Aristotle's with contemporary perspectives, the major thrust of what I have to say on the ethics of advocacy comes from an analysis of how deception is integrated with cooperative action in modern communications. I am here using both the terms "advocacy" and "deception" in loose and extended senses.[1] My analysis of the ethical grounds of advocacy does not, however, derive or depend upon my interpretations of Aristotle or his text. Rather I wish to use my interpretations of Aristotle, which make no pretension to being definitive, to illustrate my overall contention that the moral issues confronting the advocate were not attacked directly or with sufficient care in classical rhetoric, and especially in Aristotle.

Historically, advocates have attempted to justify their sins, fallacious arguments, and deceptive and diversionary tactics on the basis of expediency. The means are exonerated; only the ends count. Rhetoric in itself is never bad. It is the use people make of rhetoric that makes it ethically bad.[2] "Guns do not kill people; people kill people." For Aristotle, however, sham and spurious argument were not always expedient. What was expedient was to expose such arguments and tactics for what they really are. Consequently, Aristotle's work develops a rhetoric of exposing dirty tricks.

What seems, however, not to be considered in Aristotle is the difference between *tolerable* deceptive, diversionary, and misleading appeals or arguments and *intolerable* fallacious and sham argumentation.

Aristotle places, in my estimation, too much faith in the good sense of "natural reason" to draw such a line. For, as he says, "What is true and preferable is always by nature easier to prove, and more convincing."[3] But one can equally argue against Aristotle that the constraints of rhetorical situations quite frequently make it impossible for truth and justice to have a fair hearing in an audience enlightened by "natural reason." Insofar as *ethos, pathos,* and argumentative invention have the power for Aristotle to divert issues from truth and justice, rhetoric can and does overwhelm "natural reason." A question, therefore, that Aristotle does not confront directly is: what should be the moral constraints on the rhetor in the use of his power to overwhelm "natural reason"?

I have argued previously that both classical and contemporary rhetoric have failed to appreciate fully the *true* ethical and moral dimension of ethical appeals, their scope and effectiveness, or power in persuasion.[4] In "A Revision of the Concept of Ethical Appeal," I tried to redefine ethical appeal in an extended sense to put moral ethical qualities back into the concept of ethical appeal. I did so by calling attention to four qualities that are directly perceivable in appeals. They were qualities that not only defined an ethical mode of relating to an audience but were qualities that elicited a rational and ethical response from audiences. The four qualities were: 1) the quality displaying the speaker seeking mutual agreement with his or her audience, 2) the quality displaying the speaker as recognizing the rational autonomy of his or her audience, 3) the quality displaying the speaker recognizing the equality of the listener with him or herself, and finally 4) the quality displaying the speaker recognizing that the ends of the audience have an intrinsic value for him or her.

But my redefinition of ethical appeal, to circumscribe the *ethical qualities* of a rhetor, was limited and flawed because my analysis did not extend to the ethics of advocacy. My redefinition specified the ethical qualities of a rhetor in a specific context of argument, and not, as I had thought at the time, for argument in general. I had defined a concept of ethical appeal for a rhetor appealing for the mutual acceptance of a contention on the basis of mutually accepted premises. At the time, the limited range of my redefinition disturbed me, for I had wished to cover the ethical qualities of the rhetor in general, especially in the argumentative appeals of advocates. Moreover, it also disturbed me that the ethical qualities of the rhetor which I had identified were in part simply based upon Kant's basic principles of practical reason in dealing with other rational beings in a rational way. Thus I had in the article neither a clear conception of the grounds of my inquiry other than Kantian formalism, nor any conceivable way to relate my conclusions to the ethics of advocacy.

Much the same sort of error was made in a second article, in which I tried to treat some of the traditional problems of logical fallacies in a rhetorical context.[5] In this context, I tried to deal with the limitations of Aristotle in separating sham arguments from legitimate uses of ethical and emotive appeal, for if we take Aristotle's condemnation of diversionary tactics seriously, we must condemn ethical and emotive appeals likewise as diversionary and fallacious appeals. What I tried to show was that deceptions or fallacious appeals occur when the rhetor purports to appeal in one mode—logical, ethical, or emotive—and then shifts the appeal into another mode. Or again, the rhetor purports to be giving one sort of appeal within a mode, such as a logical appeal in the deductive mode, and then shifts the appeal into an inductive mode. Such shifts could either be deliberate or simply mistakes.

As in the first article, however, I used ideal criteria taken from Kant to delineate legitimate from illegitimate appeals. My whole analysis depended upon criteria that assumed completely explicit and open agenda between rational beings. Once again, my analysis did not relate to the ethics of advocacy, wherein appropriate rules of relationship between and within modes of appeal are *not* always observed.[6] My Kantian formalism was not able to generate criteria that would stand up when agenda are hidden, as they are in advocacy situations.

It is relatively easy, as for example in scientific discourse and especially in argument for the truth of scientific hypotheses and theory, to idealize about what *ought* to be the rational and ethical norms of participants in such discourse. But conditions of advocacy radically alter what is normative. They challenge the appropriateness of what is rational and ethical in the uses of argument and persuasion when the goals and objectives are not to make appeals to disinterested judges. Consequently, appeals for truth and justice in advocacy situations take on, in different contexts, a different light. They differ in different contexts in the life of business, in lovemaking, in law courts, and in any context where interests, loyalty, and pride complicate roles and attitudes.

What grounds do we have, then, to idealize about what ought to be the rational and ethical norms of participants in advocacy situations? I contend that both classical and contemporary rhetoric have failed to show that in advocacy situations deception and hidden agenda can be consistent or compatible with both rational and moral points of view. To see what is missing in classical rhetoric in terms of the ethical issues of advocacy, I will turn to a brief review of Plato and Aristotle. We need to see what is left out in their conceptions of rhetoric and to spot conceptual reductions that have collapsed distinctions.

In the *Phaedrus,* we find that true rhetoric is opposed to the rhetorical traditions of Plato's day.[7] The true rhetoric of the *Phaedrus* is a rhetoric that pursues truth and justice. It is a rhetoric that cannot function in advocacy situations where winning and persuasion, not truth and justice, are the ends of the rhetorical situation. As an ideal rhetoric, it suffers much the same fate in reconciling social controversy and conflict where interested parties are at odds, as do other comparable ideal notions in the history of thought (for example, Rousseau's concept of a general will and Kant's notion of a free, autonomous rational being). All such ideals generate ethical and political norms that cannot function in negotiations and compromise. For Plato, Rousseau, and Kant, when we compromise truth and justice we *compromise* in the pejorative sense of that term. All three writers ended with notoriously uncompromising ethical absolutes. And interestingly enough for my subsequent analysis of lying, all three authors had difficulty in handling lying and deception where lying might be deemed necessary, acceptable, or appropriate.

In contrast to Plato, Aristotle places rhetoric in a context of persuasion. But Aristotle, in contrast to his contemporaries, makes logical appeal and appeals to truth and justice essential to rhetoric.[8] Rhetoric as a counterpart of dialectic is a mode of invention. Both rhetoric and dialectic are powers or capacities of *finding* and *using* the available means of argument. As Aristotle phrases it, "Neither rhetoric nor dialectic is the scientific study of any one separate subject: both are faculties for providing arguments."[9] But rhetoric as a faculty is broader than dialectic in that rhetoric provides more than just arguments as the available means of persuasion. "The man who is to be in command [of the means of effecting persuasion] must, it is clear, be able 1) to reason logically, 2) to understand human character and goodness in their various forms, 3) to understand the emotions."[10] Rhetoric as a power is developed both by dialectic and ethical studies, and as Aristotle says, ethical studies may be fairly called political. Yet Aristotle turns to dialectic for what is essential for persuasion. He contends that the arousing of prejudice, pity, anger, and similar emotions has nothing to do with the essential facts, but is merely a personal appeal to the man who is judging the case.[11] Aristotle's concern is with essentials, that is, enthymeme and example. *Ethos* and *pathos* are in contrast inessential. They are nonrational appeals. But to present rational appeal in the best light, the needs of persuasion require *ethos* and *pathos* with certain audiences to win arguments on the basis of truth and justice. In the last analysis, Aristotle justifies the use of nonrational or inessential appeals on utilitarian grounds, or to use the pejorative term, on the basis of expediency.

In discussing "the current treatises on rhetoric,"[12] Aristotle contends that in focusing on forensic rhetoric they are chiefly concerned with "how to put the judge into a given frame of mind."[13] Moreover, Aristotle points out that "in many places . . . irrelevant speaking is forbidden in the law courts: in the public those who have to form a judgment are themselves well able to guard against that."[14] For Aristotle, law courts without formal procedures regulating relevancy would be less constrained by the participating parties than would political oratory "where the man who is forming a judgment is making a decision about his own vital interests."[15] Aristotle is appealing to the social and cultural facts of his own day, which appear opposite to social and cultural facts of our own. Today, we appear to believe that disinterested parties are more likely to detect manipulative and sham argument than people whose interests are at stake. This contemporary attitude is reflected in our need for disinterested professional advocates and counselors. It is reflected in the maxim that "only a fool takes himself as his own lawyer." Again opposite to Aristotle, contemporary political oratory appears to have abandoned rational and moral constraints in the name of political expediency. This reversal between forensic and deliberative rhetoric from Aristotle's day to ours may in part be the result of improved legal and formal procedures governing forensic rhetoric. But it strikes me that in any negotiations or appeals for joint commitment, the rhetorical situation requires hidden agenda and deception to at least a moderate degree, a point completely missing in Aristotle. Bargaining and compromise demand that we hide, as much as possible, the weaknesses and the facts of our position, our vulnerabilities, and the exigencies that put us in a difficult and disadvantageous negotiating stance.

Lastly in dealing with Aristotle, I find his discussion of apparent or spurious enthymemes central to the issues of the ethics of advocacy. In *On Sophistical Refutations,* Aristotle discusses four types of arguments: didactic, dialectic, examination arguments, and contentious arguments. "Contentious arguments are those that reason or appear to reason to a conclusion from premises that appear to be generally accepted but are not so."[16] Aristotle, in other words, is dealing with argumentative deceptions, arguments that deceive, mislead, or divert attention. Fallacious arguments for Aristotle, as apparent proofs or refutations, may be referred to as *ignoratio elenchi* or "ignorance of what 'refutation' is."[17] A sham argument is an argument that is not an argument, a pretend argument. In one way, all non sequiturs are fallacies, that is, spurious arguments. They simply pretend to display strict logical entailments when in fact they are not doing so. The problem in stressing the importance of logical or rational appeal is that sound arguments may be unrhetorical and unpersuasive, and spurious enthymemes persuasive but invalid logically.[18] But is there anything in Aristotle to solve this problem?

If we turn to Aristotle's discussion of apparent or sham enthymemes in the *Rhetoric,* we find a cursory summary of nine lines of argument that form spurious enthymemes.[19] In discussing the ninth line of argument, "the confusion of the absolute with that which is not absolute but particular," Aristotle presents an example of this line of argument used by Corax in the *Art of Rhetoric.*[20] It is improbable that a weak man should be guilty of an assault; and it is improbable, but not in a specific sense, that a strong man would be guilty of assault, knowing that he would be exposed to suspicion if he were to do it. Aristotle argues that the probability of the weak man's not committing assault is a genuine probability, and that the strong man's not committing assault is only a general and not a specific probability. Therefore, it is not a genuine enthymeme. It is spurious and a fraud. In modern times, Aristotle is labeling arguments from misleading probabilities as sophisms, which he condemns as having "a place in no art except Rhetoric and Eristic."[21]

Different translations and commentaries render the Greek differently. Cope and Lang interpret the phrase in their translations as "mere rhetoric and quibbling."[22] I do not wish to rest my case on differences in interpretations of this passage. But that there are differences indicates that Aristotle is puzzling to his translators. I suggest that one thing that might be puzzling them is the difficulty Aristotle has in legitimatizing deceptions, misleading statements and arguments, diversions, and other stratagems in rhetoric. What is obviously illegitimate for Aristotle is the use of these devious maneuvers in didactic, dialectic, and examination arguments where the goal is truth, not persuasion.

Hamlin makes an interesting historical comment in discussing the Aristotelian tradition of fallacies. "Cicero," he says, "wrote a great deal on rhetoric but nothing on fallacies, and his influence has tended to cut fallacies out of the subsequent rhetorical tradition."[23] Moreover, the history of the study of fallacies, as tied to logical studies after Aristotle, shifts from a problem about deception in rhetoric to a problem about logical error or mistakes in reasoning. Consequently, the study of fallacies in logic became truncated from the parent discipline of rhetoric.

Aristotle recognizes the value of logical appeals and the value of countering illogical appeals. Yet he has little to say about countering misleading and diversionary strategies encountered by the use of *ethos* and *pathos* in the context of argument. Aristotle, for example, does not deal with such traditional fallacies as abusive *ad hominem* and the psychological fallacies such as *ad misericordiam, ad baculum,* and *ad populum.* These omissions reinforce the notion that Aristotle is more concerned with formal logical errors than rhetorical improprieties. Is there then, in advocacy, any rational or legitimate use for deceptions, misleading statements, misleading arguments, diversions, the use of *ethos,* or the use of *pathos?* What possible ground, if any, is there for legitimatizing any such strategies in a rhetoric of advocacy or persuasion? I find it difficult for Aristotle to draw any line between legitimate and illegitimate uses of rhetorical ploys except on the grounds of expediency.

In giving a paper entitled "Lying and Communication," I realized that I had been confronting all along in the two previously mentioned articles, without realizing it, the basic distinctions needed to draw the line missing in Aristotle, a line necessary for the discussion of the ethical problems of advocates.[24] In my discussion of lying, I came to the conclusion that we argue differently, in different contexts, that another person has lied. It became readily apparent to me that, comparable to the case of lying, the ethical qualities of a speaker vary with different contexts of discourse; and that the sorts of considerations brought to bear on the ethical assessment of lies and liars could be generalized and extended to an analysis of the ethics of advocacy.

I wish to show now how an analysis of lying uncovers the ground for analyzing the ethical problems of advocacy that had previously escaped me. I wish to show that an analysis of lying provides a ground or principle for linking advocacy together with appeals for acceptance of contentions on mutually accepted premises, and that with such a ground we can identify the ethical qualities of the advocate.

A moral commonplace about lying is that lying is always bad. Not to acknowledge this commonplace is not to understand Kant's logic and his stringent stand on lying. A consequence of this stringency is that most ethical discussion about lying simply addresses the extenuating circumstances that excuse lying. This is the case with Saints Augustine and Thomas.[25] Augustine, for example, outlines eight degrees of lying of decreasing gravity. We see Augustine's distinctions reflected in Thomas' discussion of lies. He classifies Augustine's first four lies as mischievous lies, which are deadly or mortal sins. They are lies for which we are doomed. The remaining are less grievous. Augustine's fifth is a jocose lie whose end is giving pleasure to others. Augustine's remaining three are, for Thomas, officious lies whose end lies in usefulness. The sin of lying is thus aggravated or diminished by Thomas. Four are mortal; four are venial—pardonable or excusable. Thus, the force of the biblical injunction as interpreted by Augustine and Thomas is to condemn all lies but to allow for extenuation of lies if no harm is done and if good results from the lie. But for Augustine and Thomas lies are never good. Lying is always categorically wrong. We find the same sort of issues of extenuation and justification of "lies" arising in recent utilitarian considerations of lying. A recent book by Sissela Bok in large part addresses utilitarian issues of excuses and justifications.[26] As with the saints, Bok finds it very difficult to excuse or sanction a lie, and we have the feeling that Bok, like the saints, is not quite willing to let one off the hook for lying.

It is this matter of *letting one off* that I suggest is fundamental to the whole discussion of lying. For in one important respect, the central issue about lying is not just finding excuses or justifications for lying, but it is *in proving* that someone has *truly* lied. Many of the ethical questions about excuses and sanctions for lies presume, as did the saints, that lying is a straightforward, describable, and identifiable act. To assume without warrant that alleged lies are lies is merely to truncate the processes of argument by which we assess and evaluate lies. We especially see these difficulties in Bok. She defines a lie as an intentionally deceptive message. But fundamental to a lie, as she herself acknowledges, is the violation of the conditions of trust essential to confidence in communications. Yet these matters are never as clear-cut as Bok suggests. It is, I maintain, begging the issue to discuss alleged lies, as Bok does, as clear-cut lies. What a lie is depends, as with murder, on how we argue that the allegation is correct. What is admissable as argument in warranting the allegation that someone has lied, I suggest, is determined by both the rules and conventions of speech acts and by the norms and commitments that we accept or initiate in discourse situations.

We should first recognize that rules or conventions of speech acts are both linguistically and culturally determined. Lying requires the consideration of linguistic rules common to all linguistic communities; for example, giving erroneous advice and making false promises do not essentially vary from community to community. On the other hand, lying requires the consideration of cultural conventions or norms. Certain forms of deception and modes of speaking falsely are appropriate only in certain groups. We find, for example, a great deal of variation among different social classes and cultures about the acceptability of lying in humor, irony, deception games, negotiation, and even courtship.

In ordinary usage, moreover, we see that the term "lie" ranges over a gamut of uses running from strict to loose senses, some of which may well be metaphorical. Our looks, our actions, and even our silence can lie. Reports, promises, and even apologies lie. We lie by implication and suggestion. What is first needed in order to understand the phenomenon of lying is to analyze the wide variety of deliberate deceptions that take place by means of speech acts other than the giving of information, for to lie is not just to say only what is clear-cut and false. An analysis of lying involves, among other things, an analysis of motives, beliefs, and intentions. In sum, lying is not just simply misinforming or inaccurately reporting what it is that is the case. Lying extends to all sorts of statements and behaviors that may be misleading, deceptive, and confusing.

To my mind, the most interesting framework in which to discuss what it is to lie is found in the basic principles of discourse elaborated in the work of H. P. Grice.[27] What Grice presents in his article "Logic and Conversation" are general principles of discourse, where discourse is a cooperative effort in which the participants recognize common purpose and direction in discourse. Discourse situations, as I have tried to show elsewhere, need not be viewed rigidly as bound by the rules and norms of speech acts as analyzed in speech act theory.[28] Many discourse situations are determined not only by the rules and conventions of speech acts, but also by mutual constraints, commitments, understandings, and personal goals and objectives as mutually accepted and understood by the rhetor and his or her audience.

Grice states the cooperative principle as follows: "Make your conversational contribution such as is required, at the place where it occurs, by the accepted purpose or direction of the total exchange in which you are engaged." The key word in Grice's principle is "required," for it is the "requiredness" conditions of cooperative discourse that are fundamental to any analysis and assessment of lying. Grice's Rules of Conversation, which in part follow from the cooperative principle, are actually not nominally rules for conversation but, as he admits, the *ideal* requirements, or to use Austin's terminology, the felicity and sincerity conditions for the speech act of giving *information*.[29] Thus, Grice's theory does subsume speech act theory into its framework, but it is important to note that Grice's theory embodies a wider sociological frame of analysis.

For Grice, the rules that specifically relate to lying in the context of informing fall under his four categories: quality, quantity, relation, and manner. To illustrate, Grice's supermaxim of the category of quality is "try to make your contribution true." We may lie in giving information, using Grice's model, on two levels. We may lie directly by saying what is false in giving information; and we may lie indirectly by contextual implication. Lying can also be accomplished, again applying Grice's rules, under the category of quantity by limiting or withholding information. We lie thus by omission. Lying again occurs under the category of relation by manipulating relevance. We thus lie by diversion. And finally, under the category of manner, lying can be accomplished by obscurity, ambiguity, prolixity, and confusion. We thus lie by obfuscation. Hence we are, using Grice's principles, not limited to making ethical assessments of only straightforward or clear-cut lies. Grice's principles are especially valuable in the analysis, detection, and assessment of devious, insidious, or difficult to detect lies.

It is also possible to discover other discourse maxims for other sorts of speech acts such as promising, apologizing, praising, prescribing, and authorizing if we follow the pattern of Grice's analysis for giving information. John Searle does this sort of thing for promising in his *Speech Acts*.[30] In each sort of speech act we can charge the speaker with lying. "His promise was a lie." "His apology was a lie." "His praise was a lie." Each type of speech act, if we examine the matter carefully, has special prescribed forms of "requiredness" on the basis of which we say that a person lies in saying or doing what he says or does. In the context of charge and denial, an allegation that someone has lied has the rhetorical function of directing attention to the deceptive and misleading aspects of the speech acts brought into question. The force of an allegation that someone has lied is both directive and accusative. It is simplistic to look at such allegations as descriptive of simple acts of misinforming. Lies occur in the numerous sorts of speech acts in which confidence and trust are betrayed.

Grice, we should note, did not discuss the grounds of the requiredness conditions that determine the felicity and sincerity conditions of the speech acts except to call them "ideal." However, when he discusses the cooperative principle of discourse, discourse is assumed to be bilateral and mutual. The bilateral and mutual commitment basic to discourse situations suggests the approach to lying of the Dutch political theorist Hugo Grotius, found in his *On the Law of War and Peace*. He maintains in discussing the hearer's right to the truth, or the right not to be lied to, that the right to the truth is contingent upon the consent of the hearer. As Grotius states it: "The right of which we have spoken may be abrogated by the expressed consent of him with whom we are dealing, as when one says that he will speak falsely and the other permits it. In like manner it may be cancelled by the opposition of another right which in the common judgment of all men is much more cogent."[31]

Henry Sidgwick raises much the same issues in his *The Method of Ethics*. Sidgwick discusses as a general principle the "general right of each man to have the truth spoken to him by his followers, which right may be forfeited or suspended under certain circumstances."[32] But before discussing abrogation of the right to hear the truth, we should examine the basis of any original right to the truth in the first place.

What possible a priori basis can there be for any general right to hear the truth? Note that any agreement to talk between hostiles does not presuppose an obligation to speak truly. Negotiations between hostiles require first of all agreement about the ground rules for discussions. I am reminded at this point of the negotiations over the shape of the table in the Vietnam peace negotiations. An appeal to negotiate thus requires the setting up of mutually acceptable guidelines as to how negotiations shall take place and to what extent parties need to be truthful and sincere. We need, to put it simply, to join a community of discourse before we can have rights in it.

Deception games reflect many of these issues on agreements to tell the truth and the rights of a hearer to hear the truth about certain matters. We find, for example, in the discussion of the ethics of poker in *Official Rules of Card Games,* published by the United States Playing Card Company, that despite the demand for sportsmanlike conduct, it is part of the game of poker to fool opponents, even by lying, so long as one does not cheat.[33] Yet there are certain conventions among groups of players that prevent players from making certain kinds of untrue remarks. For example, "in nearly all circles it is considered unethical for a player to announce that he is betting or checking blind when in fact he has seen his hand." What we have in poker is conversation taking place that will make bluffing possible in an atmosphere of friendly deception. For example, it would be unfair to announce out of turn the intention to bet when actually you have no intention of doing so. Lying or deceptive remarks in poker in this last case are justified on the basis of fairness to the other players.

Note that many forums of discourse are based on similar sets of conventions and mutual understandings, some less explicit, however, than those found in poker. Deception games are a part of adversarial proceedings in love, politics, law, business, and labor relations. In each instance, negotiation and argument take place in a framework where Grice's cooperative principle is supplemented and modified by tacit adversarial codes, conventions, or understandings. An appeal for cooperation in adversarial proceedings is never a complete and outright appeal for cooperation in giving information. It is simply an appeal for a limited exchange of information controlled by the conventions and acceptances of the interested parties involved.

The differences between the conventions of advocacy and the conventions of giving advice are worth noting. If we agree to give advice, one of the strict norms is that your advice to me be given for my advantage and not for yours. If you were to do otherwise, you would not really be giving advice. The requiredness of the felicity and sincerity conditions for giving advice are thus that you recommend to me what you think best for me, not what is best for you. The norms operating on editorial pages, however, appear to violate such principles of giving advice. But there is a difference. There is tacit assent that newspapers do have a right to be advocates of their own causes. They are thus not required to give advice in the strict or ideal sense. Consequently, we should not expect them to be giving advice strictly in our interest.

The ethics of advocacy, whether in love, in marketing, in law, or in politics, depend on norms conventional to those contexts. If we participate in those affairs we should not expect any more veracity than appears mutually acceptable to the parties involved. What makes love, business, and politics doubly deceptive and frustrating is that the right to the truth is socially conventional, that it is not mutually defined and accepted by the parties involved. And it is at this point that we find what is *focal* in establishing the ethical qualities of the advocate.

Essential to advocacy and its ethics is *defining* the grounds and the conventions whereby advocacy can proceed. Aristotle recognizes this in the need to eliminate irrelevant appeals in forensic rhetoric. This need also occurs in communication involving appeals for the acceptance of contentions, as in this paper. Appeals in advocacy and appeals for mutual acceptance have different grounds. If I were, for example, to appeal for the mutual acceptance of a contention on grounds that I do not accept, it would be unethical for me to imply that I do so. For example, during the Korean War, I argued with a person over the propriety of flying the United States flag alongside the United Nations flag. I was somewhat annoyed at the patriotism of the person, so I replied, "Do you realize that

American boys are dying under the U.N. flag in Korea?" I did manage to silence the person, but I was inconsistent and guilty of the fallacy of *ad hominem* argument. *Ad hominem* as a fallacy is based on disguising agenda. One pretends to hold views in *ad hominem* that one does not hold. Basically, I had played the advocate, but I had disguised my role in a friendly agenda of mutual acceptance. It was unethical for me to have done so. One might not want to say that I had overtly lied, but I had implicitly lied. I was guilty in Aristotelian terms of sham argumentation.

Two considerations follow from my illustration. First, the agenda was disguised in the situation. The contextual implication of my pretended agenda was that I had believed my reasons. I thus violated the sincerity conditions operative in a situation in which two people wish to agree for the same reasons. But secondly, I had also wanted to have it both ways in the situation. I had pretended to argue on the basis of conventions of argument for acceptance on mutual held premises, but at the same time I had accepted for myself the liberty of being guided by the conventions of advocacy whereby I did not have to believe my reasons were true.

My contention is that the first ethical thing to do in discourse is not to lie completely about agenda. An ethical quality of an advocate is to be open about being an advocate. The paradigm sin of the advocate, I maintain, is the sin of the salesperson who says, "I am not here to sell you anything." In lying completely about agenda, the salesperson undermines any commitment to negotiate. Listening to salespersons can be advantageous to a willing customer, even if salespersons lie about certain matters. People are willing to talk to salespeople to gain information despite the acknowledged deceptions being played. With sales, just as in poker, suspected lying may betray to us what we wish to know. What first of all is unethical in sales is the unfairness of complete disguise and confusion of agenda. In business, the constraints against hidden persuasion obviously are lax, for it is part of the accepted conventions of sales strategy to disguise and confuse sales agenda, but never completely so. Note the convention in American newspapers of labeling advertisements as advertisements. Part of consumer education is to know the rules of the deception game of advertising, and part of ethical reform is to make any sales agenda open to avoid any confusion over the agenda.

Advocacy, in order to be consistent with Grice's Cooperative Principle, basically needs to be bilateral in its agenda. It is by the manipulation of agenda and by the violation of the mutually acceptable sincerity conditions of given modes of argument that deceptive, misleading, diversionary arguments become degenerate, unfair, unequal, and exploitive. And the major problem in politics and business is the degeneration of the bilateral and cooperative functions of discourse.

These considerations lead us to a second basic ethical consideration about advocacy. In that there is a tacit mutual commitment among the parties of an advocacy situation to the agenda and the conventions of advocacy, it would be unethical unilaterally to attempt to undermine or destroy these agenda and conventions. A second ethical quality of an advocate is respect for existing cooperative conventions of communication. The advocate ought not revoke these conventions lightly. The traditional modes and forums of advocacy have been built slowly throughout history. Progress has not at all been easy. And to see what has been so slowly and painfully created quickly destroyed is not pleasant. For this reason, the behavior of the advocates in the trial of the "Chicago Seven" in the aftermath of the 1968 Chicago Democratic Convention dramatized well the harm done in destroying rational modes of communication. This confrontation raised the horror of what happens when advocacy ceases to respect its cooperative and bilateral foundations and when conventions of argument can no longer function by mutually acceptable consent. Ethics and social cooperation through discourse are no longer possible under such conditions. In the case of the "Chicago Seven," legal institutions were dangerously threatened.

Intentional violations of agenda and conventions of cooperative discourse are delicate social and political problems. Protest movements flout conventions of cooperative discourse in the name of reform. When a forum of discourse becomes one-sided, corrupt, and unfair, it certainly seems justifiable to exercise extreme measures to reform it. And we often, it should be noted, refuse to talk to people with whom we find it impossible to reason. But one vital question is how far we can ever go in violating principles of cooperative discourse. Can we ever close off cooperative discourse completely?

Advocacy first and foremost rests upon a basic commitment to a cooperative framework without which no negotiation, compromise, or mutual understanding is at all possible. Even the agreement to disagree is cooperative. Insofar as there is sentiment to seek accommodation, there is the need for a framework of cooperation. We need, in making this point, to be reminded of the conventional argument against lying. Lying undermines trust and confidence in the speaker. This has been well illustrated in folk wisdom by the little boy who cried wolf. In the ethics of advocacy there is a somewhat parallel argument against those who undermine the norms and conventions of advocacy. To misuse the advocate's appeals and to corrupt the conventions of adversarial relationships is to destroy the very means necessary to negotiate compromise when the wolf is at the door. Destroying the forums of compromise destroys options and turns people back to their only recourse, violence.

We have now come full turn from Aristotle to find what appears missing in Aristotle. Aristotle recommends distinguishing between genuine and spurious enthymemes. He warns us against logical appeals that give the illusion of proof. He does not, however, do the same for ethical appeals where the rhetor gives the illusion of credibility or authority. And again he does not fully recognize the manipulative and diversionary thrust of emotive appeals in argumentation, as evidenced by the omission of the traditional psychological ones from his list of fallacies.

Yet, in defining rhetoric as the art of finding all the available means of persuasion, Aristotle must recommend selecting, compiling, and arranging arguments to gain maximum persuasive advantage. Such strategies to gain the prize need to hide the weakness of one's own position. They need to divert an audience's attention away from the strength of an opponent's argument. They need at times to instill in the audience the illusion of trust and confidence in the rhetor. And finally they need to put the audience in a receptive frame of mind that will lull their "natural reason."

In the rhetoric of advocacy, all of the above mentioned strategies have been conventionally acceptable in advocacy situations. Certain types of deceptions, certain types of misleading implications, and certain types of diversionary tactics have been acceptable and tolerable to audiences. What Aristotle misses is the *grounds* for this acceptance of deceptive stratagems in the rhetoric of advocacy. What is missing is the connection between deceptive stratagems and the cooperative principles of discourse. Without deception in advocacy little cooperation is possible. There would be little willingness to pursue cooperation where one had to reveal in every way the grounds for one's views or conclusions. The conventions of advocacy are thus a cooperative trade-off to make negotiation and compromise possible.

There is thus in the conventional norms of advocacy a strong element of "let the buyer beware." Yet even the marketplace has its codes of ethics, and sellers risk violating such conventional codes at their own peril. In part, Aristotle says as much, but his warning regards only spurious enthymemes and spurious examples.

Aristotle has much to say about spurious enthymemes. On the other hand, Aristotle's theory of example or induction is primitive by modern scientific standards of inductive rigor. And we need only to be reminded of the often quoted "lies, damned lies, and statistics" to acknowledge the extent that statistical representations have been used to display the weight of evidence in misleading ways. It is in the use of inductive fallacies that we see best dramatized the ethical issues of advocacy situations. To what extent is there any conventional prohibition against misleading statistics, especially when audiences are ignorant of statistics? To what extent does Aristotle's "natural reason" help an uneducated audience ignorant of statistics? To what extent can statistical fallacies be exposed without the sort of chain reasoning that Aristotle relegates to the sciences and not to the audiences of rhetoric? When is it thus unfair to use such manipulative statistics that are difficult to expose?

In the last analysis, a heavy critical burden is placed on audiences in the conventional ethics of advocacy. Conventions have been built around cooperative principles that permit, or at least condone, a large measure of deception. We may not like or approve of these conventions, but we need at least to start our ethical assessment of advocacy by recognizing what might be ethically right or wrong with such conventions, what social needs are fulfilled by them, and what might be possible or impossible without them. We need ultimately to recognize their value and disvalue for promoting good, harmony, justice, and the good life before we can launch any program to reform them.

The wisdom of "doing in Rome what the Romans do" is not the expediency of accepting cultural relativism usually implied by the statement. Rather, the wisdom lies in knowing that if we are to negotiate and do business in Rome, we need to operate within the framework of their conventions simply to do our business. There is no other basis of cooperation. If Arab merchants haggle, we have no other alternative but to haggle in making our purchases in their marketplaces. Thus, what is missing in Aristotle is the recognition that a rhetoric of advocacy needs to start with conventional norms and that these norms vary in different social and cultural contexts and discourse situations. What is legitimate in the way people deceive one another in a rhetoric of persuasion depends upon the sorts of cooperative and deceptive language games people play with one another. And, to put the last stone in place, rhetorical strategies *are* language games.

7
Ethos and the Aims of Rhetoric

Nan Johnson

The traditional function of rhetoric in western culture has been to provide a theory of composition and communication for oral and written discourse. The particular disposition of rhetorical theory during any one period in history reflects the intellectual and philosophical climate of that particular era; consequently, historical studies in rhetoric are also studies in the history of ideas. Those principles we consider traditional precepts in rhetoric such as invention, arrangement, syllogistic logic, style, and proof through ethos and pathos are, in fact, concepts that have been redefined and reformulated countless times since the classical period in response to changing social-intellectual milieux. Comparisons between modern rhetoric and the historical tradition are significant not only because such assessments define to what degree our ideas about language and communication have changed but also because such retrospective evaluations reveal the nature and origins of the philosophical assumptions that underlie those ideas.

When we begin to explore the substance of our assumptions we move toward a clearer understanding of the motives and aims that direct our efforts in contemporary theory and education. An examination of the historical significance of ethos in rhetorical theory is a particularly effective means of clarifying directions in modern rhetoric because definitions of the role of ethos have been linked traditionally to definitions of the aims of persuasion and the obligations of rhetorical education.[1] When we trace the status of ethos in rhetorical theories of the classical period and our own contemporary discipline, we see that variations in definitions of ethos correspond to different views of the relationship between rhetorical practice, philosophy, and ethics.

In Plato's *Gorgias,* Socrates observes that "the supreme object of a man's efforts in public and private life must be the reality rather than the appearance of goodness."[2] The philosophers of classical times laboriously honed their definitions of the moral good, and in discussing the impact of the orator they debated at length the importance of both real goodness and apparent goodness. In *Gorgias* and *Phaedrus* the nature of ideal truth and absolute goodness are central issues in Plato's argument for reformed oratorical practice; the reality of the speaker's virtue is presented as a prerequisite to effective speaking. In contrast, Aristotle's *Rhetoric* presents rhetoric as a strategic art which facilitates decisions in civil matters and accepts the appearance of goodness as sufficient to inspire conviction in hearers. Aristotle's and Plato's different accounts of the role of the speaker can be traced to their different notions about what constitutes the "Good" and what rhetoric owes the Good.

In Plato's *Gorgias* and *Phaedrus,* the role of rhetoric is defined as the instruction of ideal truth. Plato proposes in *Gorgias* that the true aim of oratory should be the "moral good," not merely persuasion as an end in itself. His indictment of sophist rhetoric in the *Gorgias* rests on the criticism that oratory so taught aims to produce gratification and pleasure, not knowledge of good and evil. The rhetorician, he argues, should be a philosopher, not a panderer, and should aim to lead the souls of his hearers to the "knowledge of ideas," not merely to belief or pleasure. Plato argues that rhetoric has the noble mission of producing order and proportion in souls. The intrinsic goodness and virtue of the speaker is a necessity if this obligation is to be fulfilled; a man is justified in embarking on a political career only if he possesses a knowledge of moral values which will enable him to improve the character of the community.[3]

Plato's stipulation that the statesman-orator be truly virtuous must be understand in terms of his general philosophy and ethical orientation. His belief that the Good represents an ideal is fundamental to the view that the speaker's virtue be obvious in thought and deed. Plato conceived of truth as that knowledge which is manifested in Ideas or Forms, first principles of reality that are eternal and universal. We human beings come to understand truth only when we ascend from the world of perception to the world of thought—a world in which we can "behold Ideas" (*ideai eide*). The idea of the Good is the highest Form of all and is evidenced, imperfectly, in nature and the lives of men.[4] The striving toward knowledge in the apprehension of Ideas, primarily the Good as an absolute ideal, is that act which liberates the soul from its confinement in the body. In order to ascend to the world of ideas, we must exert spiritual force through reason to break free from the limitation of sensory experience. As Plato explains in the *Republic,* truth is an essence beyond the scope of worldly affairs: "our true lover of knowledge naturally strives for truth, and is not content with common opinion, but soars with undimmed and unwearied passion till he grasps the essential nature of things with the mental faculty fitted to do so."[5] Reason is the guardian of the soul, the controller of the emotions, and the only faculty that affords an avenue to the Good which is reflected in harmony and order in mind and action. Dialectic, or philosophical inquiry, is the most orderly of human endeavors; relying on this image of reason in search of the Good, Plato recasts the sophistic practice of rhetoric. Dialectic discovers or identifies ideal truth while rhetoric provides instruction for the community about the application of philosophy to life.

Plato's belief that everything participates (methexis) in a higher reality shapes his ethical view that the aim of human conduct is to strive toward the Good, or universal principles which we recognize through reason and try to realize in life. Socrates observes in *Phaedrus* that rhetoric should be "the art of influencing the soul through words"; in this way, rhetoric participates in the Good by promulgating excellence through knowledge of Ideas. Without virtuous character to insure the perception and understanding of the Good, the orator could not instruct in the Forms of the Good.

Plato's definition of rhetoric's moral function and the necessity for virtuous character in the speaker are concepts which emanate from a philosophical view that defines truth as eternal and available only through rationality. Contrastingly, Aristotle defines rhetoric from a perspective that stresses the reality of particular human circumstances over the authority of "immutable" truths and ascribes a much more strategic than moral function.

Aristotle's intention in the *Rhetoric* is to formalize a technical system which will enable the student of oratory to control his art successfully. Unlike Plato, who defines rhetoric's scope as issues of good and evil, Aristotle is unwilling to stipulate a subject matter for rhetoric and emphasizes instead, rhetoric's usefulness as a faculty.

> Rhetoric may be defined as the faculty of observing in any given case the available means of persuasion. This is not a function of any other art.
> . . . rhetoric we look upon as the power of observing the means of persuasion on almost any subject presented to us; and that is why we say that, in its technical character, it is not concerned with any special or definite class of subjects.[6]

Rhetoric, in Aristotle's view, is a nonpartisan art that exists to "affect the giving of decisions" about matters that fall within "the general ken of all men" (pp. 90–91). The art of rhetoric consists of inventing arguments based on "common notions" (received opinions or enthymemes) that persuade hearers toward some specific change in attitude, behavior, or judgment.

Persuasion through the spoken word is of three kinds: ethos, "the personal character of the speaker"; pathos, "putting the audience into a certain frame of mind"; and logos, "the proof, or apparent proof, provided by the words of the speech itself" (pp. 24–25). The skillful orator utilizes one of these modes or a combination thereof as the means of persuasion. Ethos is a means of providing a persuasive argument when the speech "is so spoken" as to make the audience perceive the speaker as "credible" (p. 25). Aristotle explains that persuasion through "personal character" is the most effective means of persuasion an orator possesses but points out that it is the speech itself, not the speaker's reputation, that creates credibility. The speaker must make "his own character look right"; this is particularly important, Aristotle argues, in political and in judicial speaking situations in which an audience's trust and confidence are prerequisite to persuasion.

> There are three things which inspire confidence in the orator's own character—the three, namely, that induce us to believe a thing apart from any proof of it; good sense, good moral character, and good will . . . anyone who is thought to have all three of these good qualities will inspire trust in his audience. The way to make ourselves thought to be sensible and morally good must be gathered from the analysis of goodness already given. (II, 1, 6–18)

Aristotle stresses that conveying credibility requires acknowledgment of the accepted views and common emotions particular to different speech situations. Investing political, ceremonial, and forensic speeches with moral character requires that the orator understand human nature and emotions—in short, that he understand the Good in a variety of situations.[7] If we are to understand the true character of his presentation of ethos as a strategy of "making character" look right in varied circumstances, we must bring to Aristotle's discussion of "Goodness and Utility" in the *Rhetoric* (I, c6, 15) an understanding of his overall view of the Good and its place in his ethics.

What Aristotle means by "Goodness" in the *Rhetoric* is not the Platonic concept of the Good as the absolute transcendent ideal but something more akin to human excellence as evidenced in individual circumstances. Aristotle perceives the Good as a final level of excellence intrinsic in the motion of things as they evolve toward their final form. This human Good is evaluated in terms of received opinion or "endoxa," not immutable truth.[8] The ultimate good in human behavior is any activity which follows a rational principle, and the Good in character consists of intellectual and moral virtue (arete). Aristotle explains in the *Nicomachean Ethics* that the life of virtue is the means by which man attains the Good, or the state of happiness (eudaimonia). Complete virtue is achieved when the individual has both liberality and temperance (moral virtue) and philosophic and practical wisdom (intellectual virtue). Intellectual virtue is the result of acting rationally or practicing logic, and moral virtue is the result of the ability to choose conduct in accordance with moral custom. In Aristotle's view, morality is not an absolute; the "right thing" to do is defined in terms of a "mean" or intermediate between excess and deficiency, limits which are themselves set by "endoxa" or custom. "Virtue, then, is a state of character concerned with choice, lying in a mean, i.e., the mean relative to us, this being determined by a rational principle and by that principle by which the man of practical wisdom would determine it."[9] Aristotle remarks in the *Ethics* and the *Rhetoric* that rhetoric is related to political science. By politics he means the application of practical wisdom to the running of the state, whereas rhetoric applies practical wisdom to decision-making related to the good or health of the same enterprise. What is good is set by convention, not by nature; therefore, rhetoric, like politics, is an art dependent on knowledge of "received opinion" and the "mean."

Aristotle assumes that the rhetorician identifies the Good by analyzing the particular situation. Throughout the *Rhetoric* Aristotle stresses the importance of the orator's assessment of "subject," "persons addressed," and "occasion." Such an assessment is a major factor in the presentation of an effective ethos and is synonymous with an identification of the relative "Good" involved. In the *Ethics*, Aristotle emphasizes that the Good is not prescriptive but rather relativistic and subjective, in that it must be evaluated along a continuum of human values and situational particulars. Aristotle goes to great length in the *Rhetoric* to provide the student of oratory with information about the protocols of different speech situations, human emotions, and audience types as an aid in learning how to identify the Good and Utility implicit in different subjects and to create credible ethos in a variety of ways. Ethos is a strategy in Aristotle's rhetoric but a beneficent rather than a manipulative one; "making one's character look right" results from deliberation about the nature of the audience and the "mean" course appropriate to the subject and the situation. In other words, ethos is the result of a considered choice about how the Good is best defined and conveyed within the boundaries of received opinion.

Aristotle's and Plato's definitions of the nature and role of the speaker in effective oratory are constrained by their different notions about three issues: 1) what constitutes truth or knowledge: ideal principles or received opinion; 2) the nature of the Good: absolute perfection or excellence in final form; and 3) rhetoric's role in the discovery of truth and presentation of the Good: dialectical activity of edification in the ideal or strategic skill in the communication of human values and opinion.

Aristotle perceives excellence or the Good as a perfection of form possible through the effects of individual acts and mutual understanding; Plato defines the Good as an ideal which is only revealed to us in philosophical inquiry or spiritual edification. For Aristotle, rhetoric is an art that facilitates decision-making; consequently, "ethos" is defined as a pragmatic strategy which serves practical wisdom in human affairs. The rhetorician need not be virtuous in a Platonic objective sense, only wise about human values, opinions, and motivations. The Platonic view defines rhetoric as an art that expedites the beholding of first principles; the orator bears witness to the ideal Good by being an incarnation of virtue. Plato's philosopher-orator reveals the absolute and universal through his intrinsic state. Aristotle's citizen-orator facilitates decision and action on issues of the probable and the possible, tempering his character according to the subject and the audience.

These distinctly different conceptions in Greek rhetoric about the province of oratory and the function of character in persuasion are reflected in similarly differing presentations of the role of the speaker in the influential Roman rhetorics of Cicero and Quintilian. Quintilian defines his purpose in *Institutio Oratoria* as the "education of the perfect orator" and insists that the perfect orator is "blameless in point of character."[10] Cicero, however, who is concerned in *De Oratore* with outlining a rhetoric which serves the body politic, considers ethos to be a strategy of choosing the appropriate "token" of character.

Quintilian perceives rhetoric as an ethical activity which grounds citizens in "the principles of upright and honorable living." These principles are objective and recognizable; "surely everyone of my readers must now have realized that oratory is in the main concerned with the treatment of what is just and honorable" (XII, 1, 9).

For Quintilian, the most important quality of the orator is intrinsic moral virtue: "the first essential for such an orator is that he should be a good man; and consequently, we demand of him not merely the possession of exceptional gifts of speech, but of all the excellence of character as well" (1, 9). Moral character can be learned, Quintilian insists, and the education of the good man should be the "first and the greatest" aim of education. What Quintilian means by "good" is more closely akin to Aristotle's notion of arete or practical wisdom than Plato's concept of the Good as an ideal. It is clear, however, that Quintilian perceives the orator as a spiritual missionary who must embody philosophical truths: "it is from the thought of posterity that he must inspire his soul with justice and derive that freedom of spirit which it is his duty to display" (XII, ii, 31). Quintilian shares Plato's view that the orator must develop "loftiness of soul" in order "to speak out truly" and that edification in the "way to virtue" is the aim of oratory.

Cicero's definition of the role of rhetoric and the function of ethos is much more Aristotelian than Platonic in disposition. Rhetoric is presented in *De Oratore* (55 B.C.) as the art of speaking well, and Cicero outlines the province of oratory or "eloquence" to be matters relevant to the maintenance of "peace and tranquility" in communities and nations.[11] Cicero reiterates the Aristotelian view that the aim of rhetoric is to persuade: "to get a hold on assemblies . . . win their good will, direct their inclinations wherever the speaker wishes, or divert them from whatever he wishes" (I, lvii, 30). In addition to reproducing the major elements in Aristotle's theory of rhetoric, including the five divisions (invention, arrangement, style, memory, delivery), the three kinds of oratory, and the topics, Cicero also ascribes a strategic role to ethos, which he defines as the winning of the good will of an audience through the presentation of favorable character, principles, and conduct. However, unlike Aristotle, Cicero does not treat ethos in relation to the philosophical issue of the Good but discusses it as a strategy of style: "by means of particular types of thought and diction, and the employment besides of a delivery that is unruffled and eloquent of good nature, the speakers are made to appear upright, well bred, and virtuous men" (II, xlii, 184).

Cicero's emphasis on the importance of speakers' ability to "paint their characters in words as being upright" divorces the principle of ethos from its original place in the ethical matrix of Aristotle's *Rhetoric*. Without a recapitulation of some attending philosophical format, ethos is reduced to the status of strategic stylistic device, a long step down from its role as considered choice made in response to deliberation on the Good and Utility of a subject. It is Cicero's more narrow concept of strategy and pragmatism that colors later views of practical aims for rhetoric and definitions of the role of the speaker. Aristotle's notion of ethos as a major mode of persuasion based on a knowledge of received opinion is conspicuously absent in rhetorics modeled on a Ciceronian framework.

The contrasting views of Cicero and Quintilian about the aims of rhetoric and the function of ethos are reminiscent of Plato's and Aristotle's differences of opinion about whether or not moral virtue in the speaker is intrinsic and prerequisite or selected and strategically presented. The divergence between the perspectives held by classical rhetoricians on this topic prefigures a disagreement about the function of rhetoric and its relations to philosophy and ethics that persists throughout the history of rhetoric and that is evident in our contemporary discipline. The overall shape of the discipline of rhetoric can be understood as a composite of neo-Platonic and neo-Aristotelian views which incorporates the moral obligation of rhetoric to objective truth on the one hand and the strategic role of rhetoric in pragmatic communication on the other.[12] The status of ethos in the hierarchy of rhetorical principles has fluctuated as rhetoricians in different eras have tended to define rhetoric in terms of either idealistic aims or pragmatic skills.

In general, the pragmatic orientation of the Aristotelian-Ciceronian concepts of rhetorical aims and the function of ethos has tended to dominate the secular rhetorical arts of the postclassical period while neo-Platonic idealism has been incorporated and cultivated as a guiding principle for rhetoric mainly in the sphere of Christian rhetoric. The development of the medieval arts of ars dictaminus (the art of letter writing) and ars praedicandi (art of preaching) exemplifies a state of coexistence between moral and pragmatic rationales for rhetoric and ethos, a characteristic trend in the tradition since the classical period.[13] Ars dictaminus developed in response to a growing need for efficient bureaucracies in feudal culture, and focuses on the composition of model letters that could be adapted to the needs of numerous writers having varied intentions. Handbooks on the art of letter writing generally rely on a Ciceronian definition of ethos as a stylistic device of "painting" character in diction. Typically, ethos is treated in writing manuals under titles such as "The Securing of Good Will" as is the case in this excerpt from a twelfth century manual entitled *The Principles of Letter Writing* (1135): "The securing of Good Will (benivolentiae captio) in a letter is a certain fit ordering of words effectively influencing the mind of the recipient. . . . Good Will will be secured by the person sending the letter if he mentions humbly something about his achievements or his duties or his motives."[14]

This discussion of ethos as a device of stylistic manipulation in the service of gaining good will or favor is typical of the manner in which Aristotelian-Ciceronian approaches to the function of ethos have been incorporated into various rhetorical arts since the end of the classical period. When a medieval handbook tells us that the "ordering" of words will result in "influencing the mind," it betrays the truncation that Ciceronian rhetoric wrought upon Aristotle's complex argument outlining the correspondence between knowledge of human nature and "mean" values and strategic choice of personal deportment. The comparatively simplistic and superficial concept of ethos as a stylistic device in ars dictaminus reveals the durable influence in practical rhetorical arts of Cicero's reformulated concept of ethos.[15]

Although it is true, as the productive aim of ars dictaminus suggests, that in the postclassical era most secular rhetorics developed a pragmatic disposition in response to changing needs for literate skills, nonetheless pragmatic definitions of rhetoric and the role of ethos have never enjoyed complete dominion. Christian philosophy preserved the Platonic definition of rhetoric as a servant of an ideal truth; it generated ecclesiastical rhetoric, a mode of persuasion that maintained a customary place in rhetorical treatises on public address for over fifteen hundred years. Augustine's *On Christian Doctrine* (c. 396) was the founding document in ars praedicandi and the basic model for texts on oratory for the clergy. In *On Christian Doctrine,* Augustine insured the longevity of a concept of moral ethos by linking character in the speaker to spiritual aims for rhetoric: "the faculty of eloquence should be obtained for the uses of the good in the service of truth."[16] The "good" here referred to is the sum of Christian ideals as defined in the Scriptures, or the Word in an absolute sense. Although Augustine's rhetorical framework is Ciceronian, his philosophical orientation is objectivist in that he defines the aim of rhetoric as instruction in immutable truth. The ecclesiastical orator persuades if he has faith, piety, and speaks of the "just, the holy, and the good." Without faith, the preacher cannot interpret the Scriptures—and without knowledge of the Bible, there is no wisdom. The inner piety of the orator is a prerequisite to obtaining truth and to conveying that truth. Hence in the sphere of Christian rhetoric, Plato's sense of ethos as intrinsic and prerequisite virtue is preserved in rhetorical theory. In Augustine's view, the Christian character of the speaker is testimony to his Christian life, and that ethos is more crucial to the ability to preach than eloquence itself. "Let him so order his life that he not only prepares a reward for himself, but also so that he offers an example to others, and his way of living may be, as it were, an eloquent speech" (p. 166).

The distinctly different definitions of the function of the speaker's character in the tradition of ars praedicandi and ars dictaminus are further illustrations of the complexity that has characterized the status of ethos in the history of rhetoric. This complexity has its origins in the composite substance of classical doctrine that is itself a sum of divergent attitudes about the aims of rhetoric and the ethical role of the speaker. When we examine discussions of ethos by later rhetorical scholars such as George Campbell and Hugh Blair to whom contemporary rhetoric is more directly indebted, we see that distinctions in definitions of the nature and function of ethos continue to be linked to stipulations about the pragmatic and ethical aims of rhetoric. Both Campbell's *The Philosophy of Rhetoric* (1776) and Blair's *Lectures on Rhetoric and Belles Lettres* (1783) treat secular and ecclesiastical oratory within an overall view of rhetoric as an inclusive theory of composition and define the role of ethos with regard to persuasive purposes.

As a major proponent of epistemological views of rhetoric, Campbell devotes *The Philosophy of Rhetoric* to describing the relations between rhetorical principles and the natural processes of the human mind and behavior. In addition to addressing the philosophical and epistemological aspects of rhetoric, Campbell outlined a pragmatic program in public address in *Lectures on Systematic Theology and Pulpit Eloquence,* a volume based on his lectures to students at Marischal College and published posthumously in 1807. Campbell's philosophy of rhetoric seeks to explain how certain rhetorical strategies work in affecting the innate faculties of the mind. He defines rhetoric as an art "by which . . . discourse is adapted to its end," an art that provides the speaker with the materials to "enlighten the understanding, to please the imagination, to move the passions, or to influence the will."[17] Ethos is treated in two ways with regard to these four aims: first as a strategy in the courtroom meant to move the passions by gaining "sympathy" and second as a prerequisite virtue in the character of the ecclesiastical orator. What Campbell means by "sympathy," which he defines as "the common tie of human souls," is a response given in recognition of sincerity, honesty, and integrity. This notion of sympathy is closely related to what Aristotle and Cicero mean by good will, yet Campbell and other eighteenth century rhetoricians bring a slightly different philosophical perspective to what is involved in eliciting sympathy. Campbell perceives the gaining of sympathy as a necessary step in affecting the passions, which in turn engage the will so as to effect persuasion; ethos, or persuasion from character, is defined here as a "natural" strategy in the unfolding of mental processes.[18] This is yet another interpretation of ethos as a "strategy," in this case as a "communicative principle" that has "a foundation in human nature" (pp. 96–97). The association between ethos—sympathy—and a chain reaction of faculties is a common feature in eighteenth- and nineteenth-century English and American texts, including Joseph Priestley's *A Course of Lectures on Oratory and Criticism* (1762) and Henry Day's *Elements of the Art of Rhetoric* (1850).[19]

Primarily, Campbell's treatment of "character" focuses on a discussion of ethos as an epistemological strategy in public speaking. He advises that "for promoting the success of the orator . . . it is a matter of some consequence that in the opinion of those whom he addresseth, he is both a wise and a good man" (p. 227). A focus on the "opinion" of the hearers is typical in pragmatic definitions of ethos; the emphasis is placed much more on the speaker's need to be aware of audience needs than on the disposition of the intrinsic virtue of the orator. Ecclesiastical rhetoric, however, emphasizes the importance of the reality rather than the appearance of virtue, and Campbell's treatment of pulpit oratory is consistent with this trend. In his advice to the would-be preacher, Campbell provides a faithful rendition of Christian idealism. The sermon is defined as having the noble aim to "inspire equity, moderation, and charity into men's sentiments and conduct" (p. 110). The preacher is defined here as a "minister of grace" whose Christian virtue directly affects persuasion to action. "There is a certain delicacy in the character of a preacher which he is never at liberty totally to overlook, and to which if there appear anything incongruous, either in his conduct or in his public performances, it will never fail to injure their effect" (p. 100).

While Campbell evaluates ethos as a strategy in terms of what is "natural," Blair assesses the significance of ethos and rhetorical principles in general with regard to how expression advances Taste. In contrast to other eighteenth-century rhetoricians such as John Walker and Thomas Sheridan, who devoted their attention to elocution in the belief that control over the body and voice strengthened the faculties, Campbell and Blair share a view of rhetoric as an art of intellectual and emotional communication based on an understanding of the human mind and audience response. Blair's *Lectures* represent the most widely adapted and imitated rhetoric in the belle lettres tradition. This school of thought held rhetoric to be a general art of composition and expression in poetry, prose, and public address. Blair defines the aim of rhetoric to be the cultivation of Taste in reasoning and conduct, and his approach to oratory is to outline what constitutes tasteful speaking at popular assemblies, the bar, and the pulpit. Taste, the power of receiving pleasure from the beauties of nature and art, is described as a natural sensibility that can be improved by reason, common sense, and education. Rhetoric encouraged taste by persuading through beautiful language, or the "unassumed language of the heart."[20] Tasteful language persuades, Blair argues, because it is natural and truthful sentiment. The reasonable speaker is a good man because truth, reason, and virtue are indivisible in human nature: "seldom or never will a man be eloquent but when he is in earnest and uttering his own sentiments" (p. 100). This interpretation of the role of character in persuasion attributes epistemological, aesthetic, and ethical functions to ethos and illustrates the degree to which philosophy and poetics overlapped in belletristic thought. Like Campbell, Blair defines honesty and sincerity as those characteristics which the audience identifies with goodness. Blair, however, is more adamant about the necessity of real virtue in secular rhetoric and believes that eloquence is tied to sincerity in a substantive way, particularly in pulpit oratory. "It is of the utmost consequence that the Speaker firmly believe both the truth and the importance of those principles which he inculcates in others and not only that he believe them speculatively but have a lively and serious feeling of them" (p. 106).

In the rhetorics of Campbell and Blair we see how classical definitions of the practical and ethical functions of ethos are adapted to popular philosophical views of the eighteenth century and to expanded notions of the province of rhetoric. Despite the marked contrast between the epistemological and belletristic schools of rhetoric, a state of coexistence between pragmatic and idealist aims for rhetoric is evident in the dual focus of these rhetorics on secular and ecclesiastical oratory. Although most rhetorics of the late eighteenth and nineteenth centuries did not follow this format, notable nineteenth-century rhetoricians such as Richard Whately and Edward T. Channing continued to provide educators with a choice of points of view about the role of rhetoric and the obligation of the speaker.

Whately defines rhetoric as an "architectural" art of composing arguments, and he defines ethos as a strategy of gaining sympathy.[21] Like Campbell, Whately sees sympathy as the key to moving the Will to action, and he defines ethos as "an impression produced by the projection of good sense, good principle, and Good Will." Whately's sense of ethos as a strategy of appearance is Ciceronian, as is his concept of what the speaker is obligated to do is limited to "raising a favorable impression." He makes a point of addressing the folly of taking Aristotle's discussion of ethos to be about "real character." Whately's concept of ethos is one of the most instrumental of the influential Ciceronian trend while Channing's view is one of the more idealistic in secular rhetoric. In his lectures on rhetoric at Harvard in the 1850s, Channing defined oratory as a noble art and stressed that the central responsibility of the orator was "to gain a strong and wholesome influence over men."[22]

> It would not be going too far to say that it is not in all the graces of address, or sweetness and variety of tones, or beauty of illustration—in all the outward and artificial accomplishments of the orator, to equal or even approach the power conferred by a good character. Its still eloquence is felt in the commonest transactions of life. (P. 24)

Believing that secular oratory had a special function in a democracy—to facilitate national unity—Channing emphasizes the fact that a rhetorician must perceive himself as an individual who works with peers to solve mutual problems. Channing's definition of ethos as a beneficent commitment reflects an adaptation of the concept of the "good man" to democratic idealism.

Channing shares Blair's view that sincerity is a prerequisite to the composition and delivery of public address. Although Channing's theories of rhetoric never had the widespread popularity enjoyed by the texts of Blair, Campbell, or Whately, the particular importance of ethos and its relationship to sincerity and the arousal of sympathy was an issue raised in more influential texts of the mid-nineteenth century such as William T. Shedd's translation of Franz Theremin's *Eloquence A Virtue* (1844), Henry Day's *Elements of the Art of Rhetoric* (1850), and Matthew Hope's *Princeton Textbook in Rhetoric* (1854).[23] Theremin's *Eloquence A Virtue* emphasized the integration of ethical intention and effective expression in public speaking and prose composition. Concerned that rhetoric had ceased to be taught as a "sincere process" and was generally presented as a "collection of rules," Shedd intended Theremin's rhetoric to offer a philosophical approach to the subject which stressed the role of the speaker's moral character or "consciousness of being in the right." Theremin defines rhetoric or eloquence as the communication of "an idea of truth to an audience." From this perspective, the ethical character of the speaker is considered an absolute necessity: some exhibition of political, ethical, and religious truth is necessary in eloquence: "For the consciousness of being in the right imparts a coloring to the style, and an emphasis to the tone, which an evil conscience can imitate only in part, never perfectly; and the morally bad which peers through, will always induce a suspiciousness in the hearer" (p. 95).

Although Day and Hope incorporate several of Theremin's ideas on invention in their texts, their approach to rhetorical instruction is much more pragmatic. In *Elements of the Art of Rhetoric,* Day defines rhetoric as "address to another mind" and is clearly more interested in outlining effective skills of invention and arrangement for expository and persuasive prose than in defining ethical aims for rhetorical practice. Day's treatment of ethos is Aristotelian; he discusses the importance of inciting "good will" through the presentation of a character of "good principle" and of gaining sympathy by displaying appropriate emotions.

> The three qualities requisite in the speaker in reference to the audience as prescribed by the ancients are Good Sense, Good Principle, and Good Will . . . A character of integrity is necessary, inasmuch as just as far as the speaker shows himself unworthy of confidence, will everything he says be received with misgivings and suspicion; while the bare assertions of a reputedly honest man will often be received with the submission which is due to actual demonstration. (P. 128)

Although Day observes in his discussion of the "power of sympathy" that the orator ought to truly feel the sentiments he expresses, he does allow that the "reputation" of integrity is as effective in persuading an audience as the "actual" quality itself.

Like Day, Hope intended with the *Princeton Textbook in Rhetoric* to delineate practical skills of invention and expression. He too acknowledges the role of sympathy and gives the traditional Aristotelian-Ciceronian advice that speakers must inspire in an audience a belief in their "good will, good principles, and good sense"; the confidence of an audience that the orator possesses these elements of character is, of course, the thing essential to his power (p. 103). Hope regards the character of the speaker as potentially having great persuasive force, a force Hope defines as "presence." Presence, he explains, is "due to intellectual force, somewhat to strength of will or purpose or character, somewhat to the spiritual qualities of the man" (p. 104). (This discussion of ethos as "presence" is particularly interesting when compared to Chaim Perelman's treatment of the same issue in *The New Rhetoric,* a treatment generally regarded by rhetorical historians and critics as unique.) Like

Day, Hope emphasizes the importance of strategies that present a character which inspires confidence, thus facilitating the communication of any chosen subject. Theremin, unlike Day, perceives the character of the speaker to be a "force that develops . . . ethical impulse" (p. 63).

We observe from these samplings that the status of ethos in the hierarchy of rhetorical principles in postclassical eras is related directly to the nature of classical theory as a composite of moral and pragmatic intentions. The Platonic and Aristotelian-Ciceronian concepts of ethos represent philosophical rationales against which the aims of rhetoric in any given period can be compared and identified. Our modern discipline is marked by a composite of neo-Platonic and neo-Aristotelian views. The disposition of these views, however, is unique: pragmatic definitions of ethos and aims for rhetoric dominate rhetorical education while concepts of virtuous ethos and moral rhetoric are advanced only in theory.

Moral neutrality is the ground sought by most contemporary texts in composition when defining rhetorical purposes beyond the pragmatic aim of communicating efficiently in a variety of modes. The marked tendency of modern rhetorical texts to present strategic definitions of ethos seems to proceed from a widely held Aristotelian-Ciceronian view that rhetoric is an art of inventional, compositional, and communicative competence.[24] This view underlies pedagogical approaches which typically present ethos as a stylistic strategy of gaining audience favor and empathy. Explanations and guidelines for the use of ethos repeat traditional pragmatic advice that writers must create the appearance of sincerity in order to persuade.

The concept of ethos rarely appears in current texts by name. Rather, it is discussed under such varied stylistic headings as "tone," "writer's voice," "personal appeal," "attitude," "persona," and "credibility." Often, these are presented as preparatory considerations in the process of composing under such titles as "considering an audience," "convincing a reader," and "planning for aim and audience."[25] Contemporary definitions of ethos as "tone" or "persona" are reminiscent of Cicero's concept of ethos as the skill of "painting" character in style.

> When you write you create an identity for yourself. Using only words—no make-up, no costumes, no scenery, no music—you have to present yourself to an audience and get its attention and its confidence. You can . . . by using imagination and trying to develop a sense of tone, learn to present yourself in various ways . . . you ask, "how can I use language to make my audience believe in this character?"[26]

Many texts discuss ethos in the shape of a stylistic device (tone) and as a concern related to invention, focusing on the "rhetorical situation" or the "process of composing" or both. Such pragmatic definitions of ethos, typical of modern rhetoric, conflate the Ciceronian definition of ethos as appearance with the Aristotelian view of ethos as a choice made in response to particular audiences. As with strategic concepts of ethos in earlier historical periods, the philosophical rationale for this choice as a deliberation on the Good is conspicuously absent:

> Each time you write, you should determine the general rhetorical situation—and hence the appropriate rhetorical profile persona by asking yourself these questions: (1) For whom am I writing?, (2) What am I trying to say to the reader?, (3) What is the occasion for this particular communication?, (4) What role do I play in this particular occasion in relation to my reader? Your answers to these questions will help to bring the rhetorical situation into focus—and will help you, in turn, determine the profile that you can most effectively use in the composition that you are preparing.[27]

Modern texts advise students to correlate "persona" with assessments of the reader and the writing situation. Such advice presents ethos as a skill of stylistic adaptability to mode and audience, and typically eschews moral implications.[28]

One of the major goals of rhetoricians such as Richard Weaver and Wayne Booth has been to restore a balance between pragmatic and objective ideals as a basis for rhetorical theory and practice. Weaver argues in "Language is Sermonic" that rhetoric should be an art of identifying and disseminating immutable truth: "it has the office of advising men with reference to an independent order of goods and with reference to their particular situation as it relates to these."[29] The Platonic disposition of Weaver's view of rhetoric as an advisory art demands that the rhetorician have intrinsic virtue. The rhetorician must always have in mind "a vision of how matters should go ideally and ethically" (p. 54) in order that the aim of showing hearers "better visions of themselves" (pp. 24–25) can be achieved. Ethos is defined in this objectivist context as embodiment of truth; the speech mirrors the inner soul. Weaver believes that matters of truth and character have been neglected in modern rhetorical education. The problem with the teaching of college composition, he argues, is that instruction in rhetoric no longer aims to teach students how to speak correctly and truthfully, only correctly and usefully. In such curricula, the issue of ethos becomes merely a device of "using language to better our position in the world" (p. 189). We see in Weaver's theory of rhetoric and definition of ethos the traditional reciprocity between concepts of the province of rhetoric and the function of ethos in persuasion.

In essence, Weaver argues that *ideas have moral consequences* and that rhetoric should proceed from that hypothesis. Wayne Booth offers a similar assessment in *Modern Dogma and the Rhetoric of Assent* (1974) in which he defines rhetoric as the "whole philosophy of how men succeed or fail in discovering together in discourse, new levels of truth (or at least agreement) that neither supported before."[30] Defining intrinsic moral ethos as one of the major entries in a "repertory of good reasons" for conviction, Booth insists that communication relies on assessments of basic integrity in others (pp. 154–57). Booth criticizes educational institutions for failing to deal with ethos as a good reason; the result of this neglect, he insists, is that students are left with literate skills but no ability to determine degrees of reliability in speakers, writers, or public figures.

Despite the advocacy of influential theorists such as Weaver and Booth, there is no representative group of texts in contemporary education that defines ethos as prerequisite virtue or reiterates the neo-Platonic attitude that the rhetorician must be a good person dedicated to advancing the ideals of truth. Instruction in modern rhetoric is governed by the pragmatic attitude that rhetorical competence consists of the ability to discover topics and to control organization and grammar in expository and argumentative writing. The majority of instructors in rhetoric clearly view the issue of ethical intention to be a concern that falls outside the sphere of pedagogy, and philosophical studies in rhetoric have not succeeded in restoring to rhetorical education a focus on the moral obligations of rhetoric and the ethical responsibility of the writer.[31] In treating the principle of ethos, today's rhetorical education offers a range of alternatives narrower than that typically relayed to students in earlier periods.

The fortunes of the principle of ethos in our own era and in earlier periods in the history of rhetoric reflect the variety of interpretations left open by the classical theorists when they defined the practical and moral functions of rhetoric. A look backward at this philosophical inheritance is, simultaneously, a look forward to how the state of our own art will predispose those who follow us. What an historical examination of the status of ethos reveals, beyond the composite nature of the discipline, is the historic ability of rhetoric to maintain its position as an integral force of cultural cohesion by adapting to changing attitudes in western society about what constitutes literate communication and ethical dialogue.

8
The Continuing Relevance of Plato's *Phaedrus*

Donald C. Stewart

> *But if we are to adopt this method, it must be on condition that we all regard ourselves as rivals in the attempt to distinguish truth from falsehood; we are all equally concerned in the truth being made clear. I will tell you my conclusions; but if any of you think that I am allowing myself to assume what is not true, he must interrupt and challenge me. I am not speaking dogmatically from the certainty of assured knowledge; I am simply your fellow-explorer in the search for truth, and if somebody who contradicts me is obviously right I shall be the first to give way.*[1]
>
> Socrates

Like most of the Platonic dialogues, the *Phaedrus* begins disarmingly. Socrates meets Phaedrus outside the wall of Athens and soon discovers that the young man has been listening to a speech by Lysias. Better yet, although Phaedrus does not at first admit the fact, he has a copy of Lysias' speech, and Socrates tells him in the manner of an affectionate but firm teacher that although he understands Phaedrus' desire to practice speechmaking on him, he would just as soon have Lysias himself, represented by the speech Phaedrus carries. There follow, under the shade of a plane tree, Phaedrus' reading of the speech by Lysias, Socrates' speech on the same theme, a better one than that of Lysias, Socrates' recantation of the first speech he made, and a lengthy discussion of the soul, philosophy, and rhetoric.

How often we have seen Plato do this: begin in some quiet, friendly, casual social situation and gradually develop an increasingly complex set of ideas which lead toward a resolution of great profundity. In this dialogue, the apparent misdirection of the early sections concealed one of

Plato's most artful and sophisticated designs, and the result has been an accumulating body of scholarship on the problems of interpreting the *Phaedrus*.

Over the centuries one can discern scholarly preoccupation with three fundamental questions about this dialogue: 1) to what extent is rhetoric its subject, 2) what does Plato wish to predicate in it about rhetoric, 3) what contemporary relevance do Plato's views on rhetoric have? I plan to review representative scholarship on all three questions, citing those opinions which seem most convincing to me, and conclude with my own assessment of the relevance of the *Phaedrus* to those whose vocation is the teaching of writing in twentieth century America.

To begin, then, it is safe to say that there is now little doubt about the answer to the first question. The subject of the *Phaedrus* is rhetoric. But the dialogue did present problems in the past because it touched upon an array of topics—erotic love, rhetoric, philosophy, the afterlife, dialectics, and writing—and because there was confusion, until the nineteenth century, over its place in the Platonic canon.[2]

The dating problem was troublesome because, for a long time, it was assumed that the *Phaedrus* was an early work, possibly a statement of the educational program Plato was to establish in his academy.[3] Careful scholars of the text resolved that problem (insofar as it can be resolved) in the nineteenth century, however, by calling attention to a number of features in the dialogue which strongly suggested that it belonged among Plato's mature works: its Pythagorism; its multifarious learning, uncharacteristic of the early dialogues; the maturity of its ethical views; its exposition of Plato's method of collection and division; its perfection of the dialogue as literary art; and its dithyrambic style.[4]

Once the dating problem was settled, attention was fixed more carefully on the problem of subject matter unity, particularly the difficulty of explaining why half of the *Phaedrus* dealt with erotic love. It was not a problem for too long, however. Alfred E. Taylor: "If the real subject of the *Phaedrus* were sexual love, it is hard to see how its elaborate discussion of the possibility of applying a scientific psychology of the emotions to the creation of a genuine art of persuasion, or its examination of the defects of Lysias as a writer, can be anything but the purest irrelevance."[5]

Werner Jaeger further clarified this issue by pointing out that Eros was brought into the dialogue through Lysias' speech which Socrates examines as a piece of rhetoric. He further explains that Eros was a favorite theme for the exercises students in the rhetorical schools performed, exercises much like Lysias' speech. Finally, "the discussion of Eros gave Plato the opportunity to treat not only the form of the speech, but the question of truth or falsity, which was his chief concern as a philosopher."[6]

John Mackin, who never questions that rhetoric is the principal subject of the dialogue, adds another dimension to the subject by arguing that the *Gorgias* and the *Phaedrus* are complementary works, the *Gorgias* taking up forensic and deliberative rhetoric, the *Phaedrus* epideictic rhetoric. Claude Thompson, one of the few moderns who does not insist rigorously that rhetoric is *the* only significant subject of the *Phaedrus,* notes that its "dominant themes . . . are rhetoric, love, and the nature and destiny of the soul."[7] Intertwined with these subjects he finds subordinate motifs—imitation, inspiration or enthusiasm, and recollection —which he says echo themes and passages from other dialogues and thus enrich our appreciation of Plato's treatment of rhetoric in the *Phaedrus.* Specifically, he wants to show that there is an important connection between poetic madness and Platonic rhetoric; he says, in fact, that this divine or inspired madness is essential to Plato's true or ideal rhetoric. This is a position also shared by Richard Weaver.

Reginald Hackforth chooses to go beyond the question of the unity of subject in the dialogue by dealing with what he perceives to be Plato's purposes.

> I believe there are three purposes, all important but one more important than the others. They are: (1) to vindicate the pursuit of philosophy, in the meaning given to that word by Socrates and Plato, as the true culture of the soul . . . by contrast with the false claims of contemporary rhetoric to provide that culture. This I regard as the most important purpose. (2) To make proposals for a reformed rhetoric, which should subserve the ends of philosophy and adopt its method. (3) To announce a special method of philosophy—the "dialectic" method of Collection and Division—and to exemplify this both positively (in the two speeches of Socrates) and negatively (in the speech of Lysias). [8]

He says also that Plato's purposes are not independent of one another because he was, after all, not writing a treatise but a dramatic argument.

> Although the first or dominant purpose is most clearly discerned and most directly pursued in the middle part of the work (the second discourse of Socrates), it is present throughout, and is what gives the dialogue its unity. Once this is seen, or rather felt, by the reader, he will no longer think it necessary or helpful to ask whether the main subject is Love or Rhetoric.[9]

Hackforth pretty well settles the question about the unity of the subject in the *Phaedrus,* and his comments also offer a bridge into a much more difficult topic: exactly what is Plato predicating about rhetoric in this dialogue? That is a problem upon which universal agreement has not been reached and, because of the enormous gap in time between its writing and the present and the problems of ever getting a fully satisfactory translation of the Greek, never will be. However, there are areas of general agreement which are worth discussing at this juncture. First, the true rhetorician must have knowledge. Fakery, the appearance of knowing a great deal when one knew very little, was treated with utmost contempt in the *Gorgias,* especially at that point at which Gorgias tells Socrates that he can teach a man to speak so well that if his pupil (without knowledge of medicine) and a doctor should contend for the ear of a patient, his pupil, not the doctor would be believed. Socrates, of course, is scandalized by the very notion, and it is a theme to which he returns repeatedly in his comments on rhetoric. One must have real and substantial knowledge to speak well.[10]

That is precisely the issue which has drawn some scathing remarks about Plato and his views on rhetoric from Thomas Conley. His choice of the most significant passage in the *Phaedrus* is the one following the three speeches in which Socrates asks Phaedrus whether or not the speaker ought to know the truth of what he is speaking about. Phaedrus replies, of course, that such is not necessary; it is necessary only to know what the crowd to be persuaded deems just or unjust, good, noble, and so forth. Conley then says:

> The most striking feature of the passage is the opposition between knowledge and opinion. What we have here then is the fundamental issue in the continuing quarrel between Plato and the rhetoricians. It is in terms of this fundamental issue that everything Socrates says about rhetoric in the succeeding Stephanus pages—indeed, in the entire dialogue—must be understood. What we must conclude from this is that, contrary to what has sometimes been asserted about the *Phaedrus* and the positive contribution Plato makes in it to a theory of "philosophical" rhetoric, Plato has Socrates here set conditions for the rehabilitation of rhetoric which guarantee that it would redeem itself only by an act of self-immolation. Once we have understood that, I would contend, we come to see why any conception of rhetoric harmonious with Plato's ought to be scrupulously avoided.[11]

Conley believes that Plato never recanted the harsh views on rhetoric expressed in the *Gorgias, Politicus, Meno, Euthydemus, Apology,* and *Republic,* and that he takes an even more extreme position in the *Phaedrus.*

Convinced that Plato has offered no compromise to the rhetoricians or to Isocrates, who is, in the opinion of some, a target of some of Plato's remarks about rhetoric in the dialogue, Conley ends with as bitter a condemnation of the *Phaedrus* as one will find anywhere. Plato's view of rhetoric is a dangerous one, he says.

> Knowledge of the truth as a precondition of legitimate—or"real"—rhetoric is entirely unreasonable. In the first place, rhetoric arises from real questions and problems about matters of particular fact which need to be acted upon *now*. . . . It is also a little far-fetched to suggest that there is a way, in medicine, law, and politics alike to deal with present, past, and future questions under the rubric of truth.[12]

If Conley is right, that essentially Plato expects the rhetorician to be master of the truth in all human knowledge—and have time to debate it in ways and circumstances which are patently absurd—then he (Plato) has indeed set conditions which make it impossible for anyone to be a rhetorician or to practice his reformed rhetoric. But I do not believe that Conley is right. Strangely enough, Oscar Brownstein, who holds firmly to the position that Plato never reconciled himself to rhetoric, offers a way out of the dilemma. He argues that Plato did not expect the true rhetorician to have knowledge of everything, but he did need to acquire a method for sorting out truth from falsehood.[13] The method, of course, is dialectic.

It does not seem possible to me that there will ever be complete agreement about Plato's final position on this subject, but on several aspects of the problem there is substantial agreement. Plato had nothing but contempt for those who adopted the tricks of sophistic rhetoricians to make others believe that they had learning which, in reality, they did not possess. Plato did not expect one to master all human knowledge, but he did expect men to have knowledge of the subjects about which they spoke. The contemporary importance of this issue is crucial. The explosion of knowledge in our time has made it extremely difficult to be master of any field of knowledge. Physicists do not know all about all psychics; chemists do not know all about all chemistry; political scientists do not know all about all forms of government and particular governments around the world; students of English literature do not have mastery of the complete field; there is so much to know that one cannot encompass even his own field, much less knowledge in related or unrelated disciplines. Therefore, we who are on less joyfully intimate terms with ultimate truth than Plato was, must compromise to this extent. We can speak of that about which we do know something, and we can refrain from speaking on subjects about which we are uninformed. We have also to learn to live with those situations in which he or she who possesses knowledge is less eloquent than the fraud who pretends to know that which he or she does not. That problem is as persistent now as it ever was. In such situations, we have available Plato's best weapon: the method of dialectic, collection, and division, for checking out the accuracy and thoroughness of those who try to persuade us to adopt certain attitudes or take certain courses of action.

Another point on which there is substantial agreement is that Plato sees rhetoric's function to be the winning of souls to good causes. Much has been made of the analogy between love and rhetoric, the lover and the rhetorician. The analogy is a good one, and if one accepts Plato's method, one can see its purpose in winning souls to ultimate truth.

Actually, Plato's purpose, his method, and rhetoric's adaptability are difficult to separate. General scholarly opinion seems to be that Plato was never in doubt about what the function of rhetoric should be, but the method had to be developed. The *Phaedrus* is a mature work because in it we see the method of collection and division, the heart of dialectic, operating as Socrates takes a boy, infatuated with a silly speech by Lysias, and, by a process of defining and questioning, leads him to a mature perception of the nature of good speaking. Phaedrus, at the end of the dialogue, goes away, like Coleridge's wedding guest, perhaps not a sadder but certainly a wiser man.

Scholars also agree that Plato, the rhetorician—if I may be permitted to use that term, however briefly—saw the necessity of knowing the nature of each soul so that one could adapt discourse to each. That position also presents some problems, one of them ethical and the other practical. It might be argued that in adapting discourse to different souls, Plato is no better than the rhetoricians he castigates. But Plato is not advocating the kind of behavior which characterizes the amoral speaker whose sole purpose is to win his point. As Jaeger points out, for Plato, rhetoric must also be moral. The long road, training in dialectic, gives the rhetorician knowledge and a method for discovering truth so that he may, in the world or probabilities, help men to distinguish what is true from what is false and to make good choices.[14]

The practical point is this. Whereas Socrates can sit down by the Ilissus and deal with Phaedrus, or confront a group of three or four, as he does in some of the dialogues, what is the dilemma of the modern rhetorician when he confronts thousands of diverse souls or when he writes for a large, unseen, and not thoroughly known audience? Can the true rhetorician, this winner of souls to good causes, function successfully in such a context? The answer, strangely, seems to be that yes, he can. Certainly, one espousing evil doctrines can win over large masses. Adolph Hitler remains the classic example of the evil rhetorician who captivated millions. In "The *Phaedrus* and the Nature of Rhetoric," a chapter in *The Ethics of Rhetoric,* Richard Weaver argued that Winston Churchill represented the antithesis to Hitler, one who espoused a different set of values, certainly a better if not a perfect one, and whose force of personality rallied a nation and a world which was succumbing to Hitler's plans for "normalizing" Europe, part of which were, as we learned to our amazement and horror, the extermination of Europe's Jewish population.

The essential question, of course, is finally whether or not Plato is really promoting a vision of a reformed rhetoric or is hostile to it. Conley has said that Plato's reformation of rhetoric amounts to rhetoric's self-immolation. I understand him to be saying that Plato is either savagely ironic or else proposing that which is impossible, silly, and even dangerous in the modern world. Brownstein concludes his remarks on the *Phaedrus* by observing that Plato rejected rhetoric because it, like poetry, lies.

These positions, while well argued, are finally not convincing. The variety of interpretations of the *Phaedrus* suggests that we will never get a definitive answer to this question, but my own opinion is that the last word on this subject, despite subsequent attacks on it, still belongs to Edwin Black, who says that Plato did not despise rhetoric, but that he was opposed to the excesses of the Sophists.

> It is undeniable that Plato's preoccupation with the moral character of the rhetoric in this critique colored his positive formulations of rhetorical theory, so that he gives us not an account of rhetoric, but an account of a "true art" of rhetoric, not an account of the general social functions of rhetoric, but an account of its utility to the Ideal State. That there were actually theories and practices of rhetoric which did not fit his mold, no author has observed more brilliantly than he. But these other theories and practices were not "true" arts of rhetoric; they were "false" arts, knacks only. Plato did not deny their reality; what he denied was their moral efficacy.
>
> From our perspective in history, we are able to perceive the irony that Plato, the arch-enemy of the Sophists, was actually closer to them in his rhetorical theory than was his successor, Aristotle. Plato's repudiation of Sophistical rhetoric was neither so complete nor so thorough as his stu-

dent's, for though Plato rejected and refuted with finality the particular moral interpretation of rhetoric which the Sophists propounded, he did not reject the attempt to suffuse an investigation of rhetoric with a moral concern. It is on this point that his great disciple departed from him.[15]

College teachers of writing in twentieth century America may find these opinions about the nature and utility of Plato's rhetoric interesting to study, but they may also wonder what relevance such concepts have for their work with the students they teach, particularly when most of these students are freshmen taking the one course they most fear and despise. Actually, aspects of the *Phaedrus* have a great deal of relevance for their work, but writing teachers have historically shown very little awareness of this fact.

For example, on a purely technical level, they have failed to perceive the significance of the contrast Plato establishes between organic and mechanical unity in the organization of a piece of discourse. "*Soc.* Well, there is one point at least which I think you will admit, namely that any discourse ought to be constructed like a living creature, with its own body, as it were; it must not lack either head or feet; it must have a middle and extremities so composed as to suit each other and the whole work."[16]

In composition pedagogy this conception too frequently has been translated into the "beginning, middle, and end" or the "introduction, body, and conclusion" formulae, and the perception students have been given is of parts of a discourse hooked to each other like railroad cars with some appropriate transitions between them. Few are introduced to the idea of a concept generating and creating its own structure, something aesthetically far more pleasing and sound than the wooden, lock-step, mechanical forms they have been taught. Even the "introduction, background, argument, refutation, and conclusion" pattern which came out of classical rhetoric was often translated in this mechanical way. The only analogy which comes close to expressing the Platonic idea is that of the growing seed which contains the potentialities of the adult plant. The separate parts of an oak tree, developed from an acorn, are easily distinguished, but never separated from the concept of the entire living tree. Or one might speculate about the aesthetic limitations of an artificial Christmas tree. It is put together mechanically, the trunk first and then the branches which are hooked into it. How different such a tree is from a living tree whose separate branches cannot be conceived of as separate from the totality of the entire tree.

It is interesting that of all early writing theorists, only Fred Newton Scott noted the concept of organic unity in the *Phaedrus,* called it a fundamental principle of aesthetics, and incorporated it, via the analogy of the seed idea and its development, into his own teaching of composition.[17] In doing so, however, he was alone in his time. The only moderns to have exploited the concept are D. Gordon Rohman and Albert Wlecke, who got it from Meyer Abrams.[18]

It is not surprising that modern composition pedagogy should have missed so important a concept of Platonic theory. Any student of the past one hundred years of composition teaching in this country is aware of the fact that freshman English in particular was almost totally preoccupied with superficial mechanical correctness from approximately 1885 to 1930. So preoccupying was this tendency that grammar and punctuation drills, spelling, usage exercises, and sentence diagramming took up most of the composition class with precious little time left over for even managerial skills.

Twentieth century pedagogy had inherited a certain number of concepts—the paragraph and the forms of discourse, given their essential character by Alexander Bain; Unity, Coherence, and Emphasis, from Barrett Wendell of Harvard—but by the turn of the century these were being treated as abstractions divorced from any real social context and thus the student who was required to master them was two removes from Platonic truth and ethical rhetoric.[19] This preoccupation, particularly with various expository forms (and it still surfaces in modern textbooks) focused student attention on mastering the externals of a certain kind of paper—a narration, a description, an argument, or any of several kinds of exposition (definition, comparison and contrast, cause and effect, and so forth). Thus were created generations of students, and subsequently, teachers of writing, whose preoccupations with these forms caused them to forget the essential purposes of writing. These problems still linger with us. Whenever you read of a student assigned a comparison and contrast paper, you may be sure that regardless of what the student is comparing and contrasting, he or she will be more concerned with the formal structure of the paper than with whether or not anything meaningful is being said.

In recent decades we have begun to correct some of the deficiencies of this pedagogy. Since World War II or shortly thereafter the managerial aspect of composition began to be stressed. Students were told to be conscious of audience, of purpose, of tone, of logical organization, and so forth, all of which were supposed to direct their attention to the efficiency with which they put across the point they were trying to make. Too often, however, the ethical dimension was missing completely. Maxine

Hairston's remarks on audience and persona in the third edition of her *Contemporary Rhetoric* strike me as novel even today, because she is concerned with the ethics of rhetoric in a practical way. She tells students to be sensitive to their audiences and to use common sense when addressing them—which they can do while still maintaining their integrity. As she points out, there is no point in deliberately provoking an audience's anger just to vent one's spleen. She also encourages them to adopt many roles as speakers or writers, but she notes that they do not have to adopt any that are false to their values or beliefs. The "rhetorical chameleon" has no integrity and is not to be admired.

But a concern for truth of the kind Plato sought in the *Phaedrus* has, for the most part, been missing even from books incorporating new ideas on invention, arrangement, and style. John Mackin's *Classical Rhetoric for Modern Discourse* was an anomaly among textbooks for composition classes in that it not only presented a codified set of classical rhetorical precepts, but more importantly, because it stated baldly the central assumptions of Plato's rhetoric.

> The Socratic definition prevents a man from calling himself a true artist unless he knows values, how men incline toward or away from them, and how language can be used to help incline them toward higher values. Rhetoric is the art of inclining men and oneself toward higher values by discussion. The moral problem that accompanies rhetoric is solved by definition. If you aren't trying to move yourself and those with whom you're talking toward the good, then you aren't a true rhetorician. [p. 41]

To the teacher whose principal preoccupation is teaching students to write and develop topic sentences, to organize logically, and to edit manuscripts with sufficient skill that they will not appear to be illiterate, concern for organic forms of development and Platonic truth arrived at by dialectic must seem far removed from the classroom indeed. In this attitude teachers are nearly right but actually so perilously wrong. What they are teaching their students is that mechanical forms, such as the five-pagagraph essay, are better representations of the ways people think and more efficient vehicles of persuasion than organic forms. They are also teaching that mastery of such forms is more important than the substance of what they say. And who are the young people learning these important lessons? They are our future businessmen, politicians, educators, and technologists. And what have been the fruits in the past of such teaching? One has only to read Vance Packard's *The Hidden Persuaders,* written about thirty years ago, to see what happens to businessmen and advertisers whose sole concern is with managerial rhetoric. One is chilled by the notion that they have carefully developed a language which speaks persuasively to the consumers' unconscious minds. This is knowing your audience and addressing it appropriately with a vengeance.

We need only consider, for example, modern commercials for beer and their promotion of relief drinking, all done to sell a product at a time when alcoholism is becoming a national health problem. Or one may ask: What lessons about the ethics of rhetoric were learned by the Nixon staff which attempted to cover up the Watergate affair? Or about the Reagan administration with its continuous promises of better times just ahead as the national debt mounts, unemployment rises, businesses fail, and farmers give up homesteads which have been in their families for generations? What *have* we been teaching our students? What *are* we teaching them now? Has ethical relativism become so much a part of our thinking that we dismiss any attempt to discover the truth of a particular situation and persuade men to accept it? I do not think these are trivial questions. And I sympathize fully with the teacher who is trying to help students achieve a simple level of literacy. But I do not see why, in mastering even the fundamentals of written expression, students should not be told that what they write should be true or at least subject to the kind of examination which would test the truth or falsity of what they say.

Even if teachers are willing to ask students to subject their writing to Platonic scrutiny, however, there is one problem that we may not be able to solve. Michael Leff articulates a fundamental paradox in Plato's thinking about rhetoric:

> If, as Plato insists, truth is the only legitimate end of rhetoric, then how is rhetoric to serve this end when it must work through the medium of language? Truth exists as noumenal Form, comprehensible to the mind alone, but language is corporeal, part of the world of appearance, and there seems no direct mode of capturing internal visions of Reality in the alien medium of physical utterance. A genuine rhetoric, then, must accomplish the seemingly impossible goal of expressing the ineffable.[20]

Leff says that Plato tries to disarm or exploit this paradox in the *Phaedrus*. The essence of this position is that Plato argues for "analogical relationships between the genuine Forms of truth and the forms available in language."[21] Thus language of this kind can move the soul toward ultimate truth, despite its (language's) deficiencies. The tendency of language to do this is morally defensible because the soul, not language, is the true substance of rhetoric, a position Plato, but not Isocrates, takes. "The genuine rhetorican, in fact, destroys the very medium in which he works; his objective is to guide the auditor to a point where he can escape the prison of language and turn his soul toward a direct vision of the Reality that langauge can suggest but not encompass."[22]

The limits of language is the subject for a recent book by Winston Weathers.[23] The "communication pathos," he says, is the pathos of our era, our obsession with our failure to communicate with one another despite the vastness and sophistication of our communications technology. Our world is too vast and complicated for us to comprehend; in the face of recent scientific discoveries, the very concept of existence has become meaningless. Can we, in any meaningful way, find the words with which to express meaningful truths in this context? Is the medium itself, language, so flawed that it is not equal to the task?

These are fearsome questions in a world seeking some anchor by which to regain its psychological equilibrium. They bring us to a fundamental question that all teachers must ask about Plato and the *Phaedrus*. Are the questions about the truth and integrity of rhetoric inconsequential in the face of questions about the ability of language itself to say anything meaningful? Weathers would say no, these questions are not inconsequential.

> Flawed as the word is, inadequate as langauge is, we must still recognize that "language is without a doubt, the momentous and at the same time the most mysterious product of the human mind. Between the clearest animal call of love or warning or anger, and a man's least, trivial *word,* there lies a whole day of Creation—or in the modern phrase, a whole chapter of evolution." [quote from Suzanne Langer, *Philosophy in a New Key* (New York: New American Library, 1949), p. 83.]
>
> Whether the twenty-first century person achieves the faith and will to lift "the self" from the pathos of communication is for the future to reveal. But surely it can happen. Surely humanity will not let that "whole day of Creation" have been in vain and slip back forever into the maddening doubt that the human being may be no more than the dumb animal. Modern man and woman surely can, in the century ahead, through thoughtfulness and compassion, make their way through all the communication obstacles and articulate, not just sounds without meaning, not just the boring and the trivial, not just the correct and the established, not just the private and the personal, not just the politically and economically exploitive, but articulate the living—neither magical nor miraculous, but immensely human, that can reach somehow, though falteringly, flimsily and flawed, the other person, the other soul, the other consciousness hidden there behind the earthly garment of another human being.[24]

In that hope the ultimate relevance of Plato's *Phaedrus* and its insistent quest for truth may finally lie.

9
Issues in Rhetorical Invention
Janice M. Lauer

Two decades ago when I examined popular composition textbooks to determine the extent of their treatment of invention, my scrutiny revealed only vestiges of what had been a central component of classical rhetoric.[1] A few Aristotelian topics remained, but they had been converted into methods of development. The inventional art of beginning well, *status*, had disappeared. Judgment was taken for granted, left to the genius of the writer or to chance. The province of discourse in which invention functioned had been narrowed to exposition or polarized into personal and academic writing. These texts, later labeled "current-traditional," would be described as inventionless by theorists such as Young, Warnock, Berlin and Inkster.[2] But at the time of my study, the absence of invention went unnoticed by the majority of the profession.

Now, some twenty years later, interest in invention has escalated to the point where many textbooks offer substantial sections entitled "invention," "prewriting," or "planning." Any teacher who examines these texts, however, will discover a wide range of variation in the inventional strategies offered, a range that may confuse those interested in helping students with invention. These strategies not only differ, but they also spring from divergent conceptions of invention. Texts differ in their treatments of the genesis of writing, in their presentations of the purpose of exploratory activity, and in their determination of the types of discourse for which inventional arts are useful. I have been surprised and puzzled as I have watched these diverse conceptions of invention develop in such a short period after centuries of neglect. How much more puzzling must this array of treatments be to teachers who confront it for the first time.

One way of clarifying what may appear as a confusing mass of competing systems is to take an historical perspective on the situation. In the three sections that follow, therefore, I will discuss the background of several salient differences that now characterize the three issues mentioned above: the genesis of writing, exploratory acts and their relationship to judgment, and the province of invention. My intent is to examine these differences, analyzing their roots, not to evaluate them.[3]

In discussing these long-standing differences in invention, I do not wish to suggest that they fully explain the range of variation in modern conceptions. Elsewhere I have noted the contribution of multidisciplinary studies to contemporary theories of invention—contributions that have sharpened and shaped these theories.[4] But the major lines of divergence today were already drawn in rhetorical history: 1) current differences over the genesis of discourse reflect varying understandings of the doctrine of *status,* 2) modern disagreements about the nature and sources of judgment reenact age-old disputes over the relationship between rhetoric and dialectic, and 3) recent diverse presentations of types of discourse and topics echo a continuous controversy over the "matter" of rhetoric. In the following sections, I will illustrate these major differences in modern treatments of invention using a few representative current textbooks[5] and then examine the manifestations of these differences in rhetorical history. This examination should help teachers and scholars both better understand and more clearly distinguish among contemporary options for teaching invention.

The Genesis of Writing

One major issue involving invention concerns the genesis of discourse, the earliest phase in the art of rhetoric. This question of how best to stimulate meaningful discourse is approached by current texts in two central ways. A number of texts offer limited advice on how to begin well, frequently restating the directive commonly given by current-traditional texts: select a subject and narrow it. *Writing with a Purpose* advises writers to find real subjects within general subjects;[6] *Process and Thought in Composition* speaks of selecting and limiting as a way to begin.[7] *Classical Rhetoric for the Modern Student* directs students to select and narrow using the classical procedure, *status,* as a way of initiating persuasive discourse.[8]

A few texts, however, introduce a different kind of advice, informing students that meaningful writing begins with an awareness of dissonance or puzzlement. These texts also provide strategies to help students articulate questions to guide inquiry. *Rhetoric: Discovery and Change* urges writers to become sensitive to inconsistencies in their images of the world and to express this dissonance by posing questions that identify unknowns they need to discover to resolve their dissonance.[9] *Four Worlds of Writing* also instructs writers to determine aspects of subjects that seem inconsistent with their values or expectations and to formulate questions that capture that clash, and thus guide inquiry.[10] *Problem-Solving Strategies for Writing* tells students to determine conflicts or key issues at stake as a way of beginning.[11] *Contemporary Writing* directs students to look for subjects by searching for problems, conflicts, or unknowns.[12]

A salient difference marks these treatments of the genesis of discourse. The first cluster of texts emphasizes *selection* of a subject (or sometimes *acceptance* of a subject), often within contexts specified by the text or teacher, and *narrowing* to principal point or a subtopic. (Corbett's text goes beyond to provide a means of narrowing persuasive discourse by advising students to place subjects into classes of either fact, value, or definition.) The second group of texts highlights *question-posing* based on an awareness and articulation of *puzzlement* or *dissonance*. Neither of these conceptions lacks classical antecedents. In fact, they reflect subtle variations in the way that *status,* the earliest art governing the genesis of discourse, was perceived and used.

The doctrine of *status* has generally been attributed to Hermagoras,[13] although scholars have found traces of it in Aristotle and other earlier rhetoricians.[14] *Status* gained prominence in Roman rhetoric and remained a part of rhetorical invention through the Renaissance rhetorics of Cox and Wilson. From the outset, *status* was essentially considered a procedure for classifying issues as questions of fact, of definition, of quality, or sometimes of translation, a categorizing deemed necessary before the rhetor began to explore using the topics.

The notion of controversy was also integral to early conceptions of *status.* In *De Inventione,* Cicero said that every subject containing within itself a controversy to be resolved by speech and debate could be classified according to status.[15] In *Rhetorica ad Herennium,* Caplan translated the term *constitutio* as "issue," explaining that it signified the "conjoining of two conflicting statements, thus forming the center of the argument and determining the character of the case."[16] The Roman treatises stressed not only the idea of conflict but that of questioning. Quintilian maintained that "the essential *basis* is not the first conflict. . . . It is rather the kind of question that arises from the first conflict."[17]

The types of situations in which *status* was deemed applicable varied. *De Inventione* proposed it to initiate forensic, epideictic, and deliberative oratory (I, ix). In *De Oratore,* however, Antonius discussed it only in relation to judicial and deliberative oratory (II, xxv), having excluded panegyric from the art.[18] According to Caplan, *Rhetorica ad Herennium* used it only for judicial oratory because all of the examples came from criminal and civil cases.[19] Although Quintilian mentioned that *status* applied to all three types of discourse (III, vi, 2) as well as to definite and indefinite questions (III, v, 6), a distinction I will examine later, his discussion treats only forensic oratory. Later, in the Renaissance, Wilson also emphasized its use in forensic oratory, claiming that the issue arose from the contention of the plaintiff and the defendant, while in other discourse it arose from no contention—but rather from the discretion of the speaker.[20] In practice, therefore, *status* seems to have operated primarily in judicial situations even though in theory rhetoricians claimed a wider scope for it. As is perhaps evident, the modern view of the genesis of discourse as springing from dissonance and questions has some of the prominent earmarks of *status* discussed above but extends beyond the limited scope it generally had in practice.

Another feature of this contemporary view was prefigured in the changing relationship between *status* and the situational context. In Roman judicial oratory, the point at issue, the central conflict, was rooted in the rhetorical situation, arising from the dispute between contending parties—the defendant and the prosecutor—even though the judge or jury was the principal audience. In other types of discourse, the point of contention usually arose from the direct speaker-audience relationship, for example, senator and forum or praiser and listeners. But in the Renaissance, *status* followed the path of invention as a whole, with a consequence that Ong points out: Ramus' relegation of invention to dialectic renounced any possibility of invention within a speaker-audience framework.[21] Port Royale logicians then created a world in which thought was imagined as "ranging noiseless concepts or 'ideas' in a silent field of mental space. . . . Thought becomes private, or even an anti-social enterprise."[22] In the twentieth century when dissonance reemerges as the beginning of rhetorical inquiry, it sometimes is described as a clash between a writer and external audience, but frequently it is termed "cognitive dissonance," an internal clash between two images, beliefs, or understandings of the writer, or as the writer's inner selves engaged in investigatory dialectic.

A somewhat different sense of *status* that emerged during the Roman period has echoes in the twentieth century. Quintilian introduced the terms "basis," "point," and "standing": "The basis of the cause itself is its most important point on which the whole matter turns" (III, vi, 4). Later Isidore of Seville referred to *status* as "the point on which the case rests."[23] Alcuin continued this sense of "point," using the terms "locality of dispute" and "point on which the case rests," and he renamed the questions "conjectural position," "definitive position," "general position," and "procedural position."[24] In the Renaissance, Wilson adopted this sense of *status* when he identified it as the "chiefe ground" or "principall point."[25] The terms "point," "ground," and "basis" connote a firmer and more unilateral beginning than do the terms "issue," "controversy," "dissonance," and "questioning," which imply unresolved duality and tentativeness.

Consonant with this sense of *status*, Whately in the nineteenth century used the term "proposition," instructing communicators to lay down a proposition as an important first step and then to classify it as either fact or opinion.[26] Such a proposition, the opposite of a question, was a judgment, an answer ready to be communicated. The current-traditional textbooks of the early twentieth century called this proposition a "thesis," the ground, basis, or principal point from which writers' proceed and whose origins spring from selection and narrowing or mysteriously arise from creative genius.

Many contemporary texts with sections on invention still manifest this understanding of the genesis of discourse, while others, as discussed above, hold a quite different conception. Both views, however, have precursors in variant understandings of the doctrine of *status*.

Exploratory Acts and Their Relationship to Judgment

Another broad difference in modern treatments of invention rests in their conception of the purpose of exploration. Some offer students exploratory guides with a supportive function to aid their search for material to *develop a thesis already in hand*; others propose guides with a predominantly investigatory role to help them *prepare for discovery of theses or insights*. A representative text in the first category is *Classical Rhetoric for the Modern Student*, which explains that once students possess sharply defined theses, they face the task of developing them. The book explains that for some occasions students will profit from using a checklist of selected classical topics to gather material.[27] This type of text sees the exploratory act of invention as coming into play after the writer has a judgment; it leaves the discovery of the thesis to other arts like dialectic or to the writer's unaided talents.

The other view of exploration manifests itself in texts like *Rhetoric: Discovery and Change,* which describes exploration as the preparation of the investigator's mind for an intuition, an ordering principle, or an hypothesis.[28] *The Holt Guide* suggests the use of Burke's Pentad, especially the ratios, to facilitate discovery of a thesis.[29] *Writing* claims that just getting thoughts on paper will produce clarity of insight.[30] These texts view writing as a process of inquiry that enables writers to learn, to discover new understandings. Exploration's primary purpose in these texts is to prepare for judgment, to help writers find answers to questions they pose at the outset; its secondary function is to aid them in locating ideas, lines of argument, and material to support those judgments. These two conceptions of the purpose of exploration reflect long-standing disagreements over the roles of rhetoric and dialectic in the search for judgment, a dispute extending back to Greek rhetoric and complicated by differences among scholars as to the positions of certain classical rhetoricians on this issue.

Scholars still disagree, for example, over Plato's point of view on the sources of the rhetor's judgments. The following passage from the *Phaedrus* has been a focus of controversy.

> Until a man knows the truth of several particulars of which he is writing or speaking, and is able to define them as they are, and having defined them again to divide them until they can no longer be divided, and until in like manner he is able to discern the nature of the soul, and discover the different modes of discourse which are adapted to different natures, and to arrange and dispose them in such a way that the simple form of speech may be addressed to the simpler nature and the complex and composite to the more complex nature—until he has accomplished all this, he will be unable to handle arguments according to rules of art, so far as their nature allows them to be subject to art, either for the purpose of teaching or persuading.[31]

Commenting on this passage, Bryant asserts that for Plato "the prior assumption, of course, is that one is master of the subject and that one stands upon the truth on which one intends to persuade and that now one needs the art of persuasion."[32] Kennedy agrees with Bryant, stating that "to Plato the only valid method of inquiry into truth is dialectic . . . [that] is logically prior to rhetoric, which is the public demonstration of truth already privately determined."[33] In Cicero's *De Oratore,* Crassus criticized Plato for holding this view, castigating Socrates for separating the ability to think wisely and speak gracefully, for divorcing the tongue from the heart. Crassus called it "absurd, useless, and reprehensible—

that one class of persons should teach us to think and another to speak, rightly" (III, xvi). Enos echoes Crassus when he contends that Plato insisted on the knowledge of essences, substances, and causations as a necessary precondition for the art of rhetoric, a prerequisite with which Enos disagrees because he views rhetoric as the basic epistemic process.[34] Conley argues that Plato required from rhetoric an act of self-immolation by establishing knowledge of the truth as a precondition for legitimate rhetoric.[35] But Berger disagrees with these interpretations of Plato, maintaining that Plato saw persuasion and knowledge as erotic dialectics, involving the participation of more than one mind and hence did not reduce rhetoric to a report of prediscovered truth.[36]

Aristotle's position on this issue has also continued to be disputed. Grimaldi explains that Aristotle called rhetoric the "counterpart" of dialectic because he wished to emphasize rhetoric as a rational, intellectual activity.[37] Grimaldi considers "analogue" or "correlative" better translations because in his judgment Aristotle wished to stress the correlations between the two disciplines.[38] But Cope deems "counterpart" a poor choice to represent this relationship, preferring "offshoot" because it identifies rhetoric as a species of the general art of probable reasoning.[39] Cope's preference sees rhetoric as having a subordinate rather than coordinate relationship with dialectic. Kennedy asserts that Aristotle's "orator is usually assumed to have an hypothesis he wishes to prove."[40] Hill contends that Aristotle's idea of invention was to check through an inventory of possible premises and forms of arguments, then make a "conscious choice from a fixed stock of alternatives," and that Aristotle did not recognize creative imagination, insight issuing from the unconscious in a dream, or inspiration from above.[41] But Hughes disagrees, maintaining that Aristotelian rhetoric was both investigatory and exploratory, that the topics facilitated the making and communicating of judgments.[42] Enos takes a similar position, saying that Aristotelian invention should be reconsidered to include "heuristics not only as a composition framework for inventing techniques to facilitate meaning to others, but also heuristics as an epistemology for inventing knowledge within the rhetor."[43]

From the early days of rhetoric as a discipline, therefore, disagreement existed over whether exploration should expedite the discovery of judgment or whether it should only facilitate the location of material to support a judgment already in hand. In De Oratore, Crassus maintained that there was no merit in speaking unless what was said was thoroughly understood, that both knowledge and the art of oratory were necessary for the rhetor. But he separated their sources, explaining that if the philosopher Democritus spoke with eloquence, the matter on which he spoke belonged to the philosopher but the graceful array of words was the province of the orator (I, xi, 49). Quintilian, on the other hand, drew the investigative act under rhetoric, calling dialectic a concise form of oratory (II, xxv, 13). When Cicero and Quintilian explained the topics, they described them as aids for locating material and arguments to support and present judgments. But the political climate in which the Roman rhetoricians existed became increasingly hostile to invention of any kind. Near the end of Cicero's life and throughout Quintilian's teaching career, the oppression of the emperors militated against open-ended inquiry and even against the reasonable defense of probable judgments if they clashed with imperial conclusions. Thus Quintilian's vision of an investigative rhetoric was essentially an ideal for his time.

When Christianity pervaded the empire, the exploratory art of invention assumed another function. St. Augustine in *De doctrina christiana* converted it into a hermeneutical search of the Scriptures for material to develop sermons on Divine truths and ethical principles. Many preaching treatises of the Middle Ages continued this supportive role for exploration. Robert of Basevorn, for example, offered an exploratory guide through the Scriptures, made up of a mixture of general topics and parts of speech.[44] The medieval encyclopedic treatises of writers like Boethius and Cassiodorus listed a few Ciceronian topics in their presentations of rhetoric, but they referred the communicator to the sections on logic for purposes of inquiry.

The investigative role of rhetorical invention did not entirely disappear in the Middle Ages; instead, it took a different turn, exerting an influence on logic and theology. McKeon contends that, up to the thirteenth century, the study of logic was influenced more by instruction in the topics from the Greek rhetoricians through Cicero than by principles of demonstration from Aristotle's *Posterior Analytics*. He goes on to explain that Boethius' commentary on the *Topica* of Cicero and his own *De differentiis topicis* had the effect in the middle ages and the Renaissance of translating the problem of distinguishing principles into the problem of discovering arguments or things. McKeon also notes that the works of Boethius were used as inspiration for a scientific method of discovery.[45] Thus rhetorical invention contributed to the formulation of dialectical devices of discovery and proof and to scientific inquiry, acquiring new types of investigative roles that would become a part of composition much later.

In the Renaissance, when rhetoric regained more of its classical position in education, texts like Wilson's and Cox's devoted substantial sections to Ciceronian invention. Wilson included a short list of general and specific topics in his rhetoric, but he referred communicators to his treatise on dialectic for the major treatment.[46] But Wilson's rhetoric had little influence on practice because his text was probably limited to the Inns of Court. Of far more consequence was the work of Ramus and Talon who relegated invention of any type to dialectic and left rhetoric with style and delivery, thus silencing for centuries the debates about the purposes of exploration.[47] Ramus' tidy plan assumed an education which included both rhetoric and dialectic as companion studies, a situation that still obtained in the nineteenth century, when Whately maintained that rhetoric, an offshoot of logic, began when the process of investigation had concluded.[48] But, by the mid-twentieth century, logic was no longer a required part of many curricula, an academic situation that left current-traditional composition without a dialectical counterpart, its external invention. In fact, these texts not only lacked invention, they also inherited a negative attitude toward it from rhetoricians like Blair who considered the topics to be impediments, an "artificial system of oratory" producing "very showy academical declamations" which could only be trivial.[49]

Such was the context in which invention reemerged in the second half of the twentieth century. Many of the first exploratory guides emphasized a supportive purpose, to help writers find material, subject matter, and lines of argument to develop essays—a role exploration had more often been understood to play in rhetorical history. A few, however, stressed an investigative purpose, to prepare writers for judgment, a role often denied rhetorical invention in different periods, but one not without historical champions. Whatever differences over function these inventional efforts have had, however, they united in a common endeavor, in the face of negative attitudes, to reduce the intellectual vacuum in which composition found itself.

The Province of Invention

A final set of differences I want to examine here arises from divergent conceptions of the province or domain of invention: the type of discourse for which invention can be used, the type of material that invention can uncover, the type of judgment and topoi appropriate and useful for written invention. *Classical Rhetoric for the Modern Student* explains that although some measure of invention will operate in all four forms of discourse (exposition, argumentation, description, and narration), exploration will figure most prominently in argumentative and expository discourse, for which the general and specific topics will suggest lines of argument, while "external aids" will direct students to facts and figures to substantiate their arguments.[50] *The Holt Guide* proposes another set of topoi, an adaptation of Burke's Pentad, to help students gather resources, to discover thought for the four modes of discourse.[51] *Rhetoric: Discovery and Change* offers the tagmemic model to help retrieve material stored in the mind and to draw attention to information about any subject.[52] *Contemporary Writing* tells students that exploration is useful with any subject to "find what is in it that has worth."[53] *The Contemporary Writer* explains that exploratory techniques can be used to discover ideas, to find solutions for problems, and to develop content for writing.[54] *Four Worlds of Writing* shows students how invention operates for expressive, persuasive, and expository discourse.[55]

Harrington provides a catalog of these and other heuristic procedures that are available in texts to guide planning.[56] In a questionnaire I sent to colleges and universities concerning their teaching of invention, I discovered a wide variety of exploratory guides in use in the classroom. Thirty-three respondents reported using a selection of classical topics; twenty-four, a version of the tagmemic model; sixteen, Burke's Pentad; and eight, Rohman and Wlecke's prewriting techniques. Other procedures mentioned included brainstorming, freewriting, Pepper's four root metaphors, Kinneavy's aims and modes, Larson's questions, Gordon's synectics, the Toulmin model, Crosby and Estes' questions, D'Angelo's topics, semantic mapping, cubing, looping, clustering, and Flower and Hayes' problem solving strategies.[57] Not only do these planning strategies have different purposes, as I discussed above—some are intended to develop a thesis already at hand, while others are designed to prepare for the discovery of theses or insights—they also guide the writer to different kinds of matter: information from memory (ideas, facts, specific details, theories), data from research, imaginative creations (metaphors, comparisons, contrasts, analogies). And they prompt different kinds of conclusions with varying levels of probability: intuitions, insights, hypotheses, propositions, and theses.

The array of "matters" to which various exploratory guides lead and the range of types of discourse for which they operate thus reflect a third set of differences in rhetorical history. One disagreement centered on the extent of rhetoric's province. In *De Inventione,* Cicero identified earlier spokesmen on different sides of the debate, stating that Gorgias thought rhetoric should deal with all things while Aristotle confined it to three kinds of oratory—judicial, deliberative, and epideictic (I, v). But Grimaldi's recent commentary on Aristotle contends that for Aristotle rhetoric like dialectic had "no limited and unique subject matter upon which it must be exercised. . . . Instead, rhetoric as an art transcends all specific disciplines and may be brought into play in them."[58] He further points out that later theorists such as Alexander missed this point, hedging on rhetoric's universality.[59] Grimaldi goes on to explain that Aristotle's three types of rhetoric were not mutually exclusive because, despite their specifying definitions, they could and did contain most of the other types of discourse.[60] Hill disagrees, stating that "Aristotle's classification of kinds of speeches contains no reference to informative or expository speaking because Aristotle followed the doctrine of the *Gorgias* that rhetoric persuades without instructing, . . . a function only of demonstrative treatises in specialized fields."[61] Hill goes on to note, however, that Aristotle's distinction between rhetoric and the demonstrative sciences remains valid only if one believes in science as a closed deductive system. If, like the modern scientist, one believes that scientific truth is also probable and that the most one can know is statistical prediction of the frequency with which events occur, then the Aristotelian definition of an enthymeme based on probability loses its importance.[62] Polanyi makes this point another way by contending that scientific judgments, arrived at cooperatively by the inquirer and his accredited audience, would inevitably be informed by grounds less compelling than complete exactitude, objectivity, and explicitness, a view of the demonstrative sciences that makes them inherently rhetorical.[63]

Complementing these discussions about probability and certainty as rhetorical determiners, another issue focused the debate over the province of rhetoric—the distinction between thesis and hypothesis. Quintilian provided a succinct account of this discussion as it came down to his day: "It is also agreed that questions are either definite or indefinite. Indefinite questions are those which may be maintained or impugned without reference to persons, time, or place, and the like. The Greeks call them *theses,* Cicero *propositions,* others, *general questions relating to civil life,* others again, *questions suited for philosophical discussion,* Athenaenus calls them *part of a cause.* Cicero distinguishes two kinds, the one concerned with *knowledge,* the other with *action.* . . . Definite questions involve facts, persons, time and the like. The Greeks call them *hypotheses,* while we call them *causes*" (III, v, 6–7). He explained that Cicero at first maintained in *De Inventione* that theses belonged to dialectic and hypotheses to rhetoric, but in later works Cicero believed that the orator could speak more fully on general than on specific themes, because what was proved of the whole must be also proved of the part (III, v, 15). Crassus, in *De Oratore,* maintained that the orator could deal with any theme from whatsoever art or branch of knowledge and speak on it better and more gracefully than even the originator (I, xii). Cicero asserted at the opening of Book II that "to speak well, that is, to speak with learning, and skill, and elegance, has no definite province within the limits of which it is inclosed and restricted. Everything that can possibly fall under the discussion among mankind must be effectively treated by him who professes that he can practice this art, or he must relinquish all title to eloquence" (II, ii). Quintilian believed in a similarly broad province, stating that the material of rhetoric could be "everything that may be placed before it as a subject for speech" (II, xxi, 4). But in the Renaissance, Wilson returned to Cicero's earlier position, teaching that the definite question was the orator's proper concern while the indefinite belonged to the logician.[64]

During the Middle Ages, the subject matter of invention was narrowed in practice to the Scriptures and contents of letters. Encyclopedists like Boethius, Cassiodorus, and Isidore of Seville, however, sustained the theoretical discussion of its parameters, limiting the province of rhetoric to civil hypotheses within the three types of discourse—judicial, deliberative, and demonstrative. Alcuin resumed the discussion of probability by having Charlemagne question the genuineness of probable proof in a religiously homogeneous society. In answer, Alcuin justified probability on the grounds that it rested on beliefs accepted by public opinion.[65] Thus in a period which has often been characterized as restricting rhetoric to the preaching of divine certainties, Alcuin's treatise spoke out on behalf of a rhetorical place for probability.

McKeon traces the course of the thesis/hypothesis distinction through the Middle Ages. He contends that those who differentiated the subject matter of rhetoric into theses and hypotheses emphasized the common bases of rhetoric in human knowledge and analyzed the peculiarities of the kinds of questions asked, intellectualizing the art and changing its orientation to subject matter and its peculiarities into the problems of inquiry and understanding.[66] This intellectualizing of the art would become an ancestral strand for twentieth-century texts that emphasize the investigatory function of invention. McKeon goes on to point out that the topics became techniques for inventing arguments, means of dilating statements, and methods for discovering things.[67]

According to Grimaldi, Aristotle had long ago introduced two kinds of topics. The *particular* topics (persons, places, things) supplied *content*—subject matter for the ethical, emotional, and logical proofs in each of the three kinds of discourse—and hence had a limited extension. The *general* topics (the twenty-eight) provided the *forms* of reasoning, the ways of using generated content, and were consequently more proper to rhetoric because they transcended all specific disciplines. Grimaldi distinguishes these general topics from what he calls the common requisites (possible, impossible, past fact, and so forth) which, he maintains, have been mistaken for topics but which are, in fact, categories into which a subject must fall before further arts of rhetoric can legitimately be applied.[68] This distinction between topics that supply content and those that provide lines of argument has not clearly surfaced in modern treatments of invention, which often either mix the two or engage the writer exclusively in one kind of search or the other. Clearly, though, both kinds of modern sets of topoi have antecedants in classical rhetoric.

Many modern texts, building on classifications of discourse like Kinneavy's, Britton's, or Moffett's have extended the scope of invention to a range of types of discourse, a conception prefigured in past arguments to broaden the province of rhetoric. Extending the parameters for modern composition has, however, resulted in certain ambiguities and unstated assumptions about the issue of probability. Few texts are explicit about their epistemological underpinnings; few provide students with strategies for verifying probable judgments and hypotheses. Most texts hedge here, speaking of factuality or objectivity in expository discourse but skirting the question of whether these features necessitate propositions of certainty. Texts also dodge the problem of what constitutes an adequate level of probability for expressive writing. Rhetorical history can provide here an important caution, revealing as it does what resulted from efforts to polarize inquiry into certainty and probability: a schism that has been detrimental to both scientific inquiry and rhetorical invention.

In the above sections, I have identified some key differences in modern treatments of invention as they surface in textbooks to influence the teaching of composition: differences in conceptions of the genesis of discourse, in views of the purpose of exploration, and in positions on the parameters of invention. These dissimilarities do not constitute a uniquely contemporary phenomenon. They reflect instead long-standing and complex historical issues in rhetorical invention, an historical background which, if understood, can help clarify the differences inherent in current options for teaching invention.

10
Enthymemes, Examples, and Rhetorical Method

James C. Raymond

For Aristotle, the enthymeme was *"soma tes pisteos"* (I, 1, 1354a), literally, "the body of persuasion" in rhetoric. Along with what is commonly translated as the "example," the enthymeme was one of the two kinds of demonstration that distinguished rhetoric from other kinds of inquiry and argumentation: "all orators produce belief by employing as proofs either examples or enthymemes *and nothing else* (I, 2, 1356b, emphasis added).[1] In effect, any discussion of rhetoric that does not treat the enthymeme and the example as fundamental and pervasive techniques of demonstration is not a discussion of rhetoric as Aristotle understood the term.

And yet, from Aristotle's day to our own, the enthymeme has been misunderstood, ignored, or denigrated. In Book I of the *Rhetoric,* Aristotle complains that his contemporaries were confused about it. In particular, they failed to recognize that some enthymemes belonged to the province of *Rhetoric,* while others were appropriate "to other arts and faculties, some already existing and others not yet established" (I, 1, 1358a). The distinction Aristotle seems to have had in mind is analogous to the distinction between common topics and special topics, the former of which were ways of investigating common to all kinds of inquiry, while the latter were peculiar to particular arts or disciplines. With respect to enthymemes—those patterns of demonstration that presume upon the audience's acceptance of assumptions, often unstated—there are those assumptions that we can expect the general public to be aware of, and those that only specialists would know. When the distinction between the two is blurred, rhetoricians may be ineffective, relying on understandings beyond the grasp of their audience.

In 1932, when his translation of the *Rhetoric of Aristotle* first appeared, Lane Cooper complained of a different misunderstanding of the enthymeme. Cooper labels as mistaken "the time-honored notion that an enthymeme was a syllogism with one of the three members taken for granted and suppressed—in other words, that an enthymeme consisted of two statements."[2] Some enthymemes, Cooper concedes, do take that form. But enthymemes, according to Cooper, can also consist of one term, such as "All men are created equal," or of two terms that are not syllogistic, such as "Blessed are the pure in heart, for they shall see God" (Cooper, xxvi–xxvii). Cooper does not cite Aristotle to support this interpretation, though he may have had in mind the passage in which Aristotle says that "the maxim is part of the enthymeme" (II, 20, 1393a).

Scholarship since Cooper's translation has done little more than confirm that the enthymeme is an elusive term. In 1945, Solomon Simonson published "A Definitive Note on the Enthymeme,"[3] which, in view of subsequent articles, turns out to have been a less than accurate title. The main debate, as Richard L. Lanigan summarizes it, has been between those who hold that an enthymeme is a formally deficient syllogism (that is, a syllogism with a suppressed premise) and those who hold that it is a materially deficient syllogism (that is, a syllogism with a debatable premise).[4] There have been other interpretations, however, such as Miller and Bee's notion that enthymemes are not logical proofs, but affective proofs,[5] and Anderson and Belnap's notion that although enthymemes are sometimes valid, we can (and presumably should) avoid them entirely by being "*very* careful and always put[ting] down all the premises we need."[6]

Although no definitive definition of the enthymeme has yet emerged, there is at least some compatability among the more recent discussions of the term—enough compatability, indeed, to suggest that a consensus is on the point of developing. In "Aristotle's Enthymeme Revisited," published in 1959, Lloyd Bitzer nicely resolves the polarity between the two schools of thought by demonstrating that they are both wrong: enthymemes in Aristotle's *Rhetoric* are not limited in form to the syllogism with an implied premise, nor are they limited to syllogisms with debatable premises. Their essence, according to Bitzer, is that they are made from premises drawn from the audience's presuppositions: whether they are used in expressed or only implied syllogisms, whether they produce certitude or mere probability, is irrelevant.[7]

In *The New Rhetoric*, Perelman and Olbrechts-Tyteca have very little to say about the enthymeme as such; but their treatment of "The Starting

Point of Argument," in which they discuss facts, truths, presumptions, and other presuppositions that a rhetor must identify in an audience before constructing an argument, is clearly consistent with Aristotle's notion of the enthymeme as Bitzer understands it—namely, as reasoning from assumptions the audience shares.[8] William M. A. Grimaldi, S.J., in *Studies in the Philosophy of Aristotle's Rhetoric,* gives the enthymeme the same sort of latitude in form and degree of certainty that Bitzer would allow. Grimaldi, however, does not look for sources of enthymemes in the audience's assumptions; he is more concerned with showing that enthymemes may be drawn from ethical and emotional proofs as well as from rational proofs—and thus that they are used to gain "assent on the part of the whole person: intellect, will, emotions."[9] And finally, in his commentary on Book I of the *Rhetoric,* explaining the definition of enthymemes in I, 1, 1325a, Grimaldi quotes with approval a study by Karl R. Wallace arguing that the enthymeme is a form of reasoning that transcends the limits of dialectic. "In centuries past," Wallace observes, "when dialectic and rhetoric were still closely allied, speakers felt their reasoning ought to meet the tests of strict deductive and inductive inference. This feeling persists in modern text books on rhetoric. It now appears to be mistaken and outmoded." To which Grimaldi adds: this "is precisely what Aristotle himself is saying in the *Rhetoric.*"[10]

If we fuse what is compatible among these studies along with a close reading of the *Rhetoric* itself, the enthymeme emerges, not as a regrettable lapse into nonlogic, but as a serious attempt by Aristotle to deal with the sort of issues (those not resolvable by ratiocination or by empirical data) and the kind of audiences (those to whom it would be inappropriate to present intricate chains of reasoning) that rhetoricians face. The enthymeme is like a syllogism with some differences. The differences are these: whereas a syllogism is a formal pattern of thought with expressed premises, the major premise in an enthymeme may be implied rather than expressed because the audience is presumed to know it; and whereas the major premise in a syllogism must be an established truth, the major premise in an enthymeme may be unproved (or even unprovable) if the audience believes in it.

The enthymeme, then, is less rigid than the syllogism, both in form and in content, but not less systematic. The system is explained in detail in the *Rhetoric* (I, 2, 1357a–57b), where rhetorical proofs are divided into two major kinds, enthymemes and examples, with distinctions among several kinds of enthymemes according to the nature of the assumptions they use as major premises:

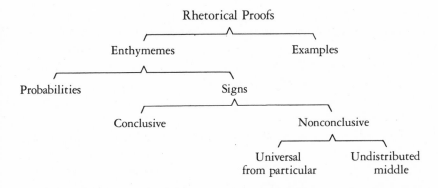

A skilled rhetorician would know that these various assumptions have varying degrees of certitude. A probability is an assumption about the way the world usually works or about the way people usually behave under certain circumstances, even though we know there may be exceptions to the general rule: the "probable is that which generally happens, not however unreservedly" (I, 2, 1357b). One example of a probability is that weak people are not likely to physically attack stronger people; thus, as Aristotle says, we might defend someone charged with assault on a stronger person on the grounds that this sort of behavior is just not likely to have occurred (II, 24, 1402a). As a modern instance, we assume that interest rates will rise if money becomes scarce, even though we know that increased rates could conceivably be prevented by other variables in the money market.

"Conclusive" signs (sometimes translated as "necessary" or "infallible" signs) are assumptions of a different sort. These are signs that have the sort of certitude "from which a logical syllogism can be constructed" (I, 2, 1357b)—which is to say a syllogism that can lead to an irrefutable conclusion. To use an Aristotelean example, we can argue with certainty that a person who has fever is ill, since fever is an infallible sign of illness. A modern instance would be the clicking of a Geiger counter as a sure sign of radioactivity. Enthymemes built on conclusive signs cannot be gainsaid, according to Aristotle (II, 25, 1403a), unless one can establish that the sign did not occur.

Of the two kinds of nonconclusive signs used as assumptions in rhetoric, one is based upon an implied syllogism with an undistributed middle term (for example, that woman must be pregnant, since she is pale), and the other is a leap to a universal conclusion on the basis of a single instance (for example, all wise men must be just, since Socrates was wise and also just). These are Aristotle's examples. He points out, of course, that the logic behind these signs is faulty; he does not imply, however, that it is always unpersuasive. Indeed, if a woman were to develop morning sickness under certain circumstances she might find this persuasive evidence of pregnancy, even though it is obviously not conclusive. And if we were told that all squirrels can bark, we might be persuaded of this fact by witnessing a single squirrel making the appropriate noise.

The enthymeme is Aristotle's solution to two ancient problems: how to reason logically with an audience that is indisposed to meticulous analysis, and how to reason logically when indisputable major premises are likely to be unavailable. These are two separate problems, obviously, but the enthymeme is the solution to them both. Because enthymemes presume upon what an audience already knows or believes, they can express in a condensed or elliptical manner chains of logical connections that would be complex indeed if the assumptions themselves had to be demonstrated. And because enthymemes build upon what the audience already knows or believes, they avoid the problem of proving their own first premises, as even science must avoid it, by presuming them.

Essentially, enthymemes may be defined as assumptions used in public discourse—assumptions both in the sense that they may be left unstated and in the sense that they may be accepted by both speaker and audience without being proven. Persuasion occurs when speakers can demonstrate that their conclusions follow from an assumption the audience is willing to accept. Whether the assumption is debatable (for example, the assumption that free enterprise is better than government controls) or not (for example, that radiation can cause genetic damage) makes no difference, provided the audience at hand is willing to grant it. Whether the assumption is implicit or explicit makes no difference: an enthymeme (for example, since the land was taken by force, it must be returned to the natives) would not become a syllogism if its major premise (taking land by force is illegal or unethical) were stated, because a syllogism, as Aristotle uses the term, proceeds from proven premises, not from assumptions.

If "enthymeme" is such an exotic term that it has managed to defy definition, "example" seems so ordinary as to require none.[11] But "example" is not a simple word. The range of its meanings in English includes a single instance representative of a group, a model for imitation and emulation, a pattern intended to discourage imitation, a precedent, a punishment intended to be a deterrent for potential culprits, or an illustration (as in textbooks) to make generalizations concrete (see *Webster's Third New International Dictionary*). Because Aristotle compares the example to induction (I, 2, 1356b), the definition often assumed in discussions of the *Rhetoric* is "a single instance representative of a group," which suggests that Aristotle considered faulty induction to be a legitimate form of demonstration in rhetoric. This pattern of thought, however, has already been described as one of the nonconclusive enthymemes (all wise men are just since Socrates was both wise and just).

The problem is essentially one of translation. The word Aristotle used is *paradeigma,* the source of "paradigm" in modern English—which is to say the sort of example used as a matrix in language learning (for example, *rosa, rosae, rosae, rosam, rosa*) so that students can infer the various forms of new words in their vocabulary by analogy to the forms of a familiar instance. Aristotle's discussion of examples as a form of proof suggests similarities with paradigms of this sort. He says that the example "is neither the relation of part to whole nor of whole to part," which Cooper (p. 14) glosses to mean the relationships of particulars to universals and universals to particulars. Rather, the example deals with the relation "of part to part, of like to like," as when two things "come under the same genus [such as two nouns of the same declension, *rosa* and *puella*], but one of them is better known than the other" (I, 2, 1357b). The point, of course, is that what we know about the better known instance—for example, that its genitive case is formed by adding a final *e*—we can infer about the less well known.

I do not mean to suggest that Aristotle had linguistic paradigms in mind, but simply that linguistic paradigms are closer to what the word *paradeigma* apparently meant in Aristotle's *Rhetoric*—namely, not just an example in the sense of an instance, but an example in the sense of a pattern. Aristotle illustrates the use of the example this way: "To prove that Dionysius is aiming at a tyranny, because he asks for a bodyguard, one might say that Pisistratus before him and Theagenes of Megara did the same, and when they obtained what they asked for made themselves tyrants. All the other tyrants known may serve as an example of Dionysius, whose reason, however, for asking for a bodyguard we do not yet know" (I, 2, 1357b).

It is significant that Aristotle does not illustrate the example with a generalization formed on the basis of a single instance, which would have lent credence to the interpretation that the isolated instance or insufficient sample is what he would have considered a major form of rhetorical proof. Rather, he cites several series of events, each of which establishes a pattern from which the audience might infer the consequence of Dionysius' request for a bodyguard.

Aristotle uses the same sort of illustrations in his more extended discussion in Book II, where he divides arguments by example into two categories according to their source: "one which consists in relating things that have happened before, and another in inventing them onself" (II, 20, 1393a). To illustrate the use of a historical parallel, he says that Darius' invasion of Greece after his conquest of Egypt and Xerxes' invasion of Greece after his conquest of Egypt may be used to support an argument that the Greeks should not allow Egypt to be conquered by the king of Persia. Illustrating the invented example (*parabole*), he says that we might argue against choosing public officials by lot instead of by ability by suggesting the consequences that would ensue if athletes were chosen for a contest in the same way, or helmsmen to guide ships at sea. Fables, he says, are also invented parallels that can be used as rhetorical proofs: Stesichorus and Aesop used them in this way, one to show why a military leader should not be given a bodyguard, the other to show why an ostensibly guilty demagogue should not be put to death (II, 20, 1393a–93b).

One aspect of the example that seems to have escaped attention is that every illustration Aristotle gives is diachronic in structure: each one is a story, an event leading to another event, like cause to consequence, not with the inexorable determinism of scientific causality, but in a pattern of probable causality, suggesting that if analogous events were to take place again, analogous consequences would be likely to ensue. Even the brief instances illustrating the invented examples are implicitly diachronic: the audience is to imagine *what would happen* if athletes or helmsmen were chosen by lot rather than by ability, and therefore what would happen if magistrates were selected by lot. Aristotle says nothing to suggest that examples must be diachronic in form; but his illustrations do confirm the notion that examples are patterns, not just instances— patterns that may well be diachronic.

The possibility that examples may be diachronic in structure explains Aristotle's remark at III, 17, 1418a, which is otherwise unexplained: "Examples [*paradeigmata*] are best suited to deliberative oratory and enthymemes to forensic." Deliberative oratory—sometimes called "legislative"—is concerned with the future. Patterns of events—examples in the form of true or at least credible stories—are our best guide to the consequences of decisions facing us in the present "because as a rule the future resembles the past" (II, 20, 1394b). Only if the example has a diachronic structure does its peculiar applicability to deliberative discourse seem apparent.

Aristotle's statement that "as a rule the future resembles the past" is, of course, an enthymeme—the kind he calls a "probability," that is, an assumption we make about the way the world generally operates. When he says that examples are appropriate to deliberative discourse because the future generally resembles the past, he is saying, in effect, that the probative force of examples is based upon an assumption, which is in fact an enthymeme. It would seem, then, that examples are, at some level, enthymemes—though on the surface they are distinctive in that enthymemes are syllogistic or at least implicitly syllogistic in form, whereas examples are patterns inferred from one set of circumstances and applied to others.

If we accept this relationship between enthymemes and examples, we can make some sense of that problematic passage (II, 25, 1402b) where Aristotle seems to contradict what he says in Book I by listing the example as one of the four "sources" from which enthymemes are derived, rather than as a separate line of reasoning altogether. In Book I Aristotle was focusing on the formal differences between enthymemes and examples (one being syllogistic, the other analogical), while in Book II he was treating the example as a peculiar kind of enthymeme, namely, a probability—the assumption that history repeats itself or, more generally, that we can extrapolate from analogies. This reading would seem to be supported later in the text where Aristotle suggests a connection between probabilities and examples by saying that they "may be refuted in the same manner" (II, 25, 1403a).

The word "example," then, does not convey precisely what Aristotle meant by *paradeigma*: it lacks the senses of pattern and analogy that are implicit in every illustration of the term in the *Rhetoric*. The choice of "example" in English translations was no doubt influenced by the use of *exemplum* in the Latin translations. But *exemplum* has senses in Latin that are not conveyed by "example" in English. An *exemplum* can be a pattern as well as an instance. It can also be a story told to influence the attitudes or behavior of its hearers. It is this meaning of the word that was used in the middle ages with reference to stories told by preachers. Erasmus was responding to this sense of the word when, referring to it as a translation of *paradeigma*, he calls it a "class that embraces the *fabula* . . . the parable or *collatio*, the imago and anology, and other similar ones."[12]

One possible solution would be to translate *paradeigma* as "precedent," a word that has respectable connotations in English (particularly in forensic rhetoric) and that describes several of the arguments Aristotle uses to illustrate *paradeigma*. Unfortunately, "precedent" suggests a factual or historical reference, whereas Aristotle explicitly includes the use of fictional and invented references.

The word "analogy" has precisely the opposite problem. Technically, "analogy" covers all of the illustrations used by Aristotle, if we consider precedent to be a particular kind of analogy. But analogy seems to be more fictive in its connotations, and therefore a more facile sort of proof than historical precedent.

Another solution is to recognize that no English word conveys the sense of the Greek accurately, and therefore to transliterate the word rather than translate it, just as we have done for enthymeme and syllogism. Precisely because paradigm is not a household word, students encountering it for the first time would have to learn its technical definition, preferably by closely reading its context in the *Rhetoric*. They would learn that analogy and pattern are key elements in this Aristotelean concept, which they might not suspect if they saw the word translated as "example." And they would learn not to misconstrue this major line of rhetorical proof as an endorsement of faulty induction.

Once we clarify the definitions of enthymeme and example it becomes possible to see them, as Aristotle did, as the methods of proof that set rhetoric apart from other lines of inquiry. Rhetoric is distinguished from dialectic on two grounds: it has a different audience (an audience indisposed to detailed reasoning) and a different subject matter (a subject matter in which we hardly ever have the benefit of universally accepted premises to reason from). Enthymemes and paradigms are appropriate to the audience of rhetoric because these lines of reasoning do not tax the attention. They are appropriate to the subject matter of rhetoric because, when we are faced with the necessity of drawing merely probable conclusions from merely probable premises, there is no way to proceed other than to reason from premises that the audience accepts or to speculate about the unknown on the basis of parallels the audience regards as credible and apposite.

Reasoning of this sort ought not to be confused with the nihilist or skeptical position that there is no truth, or at least no knowable truth, but only opinions, and that rhetoric teaches its students how to manipulate opinions rather than to discover truth. The true answers to questions raised in rhetorical discourse are, in fact, by definition not knowable in the scientific sense; rhetoric has no business investigating facts that are discoverable by science. Among the questions that are the legitimate province of rhetoric, however, not all answers are equally valid. We know this intuitively: we debate art, politics, and ethics as fervently as we do because the outcome of our debates will have consequences, often serious, that will affect the quality of our lives—in some instances, the very possibility of our being alive. Aristotle assumed that there was a truth to be discovered through rhetoric, even though it could not be discovered with the certitude of science. Its discovery, he believed, would depend upon the skill of the rhetorician: "the true and the just are naturally superior to their opposites, so that if decisions are improperly made, they must owe their defeat to their own advocates" (I, 1, 1325a).

Aristotle's *Rhetoric* is a philosophical assertion that some important questions cannot be answered by experimentation, or by logic, or by quantification because the data needed to make these methods work is unavailable. And yet, the questions must be resolved. This assertion is as important today as it was in Aristotle's time. Today there are physical scientists, behavioral scientists, politicians, and administrators who believe, as Freud did, that the scientific method is applicable to "the whole field of human activity."[13] Modern rhetoricians have already pointed out the limitations of science: Perelman and Olbrechts-Tyteca describe their own version of Greek rhetoric and dialectic as a *"break with a concept of reason and reasoning due to Descartes* which has set its mark on Western philosophy for the last three centuries."[14] Similarly, rhetoric as a discipline that deals with subjects beyond logical positivism—or "scientism" as he calls it—is the theme of Wayne Booth's *Modern Dogma and the Rhetoric of Assent* (though Booth, curiously, finds little comfort in Aristotle's *Rhetoric*).[15] And Edward P. J. Corbett finds echoes of Aristotle in both Newman and Locke, where they too discuss the value of probabilistic reasoning when the subject matter provides only probabilities as premises.[16]

If there is such general agreement among modern rhetoricians, why is the tradition of classical rhetoric reflected so pallidly, if at all, in modern classroom instruction? Aside from exceptional books like Edward P. J. Corbett's *Classical Rhetoric for the Modern Student,*[17] rhetoric and composition texts have done little to clarify the enthymeme and the example or to establish the importance of the role they played in Aristotelean rhetoric. Texts that treat reasoning at all are likely to limit themselves to the rules of induction and deduction, which Aristotle considered characteristic of dialectic, not rhetoric. Those that treat the enthymeme and the example do so briefly, almost as an appendix to logical reasoning, not as the major lines of demonstration.

One reason for this neglect, of course, has been the absence of a consensus about the meaning of these terms; as long as confusion and disagreement prevailed in the scholarly journals there could be little chance of clarity in textbooks. Another reason is the defensiveness of humanists in a culture dominated by scientific inquiry. We have not been as bold as we might have been in establishing modes of nonscientific inquiry because what is not scientific is often dismissed as not rigorous. Now that there is more of a consensus and less defensiveness among scholars, there is still another problem—in fact, one of the problems that rhetoric itself is supposed to be able to solve: how do you explain a complicated subject like rhetorical reasoning to an audience of students who are impatient with detailed analysis?

My own suggestion would be to abandon the terms "enthymeme" and "example" in favor of "assumption" and "paradigm." We could explain to our students that when they deal with issues that cannot be resolved by science or pure logic, they persuade and are themselves persuaded through these two means. When we teach critical reading, instead of asking our students to evaluate an argument on the basis of its logic alone (which would suggest, contrary to the Aristotelean tradition, that a geometrical style of reasoning is capable of resolving the issue), we should teach them to identify the assumptions, both explicit and implicit, that the presumed reader of the text is expected to share, and to locate the paradigms, if any, that form the basis of the argument. Thus, the ultimate question to ask in analyzing a piece of persuasive writing is not "Are its arguments valid?" but rather "What would a reader have to believe in order to find the arguments persuasive?"

If Aristotle is right, we should have no trouble illustrating the use of assumptions and paradigms in the daily editorial page, or in the "persuasive" essays in our rhetorical readers, or in any discussion of politics, ethics, or art. Judicial opinions and the *Congressional Record* are particularly rich sources of material. There we will, of course, find other kinds of evidence as well—factual information, even local instances of dialectical reasoning; but if the overall issue is a rhetorical one, the data and the analysis will persuade or fail to persuade not because of their own probative force, but because they will be presented in the context of assumptions and paradigms that readers will either accept or reject.

Persuasive writing is the inverse of critical reading. Once students understand that readers are persuaded when they see a writer's conclusions as the logical consequence of their own assumptions (reasoning from enthymemes) or as extrapolations from analogous situations (reasoning from paradigms), they can learn to analyze their audiences with some sophistication, estimating what sorts of assumptions a specific audience is likely to have, what sort of paradigm it is likely to consider persuasive.

Whether we ought to teach formal logic along with rhetorical reasoning is a moot point. Aristotle observes that "he who is most capable of examining matter and forms of a syllogism will be in the highest degree a master of rhetorical argument, if to this he adds a knowledge of the subjects with which enthymemes deal and the differences between them and logical syllogisms" (I, 1, 1255a). Edward Corbett, however, has pointed out that even after we teach formal logic, our students are "still capable of writing a discursive argument that flagrantly violates one or more of the rules of deductive reasoning."[18] Perhaps the intricacies of formal logic and the distinctions among various kinds of enthymemes ought to be reserved for our more capable students—those in advanced courses or honors sections. All students, however, ought to be able to learn at least the limits of science and the limits of logic, by learning to distinguish between those questions that ought to be answered by scientific inquiry (for example, whether radiation will affect the structure of amino acids) and those that must be resolved through rhetorical reasoning (for example, questions that depend upon taste, or upon value judgments, or upon speculation about future events that can be affected by human choices or human error).

In short, they can all learn that the subject matter of a discussion determines the nature of the proof possible; no methodology, neither science, nor logic, nor even rhetoric, is universally applicable. This is precisely the point Aristotle makes in the *Nichomachean Ethics*: "It is the mark of an educated mind to expect that amount of exactness in each kind which the nature of the particular subject admits. It is equally unreasonable to accept merely probable conclusions from a mathematician and to demand strict demonstration from an orator."[19] In an age of uncritical reverence for the possibilities of science and technology, our ability to make this basic distinction understood—or more specifically, our ability to establish rhetoric as systematic reasoning about basic questions beyond the limits of science—may well determine whether we become the masters or the victims of our other kinds of knowledge.

11

An Adequate Epistemology for Composition: Classical and Modern Perspectives

John T. Gage

Epistemologies of rhetoric, in their extremes very different, provide assumptions for how any system of rhetoric is used, whether to describe the effects of language or to prescribe principles for learning to write. In the case of pedagogy, it is important to ask how formal means of teaching composition imply epistemological assumptions, that is, what those means seem to tell students about the nature of knowledge and its relation to the rhetorical tasks they are taught to master. Recognizing that classical rhetorics addressed this concern, although at times indirectly, sheds some light on the form this problem takes in contemporary methods of teaching writing. The following essay will take up the general question of rhetoric's epistemological implications in part 1, illustrate how concepts developed and used in classical rhetoric and contemporary composition are based on epistemological assumptions in parts 2 and 3, and suggest finally in part 4 how composition teaching might benefit from more attention to the kinds of assumptions about knowledge it passes on to students of writing.

1. Rhetoric and Knowledge

The relationship between rhetoric and knowledge has always been problematic, no less so today than in the classical period. Systematic thinking about rhetoric emerged in the fifth century B.C. out of the paradoxes discovered by sophist philosophers in their contemplation of the relationship between language and belief. Their discoveries often took extreme forms of relativism, as in Gorgias' famous first principles: Nothing is; even if it is, it cannot be known; even if it can be known, it cannot be made meaningful to another person. While such principles seem contradictory, they at least had the salient effect of making subsequent rhetoricians aware, in the words of G. B. Kerferd, that

> the relationship between speech and what is the case is far from simple. While it is likely that fifth-century thinkers all were prepared to accept that there is and must always be a relation between the two, there was a growing understanding that what is very often involved is not simply a presentation in words of what is the case, but rather a representation, involving a considerable degree of reorganisation in the process.[1]

These words describe a legacy of philosophical thought with which even the earliest theorists of rhetoric had to contend: that in the use of language to describe reality, reality undergoes interpretation. Knowledge needs language as much as language needs knowledge.

With the necessity of responding to sophistic relativism in the background, systems of rhetoric seem to have grown in two general directions, which can be expressed, at the risk of oversimplification, as two ways of regarding the relationship between knowledge and rhetoric. One is that rhetoric consists of techniques for successfully communicating ideas which are either unknowable or are discovered and tested by means which are prior to or beyond rhetoric itself. This is the view assumed by the writers of the handbooks of persuasion, which consist of technical means of presenting any case. Such a perspective on the function of rhetoric owes an obvious debt to the speculations of the Sophists, in the sense that it treats persuasion skeptically, as having no essential bearing on what is finally true. Given this view of language use as independent of the means by which knowledge is generated and validated, if it can be, rhetoric was viewed as a technical application of linguistic forms without necessary regard for whatever may or may not make the ideas expressed knowable.

The other way of regarding this relationship is to view rhetoric itself as a means of discovering and validating knowledge. The purposeful use of language, in other words, can be seen as what makes knowing possible. This perspective also owes something to the sophistic tradition, namely the idea that language necessarily affects the truths that it is about. From this perspective, rhetoric aims at knowledge, or makes it available. Rather than producing persuasion without reference to truth, rhetoric aims at producing mutual understandings and therefore becomes the basis for inquiry into sharable truths. The end of rhetoric from this point of view would not be to argue any case, but to assemble the means by which mutually believable conclusions can be distinguished from those that do not earn assent. In this view, rhetoric has knowledge as its goal, rather than operates on knowledge as raw material.

Each of these views can be found in classical and modern rhetoric in many forms, whether acknowledged or not. The history of rhetoric and composition includes many changes that have been brought about by the influence of more variables than this philosophical one, of course. Yet, in light of this distinction, it is possible to observe how the concepts stressed in a given approach to rhetoric imply a stance toward how knowledge is discovered and how rhetorical techniques affect it. Toward this end, I will look at the fate of three central concepts in classical rhetoric and in some contemporary approaches to composition, and suggest in each case what the role of these concepts implies about the epistemological status of rhetoric. The concepts I have chosen are *dialectic, enthymeme,* and *stasis.*

2. Dialectic, Enthymeme, and Stasis in Classical Rhetoric

The writers of handbooks of persuasion were masters of the art of *eristic,* which consisted in assessing an adversary and using techniques of language for "seeking victory in argument."[2] Underlying this purpose was the prerequisite that the orator must know how to adjust his *case* to an audience, but there was no necessity that he must also adjust *what* he wished to argue. The eristic view of rhetoric, in other words, aimed at winning any given case, and knowledge of the truth was no more than a means to that end—to be used if warranted or hidden if necessary. In the handbooks, formulaic devices were made available to the rhetor, to be used in defense of typical propositions before typical audiences. Objections to the technical devices which the handbooks prescribed were not directed at their efficacy so much as at the possibility that they could be applied equally on behalf of true or false propositions, and in their application carried no necessity to make such a distinction. In such cases, to *seem* to know was as good as knowing. Plato wished to distinguish such "false" arts from a "true" art of rhetoric on the basis of whether the rhetor knew the truth of the case he argued. This distinction made the true art of rhetoric, for Plato, identical to dialectic.[3]

Aristotle was likewise motivated to describe an art of rhetoric which made knowledge its object. Although his *Rhetoric* makes use of many of the categories of the handbooks, rather than condemns them as Plato had done, it was not written as an eristic art for arguing any thesis. As William M. A. Grimaldi has written, the *Rhetoric* functions "as a method of communication . . . between people as they seek to determine truth or fallacy in real situations."[4] Toward this end, Aristotle also based rhetoric on dialectic, but unlike Plato he did not view these arts as identical. This was because Aristotle recognized the legitimacy of inquiry into real knowledge of a probable, contingent kind.[5] He saw rhetoric as the "counterpart," or likeness, of dialectic in this realm of probable knowledge, where differences of opinion do not necessarily constitute differences between right and wrong. Assent, as agreement reached when all the "persuasives" (*pisteis*) have been considered, could constitute a legitimate kind of knowledge. "The function of rhetoric," Aristotle asserted, "is to deal with things about which we deliberate, but for which we have no systematic rules." He did not mean that we need systematic rules, but that for issues of knowledge about probable and contingent reality which people do deliberate, human nature being far from purely rational, we must learn to reach agreement without such rules, since for this kind of knowledge the strict rules of dialectic will not work. "But we only deliberate about things which seem to admit of issuing in two ways," he went on to say, and "as for those things which cannot in the past, present or future be otherwise, no one deliberates about them."[6] We deliberate rhetorically, that is, about such things as no other means besides rhetorical agreement can establish as true, and we are motivated to do so by the necessity of discovering knowledge in such agreement. As Grimaldi comments about the relationship of the *Rhetoric* to Aristotle's philosophy:

> The constitutive elements of this environment admit neither absolute knowledge nor absolute assertion since their very contingency asserts that change is possible and this very fact of change may very well condition what can be said or known about them. Such factual evidence and such contingent situations admit a probable knowledge about themselves, and they demand deliberation and considered discussion consequent upon which we are able to assent to their probable truth.[7]

The rhetoric which emerges from the recognition of "probable truth" as real knowledge is like dialectic insofar as the aim is an exchange of ideas among parties whose mutual goal is the discovery of such knowledge. The rhetor, as one party to this exchange, considers the contribution of what the audience knows as making the discovery of this sort of knowledge possible. That contribution is discovered in "invention." In the words of Richard McKeon, "The topical analysis of statements and arguments or the use of language in the process of dialectical question and answer is directed to clarify the implications of opinions more or less commonly held and to discover new propositions and principles."[8] Aristotle himself distinguished this art of discovery from that of sophistically "making the worse case appear the better," by saying that it applied to "real" as opposed to "apparent probabilities."[9]

Rhetoric as a form of dialectic implies an attitude toward knowledge that is important to my argument in this paper. Dialectic implies that knowledge can be created in the activity of discourse, because it is potentially changed by that activity, either as discourse gets closer to it or as it emerges in the interaction of conflicting ideas. From this point of view, knowledge can be considered as something that people *do* together, rather than as something which any one person, outside of discourse, *has*. Knowledge can be said to be valid, that is, to the extent that it can be shared,[10] and is likely to need modification when minds bring new understandings to anything thus known. Rhetoric can be viewed as dialectical, then, when knowledge is seen as an *activity,* carried out in relation to the intentions and reasons of others and necessarily relative to the capacities and limits of human discourse, rather than a *commodity* which is contained in one mind and transferred to another. The Platonic ideal of rhetoric as pure dialectic required that it be *performed,* by "congenial souls" whose mutual aim is to know. The "erotics" of rhetoric that emerge in the *Phaedrus* depend on the condition that the rhetor's object not be to force his knowledge onto a passive other, since by that means he cannot come to know, but that mutual "lovers of knowledge" can through dialectic arrive at knowledge neither alone could possess.[11]

Although Aristotle's *Rhetoric* differs from the *Phaedrus* in tone and temperament, and certainly in the ultimate status of the kind of knowledge with which it deals, the close association of rhetoric and dialectic in Aristotle is in line with Plato's critique of the deficiencies of the handbooks of persuasion. In the world of probable knowledge with which *Rhetoric* deals, real understanding results no less from the influence of the audience on the knowledge of the rhetor.

The centrality of the concept of the enthymeme in the *Rhetoric* derives from this view of knowledge. Aristotle sought to analyze the process by which agreement comes about; he did not, therefore, toss aside as mere tricks the techniques advocated by the handbooks, as Plato had done. Rather, he attempted to view these techniques in relation to the causes that account for agreement. To do so, according to his methods of analyzing anything, he needed a term for the final cause of persuasion that would function teleologically in relation to those familiar techniques, viewed as formal causes. He adapted the enthymeme as an architectonic principle, one which embodied the dialectic of rhetorical discourse and allowed the techniques of the handbooks to be ordered according to this end. The enthymeme brings together the dialectical considerations necessitated by the rhetor's search for mutually agreeable grounds for probable knowledge. It is Aristotle's term for the basic "unit of all persuasive discourse," carried on, like dialectic, by "those who discuss things together in the spirit of inquiry."[12]

The difference between an enthymeme and a syllogism, besides the fact that an enthymeme addresses probable truth, is that the premises which go into making it are derived from, or contributed by, an audience which does not already share the conclusion. The enthymeme cannot be constructed in the absence of a dialectical relation with an audience, since it is only through what the audience contributes that the enthymeme exists as such. It is, in one sense, a necessary compromise between what one who wishes to persuade may want to say and what an audience will allow to be said. But it is, in another sense, an adjustment of what one who wishes to "discover the means" of persuasion knows to what is known by others. Thus, Aristotle viewed the enthymeme as the essential "body" of rhetorical proof, as a sort of metonymy for the whole rhetorical activity of discovering a basis for mutual judgment. In addition to being a device for constructing parts of a logical proof, the enthymeme represented for Aristotle the basic form of reasoning which determines the other choices the rhetor must make.[13] It defines a way to think about such choices as establishing the previously unknown (or unshared) on the basis of the known (or shared).[14]

The enthymeme functions in Aristotle's treatise on two levels: locally, as a formal structure for argument (as in the distinction between enthymeme and example as deductive and inductive strategies), and teleologically, as the theoretical basis for inquiry into probable knowledge. Subsequent rhetorics, lacking the dialectical perspective that characterized Aristotle's sense of the whole art, adopted the enthymeme in the first sense from Aristotle but neglected it in the second sense. Hence, the enthymeme was often made a formula for expression rather than a dynamic of thought, and as such was subordinated to other formulaic categories.[15] For instance, Quintilian (who chided Aristotle for reducing all of rhetoric to invention) prescribed the enthymeme as a recommended option in the context of syllogistic argument, which is consistent with his view of dialectic as a formal subcategory of rhetoric: "concise speech."[16]

A similar fate can be described for the concept of stasis in classical invention. Stasis in its original sense also embodied the dialectical intentions I have described as underlying one view of rhetoric. Stasis in its most frequent applications, however, was reduced to a technical formula for coming up with commonplaces, things to be said in given contexts. Aristotle had no elaborate systems for discussing stasis, such as those developed by Hermagoras and others and catalogued by Quintilian, but antecedents for such systematic treatments are found in Aristotle.[17] His introduction to the use of topoi asserts the principle underlying stasis theory. "First of all," Aristotle wrote, "it must be understood that, in regard to the subject of our speech or reasoning . . . it is necessary to be also acquainted with the elements of the question." Otherwise, "you will have nothing from which to draw a conclusion."[18] What is essential in this comment is that until the speaker or reasoner is clear about what question is being addressed, the search for reasons has nothing to progress towards. Conclusions can be discovered, knowledge can be created in rhetorical discourse, only in the context of an issue which requires deliberation to answer. Thus, undergoing topical invention in light of a question is a very different matter from finding topoi to confirm an already determined conclusion. The topoi which Aristotle discusses, then, must be seen in the context of the prior need to discover an answer, a context which makes it necessary to adjust the topoi to fit the question rather than to accept them at face value as applicable or otherwise true. Thus, as Grimaldi points out, Aristotle developed the topoi not as potential things to be said in a speech, but as a "method devised to supply both the content for the critical examination of the subject and the general inferential statements which would present legitimate forms of deductive reasoning" in relation to an audience. It was not until after Aristotle that the topoi became "mere mechanics of invention, i.e., ways and means of developing and enlarging on a theme."[19]

The implication of stasis theory that will be most important to my analysis later is that it locates the intentional cause of the investigation of potential conclusions in the desire to resolve real questions of disagreement. Classical invention, in this context, was not carried out for the purpose of "finding something to say," but for the purpose of investigating reasons that might be applied to the solution of a given question. It was undertaken only in the face of a disagreement, a question which was not itself the rhetor's invention but the outcome of his presence in a conflict of belief. In this way stasis theory acknowledged the dialectical source of knowledge which rhetoric might lead to: it defined what the rhetor needed to discover, not by his own choice but by virtue of a conflict between what he already knew and the knowledge of others. After cataloging the many complicated forms that stasis theory had taken, Quintilian dismissed them as "mere laborious ostentation," and came around, as Aristotle had done, to the position that "a clear view of the main issue of a dispute" is sufficient.[20] The sort of knowledge that Quintilian understands rhetoric to develop, at this advanced stage in the orator's education, is *iudicium,* a power similar to Aristotle's *dynamis,* when it refers to the ability to discern warrantable conclusions.

The concepts of dialectic, enthymeme, and stasis played central roles in classical rhetoric when they were necessary to the very definition of rhetoric as a mode of knowledge. From the viewpoint I have contrasted with this one, of rhetoric as techniques adaptable to any conclusion which do not at the same time affect that conclusion, these concepts no longer need to occupy any central position. As it happened, each of them was reduced to technical formulae functioning alongside other devices as options.

3. Dialectic, Enthymeme, and Stasis in Contemporary Composition

The simplest way to describe the fate of these same concepts in contemporary methods of teaching composition would be merely to say that they are neglected. Although other classical terms and categories have managed to find their way into contemporary pedagogy nearly unchanged, these have largely disappeared, or else they have been relegated, as in some classical rhetorics, to the status of techniques, rather than providing architectonic principles for organizing considerations of technique. I will try to describe the form that these concepts have taken, but to do so I must first account for the general hypertrophy of rhetoric-as-technique that seems to accompany the atrophy of rhetoric-as-inquiry.[21]

Historical reasons for shifts in emphasis in rhetoric from philosophical to technical and back are beyond the scope of my analysis here. The seeds of the difference I am describing were in classical rhetoric from the beginning, in its different reactions to epistemological issues. Yet there are always historical reasons associated with such changes, although I cannot enter here into even the recent history of educational philosophy and the variety of rhetorics it has engendered. It may be illustrative to recall that Roman rhetorical education, with its greater emphasis on technicalities of style, at the relative expense of invention in Aristotle's sense or dialectic in Plato's, existed in the context of Roman government. In practical oratorical contexts in which the outcome of public debate did not determine social policy, unlike the situation during the "golden age" of Greek democracy, and the status of the orator was measured by conventional signs of nationalist virtue, rhetorical training naturally became directed more toward formal criteria than rational inquiry—as Quintilian in his old age lamented. In such contexts, as Aldo Scaglione has argued, training in rhetoric is "concerned only, or chiefly, with brilliance of exposition, empty formalism, and unconcern for the intrinsic validity of the issue at hand."[22]

Whether our society's expectations affect our rhetoric in the same way is not easily answered, but another consideration—which Scaglione's descriptions of changes in the rhetorical tradition illustrate rather than argue—is apparent. As inevitable changes occur in the way in which rhetoric is used, analysis of the varieties of forms and structures of discourse multiply, becoming more subtle and complex and supporting the temptation to suppose that because a structure can be analyzed and defined it should therefore be prescribed as a model for the incipient composer. In the history of rhetoric, every sort of structure that could be distinguished, labeled, and quibbled over—from the types of orations and their proper number of parts to the nearly endless and contradictory catalogs of figures of speech—has been formalized and added to the potential list of forms the student writer must know. We are the inheritors of all such descriptions. Considerations about form had once been subordinated to the organic necessities of inquiry, or, in the case of Aristotle, described as causes of persuasion rather than prescribed as devices; but forms understood in these ways can easily become "empty formalisms" when the function of inquiry is eliminated and teaching writing becomes defined in terms of practice in the range of possible forms, even without the manipulative motive of the sophistical handbooks. This impulse is ever present in the rhetorical tradition, and is part of the legacy of classical rhetoric as it impinges on teaching writing today. The issue is as old as, and older than, Crassus' claim in Cicero's De Oratore that eloquence is not born of artifice but artifice of eloquence.[23]

"Eloquence" is assumed to be born of "artifice" when the structures of discourse are abstracted from analysis and prescribed as imitable forms.

Many current methods of composition take this relationship for granted, whether they work up from structural models of sentences (as in "sentence combining") or down from structural models of whole kinds of compositions (as in "modes of discourse"). Frank D'Angelo has aptly shown how all such structural considerations must be related to each other, and he argues that knowledge of these relationships can provide the basis of competence in their use. He appeals to the distinction in contemporary epistemology between knowing *that* and knowing *how* to justify the teaching of "paradigms" which exist in discourse because they reflect mental patterns.[24]

Teaching methods which prescribe formal models, whether they are ancient or new models, assume that the ability to select and adapt such patterns to new writing contexts is learned on the basis of prior knowledge *of* the patterns. This assumption is questioned, however, by the very epistemologists who have given us the knowing *that* / knowing *how* distinction. Gilbert Ryle, for instance, concludes from this distinction that "efficient practice precedes the theory of it." Since a paradigm or a maxim drawn from it is "inevitably a proposition of some generality," Ryle argues, "it cannot embody specifications to fit every detail of the particular state of affairs." Thus, in actual use, when the purpose is not to imitate patterns, but to use them, "knowing how to apply maxims cannot be reduced to, or derived from, the acceptance of those or any other maxims."[25] The ability to know *how* to choose and adapt a pattern or principle to a given case, then, belongs to the realm of knowledge Michael Polanyi has called "tacit," and is learned as a function of confronting tasks with the intention of accomplishing some practical end which such tacit choices will serve as means.[26]

Thus, the question is also what *kind* of competence is assumed by formalist methods to constitute writing ability. It often seems that the skill sought is the skill of making formal patterns, under pressure of the intention of making them, rather than the skill of using them to achieve some other intention. This appears to be the case because such formal patterns, as abstracted from discourse by analysis, seem to remain stable independent of the audience and of the quality of ideas that can go into them. The skill of making them, at any rate, does not depend on the skill of knowing what form warrantable ideas must have. The test of whether such methods can lead to the possibility of this knowledge is whether they are able to be practiced equally well with or without a real audience to whom the ideas are directed.

Rhetoric is dialectical, or like dialectic, insofar as it assumes an active audience which motivates the composer's inquiry into possible knowledge, rather than a passive audience to which prior knowledge is meant to be passed on. Modern composition methods, as well as ancient ones, do not neglect to advise writers that they must "know their audience," but the difference I am suggesting is not necessarily a difference between knowing one's audience and not knowing it. It is a difference between how and at what stage that knowledge is used to inform the composing act. In contemporary composition, knowing one's audience is usually viewed as a rhetorical consideration in the sense that one must adapt one's way of making a case to the "needs, interests, personality, values"[27] of a particular audience, but not in the sense that a particular audience contributes reasons which determine *what* that case must be or motivates the inquiry. In the familiar "rhetorical square," for instance, diagrammed at the beginning of many textbooks, audience is one element of the abstract schema which illustrates the communication process. It is a separate but equal element, to be considered along with "persona," "argument," and "purpose," or some variety of these. This is not incorrect, of course, but this schema is often used to construe the causal relations between these parts in a particular way. Which comes first? On this the textbooks seem to agree: purpose. Thus, *after* a writer decides on a purpose, the next question becomes "Who is my audience?" and then "What persona and argument do I make?" The implication that I am suggesting about this otherwise neutral way of schematizing rhetorical elements is simply that a writer's audience is not seen as contributing to, or determining, a writer's purpose; the decision to discuss or to argue one thing or another is not made because the audience is present already, asking the same question. This leads to enforcing the idea that writing exists for the purpose of "winning," or of bringing a passive audience around to accepting a purpose which is wholly the writer's and none of its own. In one textbook, following a discussion of the need for balance among these elements, an "audience-centered argument" is described as one which "seems more a sales talk than an expression of opinion."[28] By implication, then, the expression of opinions should not be "audience-centered." In the dialectical definition of rhetoric, from the viewpoint that rhetoric arrives at knowledge rather than operates on it, there can be no purpose without an audience which contributes centrally to making it one.

The theoretical separation of audience and purpose as independent variables can lead to forms of pseudo-dialectic which further isolate the writing process from the investigation of potential truths. A recent article on how to teach the concept of audience begins like this:

> Students can . . . fail to produce a successful composition because they have little or no knowledge of their readers. . . . The problem for student writers comes from the fact that their audience is unseen, a phantom. It is *always*, to use Walter J. Ong's term, "a fiction," a creation of the writer's mind. Students, like all writers, must fictionalize their audience.[29]

To make this possible, the authors of this article advocate "a heuristic model for audience analysis," a checklist of features which the writer's fictional audience is fictionally imagined to have. The kinds of criteria defined on this checklist range from the reader's imagined values about money and cars to that reader's imagined attitudes about the writer. Nowhere on this checklist are any places to define the reader's specific ideas on the specific issue about which the author wishes to write, or that reader's reasons for holding them. The reader being defined is an all purpose reader, not one who is imagined to read out of any mutual concern for the problem at hand but who is invented to play the role of vessel into which the writer's already decided ideas may be poured, presumably in order for student writers to practice the kinds of adjustments that real writers supposedly make. More basically, these authors construe Ong's term "fiction" to imply that writers go through something like this "heuristic" in order to overcome the inevitability of addressing an "unknown" audience. Ong, needless to say, did not make up such an audience for himself when he wrote his persuasive article, even though he knew that you and I may differ in peculiar likes or dislikes which he could not know. His audience was quite real in one sense: he wrote his article to address critical questions that real people were really engaged in debating, and he wouldn't have written it at all, or searched for his own answer, if they had not been. His audience is a "fiction," according to his own logic, simply because he had to address a composite of readers who must be represented in the writing as willing to engage in the exchange of ideas according to certain assumptions and by means of certain arguments. Ong's "fictional" audience is a collective of minds.[30] The fictional audience defined by the advocates of this heuristic is an individual with peculiar traits which seem to act as obstacles to the writer's expression rather than as resources for the writer's thinking. Even if such a fictional audience were to be defined to terms of fictional reasons, the result would be a pseudo-dialectical relationship predetermined to guarantee that the writer's reasons prevail.[31] In terms of my own earlier distinctions, such a method for teaching students to "know their audience" can only separate them from any sense of writing as the discovery of mutually validated reasons in the context of the need to discover collective truths.

Elements of dialectic which are distorted by such approaches to the audience have reentered composition methods under psychological rubrics which, although quite valid, are usually set against classical rhetoric rather than viewed as consistent with it. The most popular of these is the "Rogerian approach" to argument, after Carl Rogers' essay, "Communication: Its Blocking and Facilitation." It is precisely the motive of arriving at mutual understandings which Rogers advocates, and the impulse to adopt his approach follows, for good cause, from the eristic formalism of traditional rhetoric as interpreted in textbooks. The theory itself, and some presentations of it, are consistent with the classical tradition in its dialectical dimension. The potential effect, however, of presenting it as an alternative to classical persuasion may be to reinforce the eristic use of reasoning. Here it is the context in which Rogers' ideas are placed that is relevant. Before presenting the option of Rogerian argument to students, most textbooks follow the example of Young, Becker, and Pike by detailing the classical categories of persuasion first. These authors then introduce Rogers to the student by discussing "the limitations of classical argument" in situations involving "strong values and beliefs," and they say that in such cases "logical demonstrations may seem irrelevant and conventional argumentative strategies suspect."[32] If "traditional argument" is the category under which logic is discussed, and if Rogerian argument is said to be an alternative to it, the strong implication is that logical forms of reasoning aim at manipulation only and at understanding not at all. It is the interpretation of classical rhetoric in its eristic rather than its dialectical dimension that gives rise to the need for such alternatives to it, rather than any failure of classical rhetoric as a whole.

Moreover, rather than providing a corrective to the abuse of rhetoric, the concept of a rhetoric of understanding can engender an alternative set of formulaic strategies which the student can apply to an eristic intention. One contemporary textbook, for instance, labels Rogerian rhetoric an alternative "format," and prescribes its ideal paradigmatic structure. While cautioning against the possibility that this method can also be used "manipulatively," the author says that its "objective is truth, not victory."[33] Despite this caveat, the reduction of this intention to empty formulae might serve to make more emphatic the implication that Rogerian strategies manipulate better because they appear not to. The dilemma illustrates the always difficult relationship between wisdom and eloquence. In this case, one is tempted to reply as Quintilian did, by saying that while "philosophy can be easily simulated, eloquence cannot."[34]

Perhaps because of more serious attention to Aristotle, the enthymeme is beginning to be rediscovered in composition textbooks. As in the case of the interpretation of Aristotle by Roman rhetoricians, however, it has been employed in one of the senses Aristotle meant, as the rhetorical equivalent of deduction and therefore a "local" structure, but not in the more basic sense as an architectonic principle underlying the whole rhetorical situation. The reasons for this, apart from using historical interpretations of Aristotle, are no doubt tied to the ways in which audience is conceived in the textbooks, since the role of the enthymeme as the "body" of all rhetorical proof is to represent the contribution of the audience to what the rhetor must argue, to what will constitute warrantable reasons and to what may be left unsaid. The role of the enthymeme in concentrating the activity of discovering sharable knowledge is neglected when it is taught merely as any syllogism with one part missing,[35] that is, as a form to be filled in with the writer's *own* ideas.

A recent textbook tells students that syllogisms and enthymemes "will allow you to trace the pattern of your own thinking and test both its truth and validity; thus you can correct weaknesses before you actually put them in writing." This advice begins to do justice to the enthymeme in its more basic role, yet it is still one's *own* thinking, as this textbook subsequently demonstrates, that is being tested for truth and validity, by its ability to be cast into logical forms rather than by virtue of its relationship to the thinking of others.

In this same textbook, the syllogism is recommended as a way to think through a whole argument and thereby become the basis of structure. In such fashion, structure is not prescribed as a paradigmatic formula, but derives organically from the logic of ideas.[36] Were this advice to include the suggestion that the enthymeme could also be so used, if the probable basis of the reasoning were derived from the ideas of the audience and the *conclusion* adjusted accordingly, a method of teaching structure would have been created that would be very close to Aristotelian rhetoric in its dialectic context. Aristotle's definition of the necessary parts of a composition, unlike the prescribed divisions of the handbooks which he calls "absurd," is in fact an enthymeme.[37] Only one available textbook that I know of has followed Aristotle in defining structure enthymematically, so that the students must consider the dialectic source of their ideas at every step in composing. It is no coincidence that in this textbook we read:

> What we have instead of the single answer to each question that many of us would like, is an extended dialogue . . . in the course of which many answers are proposed. . . . It is probable that large numbers of human beings will continue to dislike this situation. The problem is that we must act, and our acts must be based upon answers, answers, conscious or not, to the questions considered in the great human dialogue. . . . It would be very comfortable to be able to act on the basis of immutable truth, but it is not available to us. [38]

In my conclusion I will discuss why I think it is rare to find such acknowledgments of this epistemological premise in composition textbooks. For now it is sufficient to observe that the probable and contingent nature of the sorts of ideas that we argue, that we are forced to rethink and rediscover in the presence of other minds, is neglected in composition methods, with or without mention of the enthymeme. Yet the enthymeme was made central by Aristotle specifically to acknowledge that the ideas we can claim with confidence are not our own property, but such as we are able to forge through the rhetorical acts we perform.

I find little use in contemporary textbooks of stasis theory, although I do find discussions of the "question at issue" and, of course, "invention." Indeed, there is no need to give an old name to these old ideas. It is useful, nonetheless, to compare how these concepts are used to the function of stasis as I have already described it in classical invention. [39] "Invention" in most textbooks, rather than a matter of exploring questions of dispute, has come to be equated with finding a topic and things to say about it. By defining invention as a search for something to write *about* and as procedures for exploring possible aspects of that subject once discovered, many of the latest heuristic systems are applied to subjects independently of the need to consider the beliefs of one's audience on any question involving that subject. Insofar as this is the case, such systems neglect the concept of stasis that gives rise to classical invention as part of a rhetoric of inquiry into justified knowledge. Knowledge is assumed to be a function of the subject itself, rather than a product of possible interpretations. [40]

One implication of such invention systems, in which it is a subject rather than a question which is investigated, is that student writers must first be taught how to find an intention. The implication of stasis theory, as I have already discussed, is that intentions result from situations of conflict of knowledge, which are the mutual invention of the writer and the audience.[41] When invention follows from the intentions in such situations, no means of inventing an intention seem necessary. When, however, the rhetorical situation of composing shifts from the need to resolve conflict by finding potentially shareable truths to the need to practice using predefined forms, then the necessity of "finding a topic" arises. In a sense, then, the need for systems which teach students how to discover a subject has developed out of the formalist, prescriptive tradition of rhetorical analysis. The prior existence of a conflict of knowledge gives rise to the need to search for forms, in stasis theory. In contemporary invention theories, often, the prior existence of a form gives rise to the need to search for a subject to fill it. A good or bad idea or reason will succeed indifferently if the intention, as the "final cause" of the writing assignment, is to fill in a form.

4. Composition as Knowing

I have not set out in this essay to argue that writing *is* an activity directed toward the discovery of warrantable knowledge, but only that it can be viewed as such. Obviously, writing can be viewed as many things. The classical tradition of rhetoric offers us two views, at least, of writing along an epistemological axis, each suggesting ways of teaching composition consistent with its assumptions about knowledge. I have tried to illustrate that theories of teaching in which forms are prescribed as models imply a certain status for knowledge in the rhetorical act, and that as a static, predetermined and, to some extent, unexamined *thing* to be transferred unchanged from one mind to another by means of the form. In doing so, I hope I have not avoided the question of how composition might be taught as a skill and yet depend on a probable, contingent, cooperative sense of knowledge, even though I have only implied the answer by illustrating the neglect or interpretation in contemporary methods of the classical concepts of dialectic, enthymeme, and stasis.

In these illustrations, we have seen that the technical formulae of classical rhetoric are shared by both epistemologies. They can be viewed as descriptions of how people *do* manage to create knowledge in discourse as easily as they can be prescribed for the purpose of winning a debate or of learning to write. They can also be prescribed for the purpose of learning how to transform knowledge through discourse, but in that case the formulae must be seen for what they are in a dialectical light, not as devices to be mastered, but as activities that people will perform, without having to be taught how, when they in fact desire their discourse to lead to more certain knowledge with others. The art of composition, seen from this angle, is an art of knowing, to be measured as such, and not a competence in the many kinds of formal patterns that analysis might be able to identify.

Measuring success in the achievement of formal competency is relatively easy compared with the prospect of measuring success in the art of knowing, an art which none of us has mastered to our satisfaction. This fact will always recommend formalistic teaching methods so long as we must measure what students have learned on the basis of competencies. There is no easy way to avoid this problem. I am not suggesting in this paper that one view of writing, any more than one view of knowing, should prevail. But I do wish to end by suggesting that viewing our methods in light of the epistemological assumptions they depend upon might change our students' attitudes toward the difficult, but immanent, problem of knowing.

No doubt our students do not possess all of the competencies they will require when they discover that they need to engage in rhetoric for the purpose of finding out what they can know through inquiry into the reasons of others. But in teaching these skills, when we must, in the absence of that purpose, we are implicitly recommending other purposes which we may not intend. Students, like all of us, already have confidence in their own ideas, for reasons which they often have not examined. They are confident because they have been taught that truth is confirmed only privately by irrational means, or because they have been taught that truth is confirmed only by experts who possess the "facts." In either case, such confidence in the validation of knowledge *outside* of discourse leads to another kind of confidence, the attitude that reasons *in* discourse are mere rationalizations, for irrational drives or for unconfirmable opinions, and serve only to make it possible to win. Perhaps our students accept these confidences so readily because they are present in the conduct of much of the discourse they have encountered.[42] But because of them, students may think that the reason they are being taught to write is so that they can put ideas, acquired and proven by other means, into the correct form. They rarely view learning to write, at any rate, as learning how to know when to make up and change their own minds, a skill for which, as Aristotle said, we have no systematic rules. The methods by which students have been and will be taught to compose can confirm their confidence in knowledge unchallenged by the uncertainties of agreement. But those methods, adjusted to the purpose, can also address the problem of this confidence, if it is a problem, by bringing the uncertainties and necessities of inquiry about grounds for agreement into the open. The epistemology of agreement may not address some of the clerical writing tasks these students will be required to perform in the business of their lives, but it may nevertheless prove more adequate to the conflicts and cooperations that are necessary to improve the condition of the human parliament, as Kenneth Burke called it, that we are all born into.

12
Symmetrical Form and the Rhetoric of the Sentence
Richard L. Graves

Historically, the style of writing attributed to Gorgias has been regarded as artificial and contrived. Indeed, the adjective derived from his name carries with it a strongly pejorative connotation; whatever is "Gorgianic" is said to be there only for effect or to make an impression, a thin veneer with no substance at all. In the *Art of Persuasion in Greece,* George Kennedy reminds us that one of the problems with the Gorgianic figures— "antithesis, isocolon, parison [parallelism of form], homoeoteleuton, and others of that sort"—is that they are too conspicuous. "Most ancient and modern critics," he writes, "have regarded them with disfavor; if the highest art is to conceal art, as has often been claimed, the devices hardly qualify, for they are extraordinarily conspicuous."[1] One of those ancient critics which Professor Kennedy cites as looking upon the figures with disfavor is Quintilian, whose full commentary on the subject deserves our attention: "The old orators were at great pains to achieve elegance in the use of words similar or opposite in sound. Gorgias carried the practice to an extravagant pitch, while Isocrates, at any rate in his early days, was much addicted to it. Even Cicero delighted in it, but showed some restraint in the employment of a device which is not unattractive save when carried to excess, and, further, by the weight of his thought lent dignity to what would otherwise have been mere trivialities. For in itself this artifice is a flat and foolish affectation, but when it goes hand in hand with vigour of thought, it gives the impression of natural charm, which the speaker has not had to go far to find."[2]

The central thrust of Quintilian's comment is that it is not the figures themselves but their excessive use which can lead to foppish writing. Quintilian rightly condemns their merely ornamental use as "flat and foolish affectation," yet his criticism is mixed. There are times, that last cryptic sentence implies, when their use is justified, notably when the style grows "naturally" out of the subject matter at hand. Kennedy himself seems to reserve a modicum of praise: "Yet in his own age the style of Gorgias did not seem in poor taste. There was then a general desire to create a literary prose."[3] The tendency of our age, it seems to me, has been to accept the negative connotation of Gorgianic figures uncritically and not give due consideration to the possible positive effects. In order to gain a full understanding of the figures, I believe it is necessary to see them not in a narrow, restricted way but as part of a larger perspective. It is necessary to see them as part of the continuing human concern with the idea of symmetry, an idea which is rooted in our physiological being and touches many aspects of our collective lives.

It may be that the worst examples of Gorgianic figures represent a kind of imperfect individuation of the Greek idea of symmetry, an idea which was so well expressed in their architecture. But although a particular individuation may be flawed, the concept itself may still be valid. The concept of symmetry seems to be a part of what Kenneth Burke calls "the innate forms of the mind." Burke suggests that certain basic thought patterns, such as contrast, comparison, balance, repetition, and so on, parallel "certain psychic and physical processes which are at the roots of human experience."[4] Burke's basis for calling them "innate" is that they are closely tied up with the rhythm of bodily processes: "The appeal of form as exemplified in rhythm enjoys a special advantage in that rhythm is more closely allied with 'bodily' processes. Systole and diastole, alternation of the feet in walking, inhalation and exhalation, up and down, in and out, back and forth, such are the types of distinctly motor experiences 'tapped' by rhythm. Rhythm is so natural to the organism that even a succession of uniform beats will be interpreted as a succession of accented and unaccented beats."[5]

Moreover, we see the concept of symmetry expressed everywhere, all around us in all kinds of human institutions. For example, the idea of justice carries with it the idea of balance and symmetry. We believe that the punishment should always be related to the crime. This idea is reflected in the maxim "An eye for an eye, and a tooth for a tooth." At least part of the success of this maxim is derived from the condition laid down by Quintilian: the symmetry in the form reflects the "vigour of thought," or what we may describe as the psychological symmetry inherent in the concept. It is not surprising then that symmetry should also be a major concern of the arts. Suzanne Langer describes symmetry as a fundamental principle of art. "The second great function of design," she writes, "which may be the more important, at least if we measure its importance by its influence on the further potentialities of art, is the establishment of symmetry, or correlation of counterparts, which creates the axis as a structural element."[6] Langer goes on to explain the role of right and left in relation to a median, and the function of vertical and horizontal planes. However, her most interesting contention is that symmetrical form is not only fundamental to human experience but capable of expressing "our deepest vital feeling." She writes, "The safest device to achieve living form is symmetrical composition." Thus seen, symmetry is not merely a cold, static form, but, rather, a potentially dynamic, life-giving force.

It is important to note that the ideas about symmetrical form which have been discussed thus far—ideas from classical rhetoricians as well as from Kenneth Burke and Suzanne Langer in our own time—are all based in personal experience, or more accurately, in personal intuition. They appeal to our experience and sense of logic for corroboration, and they are supported by the weight of scholarly prestige, tradition, and authority. It is possible, however, to express these same philosophical constructs in quantitative terms, put them into a research design, and test their validity empirically.[7] Although these same constructs may appear foreign to us when they are expressed quantitatively, the results of empirical testing can yield untold benefits for our field. A series of studies conducted by the perceptual psychologist Fred Attneave, for example, sheds further light on the question of the function of symmetrical form.[8] His research deserves our careful attention.

Attneave was interested in studying, in quantitative terms, a belief long held by Gestalt psychologists, namely, that symmetry has a positive effect on memory. "Are regular figures better remembered than irregular ones simply because they contain less information to be remembered," he asked, "or does their superiority persist even when information is held constant? In other words, which is remembered more accurately; a large, well-organized figure, or a small, poorly-organized figure containing the same amount of information?"[9] In order to test that theory, Attneave devised a series of three experiments in which subjects were asked to recall certain nonverbal patterns ("patterns of dots presented in rectangular matrices") which had been presented to them. Two kinds of variables were included in the experiments: 1) the amount of information, that is, the size of the pattern, and 2) the level of symmetry.

In the first experiment, labeled "Immediate Reproduction," Attneave presented a series of patterns to 149 subjects divided into five groups. The patterns were arranged as follows: 1) a twelve-cell grid with six dots randomly arranged, 2) a twenty-cell grid with nine dots randomly arranged, 3) a twenty-cell grid with ten dots symmetrically arranged, 4) a thirty-five-cell grid with nineteen dots randomly arranged, and 5) a thirty-five-cell grid with seventeen dots symmetrically arranged. Each group was shown a different class of patterns, and subgroups within each were shown reverse image patterns as well as the patterns in reverse order.

In the first experiment Attneave found that slightly fewer errors occurred with the symmetrical patterns. However, in the second experiment, labeled "Delayed Reproduction" (which increased the length of the viewing time), the symmetrical patterns were clearly easier to remember, even when the amount of information was increased. The clear superiority of the symmetrical patterns was also evident in the third experiment ("Identification"), which required subjects to identify the various patterns with arbitrarily chosen names.

Although Attneave was cautious in reporting his findings, he did observe what might be called a consistent tendency toward the symmetrical pattern being easier to remember. He writes, "The further finding that symmetrical patterns are more accurately reproduced than random patterns with the same number of elements (and accordingly more information) may be taken to indicate that some perceptual mechanism is capable of organizing or encoding the redundant pattern into a simpler, more compact, less redundant form."[10] The implications of studies such as these for comprehending, and therefore composing, a text are intriguing. It seems only a matter of time before we gain a fuller understanding of not only the subtle influences of symmetrical form on the learning process but the nature of the "perceptual mechanism" itself.

Let us now consider briefly the role of symmetry in the teaching of written composition. During the past twenty years, three major theories of the sentence have been advanced, all of which offer significant help to the young writer. Since all three are concerned with the control of elements inside the sentence, it is appropriate to classify them as *syntactic rhetorics*. The first of these is the generative rhetoric advanced by Francis Christensen in 1963. The major importance of this work is that it illustrates so well the function of asymmetrical form—the cumulative sentence with its short base clause and jungle of appended, nonclausal modifiers. The second major theory appears in Edward P. J. Corbett's well-known text, *Classical Rhetoric for the Modern Student*. In that text Corbett reminds us of the classical concept of form which appears in sentence schemes, and especially of the power which can be derived from repetition and rhythm within the sentence. The third major theory is that which is inherent in sentence-combining activity, an activity which makes students aware of the dynamics of the embedment process within the sentence. Although all three of these syntactic rhetorics employ the idea of symmetry, not one (with the exception of Corbett) treats it directly.

Even though these syntactic rhetorics fail adequately to emphasize symmetry, their strategies are clearly superior to more traditional approaches, which typically present students with examples of flawed parallelism and ask them to mend them. The difficulty, as we know, is that simply asking students to correct examples often does not stimulate a genuine understanding of a concept. More importantly, such exercises rarely promote the kind of active learning that the teaching of writing requires.

Attneave's experiments and Burke's comments on innate form suggest the potential fruitfulness of efforts to develop a syntactic rhetoric based on symmetry and parallelism—one which could, in combination with other related activities, serve as a powerful heuristic tool. As a beginning for this obviously demanding project, I offer here a tentative outline of the structure of parallelism in the English language. Using this simple guideline, the resources already provided by current syntactic rhetorics, such as sentence-combining, and other activities such as imitation, teachers can themselves develop direct exercises designed to increase students' understanding and control of this powerful linguistic resource.[11]

Below is an outline of the structure of parallelism in the English language. The outline and accompanying examples are the raw material for fashioning a curriculum which is both compassionate and intellectually honest. Parallelism is shown as consisting of four major categories: 1) the repetition of key words, 2) the use of opposite words, 3) the repetition of grammatical elements, and 4) combinations of these, in which selected elements function together. The examples below are drawn from a broad range of the resources of the English language and are intended to be representative. The italicized words in each example illustrate the kind of parallelism being described; in the examples of combinations the first element mentioned is italicized except where noted.

1. The Repetition of Key Words

1. Basal Repetition—the repetition of key particles, especially prepositions and articles

I have a dream my four little children will one day live in a nation where they will not be judged *by the* color *of their* skin but *by the* content *of their* character.

Martin Luther King, "I Have a Dream"

2. Conceptual Repetition—the repetition of major conceptual terms, particularly nouns, verbs, or adjectives

There warn't no color in his face, where his face showed; it was *white*; not like another man's *white,* but a *white* to make a body sick, a *white* to make a body's flesh crawl—a tree-toad *white,* a fish-belly *white.*

Mark Twain, *The Adventures of Huckleberry Finn*

3. Parallel Modification—the same word modifying two different words in the sentence

False face must hide what the *false* heart doth know.

Shakespeare, *Macbeth*

4. Isocolon—precise word-for-word repetition of two or more members (phrases, clauses, and so forth) with the exception of one or two words

He did not know the Somali proverb that says a brave man is always frightened three times by a lion; *when he first* sees his track, *when he first* hears him roar and *when he first* confronts him.

Hemingway, "The Short Happy Life of Francis Macomber"

2. The Use of Opposite Words (Anthithesis)

The *rich* ruleth over the *poor,* and the *borrower* is servant to the *lender.*

Proverbs 22:7

3. Repetition of Grammatical Elements

1. Nominal

The hazy *sunlight,* the warm and drowsy *air,* the tender *foliage,* the opening *flowers,* betokened the reviving life of nature.

Mark Twain, *Life on the Mississippi*

2. Verbal

Suddenly one of these gypsies, in trembling opal, *seizes* a cocktail out of the air, *dumps* it down for courage and, moving her hands like Frisco, *dances* out alone on the platform.

F. Scott Fitzgerald, *The Great Gatsby*

3. Participial

They move in orderly lines around the box, *crowding* one another precisely, without injury, *peering* down, *nodding,* and then *backing* off to let new people in.

Lewis Thomas, The Lives of a Cell

4. Infinitival

Manny Greenhill is hoping to get Miss Baez *to write* a book, *to be* in a movie, and *to get around* to recording the rock 'n' roll songs.

Joan Didion, "Where the Kissing Never Stops"

5. Gerundive

And with her cries came the sound of hoofs, and the *beating* of wings and the *roaring* of lions.

Khalil Gibran, The Prophet

6. Adjectival

His features are *strong* and *masculine,* with an Austrian Lip, and arched Nose, his Complexion *olive,* his Countenance *erect,* his Body and Limbs well *proportioned,* all his Deportment *majestick.*

Swift, Gulliver's Travels

7. Adverbial

The Bible's account of Moses is, alas, as *geographically* perplexing as it is *spiritually* enlightening.

National Geographic

8. Prepositional

To counteract any evil result of that bad conjunction he walked quickly *past* the ranch house, *through* the chicken yard, *through* the vegetable patch, until he came at last *to* the brushline.

John Steinbeck, The Red Pony

9. Clausal

There are thousands *who* are in opinion opposed to slavery and to the war; *who* yet in effect do nothing to put an end to them; *who,* esteeming themselves children of Washington and Franklin, sit down with their hands in their pockets, and say that they know not what to do, and do nothing; *who* even postpone the question of freedom to the question of free-trade.

Thoreau, "On the Duty of Civil Disobedience"

4. Combinations

1. Basal and Conceptual Repetition (both italicized)

   As men's prayers *are a disease of the* will, so *are* their creeds *a disease of the* intellect.

   Emerson, "Self Reliance"

2. Parallel Participles and Basal Repetition (both italicized)

   Blinded by the glare *of the* headlights and *confused by the* incessant groaning *of the* horns, the apparition stood swaying for a moment before he perceived the man in the duster.

   F. Scott Gitzgerald, *The Great Gatsby*

3. Parallel Participles and Antithesis

   We have before us a blameless and noble spirit *stricken* to the earth by malign powers, *but not conquered; tempted, but grandly putting the temptation away; enmeshed by subtle coils, but sternly resolved to rend them* and march forth victorious, at any peril of life or limb.

   Mark Twain, "In Defense of Harriet Shelley"

4. Antithesis in Isocolon

   Power corrupts the *few*, while *weakness* corrupts the *many*.

   Eric Hoffer, *The Ordeal of Change*

5. Parallel Nouns and Verbs in Isocolon

   With mine own *tears* I *wash* away my *balm*,
   With mine own *hands* I *give* away my *crown*,
   With mine own *tongue deny* my sacred *state*.

   Shakespeare, *Richard II*

6. Antithetical Adjectives in Isocolon

   Now am I *humble*, who was once *proud*;
   Now am I *silent*, who was once *loud*.

   Janis Ian, "Light a Light"

7. Antithesis and Parallel Verbs in Isocolon

   If a free society cannot *help* the many who are *poor*, it cannot *save* the *few* who are *rich*.

   John F. Kennedy, "Inaugural Address"

8. Parallel Modification and Parallel Nouns, with Antithesis and Basal Repetition

Let us focus instead on a *more* practical, *more* attainable peace based not on a sudden *revolution* in *human nature,* but on a gradual *evolution* in *human institutions.*

John F. Kennedy, "What Kind of Peace Do We Want?"

9. Antithetical Infinitives in Isocolon

It takes one some little time to find out that phrases which seem intended *to guide* the reader aright are there *to mislead* him; that phrases which seem intended *to throw light* are there *to throw darkness*; that phrases which seem intended *to interpret* a fact are there *to misinterpret it*; that phrases which seem intended *to forestall prejudice* are there *to create it*; that phrases which seem *antidotes* are *poisons* in disguise.

Mark Twain, "In Defense of Harriet Shelley"

Even this brief description of the four major categories of parallelism reveals how pervasive principles of symmetry are in our language. And their pervasiveness argues strongly for our including the study of parallelism and symmetry in our writing curriculum. We must be certain, however, that such principles are taught not as sterile forms to be imposed, willy nilly, on the "content" of sentences, but as major means through which we perceive and structure reality.

Greek art, architecture, and oratory all reflect the importance of balance and symmetry. And the Greek rhetoricians gave us our first full accounting of these principles in language. We can learn much by returning to these ancient authors' discussions and using their insights to inform our teaching of sentence rhetoric. Students can begin, perhaps, by discovering examples of parallelism in newspapers, magazines, and even textbooks. They can then go on to create symmetrical structures, seeing for themselves how parallelism—and purposeful "faulty" parallelism[12]—focus our attention and influence our understanding of particular sentences. Extensive *exercitatio,* accompanied by instruction in the *ars* of symmetry, can lead students back to the principles adumbrated by Greek rhetoricians, and forward into new areas of language play. Thus does the work of the classical rhetoricians nicely balance our teaching of modern discourse.

13
Figures of Speech in the Rhetoric of Science and Technology

S. Michael Halloran and Annette Norris Bradford

In a move to halt the depletion of "our most precious terrestrial resource," Darwin Crum of the ASCG (the American Society for the Conservation of Gravity) has postulated an alternative to the Newtonian concept of gravity. According to a note in the magazine *Science 81*:

> ASCG conceptualizes the force as a bunch of machine screws called LIGRE-FITES extending from the center of the Earth to the stars. Since the LIGREFITES pass through the nuclei of all atoms, the electrons spinning around each atom screw themselves down to Earth. Lead is thus heavier than magnesium because it has many more electrons. "Hydrogen and helium of course spin in a left-handed direction and hence rise upward on the LIGREFITE." The problem is that the delicate threads of the LIGREFITES wear down. In response, the ASCG is researching alternatives, such as "synthetic gravity, artificial gravity, or new gravity mines." Crum's even talking about black hole towing.[1]

Even the most wooly headed humanist will recognize the LIGREFITE theory as a joke, a parody of real science. But why? How does one recognize it as deliberate parody rather than just a wacky idea? We believe that, like a literary parody or a cartoon caricature, the LIGREFITE theory works by distorting a salient feature of the original for comic effect. As the caricaturist fixes on Jimmy Carter's smile and the literary parodist on Hemingway's curt intimacy, Mr. Crum of the ASCG has exaggerated a real scientific theory's peculiar way of exploiting metaphor. And just as the skilled caricaturist or parodist can teach us to see more clearly the salient features of his or her victims, so too Mr. Crum points up an important feature of many, perhaps all scientific theories: their essentially metaphorical character. Scrutinized closely, a theory more often than not turns out to be a figure of both thought and speech, pressed hard and elaborated in great detail.

The claim that scientific theories have something in common with rhetorical tropes has been made elsewhere,[2] though it is a fairly recent and still controversial development in the philosophy and psychology of science. From the side of rhetoric, a long-standing tradition holds that devices of eloquence are inappropriate for scientific discourse, and the standard textbooks in scientific and technical writing continue to take this position. We hope in this essay to suggest that a judicious use of figures—both schemes and tropes—is warranted in scientific and technical writing. We want to undermine the pedagogical tradition that simply rejects the use of figures in writing about science and technology, and to open up a field of research toward a better understanding of what would constitute "judicious" use of figures. Our approach is analytic and speculative rather than empirical, and our aim is more exploratory than demonstrative.

We begin by sketching the antifigurist tradition in scientific and technical writing, and then turn to a representative field of scientific inquiry—molecular biology—to illustrate the role of metaphor in the formulation and communication of scientific ideas. Next, we examine the role which schemes can play in enhancing the comprehensibility of scientific and technical prose. Finally, we develop an argument that the antifigurist tradition places unnecessary constraints on scientific invention and communication. Figures are useful in scientific/technical discourse: schemes because they enhance comprehensibility, tropes because of their expressive and heuristic power. While acknowledging the stylistic constraints imposed by scientific and technical writing practices, the technical writing teacher can advocate the judicious use of figures and perhaps introduce more artistic pedagogical techniques.

Modern science has been slow to acknowledge its use of figurative expression, probably due to the long-standing tradition which contends that the figures are not suitable for scientific and technical discourse. Aristotle's famous line "Nobody uses fine language when teaching geometry"[3] is but the first of such edicts. After the proliferation of figure study and the overuse and abuse of figures during the Renaissance, the emerging sciences of the seventeenth century divorced themselves entirely from the ornate Renaissance style, opting instead for the plain style which today remains the hallmark of scientific and technical writing. Francis Bacon attacked rhetorical devices because they led men to "study words and not matter" and made detection and correction of error difficult.[4] Thomas Sprat in his *History of the Royal Society* attacked rhetorical ornament as being "in open defiance against Reason" and indicated that members of the society were resolved "to reject all the amplifications, digressions, and swellings of style: to return back to the primitive purity, and shortness, when men deliver'd so many things, almost in an equal number of words."[5]

Yet there was ample and justifiable reason for Bacon, Sprat, and their fellow members of the Royal Society to condemn the prevailing scientific style. Fostered by the new empiricism and attention to methodology, the infant "modern science" was born into an era where style did little to enhance comprehension. The prevailing style emphasized rhythm and rhetorical ornamentation above comprehensibility and advocated that ideas be framed in long, involved, and obscurely worded sentences. But this problem was minor compared to the tradition of scientific expression which Bacon sought to uproot. During the Renaissance, when science was viewed as one short step above witchcraft, scientists were often prosecuted as heretics and punished accordingly. Galileo was only the most celebrated case. Therefore, written expressions of emerging scientific theories such as those of Kepler were committed to a language bordering on the mystical: convoluted enough to confuse the superstitious yet comprehensible enough to transmit ideas to other members of the scientific community. Renaissance scientific style, then, was a confusing verbal smoke screen, a cloak of mystical gibberish with the antithetical goals of expression and obscurity.[6]

But modern writing theorists also condemn figures based on this seventeenth century plain style tradition. Figures by definition violate the traditional style, language, and purpose of technical writing. Schemes achieve their effect by embellishing standard syntax, tropes by exploitation of ambiguity.[7] Both kinds of figures can add personality and individuality to technical prose. But embellishment, ambiguity, and authorial intrusion are violations of "correct" scientific and technical writing style, and modern textbook authors are quick to condemn them. Ulman and Gould, for example, find that the only style which fulfills the objectives of technical prose "is simple, direct, and unadorned." They caution students, "Don't get the idea that an elaborate or elegant style will impress people with your erudition. For every reader impressed by your bombast, ten will be annoyed or even left wondering what you are trying to say."[8] Warning against the view of style as "mere literary trick" or "mannerism," scientist Donald H. Menzel and his colleagues emphasize that style "does not depend on ornament or ostentation."[9]

But the ambiguity of figures—especially the tropes—is the most important objection to their use in scientific and technical writing. Ambiguity affects not just form but meaning as well. Scientist Waldon Willis calls the figures "nothing more than tricks of meaning or word order."[10] These "tricks" are possible because the interpretation of many tropes such as metaphor is open-ended, that is, capable of supporting several logical interpretations. But one of the primary characteristics of scientific and technical writing is the author's intention to convey one meaning and only one meaning in what he says. An ideal scientific language should be as concrete and exact as mathematics. Thus, while unambiguous interpretation in aesthetic writing "is not necessarily even desirable," technical communication is "the world of pure symbol" and "a precise meaning is essential and indispensable."[11]

Still another objection to figures in scientific and technical writing is based on propriety and the role of the writer in scientific prose. Figures can add individuality and personality to a writer's style. But the plain style tradition demands that the writer subvert his individuality to the high calling of his content. The writer must remain in the background of his work, necessitating the sometimes confusing and complex use of passive voice constructions which most people associate with technical writing style.

These condemnations found in technical writing textbooks but mirror the attitudes expressed in broader areas of inquiry such as philosophy and discourse theory. Analytical philosophy, for example, in its attempt to rid language of ambiguity and thus make it a suitable tool for scientific use, views figures as a major problem. Paul de Man points out that "philosophy either has to give up its own constitutive claim to rigor in order to come to terms with the figurality of its language, or . . . . it has to free itself from figuration altogether."[12] James Kinneavy likewise finds that the figures are ill-suited to reference discourse, the category in which he places scientific and informative writing. "Science usually prefers the literal to the nonliteral term," Kinneavy writes,"—that is, figures of speech are often out of place in science." But in the same discussion, Kinneavy says, "Of course, models and analogies are nonliteral terms and are necessary in science, so again the injunction cannot be absolute."[13]

In noting the role of "nonliteral terms" in model-building, Kinneavy suggests the fatal flaw in science's argument against figures: science, contrary to its own contentions, is not just "the presentation of objective information gleaned from observation."[14] No synthesis could ever be achieved, no models postulated, no paradigms established if science relied wholly upon "careful observation" for its theories. Model-building requires an inductive leap; carefully recorded examples must be synthesized into a logical premise, and then be further verified and expanded by traditional scientific method. For this, science must exploit the power of metaphor; it must shape its expectations, choose its experiments, and interpret its data in a realm of thought outside the literal world.

Neither the ancient nor the modern condemnation of figures has been successful in eliminating these devices from scientific and technical writing. Tropes exist because science must build models; schemes exist because these models must be explained and understood. Aristotle's criticism of the sophistic use of figures was based on the excessive use of schemes, yet Aristotle recognized the power of metaphor and is, in fact, the first major theorist of metaphor. Later rhetoricians such as Cicero and Quintilian explicated further the correct and judicious use of figures in prose. Even Bacon, the father of modern scientific writing style, did not practice what he preached; his own style was highly figured. Thus, condemning figures proves to be easier than eliminating them. For all it protests to the contrary, science has and does rely on the power of figures.

We turn now to a specific example of scientific invention and communication to illustrate the role of rhetorical tropes in science. In 1953 James Watson and Francis Crick proposed a model of the DNA molecule which suggested an explanation of the process by which the specific traits of an organism are determined in one generation of cells and passed on to the next.[15] According to their model, a molecule of DNA consists of two strands wound around a common axis, bound together by a chemical force called hydrogen bonding. Each strand contains a sequence of bases that bond with corresponding bases on the other strand in such a way that the sequence on one strand can vary in any way it wants, and yet this sequence will automatically determine a corresponding sequence on the other strand. Only four different bases are involved, and according to the Watson-Crick model the sequence in which they are arranged determines the characteristics of the organism of which the cell is a part by controlling the production of enzymes in the cell. These characteristics can be passed on from one generation to the next because when the cell divides the two strands of the DNA molecule separate, and each single strand can then control the production of an appropriate corresponding strand.

In this sketch of the famous double helix, we have deliberately avoided a metaphor that appears in every popular discussion of DNA we have encountered: the notion of a genetic "message." Accounts of molecular biology for lay audiences invariably speak of a genetic "code" in which the DNA molecule "transmits" "information" that is "transcribed" onto other substances in the cell and thus "translated" into the characteristics of a specific organism. The arrangement of bases on the strands of the molecule constitutes a message that is read intuitively by the cell, and can be decoded and now even rewritten by researchers. This version of the double helix is by now familiar to most educated people. We believe that our own version is poorer for its avoidance of the message metaphor, and we offer it simply by way of illustrating a point. The metaphor can add presence and life to an idea that is otherwise remote and lifeless. Those four bases somehow take on a heightened reality when seen as letters in an alphabet used to spell out instructions to the machinery of the cell. (The notion of cellular "machinery" invokes another important biological metaphor which we do not consider in this paper.)

The power of the message metaphor is illustrated by an article that appeared in a recent issue of *Science 81,* dealing with the discovery that the strands of the DNA molecule contain segments of apparently irrelevant or "meaningless" material. To the lay reader, the intended audience for *Science 81,* this fact might well seem no more than mildly interesting, so the writer faced a problem: how to dramatize the importance of this discovery which to molecular biologists is very nearly as revolutionary as the original discovery of the double helix. He began his article in this way:

> Try to keep reading this paragraph no matter what *lkjdf asdflku oirnmr kf* strange interruptions occur. You may wonder that a writer would *oiudl msd kjhltf* use such an oddly fragmented way of conveying *hofoie lknnwer lewwe* his meaning. But biologists today are trying to get used to the even odder fact *llknr smnlwrdf ifet* that genes do something very similar. It now appears that the genetic sentences that *erjndfu jnunww oisdfaserg* convey the instructions for you or a frog or a daisy *lkromswer nbwer lkhsf* are broken up by lengths of what may be genetic gibberish.[16]

The paragraph works by asking us to see the process of genetic communication in terms of a communication process with which we are more familiar, a process we are in fact enacting at the very moment of seeing the less familiar one through the lens provided by the writer. Further, it *estranges* the familiar process of reading, makes the very action we are performing an object of wonder in order to intensify the light it sheds on the less familiar process of genetic communication. By calling attention to the structure of reading, it helps us to see something about the structure of genetic communication. By itself the paragraph does not explain the significance of the discovery it introduces, but it engages our attention, focuses our vision in the direction that will lead to a fuller explanation. Because the strings of gibberish interrupting the meaningful prose of the paragraph seem bizarre and dysfunctional, we are prepared to accept the idea that strings of "gibberish" interrupting genetic "sentences" might be equally bizarre and challenging to researchers.

The author of this very recent article did not invent the message metaphor for DNA. In fact, the metaphor had figured prominently in popular treatments of molecular biology for many years before the particular feature of DNA he tried to explain was even suspected by researchers. The Life Science Library volume on *The Cell,* for example, speaks of the DNA code as "The Alphabet that Spells Life" and notes that "All the DNA instruction for a human being, if spelled out in English, would require several sets of a 24-volume encyclopedia."[17] This was published in 1964, and the existence of "genetic gibberish" within the pages of the book of life was first hinted at in 1977. We think it is worth pausing over the fact that a metaphor which seems peculiarly apt for explaining a discovery made in 1977 had been widely current in popular accounts of the field for years before. To us, this suggests that the message metaphor may be more than a convenient device for giving lay audiences a vague understanding of DNA.

And if we turn to the more technical literature of molecular biology, we find that the message metaphor appears there as well. An article in the journal *Nature* by one of the principals in the discovery of "genetic gibberish," contains this passage:

> The notion of the cistron, the genetic unit of function that one thought corresponded to a polypeptide chain, now must be replaced by that of a transcription unit containing regions which will be lost from the mature messenger—which I suggest we call introns (for intragenic regions)— alternating with regions which will be expressed—exons. The gene is a mosaic: expressed sequences held in a matrix of silent DNA, an intronic matrix.[18]

The author of this passage, Walter Gilbert, is somewhat more inclined toward figurative flourishes than some other molecular biologists. His references to the gibberish segments as "silent DNA" and to the gene as a "mosaic" do not so far as we know appear elsewhere in the literature, and in another passage of this same article he speculates that the introns might be "both frozen remnants of history and the sites of future evolution." But while Gilbert may be more fanciful than his colleagues—more rhetorically artful, we might say—his reliance on the message metaphor is by no means atypical. We have found that terms such as "expression," "translation," "transcription," "messenger," even "editing" and "reading" are used to describe the working of DNA in articles by different authors in such journals as *Science, Nature, The New England Journal of Medicine,* and *Scientific American.* [19] On the basis of a good sample of this literature, we believe the metaphorical idea that DNA transmits a message from one generation of cells to the next is central to modern research in molecular biology. The standard model of DNA is in essence a metaphor, a figure of both thought and speech.

The earliest appearance of the message metaphor that we have found is in two of the four papers in which Watson and Crick presented their discovery of DNA's structure to the scientific world in 1953. The metaphor does not appear in the papers or sections of papers that concentrate on the structure of the molecule, but only in those passages where they begin to speculate on how the molecule might perform its function of specifying the characteristics of organisms. In one paper they say that "it therefore seems likely that the precise sequence of the bases is the code which carries the genetical information"; in another, "that its [the cell's] specificity is expressed by the precise sequence of the pairs of bases." [20] These references to *code, information,* and *expression* seem to be the first tentative hints that the genetic process might be viewed as communication.

It might be argued that to the biologist the idea of genetic communication is not a metaphor but a literal theory, that the genetic process is not *like* communication, it *is* communication. Consider, for example, this passage from an essay in a special 1972 issue of *Scientific American* devoted entirely to the subject of communication:

> The capacity to communicate is a fundamental feature of living cells. . . . The genetic information of an organism is embodied in the precise sequence of the four kinds of nucleotide base—adenine, guanine, thymine, and cytosine—in the DNA molecules of the nuclei of its cellular constituency. The meaning of that information is the specification of the precise sequence of the 20 amino acids in a myriad of different kinds of protein molecule. It is the ensemble of cellular proteins that functions to make the cell what it is: an engine built of highly specific structural members and

enzymes that carries out a complex network of catalytically facilitated metabolic reactions. In the course of cell reproduction the parental DNA molecules are replicated and each of the two daughter cells is endowed with a complete store of the genetic information of the mother cell.[21]

Our guess is that the author would be willing to label certain notions in this passage metaphorical: that the cell is an engine perhaps, certainly that cells stand in a mother-daughter relationship. But the idea that DNA communicates meaningful information seems to be put forward as a literal claim.

The central point to be made in answering the objection is this: a metaphor is not necessarily a *mere* metaphor. Lakoff and Johnson have pointed up the existence of metaphors that serve to organize fundamentally our everyday experience of the world;[22] for example, much of what we say and think about the experience of arguing is grounded in the metaphor *argument is warfare*. These "metaphors we live by" are so integral to our experience that we recognize them as metaphors only through a conscious effort. Most of the time we use them as literal truths; in an argument, for example, we devise a *strategy* to *attack* an opponent's *position* and thus *defeat* him. While we don't think consciously about an argument-warfare analogy, our experience of warfare serves to organize our experience of arguing. (Note that it is not necessarily the more familiar experience that serves to organize the less familiar; for most people, warfare is a purely vicarious or imaginary experience.)

The message metaphor is in the world of science a similarly fundamental metaphor, a metaphor to think and work by. It has become basic to molecular biology's way of interpreting experience—so much so that it has set the agenda for much of the research done in that field since Watson and Crick's discovery of the double helix. One of the great questions that occupied biologists throughout the 1950s and into the sixties had to do with what we might call the morphology of the genetic code. The metaphorical basis of this work is perhaps most apparent in Crick's effort to devise what he called a "comma-free code," a morphological scheme in which the boundaries between meaningful units—"words"—on the DNA molecule would not have to be marked by discrete spacing elements—"commas."[23] His solution turned out to be mistaken, but what interests us here is his way of conceptualizing and expressing the problem. The experience of communication through language served as an organizing perspective on the working of DNA.

Not all scientific metaphors are similarly fundamental. Many of the tropes that appear in scientific writing are of quite local and limited application: the DNA molecule, for example, can be likened to a spiral stairway, or a pair of intertwined coil springs, or a zipper. Watson and Crick in fact used the image of a zipper to suggest how the two strands of the molecule might come apart during cell-division, and the same metaphor appears in both the Life Science Library volume *The Cell* and the *Science 81* essay we quoted from earlier.[24] The image of the zipper provides a useful perspective from which to view this quite specific aspect of the DNA molecule, but if one tried to apply it beyond this single aspect the result would be something like the LIGREFITE theory of gravity. When used to explain how the strands of the DNA molecule fit together and come apart, the image of a zipper is a *mere metaphor* (which is not to say that it is rhetorically useless). The idea that DNA encodes a message is more than this. Its field of application opens far beyond one specific aspect of DNA; it has served to pose questions as well as to organize and illustrate what's already understood. The failure of Crick's idea for a comma-free code, for instance, did not discourage others from looking for "commas," boundaries between the "words" in genetic "sentences." The message metaphor continued to serve as a heuristic for research in the field.

Other fields have their own heuristic tropes. In cognitive science, for example, *the brain is a computer*. In quantum physics, *particles are waves*. (Here is an instance of oxymoron.) The pervasiveness and importance of heuristic tropes has led one scholar to suggest that "perhaps a rhetorical analysis could be used by scientists to help generate metaphors tailor-made to the scientific task at hand."[25] What we suggest is not quite so ambitious. Since tropes do play a role in scientific invention, it seems whimsical to persist in proscribing their use in scientific and technical writing. We believe that the *Science 81* piece quoted above illustrates an important principle of scientific popularization: reveal to your audience the central heuristic trope(s) of the field you are writing about. And "mere tropes" have their own uses in writing about scientific subjects for both professional and lay audiences.

Thus far we have concentrated on tropes, but this is not to deny the utility of the schemes. Perhaps less discussion of these figures is needed since many of the classical schemes—parallelism, antithesis, and apposition, for example—have been incorporated into handbooks as devices of syntax and usage. But the more elaborate schemes such as antimetabole, epistrophe, and anastrophe have largely disappeared from writing pedagogy, particularly the teaching of technical writing.

The reason for this disappearance is the emphasis which scientific and technical writing places on "plain and simple prose," on what Richard Lanham would call the transparent style.[26] Yet the complex subject matter of scientific and technical prose demands the use of devices for creating regularity and predictability. Such devices as frequent headings and numbered and bulleted lists have become standard means by which technical writing strives to achieve regularity. (Listing and bulleting are simply visual expressions of parallelism.) The putative function of these devices is to achieve transparency and thus to maximize readability.

But readability turns out to be a paradoxical notion. Up to a point, efforts to regularize and simplify prose—to achieve "transparency"—will make prose more readable. But beyond this point, the result is to *diminish* readability. When prose becomes too regular and predictable, readers lose a sense of what's important in it. Emphasis disappears and the audience becomes *bored*. We believe that the ideal of *comprehensibility* expresses better the desired effect of well-written scientific prose. Readability is a text-based measure which ignores the conceptual relationships in the prose, even the meanings of the words. Comprehensibility, on the other hand, is a reader-based measure concerned with subtle aspects of syntax, relative difficulty and density of ideas, levels of abstraction, style, cadence, and structure.[27] Comprehensibility recognizes that tempos should vary within a piece of well-written prose. The reader needs on occasion to be slowed up, his attention caught by a hook of rhythm or syntactic deviance that says, "Pay close attention here."

Understood thus, comprehensibility is rooted in something like Kenneth Burke's notion of form as "the creation of an appetite in the mind of the auditor, and the adequate satisfying of that appetite."[28] And Burke's notion of form was anticipated centuries ago by Cicero, whose *Orator* suggests that the function of style is to shape a curve of audience response.[29] Like the other great classical rhetoricians, Cicero knew that syntactic figures can do precisely this: they shape the audience's ongoing awareness of a message. The more elaborate schemes are devices of emphasis built on balance, repetition, omission, and inversion, devices which can slow the tempo of prose and point up passages meriting special attention. They are subtle, intrinsic to the text (as opposed to the extrinsic nature of headings, and so forth), easy to incorporate into a writer's style, and equally effective for lay or professionally learned audiences.

This is not to suggest that a classical or Renaissance typology of schemes could simply be imported into a technical writing course. There is a substantial difference between modern scientific and technical communication on the one hand and the modes of discourse for which classical rhetoric was developed on the other. In the discourse of classical rhetoric, what Frye calls the radical of presentation is oral;[30] even when recorded in writing or print, as for example in the text of a speech by Demosthenes or Cicero, the words are addressed ultimately to the ear. In scientific and technical writing—and indeed in much modern discourse that falls outside this category—the radical of presentation is visual; even when the words are spoken, as in a presentation at a conference or seminar, they may be addressed ultimately to the readers of a journal or a volume of proceedings. The classical schemes create auditory patterns that can work powerfully to shape an audience's response, but in the primarily visual economy of the technical writer, they may seem extravagant. Consider, for example, this familiar passage from the King James Version of the Bible:

> And God said, "Let the earth bring forth living creatures according to their kinds: cattle and creeping things and beasts of the earth according to their kinds." And it was so. And God made the beasts of the earth according to their kinds and the cattle according to their kinds and everything that creeps upon the ground according to its kind. And God saw that it was good.

In a just slightly whimsical mood, one working technical writer suggested that this passage might in her own professional world be rendered thus:

> God said, "Let the earth bring forth the following living creatures:
> • Cattle
> • Creeping things
> • Beasts."
> Then God made those living creatures, and saw that it was good.[31]

The Gospel according to technical communication lacks the auditory magic of the King James Version. But by means of a simple visual device it achieves emphasis and organization more economically than the original. The bulleted list serves as a visual scheme. A more subtle and complex visual scheme is illustrated by the "genetic gibberish" passage from *Science 81* quoted earlier. Here the printed text becomes an icon as well as a discursive message, and the iconic character of the text interacts with its discursive message to make a point vividly and economically. The printed text enacts the message metaphor for DNA as well as expressing it.

The standards of propriety in technical writing call for heavier reliance on visual devices such as these than on the primarily auditory schemes of classical rhetoric. But the distinction between the visual and auditory modes is by no means tidy and absolute. While classical rhetoric was primarily auditory, it had important visual dimensions as well. Recall that clarity was always regarded as a major stylistic virtue, and, like Lanham's notions of transparency and opacity, clarity invokes a visual metaphor for the verbal medium. Similarly, the orator relied upon a complex technique of visualization to memorize a speech. While technical and scientific writing is primarily visual, no writing can ever divorce itself entirely from the auditory mode. The ultimate radical of presentation for any text is the human voice, as our persistent use of the term audience—the ones who audit—suggests. An important area for investigation in the rhetoric of science and technology would thus be the relationship between visual and auditory modes in the processing of texts.

The notion of propriety brings us to a pedagogical problem with which we will conclude. Scientific and technical disciplines tend to be rigid in enforcing stylistic constraints, and their constraints tend to be narrow. A Walter Gilbert can get away with talk of genes as mosaics, of "silent DNA" and "frozen remnants of history." But the average beginning scientist or engineer may not get published if he or she strays far from the leaden impersonality that characterizes most technical prose. As rhetoricians we may know that figures inevitably appear in scientific and technical writing, and that a more liberal and artful use of them could produce more forceful, emphatic, communicatively powerful writing. But *we* won't be editing the technical papers or evaluating the proposals and reports our students will have to write in their professional careers. The rhetorical norms to which these students will have to adjust are in many cases deplorable, but they exist. What is the teacher's responsibility in a course intended to prepare students to write as scientists and engineers are supposed to write?

Some would write over the door of a technical writing class, "Abandon art, all ye who enter here." A respected authority in the field has argued strenuously that what students want and need from a technical writing course is rote indoctrination in certain established conventions. [32] According to this view, a technical writing teacher would serve students badly by encouraging them to experiment with schemes and tropes, or indeed to exercise the smallest degree of rhetorical originality. The purpose of a technical writing course is to train students to conform meticulously to "mil specs" and/or whatever other norms are appropriate. An obvious practical problem with this view is that one cannot know infallibly just which sets of norms will be appropriate for a given group of students. Rhetorical norms vary widely from one technical field or industry to another, and the student who has simply been indoctrinated to the norms of one field—for example, to the specifications of the United States Department of Defense—may be worse than merely ignorant if his or her career takes him or her into another field.

At the very least, then, technical and scientific writing students should be taught to understand the rhetorical principles upon which the writing norms of a field rest. We believe that it is also possible to teach them to take a critical view of the particular norms of this or that field, without thereby disabling them for work in that field. Indeed, if a student really understands rhetorical principles, he or she will inevitably question (but not necessarily disregard) some of the more mindless conventions that are enforced in certain fields. For example, a student who understands the notions of emphasis and comprehensibility will see the futility of insisting upon an inflexible maximum sentence length. A student who understands the subtle relationship between form and content in discourse will know that one may not be able to meet a certain readability criterion without doing conceptual violence to the topic at hand. If this same student has learned some of the classical schemes and tropes, he or she may recognize their potential usefulness in solving the rhetorical problems of a given scientific or technical field.

Our most general point is simply that classical rhetoric has much to say about technical and scientific writing. It offers specific tools, such as schemes and tropes, but beyond these it offers the critical perspective that transforms craft into art. As rhetorician, the technical writer will recognize the writing norms of a given field as constraints to be taken seriously, but not slavishly. He or she will bring to his or her work the quality that Cicero called tact (*aptus*),[33] an attunement to the complexities of the given situation allowing him or her to judge when to conform and when to be creative.

14

Classical Rhetoric and the Basic Writer

Lynn Quitman Troyka

Aristotle wrote, "All men desire to know." For all of humankind, this desire is among the central pleasures of life. Infants learn at staggering rates, constantly striving to observe and make sense of their world. Yet many teachers bear sad witness today to the fact that some students seem to have given up, that they seem to have lost their inborn desire to know. Scholars of education have devoted careers to the investigation of this alienation, but debates about its causes rage on nonetheless.

I believe that no person ever loses the "desire to know." When we give human beings who think that they *cannot* learn the hope that they *can,* they will cautiously try again. My evidence is derived from a decade-and-a-half of teaching Basic Writing to college students. These students have little sustained control over sentence structure or paragraph development, and thus they have had few successful experiences with academic writing. These students have taken a battery of placement tests and have been told, in most cases, that they must take what amounts to remedial reading, remedial math, and remedial writing. In spite of this discouraging news, these students risk their self-esteem once more by enrolling in the required courses.[1]

Perhaps their motivation comes from the realities of the job market, or from the pressure of their families, or from sheer will to gain more control over their lives. But motivation is not enough. How many of us have seen eager students trying hard, indeed straining, to master the material but unable to learn? Motivation is, therefore, a necessary but not sufficient condition for learning, for fulfilling the desire that Aristotle recognized over two thousand years ago.

Frank Smith, a synthesizer of much of today's research and speculation in education, develops a carefully reasoned and, from the perspective
of my experience, useful argument that extends our understanding of how
learning takes place. Smith's thesis is too complex for facile condensation,
and so he deserves to be read in his entirety.[2] For my purpose here, I shall
focus on one of his summarizing statements which tells us that *people
cannot learn when they expect that they cannot.*

> Learning occurs when a learner *engages* with a demonstration, so that it, in
> effect, becomes the learner's demonstration. . . . Engagement takes place
> in the presence of appropriate demonstrations whenever we are sensitive to
> learning, and sensitivity is the absence of expectation thatlearning w
> ll not take place. Sensitivity does not need to be accounted for; its absence
> does. Expectation that learning will not take place is itself learned. The
> ultimate irony is that the brain's constant propensity to learn may in fact
> defeat learning; the brain can learn that particular things are not worth
> learning or are unlikely to be learned.[3]

Basic Writers need more than to be highly motivated. They need, in
Smith's terms, to "expect that learning will take place." Such expectations are particularly difficult for teachers to elicit in students previously
discouraged by experiences that have taught them that they are unlikely
to learn. Exhortations from teachers do not help raise students' expectations that they can learn, for such earnest reassurances are rarely believed
and serve, in addition, only to enhance the self-consciousness that defeats
fragile renewal of the expectation that learning is likely. "Demonstrations" do help, as Frank Smith explains. Demonstrations sweep reluctant
students along, immersing them in the endeavor so that "engagement
takes place." Only in retrospect do the students realize that they have
learned—and thus that they no longer need to be quite so sure that
learning will *not* take place. The expectation to learn must be preconscious, not a straining to confront the material but rather a relaxing to
embrace it.

I come now to my main point: among the most effective sources for
"demonstrations" to help Basic Writers revive their confidence in their
natural powers to learn is classical rhetorical theory. The great value of
classical rhetoric for Basic Writers is that it derives from observations of
the art of persuasion as it operates in real life. It is "relevant" for modern
students. Classical rhetoric provides a rhetorical situation given whole,
not atomistically as in other models of rhetoric.

As Edward P. J. Corbett says in *Classical Rhetoric for the Modern*

Student (*CRMS*),[4] "The student cannot escape rhetoric, no matter what his vocation in life is. Every day of his life, he either uses rhetoric or is exposed to it" (p. 40). Thus, demonstrations built on classical rhetorical theory can lead Basic Writers, gently and naturally, into observations of their personal experiences. Such seemingly self-evident insights permit students to make conscious connections between what they know and what they are learning—and hence they begin to expect that they will learn.

Here is an example. Early in a recent semester, my class of Basic Writers had just learned about the six parts of classical persuasive discourse. They had read, first, Corbett's summary of *dispositio* in *CRMS* (p. 38). Second, they had read Ross Winterowd's "Structure as Heuristic," a brief explanation of classical form in *The Contemporary Writer*.[5] One student who had been listening to the discussion about the readings but had not participated wrote this in his journal that night. I offer it here for its content; I shall come to the matter of English error presently.

> Corbett says Aris. did'nt sit in his office dreaming up principles. Well, he's right. I saw some rhetoric today. My math teacher was mad and told us why we needed his course. Then he started to argue against the arguements against what he was saying. At first I did'nt know why he was going on and on. I thought about Corbett's ios and iums and I listened. Maybe my teacher did'nt know he was working rhetoric, but I did. Like Winter-[owd] says it worked well for more than 2,000 years.
>
> Eddie[6]

Here is another example. This student participated enthusiastically in the discussion of the readings, but argued that classical form is too long-winded. She then wrote in her journal:

> My sister is a natural at *confutatio*. (How's *that?* I copied the spelling off the sheet.) She always thinks she knows what my father is going to say when she asks for something. She says "I know you're going to say so and so, but your wrong." Tonight, I decided to test it out and when she started in about her boy friend, I told her not to say he was wrong, I told her to prove he was wrong with an example. She got mad at me for interferring but later she came over and asked me to help her with examples for next time. Maybe it makes sense. No promises.
>
> Laura

Before I continue to explain the uses of classical rhetoric for Basic Writers, I want to discuss the matter of English error and the resulting proper content for a Basic Writing curriculum. The journal entries above reveal students who make spelling errors, who punctuate sentence boundaries incorrectly, and who write with less than a sophisticated style. Even with allowances for the fact that the extracts are journal entries and therefore are not to be read as finished prose, readers can discern students who surely need a course in Basic Writing. What, then, constitutes a proper curriculum for such a course? Without any doubt, Basic Writers must work on grammar, usage, and syntax because their errors interfere with clear communication and because their errors mark them as "illiterate" by most of educated society. The study of such matters, however, is most successful and best recalled for use in actual writing, when the study is undertaken in the service of rhetoric, of the elaboration of ideas, and of the development of academic forms of cognitive engagement.

What Basic Writers need more than anything, therefore, is experience with intellectual endeavors of the mind. Along with work on grammar and usage, Basic Writers need to explore concepts with close-in intensity. They need to immerse themselves in, and gain confidence in their abilities with, the demands and pleasures of careful reasoning. They need to be exposed to notions that help them conceptualize their everyday lives and their abstract thinking. Mina Shaughnessy, in *Errors and Expectations,*[7] her modern classic about Basic Writing, reminds us that, although her trenchant analyses concentrate on the sentences that Basic Writers produce,

> What *is* basic to the Basic Writing student [is] "beyond the sentence." . . . The student is almost certain to find his progress beyond the sentence more gratifying, for it seems to link him more directly to his recognized powers and, therefore, to the deepest purpose of education as Dewey has defined it: "the transformation of more or less casual curiosity and sporadic suggestions into attitudes of alert, cautious, and thorough inquiry." (p. 274)

Further, Andrea Lunsford argues in "Cognitive Development and the Basic Writer,"[8] that teachers need "to foster conceptualization and analytic thinking" (p. 41) in Basic Writers. To that end, she offers specific techniques that range from special studies of verbs to essay writing, all designed to enhance cognitive development.

Too often, however, such well-argued advice from experts in Basic Writing is not heeded. In so-called "remedial writing" classes today, the prevalent instructional orientation ignores all that is currently known about cognition and learning. With the best of intentions, many teachers faced with classrooms of Basic Writers think that their students should begin at what seems to be the simplest beginning: word identification. Once the parts of speech, the verb tenses, and the agreement rules have been learned, the student can proceed to a study of sentence structures. Only later can these students move on to the paragraph or larger unit of written discourse. Such a progression does a disservice to Basic Writers, but the evidence of its tenacity is easy to find. Witness many college catalogs which show a Basic Writing sequence that starts with a semester for the study of the word and the sentence, followed by a semester on the paragraph, which precedes another semester to study essay and report writing. In addition, college Basic Writing texts that move from the word to the sentence and—sometimes—to the paragraph, with only rules and drills, sell briskly.

This atomistic inductive sequence for Basic Writers is ill-advised. As I have reported elsewhere, my research concerning cognitive styles, a technical term for the ways that people learn, reveals that most Basic Writers learn best with a deductive instructional approach.[9] Most are holistic thinkers who can move easily from seeing an overview of what they are studying toward seeing the details of the material. They assimilate new information when the overall context has been explicitly demonstrated and is always at hand. Therefore, segmented rules with no over-arching framework are rarely remembered beyond the drill stage. Frank Smith gives us another reason why atomistic presentation of material is not advisable, especially for unsure learners. He explains that learning is the act of *relating that which is already known to that which is unknown.*

> [People] try to make sense of the world by relating all their experiences to the theory of the world in their heads [i.e., cognitive structure], a theory they have been developing and testing since birth. This theory becomes the constellation of beliefs and attitudes and expectations that children bring with them to school; it constitutes the prior knowledge upon which they will depend if they are to make sense of instruction and instructors. It is the child's theory of the world that the educational process endeavors to build upon, modify and elaborate.[10]

Basic Writers do not come to college ready to forget all that they have ever learned, correctly or not. In the parlance of computer intelligence, people's memory banks cannot be assumed to have been erased when they enter a Basic Writing class.

As teachers of Basic Writing, therefore, we must use our students' prior knowledge as the infrastructure onto which students can build new learning. In order for us to facilitate this new learning, we have to recall what Frank Smith has said: "Learning occurs when a learner *engages* with a demonstration,"[11] an occasion that totally engrosses the student to the point that all self-consciousness about learning temporarily dims because the material to be learned occurs as a natural part of the experience.

Thus, only "demonstrations" of the utility of grammar, usage, and syntax can justify their mastery. Classical rhetorical theory offers excellent opportunities for such demonstrations. When students perceive that rhetoric enables them to sway an audience, to exert some positive control over that audience and, by extension, over their environment, they have a purpose and context for learning language precisely.[12] The ability to cope with, and thrive in, today's information-based, language-oriented mainstream is no small payoff for students who think that their problems with grammar preclude them from full participation in society. As Martin Nystrand points out, "Language use [is] a unique and powerful strategy for knowing in its own right. Language, once acquired to any degree, is an event which imposes order on world and self."[13]

Within classical rhetoric, the subjects of the effects on audience (Books 1 and 2 of Aristotle's *Rhetoric*), and of the appeal of fables for popular audiences (Book 2 of Aristotle's *Rhetoric*) rarely fail to elicit animated interest in Basic Writers. These aspects of classical rhetoric strike a particularly responsive chord in Basic Writers who are black Americans. Black Americans who have been reared in the black American oral tradition use structured verbal and rhetorical strategies with deft experience that springs from their linguistic roots, as Edward Anderson explains in "The Uses of Black Rhetorical and Verbal Strategies in Teaching Composition."[14] These strategies range from black folk tales, folk sermons, and ballads to mainly urban ghetto-structured, oral exchanges such as rapping, running it down, jiving, shucking, copping a plea, sounding, and signifying. Similarly, Geneva Smitherman tells us in her landmark book *Talkin and Testifyin*:[15]

> We must look to the "original contributions" of the folk—their folklore, folk utterances, songs and tales of folk expression—to complete our definition and understanding of Black English. Comprising the formulaic structure of these contributions are verbal strategies, rhetorical devices, and folk expressive rituals which derive from a mutually understood notion of modes of discourse, which in turn is part of the "rich inheritance" of the African background. (P. 103)

The ease with which students from such traditions take to classical rhetorical theory is, therefore, not surprising.

That Basic Writers of all backgrounds would find much that is familiar in classical rhetoric would not have surprised Shaughnessy, for she suggests seven "types of written statements that give rise to fairly predictable patterns of elaboration."[16] She then cites her source:

> Most of the thought patterns we have been reviewing here are familiar to many teachers already as the topics of rhetoric, yet the presentation of the patterns [here] in the form of statements rather than names not only helps the student understand and remember them but demonstrates how form, rather than being an arbitrary frame one imposes on unruly content, lies embedded in the thesis or matrix statement that conventionally heads up a paragraph or essay.[17]

Andrea Lunsford makes additional, more extensive connections between classical rhetoric and the teaching of Basic Writing in "Aristotelian Rhetoric: Let's Get Back to the Classics."[18] Lunsford proposes that Basic Writers will benefit not only from Aristotle's discussion of *topoi* but also from his ideas about metaphor, *imitatio* (imitation exercises), audience, *controversiae* (arguing two sides of a question), and *prosopopoeia* (impersonation). Lunsford's generous menu of suggestions is further enhanced by her insight that Book Two of the *Rhetoric* "offers us a *method* of learning about our students and hence about our own craft" (p. 6) by sharpening our powers of observation and classification.

I would like to extend these excellent ideas by suggesting that specific sections of Corbett's *CRMS* offer particularly fine texts for teachers of Basic Writing to use with their students. No book has been more responsible for the current revival of interest in classical rhetoric in today's composition studies than has *CRMS*. And of special importance for Basic Writing students is Corbett's friendly, optimistic tone, along with his material that clearly draws on everyday experiences that relate to students' lives. *CRMS* provides Basic Writers with sensible "demonstrations" that engage them without making their learning self-conscious. Though Corbett speaks not to Basic Writers when he addresses the audience of students for whom he is writing, he surely appeals to them. Here is an entry from a class log, written by a student who was asked to record very briefly what she liked best so far and why. This student was a practical nurse:

> The part I liked best so far is "The Relevance and Importance of Rhetoric for Our Times." I want to go on to be an RN (not an electrical engineer, Corbett, but I get the idea.) I be convincing patients to take their Rxs or do like the dr. says. Rhetoric is the POSITIVE APPROACH TO PROBLEMS. It's

building up something, Corbett says. Which is what I am with my patients. He shows me how to convince them (or at least try more than just tell them.) I think Corbett would like to know that he helps me with the patients. He's smart, not starch (which I hope for me stops at my uniform). Too bad he's from Ohio.

Stella[19]

CRMS can be made accessible to Basic Writers, but because many of them do not have strong reading skills, teachers might want to provide glossaries, or, at times, adaptations with simplified vocabulary. The choice of sections from CRMS might vary somewhat according to the level and needs of the students, but I rarely fail to use certain sections. I have mentioned above the effectiveness of Corbett's discussion of *dispositio* (p. 38), and "The Relevance and Importance of Rhetoric for Our Times" (pp. 40–44). Corbett's discussion of "The Emotional Appeal" (pp. 99–107) is a favorite also, especially when shortened slightly, though never at the expense of his unique voice coming through. One student was especially impressed by the notion that emotions are best aroused indirectly. She focused on this statement (p. 101): "We cannot arouse an emotion, either in ourselves or others, by thinking about it. We arouse emotion by contemplating the object that stirs the emotion." Here is what she wrote in part of an essay before and after she had read about *pathos*:

Before:

I think mothers should work. Those that have to of course should work. Those that don't have to should if they want to. It's a free country. The kids get along fine. I should know. My mother worked and I turned out OK.

After:

The apartment was usually empty when I came home from school. Cookies were on my private plate. When I ate them I knew my mother put them there for me. Or asked me to before we left for school in the morning. Each chocolate chip was soft. I pretended they felt like her kiss on my cheek. We had a game where I'd leave one chip on my plate. When she came home from work she saw the chip and that was my hello kiss to her. Maybe if she was at home all the time I would not have realized it. I missed her sometimes, but I know that I turned out OK. So, it should be OK for mothers to work.

Joann

Joann's "after" sample might have been achieved if she had been told to use narrative, or to be more specific, or to draw upon her own experience in greater detail. Yet the "demonstration" that helped Joann revise her work is far more effective than any modern prescription. In learning about classical rhetorical theory, Basic Writers are given access to more than techniques of writing; they are given access to the underlying rationales for choices they can make as they write.

Here is a final example. The students had been writing about the need for prison reform. They had been asked to keep a log that recorded their process in making decisions for subsequent revisions. The first version of the essay was written early in the semester. A revision was required after the class had studied an adaptation of Corbett's discussion of the parts of a discourse, with particular emphasis on *confutatio* (pp. 323–25). About three weeks elapsed between the two versions, a time during which other writing was done but the prison reform arguments had been set aside deliberately. The following log accurately reflects what this student did in his two essays.

> The first time that I argued for better prisons, I said we need them for three reasons: (1) protect new prisoners from hardened criminals (2) prepare criminals for jobs on the outside (3) give prisoners back their self respect by treating them like human beings, not animals.
>
> The second time I tried to think about *confutato* which made it harder to write. I had to think of the opposite and write about it & I tried to make my points from before.
>
> 1. Criminals are all alike. No they aren't. Some did not do much, but they are with rapists and murders. Prisons are criminal factories today. So, protect new prisoners from hardened criminals.
>
> 2. Criminals deserve to be punished. But being locked away is enough, unless it was a bad crime that draws a life sentence. If criminals are not prepared for jobs on the outside, they will go back to the life [of crime].
>
> 3. Prisons are not country clubs. But human beings have to be treated with respect or they will lose it. Then they will be criminals forever.
>
> The second version is better because I tried to get into the reader's mind. It took longer to think about. Also, in my second essay, I tried an emotional appeal in my conclusion because I was at Attica for three years for possession [of drugs]. Maybe that is also establishing my authority. I don't know.
>
> Sal

While Sal was not entirely successful in his attempt to broaden the sophistication of his discussion, he did make real progress. Again, he was not trying out a technique; rather, he was applying his growing insight into how academic persuasive writing operates and how communication can be shaped for greater impact.

My central thesis is that classical rhetoric is among the most effective sources[20] for arranging "demonstrations" that elicit in Basic Writers the expectation they they *can* and that they *will* learn. This learning begins with exposure to concepts that engage Basic Writers in the practice of reasoning expected of students who write for academic purposes. Grammar, usage, and syntax—the obvious subjects that Basic Writers need to master—are best learned and retained when they are taught in a rich context of ideas that seek expression and elaboration. Basic Writers in college, daily determined to move into the mainstream of the academic college community, "desire to know" and are willing to risk much of their self-esteem to learn. Aristotle would have understood them well.

15
Classifying Discourse: Limitations and Alternatives
Richard L. Larson

One can't tell for sure whether the penchant for dividing discourse into kinds and classes that theorists and teachers of rhetoric and composition have displayed in the last two centuries should trace its roots to classical rhetoric. It is certainly true that classification was an important function of classical rhetorical theory, and recent theorists can find ample precedent in the work of classical rhetoricians for the effort to make the teaching of rhetoric easier by identifying and naming categories of discourse. Aristotle and others created the categories of epideictic, forensic, and deliberative rhetoric, and Aristotle divided the appeals used by a rhetor into those from rational argument, those from emotions, and those from the character and probity of the speaker. He added that within rhetorical argument there are essentially two classes, that derived from example (broadly speaking, induction), and that derived from the enthymeme (broadly speaking, deduction). Indeed, carrying out his characteristic impulse to organize and classify the data of experience as a way of reaching for truth, Aristotle identified and described ways of locating arguments and ways of relating arguments to the interests and inclinations of audiences. Cicero and Quintilian accepted and elaborated in their own way the division of rhetorical discourse into kinds, and further divided into classes the various questions that rhetorical discourse treats. Edward Corbett's own *Classical Rhetoric for the Modern Student* draws upon these classifications, and even more systematically breaks down the questions that rhetorical discourse can address as well as the sources of data and argument one might use in dealing with these questions.[1] The study of rhetoric as a teachable art began, it would seem, with the effort to put into categories the finished products of the rhetor's art as they were seen in the societies in which the theorists moved. Classical theory developed around taxonomies of discourse, and despite the fact that the categories arrived at by recent rhetoricians hardly match those of Aristotle and Cicero, classification of discourse is still one of the questions at the heart of the rhetorical enterprise.

A recent inquiry into one effort to categorize discourse is Robert Connors' "The Rise and Fall of the Modes of Discourse."[2] Connors locates the beginnings of the theory of "modes"—narration, description, exposition, argument—in an 1827 text by Samuel Newman, shows how the "modes" won out (as a system for clasifying discourse) over Hugh Blair's set of more literary categories, shows how Alexander Bain adopted them in his *English Composition and Rhetoric,* and traces their permutations (along with those of the "methods of exposition") through the rhetoric texts that taught writing to college students through the 1950s.[3] If one can have any argument at all with Connors' informative historical study, it is with his contention that the "modes" have been abandoned by teachers and theorists. As one who regularly reads manuscripts of articles submitted for publication in a professional journal as well as manuscripts of books submitted for commercial publication (and who before that read widely in the literature on rhetoric and composition in order to prepare annual bibliographies), I can testify to the persistence of the nineteenth-century "modes," or of classificatory systems closely akin to them, in the thinking of scholars and teachers right up to the present day. The modes furnish many teachers, it would seem, with a handy brief system for dividing up examples of writing—a system that ostensibly simplifies or even solves the problem of planning a text or organizing a course in writing.

But whether or not one agrees with Connors that the "modes" are dead or moribund, the impulse to organize thinking and discussion about discourse by finding systems of classification is very much alive. Let me glance at a few manifestations of the impulse, some well known, some less well known. Among those less well known is one that classifies discourse as "subjective" or "objective," or that differentiates "perceptual" from "conceptual" discourse. One example of a theorist who develops such classifications is George Bramer, who has argued that one can distinguish between "subjective" discourse, in which the writer is personally "involved," on the one hand, and "objective" discourse, from which the writer is "detached."[4] This principle of division also holds that pieces of discourse are either made up primarily of details observable to the senses and direct interpretations of those data, or primarily of ratiocinative constructs not based on sensory observations. Bramer even identifies perceptual and conceptual varieties of "subjective" discourse and similar varieties of "objective" discourse. Not many theorists or teaching texts are organized around precisely these classifications, but many teaching texts take for granted some such distinction when they discuss argument and style.

Another principle for classifying discourse, less well known as theory but influential in teaching practice, divides pieces into "familiar" essays and those that presumably reflect greater distance between author and reader. In his "Aesthetic Form in Familiar Essays," Howard Brashers characterizes at some length the features of that breed of essays he calls "familiar," though he does not go into much detail on writing that is not "familiar."[5] Quite a few teaching texts used in the schools, without necessarily using Brashers' characterization, treat "familiar essays" as a distinct genre and ask students to write them. Some college rhetoric-readers also treat "familiar essays" as a distinctive genre. Brashers, at least, undertakes an analysis of the form to derive its distinctive features. Many books do not, leaving to teacher and student the task of saying how one knows whether or not an essay is "familiar."

But probably the plan best known today for dividing up the members of the universe of discourse was advanced by James Kinneavy in *A Theory of Discourse*.[6] If any taxonomy of discourse has indeed displaced the "modes," which Connors thinks are no longer influential, it is Kinneavy's taxonomy. *A Theory of Discourse* draws heavily upon readings in and interpretations of theories of discourse and rhetoric, not to mention moral philosophy and philosophies of knowledge, from Aristotle to the present day. Though neither Kinneavy himself nor any disciples have produced a successful and influential teaching text built around his taxonomy, Kinneavy's taxonomy shapes the thinking of (or is at least given credit by) many who present papers at professional meetings, submit manuscripts about rhetoric for publication, and say they are reflecting fresh views of discourse in proposals for "new ways" of teaching rhetoric. I cannot here present the details of Kinneavy's complex theory, but since his approach seems to epitomize the assumptions of those who argue the value of such a taxonomy, I must mention at least a few of Kinneavy's major categories.

Kinneavy derives his argument, as I understand it, from the concept of a "communications triangle," which supposedly diagrams the interactions among elements in a communication. At one apex is the "writer" (or, one assumes, the speaker), at a second apex, the audience, and, at the third, the subject of the discourse. Discourse in which the writer is perceived to focus upon the details and contours of his or her subject is identified as "referential," a category further subdivided into "informative" (discourse designed to give full, accurate, and fresh information about its subject); "scientific" (discourse designed to present with impeccable precision the findings of empirical inquiry); and "exploratory" (discourse designed to exhibit efforts to work through a problem). Discourse in which the writer is perceived to focus upon disclosing his or her feelings or opinions (or those of a group) is designated "expressive"; Kinneavy has an elaborate structure of criteria, derived from existential philosophy, for judging such discourse. Discourse in which the writer is perceived to focus attention upon the audience—upon shaping the thoughts and feelings of that audience—is designated "persuasive." Still a fourth category of discourse operates without focus on one of these three apexes and depends for its distinctive qualities upon a network of internal relationships among language, sound, *personae,* characters, and so on: this is "literary" discourse. Kinneavy and his followers, in effect, propose that this taxonomy, based upon the identification of a writer's "aims," guide not only research into the characteristics of discourse but also designs for teaching the composing of discourse.

Now of course the impulse to group instances of discourse into classes responds, understandably enough, to our desire to gain some kind of control over the vast multitudinousness of the universe of discourse; human beings need to categorize and organize phenomena in order to discuss them. There may even be procedural advantages in such categorization for those who want to conduct research on the workings of discourse; we can't yet tell, because few researchers have carried such research very far or made significant use of schemes of categorization. Furthermore, every effort at constructing a taxonomy enjoys some surface plausibility. The "modes," as Frank D'Angelo observed in *A Conceptual Theory of Rhetoric,* arise from the recognition that writers do indeed sometimes describe, they do sometimes narrate, they do sometimes explain, and they do sometimes hope to persuade—and that when undertaking these purposes discourse may have some distinctive features.[7] D'Angelo went on to argue that the standard patterns identified in much discourse—defining, classifying, comparing, and so on—originate from classical *topoi* (procedures for generating or arranging data for use in discourse) and reflect essential ways in which the human mind works. One can argue, further, that some discourse is indeed made up largely of details recorded from sensory observation, that some discourse (philosophic reflection, for instance) may contain mostly nonsensory exploration, that some discourse seems to reveal the writer's wish for a closer relationship with the reader than other discourse (if the metaphor of "relationship" is at all useful), that some discourse does seek to record procedures and facts so that others can follow the procedures and confirm the facts, and so on. That is, one can acknowledge that almost any of the principles for classifying discourse offered to us these last two centuries arises from honest analysis of what writers (and speakers) do, though of course the same writing may contain several or all of the features that are alleged to identify positively members of different classes of writing in the same scheme. More on this point later.

The limitations in these categories of discourse do not emerge, then, from theorists' derivations of the categories. Rather, they emerge from the inferences and conclusions drawn from those origins: that a finished piece of discourse can be classified into a box on a taxonomic chart; that in so classifying, a theorist has made a useful statement about that piece of discourse; and—even more significant—that one can employ these categories to erect a structure for teaching others to produce discourse. The categories are often presented in the professional literature, not to mention in teaching texts, as if, rather than being classes derived in order to facilitate inquiries about rhetoric, they had some objective existence—and some control over the behavior of writers—that makes them individually worth attention. Many scholars, and many teachers, using these systems of classification, rarely ask whether in our experience of a work we perceive that work as belonging to a particular classification. Instead, they present individual works as examples of a class of works, rather than distinctive wholes that demand distinctive responses and invite detailed, rounded examination. And teaching texts tend to present opportunities for composing as occasions for the writer to try to match in his or her own work the properties of the members of a class, rather than as occasions for responding to a specific rhetorical situation. One needs, therefore, to look critically at the proposed taxonomies of discourse in order to recognize their theoretical and practical limitations, even while taking account of their attractions.

Since the four forms, or "modes," of discourse are alive and well in many texts and many syllabi, consider James Britton's comment on this taxonomy in *The Development of Writing Abilities (11–18)*.

It is the taxonomy [of the four forms] itself that reveals the basic weakness. The categories, supposedly based on the purpose or intention of a given piece of writing, are seen only in terms of the intended effect upon an audience. Yet narrative can scarcely be seen as an intention in the same sense as persuasion or exposition might be. We can perceive widely varying intentions in different narratives such as a fictional story, a factual report of events, a scientific account of a sequence of events, . . . and a narrative contained within an advertisement. . . .

. . . More generally it can be said that the four categories are not equal in status. If it is the intention of a given discourse to persuade or to explain, then on this criterion the narrative and descriptive categories can be conflated with the other two. IT is no difficult matter to find narrative or descriptive writing which has as its dominant function calculated persuasion or highly didactic explanation. [8]

How one organizes a rhetorical theory, a curriculum, or a teaching text around categories that exhibit such conceptual shortcomings is hard to explain.

Conceptual problems limit the usefulness of other categorizations, too. It is possible, for example, to say that some discourse records more of the writer's individual feelings and perceptions than other discourse. But almost every piece of discourse records the writer's perceptions and selections from among the data available, and most successful writers are typically credited with the ability to move skillfully among levels of abstraction—to combine data with interpretations of data and generalizations about data (topics, questions, theses, inferences, conclusions). How one erects a workable distinction between "subjective" and "objective" discourse, then, is hard to imagine. Similarly, although some writers at times imply by their language (and by what they say) a preference for a closer, more relaxed social relationship with their readers than they seek at other times (or a closer relationship than some writers seek at any time), the line between discourse one would call "formal" and discourse one would call "informal" is faint and wavy. Tones, stances, and implied relationships with readers change within single pieces of discourse; indeed, one of the powerfully subtle rhetorical strategies available to skilled writers is the ability to signal emphasis through changes in *persona,* stance, and tone of voice. For some discourse, a classification based upon one section might have to be changed after examination of another section.

Even James Kinneavy's classifications, though worked out more subtly and with the support of far wider inspection of theories about rhetoric and discourse than the classifications just glanced at, break down when we try to use them as a framework for organizing our perceptions of the universe of discourse. Kinneavy, of course, admits that his categories leak; he would argue for classifying a piece of discourse on the basis of its "dominant" aim. But all of us, I would think, have experienced pieces of discourse that exhibit many features and achieve several effects that he ascribes to different classes of writing. To take a couple of obvious examples, the Declaration of Independence, which Kinneavy views principally as "expressive" discourse (does not *all* discourse "express" something of a writer's attitudes and outlook?), is surely more than just a revelation of the principles and political assumptions of a people as distilled by the drafters. It is an effort to win the assent (and assistance) of others, and to move the feelings of readers, by explaining the reasons for an action. It assembles factual information about the experiences of a group and the behavior of an adversary, and at the same time it is viewed by some scholars as an archetype of syllogistic reasoning —a form of argument. And how are we to classify a successful piece of satire, like *A Modest Proposal?* The *Proposal* is surely argument—albeit indirect argument—but it is in part a factual report on social and economic conditions. Yet it is equally "expressive," disclosing its author's feelings about the actions of absentee landlords. And at the very same time it is "literary" discourse, depending for its effect upon the internal connections of structure, data, voice, and language. One could argue over where on the communications triangle to place the *Proposal.* But does it matter?

Placing pieces of discourse into boxes on taxonomies, I would argue, fails to respond to a reader's experience of the piece as read. And for those who teach composing, the advantage offered by these taxonomies—the advantage of helping to formulate a neat, convenient curriculum—is an illusory advantage. It is gained at the price of ignoring all that happens within the writer before the piece of discourse is finished, and of making writers think that writing is the production of discourse that meets predetermined, inflexible specifications. That implication probably rings false in any writer's experience and ignores the fact that writers write individual pieces in order to say particular things to readers for specific reasons. Taxonomies as frameworks for teaching, then, threaten to cause the act of composing to seem mechanistic, formulaic, artificial. They may foster composing of the kind of pieces that William Coles in *The Plural I* calls "themewriting," but they do little to help writers understand the act of composing or enlarge their abilities to communicate with readers for specific reasons.

As an alternative to taxonomic views of discourse, one seeks, I think, a more flexible, supple plan for describing discourse—one that would inform its users more reliably than taxonomies do about the distinctive features of a piece and that might, thoughtfully used, act as a paradigm for writers and speakers faced with the need, or desire, to create discourse. Such a plan might identify elements that almost any discourse might exhibit—that is, generalizable elements—but elements whose distinctive forms will vary from example to example. One might seek, in one's descriptive plan, ways of describing the "range of variation" (to borrow a term from Richard Young) in each element; that is, one might seek to define scales or "continua" along which these elements vary from discourse to discourse.

One notable effort to build such a flexible descriptive plan—less well known, I think, than it deserves to be—is that put forth in detail by James Moffett in *Teaching the Universe of Discourse*.[9] Moffett identifies two dimensions along which any discourse can be defined: 1) the distance of writer from reader and the relative familiarity of writer with reader (the closest audience to the writer is the writer himself or herself; the most distant is a large, variegated audience whose members are largely unknown to the writer); 2) the degree to which the materials of discourse are abstracted from immediate experience—what Moffett calls their "abstractive altitude" (the least abstract materials are direct reports of what is happening as it happens; the most abstract utterance is a generalized statement about events that have not yet taken place or ought to be made to take place). Any piece of discourse locates itself somewhere along each dimension; locating the piece on each dimension constitutes an exact, if introductory, description of that piece. Though rudimentary, the technique squares, I think, with our experience of how discourse works, and it can be made (Moffett has made it) into a framework for teaching discourse that squares with writers' perceptions and their cognitive development as human beings.

When James Britton (whose comments on the four "modes" I quoted a few paragraphs earlier) and his colleagues at the University of London sought a model for describing discourse that would facilitate study of the writings of children and adolescents, they adopted and extended Moffett's theories. They retained his assumption that a useful way to describe discourse is to identify the dimensions of writing, the scales or continua, on which one can locate almost any piece of writing. The scales developed by Britton and his colleagues are much more complex than Moffett's scales; they exhibit fine gradations and tight discriminations between points along them. Without giving the details of Britton's system, I will mention here the principal dimensions he cites: the distance and relation between writer and audience (from writing for oneself alone through writing for trusted individuals to writing for an unknown audience of indeterminate size); and the purpose for writing (from immediate "transactional" writing, in which the writer is a participant in an action, through "expressive" writing, which presents the writer's reactions, feelings, preferences, speculations, and so forth, to "poetic" writing, in which the writer contemplaces events almost entirely as a spectator, seeing how the parts fit together). Although the scale from writing as participant to writing as spectator may roughly parallel the scale between transactional and poetic writing, the two scales can be, and often are, set out separately, since each helps clarify the other and the two together may help clarify what is going on in a piece of discourse. Transactional writing, Britton adds (evidently following Moffett), can be scaled from writing that records events directly to writing that offers hypotheses, theories, proposals. Britton's scales, in their detailed intricacy, offered his research staff a plan for the scoring of students' essays that seemed plausible and reliable to the researchers. How well they describe professional writing or adult discourse may await further investigation.

But devising one or two scales is not a self-evidently preferable replacement for building taxonomies of discourse. The points on a single scale can too easily become the boxes in a taxonomy. Moffett's scales have not, so far as I know, suffered that fate, but Britton's scales have, possibly because his theoretical scales are better known as such than Moffett's. It is all too easy, one finds, to make of "transactional" writing a box within a taxonomy, and even easier (perhaps because the term echoes one offered by Kinneavy) to extend "expressive" writing from a range of points to an enclosed box. The temptation to make "expressive" writing into a category increases when one wants, as Britton does, to see teachers and schools encourage and elicit writing that has many of the features Britton associates with "expressive" writing. Accordingly, one hears from Britton's followers the assertion that "expressive" writing is an identifiable kind of writing, even if they acknowledge that some features of expressive writing might also characterize the "poetic." We need, perhaps, an analytical framework that might describe—and encourage users to describe—several dimensions and forms of "expressive" writing rather than using "expressive" as a univocal adjective. Indeed, we need a framework that will enable each of us to *describe* more precisely any example of discourse, regardless of how someone using the taxonomies I have discussed might *classify* it.

Accordingly, I propose that we adopt the approach originated by Moffett and extended by Britton—that of defining dimensions or scales on which discourse can be located—but that we extend that approach to the defining of several different scales on which we can locate discourse, and that we take the approach in a slightly different direction from that followed by Moffett. I suggest that by redirecting and extending the study of dimensions (obviously I use the term metaphorically) of discourse we can locate and define with some precision a rhetorical profile of any piece.

I think I can identify seven dimensions of discourse, each capable of being described as a scale or continuum along which a piece can be located. One dimension might be *the occasion or stimulus for writing*; the scale might run from discourse that is wholly self-generated in response to a need or impulse perceived by the writer to discourse that is produced entirely on the demand of another. A second dimension might be *readers' expectations*; the scale might run from discourse expected by readers who are anxious to receive it to discourse not expected by its readers and actively not wanted by them. A third dimension might be (à la Moffett) *the distance, character, and attitudes of the audience*; the scale might run from the writer as his or her own exclusive, and willing, audience to an audience of unknown size and composition, likely to be displeased by the subject or alienated by the writer's views. A fourth dimension might be *the writer's goal —the reaction or response desired in the readers by the writer*; the scale might run from the audience's accepting and taking note of what is said to the audience's moving immediately to act exactly as the writer advises. A fifth dimension (again à la Moffett) might be *the abstractive altitude of the subject matter*; the scale might run from an immediate record of direct sensory experience to inferential statements about events that might or ought to occur at a later time. A sixth dimension might be *the density of detail required*; the scale might run from discourse in which few or no data are required in order for the reader to grasp the piece, to discourse in which there must be a dense presentation of data in order for readers to understand the piece. A seventh dimension might be *the extent to which the individual writer's idiosyncratic perceptions, comments, and feelings permeate, or can permeate, the discourse*; the scale might run from discourse made up entirely of the individual writer's uncorroborated observations, opinions, and feelings to discourse made up entirely of verifiable facts and empirically confirmable generalizations. My list is not necessarily exhaustive; others might suggest additional dimensions, and the same or other readers might suggest removal of one or more of my seven dimensions from the list. Regard the list, if you will, as a list in process. That is what it is.

If one were to locate a piece of discourse, or the demands of a piece of discourse in preparation, on each of these scales or continua, one might have a description of the piece that one could use in research, not to mention a description that might guide composing. One would have, that is, a "rhetorical plot," or a rhetorical "profile" of the piece that exists or the one that is to come into being. For analysts and students, the profile would permit further investigation into the strategies and workings of the completed piece; writers beginning the work of composing would have a definition of the problems they faced. (I think that the kind of description suggested here would be consistent with the findings of Linda Flower and John Hayes that the more successful writers have good, complete definitions of the problems they must solve in composing.)[10] One might want to recognize, of course, that discourse is fluid; in the course of developing, a piece might—in the perceptions of its reader or its writer—shift its position on one or more of the scales. Discourse most probably does not remain, throughout its length or the process of its composition, frozen in a single profile on all dimensions.

This proposed construction of a rhetorical "plot" or "profile" for existing discourse and discourse-to-be does not simplify the task of discussing examples of discourse, nor does it simplify the task of composing or teaching composing. But it can give much clearer direction to both analysis and creation than the more rigid taxonomies give. It can give analysts guidance in interpreting the discourse they read, and it can give composers guidance in sizing up what is required in the writing that, now and in the future, they will have to do. It can assist scholars in building a more adequate pedagogical rhetoric—one organized around ways of responding to circumstances with varied rhetorical profiles rather than around making pieces of discourse conform to the supposed characteristics of uninformative classifications of discourse.

Our forbears in the study of rhetoric were teachers; they classified discourse in order to help them teach rhetoric, in order to help them lead their pupils to understand how to make discourse. Whether or not their impulse to classify and create taxonomies can fairly be said to have "influenced" us, we seem to have carried out the same impulses in our rhetorical theories these past two or three centures. The impulses are active, even decisive, in much of what we read today about rhetoric, in descriptions of theoretical frameworks and in teaching texts. I suggest that we now need, not necessarily to lay aside, but to get beyond, the impulse (possibly inherited from our ancient predecessors) to create enclosed boxes—boxes with labels for rhetorical categories—that can be assembled into taxonomic frameworks. Older theorists left us much to think about in their discussions of rhetoric. Using the scales I have suggested in order to describe the dimensions of a text or a rhetorical task might assist us in getting beyond where they took us; that is, using this multidimensional plan for describing a rhetorical situation might help theorists advance their analyses of finished texts. It might also help composers (of any age) to define more clearly each task that faces them as practicing rhetoricians, so that, having defined a problem well, they can hope to solve that problem effectively.

16
Why Write?
A Reconsideration
Richard Young and Patricia Sullivan

Why write? Why not speak instead? Plato gave answers to both questions in the *Phaedrus*: "We shouldn't," to the first; "We should," to the second—at least when we are concerned, as philosophers and rhetoricians, with original thought and getting at the truth. In a discussion between the Egyptian king and the god Theuth, writing is attacked for two reasons. First, it weakens the memory. The fact is, the king argues, that "this invention will produce forgetfulness in the minds of those who learn to use it, because they will not practice their memory. Their trust in writing, produced by external characters which are no part of themselves, will discourage the use of their own memory within them." In writing, he says, "You have invented an elixir not of memory, but of reminding." Linked with this criticism is a second charge: if we embrace writing as a vehicle for philosophic thought, we abandon dialectic, an oral art, which was for Plato the only reliable means for discovering truth. Those who rely on writing as their source of knowledge, the king says, will be widely read without the benefit of a teacher's instruction "and will therefore seem to know many things, when they are for the most part ignorant and hard to get along with, since they are not wise, but only appear wise."[1] That Plato put these arguments in the mouth of an imaginary king suggests he may have had equivocal feelings about the new invention. Though Plato wrote, he may well have believed he lost something by doing so.

For different reasons, the questions (i.e., Why write? and Why not speak instead?) are being asked again. In an electronic age, it has been argued, writing is becoming in many ways a dispensable art.[2] Radio and television are replacing newspapers and books; the telephone is replacing letters; interactive cable programming may replace theaters and live performances; voice-activated computers may well replace writing by hand or typewriter, and so forth. More efficient and perhaps more effective inventions for recording and transmitting information are becoming available almost daily.

The arguments for the continuing value of the written word have been numerous and varied.[3] Some are institutional—records must be kept, data preserved. Some are vocational—writing skill makes one more employable. Some focus on special features of written discourse—it decreases redundancy and increases precision, and it enables the reader to ponder and refer back to the discourse repeatedly. Most of the arguments in the "Why write?" controversy focus attention on the value of the completed text. Though their implications are formidable for education and society as a whole, as formulated they are not particularly interesting to the rhetorical theorist. For they do not address the question in a way that raises fundamental issues, as, for example, Plato did.

But if the focus of attention is shifted away from the text to the activity of writing—a shift that characterizes much of the recent work in the discipline of rhetoric—more interesting arguments emerge. Take, as examples, the insistence of Gordon Rohman, Ira Progoff, and others that the activity of writing is a powerful means to self-realization;[4] James Britton's view that writing is a means for developing important intellectual abilities, including the ability to speak effectively;[5] and David Olson's argument that the experience of writing makes us not only more perceptive readers but more willing to challenge the authority of the written word.[6] What these arguments share is the idea that writing enables us to think in ways that are otherwise improbable, or difficult, or even impossible. The idea is most elaborately and elegantly developed in Walter Ong's work; for example, in *Rhetoric, Romance, and Technology*, he argues that

> human thought structures are tied in with verbalization and must fit available media of communication: there is no way for persons with no experience of writing to put their minds through the continuous linear sequence of thought such as goes, for example, into an encyclopedia article. . . . Until writing, most kinds of thoughts we are used to thinking today simply could not be thought.[7]

In Ong's statement we find still another answer to why we write: one important reason we write is to enable outselves to engage in a kind of thinking that would otherwise be beyond us, that is, extended thinking in which ideas are linked by complex logical and linguistic connections.

However—as often happens when looking for fundamental answers to fundamental questions—this answer raises new questions. The most importunate of these is why it is that without writing human beings are barred from an extremely valuable kind of thinking. The answer we want to propose here leads us once again to a consideration of the relation of writing and memory. What are the links between writing and memory? Does writing impede (as the Egyptian king argued) or extend (as Ong and others argue) the possibilities for thinking?

Let us consider the links between writing and memory, first, by means of a short digression. Compare the following multiplication problems:

$$
\begin{array}{cccc}
6 & 68 & 96 & 6723 \\
\times\, 7 & \times\, 7 & \times\, 87 & \times\quad 376 \\
\hline
\end{array}
$$

How do these tasks differ? We can supply the first answer "off the tops of our heads" since we have memorized multiplication tables up through 10 or 12. We probably can work the second problem in our heads; but it requires a bit of time and concentration. However, unless we have had special training in mathematical problem-solving, we cannot work the third and fourth problems without the aid of pencil and paper.

Why is this so? None of the problems are, after all, very difficult. Even the last problem is only grade-school arithmetic. A plausible answer to this question can be found in psychological studies of short-term memory. By "short-term memory" we mean the part of the memory system that retains information without rehearsal for only a brief period of time, the part that can usefully be called "working memory" because it holds only the knowledge currently being used.[8] Long-term memory, by contrast, is the relatively permanent store in the memory system. While psychologists propose differing conceptions of human memory, they generally agree that short-term memory is the major bottleneck in human thinking processes, for it can hold only a few units of information at any one time and loses the information it is working with unless that information is rehearsed. The number and size of those units is debated. George Miller, in a seminal article "The Magical Number Seven, Plus or Minus Two: Some Limits on Our Capacity for Information Processing," argues for a capacity that ranges from five to nine units.[9] Thus, in carrying out an intellectual task—for example, remembering lists of words, summarizing a text, forming judgments, reasoning logically—we can juggle in our minds at a particular moment only seven units of information, plus or minus two. If carrying out the task requires that we work with more units of information than our short-term memories can reasonably accommodate, then we need to use some sort of aid to memory, like an abacus or pencil and paper.

It is possible to extend the capacity of our short-term memory somewhat by grouping several uncomplicated units of information into fewer but more complicated units; although the number of units we can juggle remains limited, the amount of information we can process is increased. When information we are working with is familiar or becomes more familiar as we work with it, we tend to develop larger categories to handle it so that we can use our minds more efficiently. This phenomenon has been repeatedly demonstrated in a variety of ways in psychological studies. For example, we can remember more letters organized into words than we can letters in unrelated strings, and also more letters in familiar letter strings than in unrelated letter strings. Take the following lists as an example; both contain the same letters, but the second is much easier to remember because those letters are initials that are familiar to us: 1) FBC IIB RCB MIA MAW; 2) FBI CIA IBM RCA BMW.[10] And we have good reason to believe that the generalization extends to language units larger than the word. For example, Herbert Simon extends to the phrase the argument that meaningful grouping of material increases our total capacity to remember.[11] He observes that memory for a list of isolated words differs from the memory for those same words grouped into meaningful phrases. Take the words: Lincoln, milky, criminal, differential, address, way, lawyer, calculus, Gettysburg. So arranged, the list is difficult to remember. But rearrange them to read—Lincoln's Gettysburg Address, Milky Way, criminal lawyer, and differential calculus—and they become more memorable. As the rearranged letters and phrases suggest, familiarity with both meaning and organization of the information can affect our memory of it. While the limits of short-term memory can be demonstrated at the various levels of language—the letter, the syllable, the word, the phrase, the clause, and so on—our familiarity with particular language structures helps us remember more than we would expect to remember given the small number of units Miller postulated.

Consider again the multiplication problems posed earlier. The first multiplication problem ($7 \times 6 = 42$) is for most of us not a problem at all since we memorized the answer years ago. The second problem (68×7) requires that we perform several steps, each step adding a new unit of information.[12] In this problem, it is highly unlikely that we have performed this particular computation often enough to have memorized the answer, so we probably have to use six or so units to perform the steps in the multiplication (depending on the algorithm used in the computation). But we have not crossed the threshold where pencil and paper become necessary. We do cross the threshold when solving the remaining two problems; one can confirm this by actually working the problems and noting how many separate numbers we must attend to (and how many steps we must perform) before we arrive at a solution. There are, however, people who can perform complex mathematical operations in their heads by using one or another system that reduces the strain on short-term memory.[13] Some lightning calculators, for example, have a mnemonic system that stores the partial products of multiplications in number-associated words and then retrieves the words for final summing. These people have found a way to organize the information into larger units, but they have not escaped the fundamental limits of short-term memory. Even lightning calculators would find complex problems in trigonometry or calculus beyond the scope of their mnemonics.

This digression into memory research in psychology suggests several points that seem relevant to the activity of writing. First, simple mental tasks can be carried out without the aid of pencil and paper, "simple" here being defined in terms of the number of separate units of information we must hold in our short-term memory while performing the task. Second, when mental tasks become sufficiently complex, that is, when they require that we hold more than seven or so separate units in our minds at one time, we must use some sort of memory aid. Third, the mind has a strategy for aiding memory, for as material becomes more familiar, we tend to organize this material, making the size of familiar units larger than the size of unfamiliar units. Fourth, and for our purposes most important, without aids to memory there are mental acts we cannot perform, thoughts we cannot think, inquiries we cannot engage in.

These are reasonable points to make about math problems, where the task is to apply an algorithm to a set of numbers. As we have seen, they apply, at least to some extent, to understanding and remembering prose as well. But some might argue that the psychological principles we have noted do not capture the complexity of composing text. Hence, we must consider whether this work on the limits of our information processing ability helps us better understand the production of discourse and the relationship between the activity of speaking and writing.

What reasons do we have to believe that similar memory limits exist in thinking and composing with natural language? There is no system for rating how various kinds of thinking and composing in language tax short-term memory. But we do recognize that some tasks are simpler than others and that some types of discourse are easier to produce than other types.

As an example of language use—and thinking—that does not tax short-term memory, consider the following passage from Dostoyevsky's *Diary of a Writer*. It is a conversation of a group of drunks consisting entirely of one unprintable word.

> One Sunday night I happened to walk for some fifteen paces next to a group of six drunken young workmen, and I suddenly realized that all thoughts, feelings and even a whole chain of reasoning could be expressed by that one noun, which is moreover extremely short. One young fellow said it harshly and forcefully, to express his utter contempt for whatever it was they had been talking about. Another answered with the same noun but in a quite different tone and sense—doubting that the negative attitude of the first was warranted. A third suddenly became incensed against the first and roughly intruded on the conversation, excitedly shouting the same noun, this time as a curse and obscenity.[14]

And so on, until each one of the six had spoken his very brief piece. The conversation of the drunks is, admittedly, an extreme example, but it serves to mark one end of a rough spectrum of thinking and composing tasks, a spectrum we would like to consider for the next few pages.

Dostoyevsky's narration of the incident, which included the drunken utterances, is obviously more complex and difficult to produce than the utterances themselves, but it too could have been produced without the aid of pencil and paper. A piece of writing such as his brief account displays organizing strategies that are closely connected with informal oral tale-telling: a scene to be reconstructed, a number of characters with simple lines, and a listing of their interaction—from character one to character six—with the narrator interjecting comments about the situation. In composing simple narratives of this sort, we can locate and recall the appropriate events in our long-term memory without straining our working memory at all. (The recollection is analogous in some ways to our recall of math tables.)[15]

However, composing original, complex, and orderly discourse that is not narrative and that is much more extensive than Dostoyevsky's brief account is also possible without the aid of pencil and paper. Charlotte Linde and William Labov, for example, asked approximately a hundred New York apartment dwellers to give impromptu descriptions of their apartments so that a listener would understand where everything was.[16] The task required them to think on the spot; they were not recalling something they had heard or said before, though they were very familiar with the subject. Interestingly enough, while various strategies were used for organizing the details of the descriptions, nearly everyone carried out the task in a similar way; they constructed a verbal tour of the apartment: "You walked in the front door. There was a narrow hallway. To the left, the first door you came to was a tiny bedroom. . . ."[17]

Such lengthy descriptions appear to be inconsistent with the argument we have been developing; but several things should be noted before jumping to that conclusion. First, all the people giving the descriptions had detailed, long-term memories of the layout of their apartments. Second, a step-by-step movement through the apartment (for example, front to back) gave them a simple strategy not only for relating the parts but for reducing the number of parts they had to hold in their minds, since once a step was completed it no longer need be attended to. Finally, by grouping details by location (for example, room-by-room), they could reduce the complexity of the task.[18] This tour strategy produces a chain-like structure for the discourse. It is similar to an ancient strategy for organizing long narratives, in which the singers, as Albert Lord has demonstrated, memorize chunks of discourse that they then string together into an extended tale. Auerbach regards this method of paratactic organization, which is found frequently in early Western literature, to be a fundamentally oral structure.[19]

The apartment descriptions might be thought of as an intermediate stage in our spectrum—a stage where famliarity with the material and a strong set of organizational conventions help reduce the strain on short-term memory. Another illustration of this stage can be found in John Gould's research on speaking, dictating, and writing at IBM's Thomas J. Watson Research Center.[20] In several studies in which people were asked to speak, dictate, and write short messages (one-page letters and essays, summaries of daily events) no significant differences in quality were apparent as a result of changing from one mode of production to another. Nor was there any significant difference between the quality of those works and the quality of text produced by so-called "invisible writing," that is, writing done with a wooden stylus on carbon paper, a procedure which produces a permanent text but prevents the writer from viewing what has been written.

How are these results to be explained? If short-term memory does place limits on the amount of complexity a writer can handle while composing, then there ought to be some evidence that Gould's tasks did not push writers beyond the limits of their memories. Comments by

Gould suggest that this was the case. For example, his remark that "in these fairly routine letters, participants seemed to produce a series of 'units,' e.g., inside address, return address, salutation, introductory sentence, successive required information items, and closing. Each 'unit,' once completed, was generally left intact [i.e., no major revisions were made in a written or spoken unit once it was produced]. In this sense their style on these formal letters resembled a chaining of loosely related events that often occurs in the informal personal letter."[21] This method of completing one relatively small part of a conventional form before moving on to the next reduces the strain on short-term memory, as does the general familiarity with the form. If our argument is sound, we can explain both results—Linde and Labov's and Gould's—by saying that the intellectual tasks could be managed in ways that did not put excessive strain on short-term memory.

It is easy to imagine that these tasks could be spoken as easily as they could be written: they seem to be normal, almost routine kinds of thinking and communication. But what happens when we engage in a kind of thinking that is still more sophisticated, when we must hold in our minds many units of information and their relationships, as we must when we are creating, say, a sonnet or a philosophical argument? We look for a pencil and paper. We simply cannot engage in such inquiries in our heads or talk them through out loud. If we try to do so, we find ourselves getting muddled and saying things like "Now where was I?" and "What was I going to say next?" We exceed the capacity of short-term memory. What is at issue here is not the number of units of information one can isolate in a completed discourse or the length of the discourse, but the number of units and their relationships that must be juggled at any moment as we shape the poem or argument.

The real test of the importance of writing to thinking comes with thinking that strains short-term memory so much that some sort of prompt is required if we are to carry out the task successfully. With such thinking we need reminders of where we are and have been, a kind of supplementary working memory. It is this kind of thinking or writing —one is not sure which—that Carl Bereiter calls "epistemic writing."[22] In reporting on a series of experiments carried out at the London Institute of Education, James Britton has described a spectrum of thinking and composing tasks similar to the one we have been exploring.

> On one occasion, four members of . . . [the] research team tried writing with worn-out ball-point pens. We couldn't, therefore, see what we had written, but we used carbon paper so that what we wrote could be read

later. We were acutely uncomfortable. When we wrote letters to an absent member of the team about what we were doing, and when we reported recent experiences in a straight-forward narrative, we were able to complete the task with only a few blunders; but when we tried to formulate theoretical principles, even on a topic very familiar to us all, and when we tried to write poems, we were defeated. We just could not hold the thread of an argument or the shape of a poem in our minds, because scanning back was impossible. As we expected, the carbon copies showed many inconsistencies and logical and synctactical discontinuities. They were, in fact, useless.[23]

In some of the tasks Britton describes (formulating theoretical principles, creating a poem), writing and thinking appear to be inseparable. The tasks require the creation of discourse that is both linguistically and conceptually original; when carrying out the tasks, one cannot write down what is already known, nor is it sufficient simply to let the words come without reference to the complexities of the linguistic structure being shaped. As one veers into the unfamiliar, the shaping that goes on at the point of utterance (to borrow Britton's apt phrase) necessarily entails a great deal of trial and error activity with relatively small units of information and frequent reflexive reference to what has aleady been shaped. In such tasks, writing serves, in Vygotsky's words, as an "extracortical organization of complex mental functions."[24]

Our discussion suggests several observations. First, if we can use chronological time as the structural principle in composing, there is little strain on memory: we simply conjure up the events in order of occurrence. Second, if we can group information in a composing task into units that we can then string together according to some simple ordering principle, we can reduce the strain on short-term memory. Third, if the units to be used themselves have conventionally prescribed components, this also helps us manage short-term memory. But, fourth, if the task asks for the analytic/synthetic thinking necessary to invent theoretical principles or the linguistic and conceptual originality now prized in poetry, pencil and paper appear necessary.

A consideration of the relationship between writing and memory draws us quickly into questions about the activity of composing and the art of composing—questions that can only be answered by careful research. For example, does an understanding of this relationship help us explain variations in composing performance from task-to-task or person-to-person? More specifically, is the ability to manage memory efficiently and effectively during the act of composing likely to increase the writer's success in composing? If so, is a writer's ability to manage memory during the composing process best explained by individual differences (like talent, or experience, or training)? Or by the nature of the genre being produced? Or by the strategies the writer uses to find ideas, shape them into a text, and revise them? (These possibilities are not, of course, mutually exclusive.) Generally speaking, it would be useful to know how much can be explained by natural differences among minds, by formal training, by the kind of product being created, and by the writing process used.

As we saw earlier, there is a strong relationship between what happens during composing and the kind of discourse being composed. Some kinds of discourse, for example, appear to tax short-term memory more than others, although at the present time it is difficult to be more precise as to how and why. If indeed writing an argument taxes memory more than writing a narrative does, what features of argument contribute to this heightened difficulty? This line of inquiry, that is, the relation of composing to the genre being composed, also has implications for class-room instruction (as do all the others mentioned). For example, if, as some have argued,[25] novice writers tend to focus on relatively small units of thought and discourse during composing, with a resultant strain on short-term memory, then genres that place little strain on short-term memory would seem more appropriate assignments in the earlier stages of education. Assuming the relationship between discourse type and ease of composing to be anywhere near as strong as it appears to be, we must be disturbed that genre study has received relatively little attention in rheto-rical research.

We also know little about how mode of production affects thinking and writing. Gould's experiments with taping, dictating, and writing are interesting, but they barely scratch the surface. Carl Klaus raised this issue some years ago by way of an illustration of how limited the English teacher's knowledge is about writing and the teaching of writing. When Klaus asked how the mechanical implements used in writing (such as pen, pencil, or typewriter) affect the process of writing, he found alterna-tive positions that lead to contrary teaching practices, but he could not find conclusive support for one position or the other. One position as-sumes that mechanical implements impede "the flow of words" and, therefore, that teachers should have students dictate their compositions. But dictation can sound like talking rather than writing if the message has not been previously thought through. The alternative position as-sumes that the implements constitute "an external storage device which supplements the writer's limited short-term memory." This second position contends that pen and paper "enable a writer to control the chaotic flow of language as it arises in the mind," and thus suggests that dictation may have subversive effects in classroom instruction.[26] Our lack of information about the effects of even such basic modes of production is particularly distressing, since we are entering an era when the word processor and computer are introducing new capacities and complexities into the composing process.

Since our intent here in raising such questions in this essay is only to suggest the richness of this unploughed field, we will limit ourselves to one more line of inquiry for research. The relationship between memory and the activity of writing suggests the possibility of a modern art of memory, roughly analogous to the classical art but focusing on the interaction of writing and memory at the point of utterance. (The classical art, by contrast, was an art of recollecting what had already been produced.) A modern art of memory might provide explicit strategies for increasing the power of short-term memory and for accessing long-term memory more effectively. But a "modern art of memory" might be only another name for an art of invention approached from a new and interesting direction. English teachers tend to regard invention as primarily a process of retrieving what is already known, that is, an art for accessing information stored in long-term memory (or in libraries, which serve as ancillary memories). We are less likely to see the relationship of invention to working memory, where it can offer strategies for combining smaller units of thought and discourse into larger units (for example, extended definition, categorization, comparison and contrast) and strategies for suppressing stereotypic responses to the issue at hand that are stored in long-term memory (for example, a strategy that requires us to take multiple perspectives on the issue).

Why write? One important reason is that unless we do there are mental acts we cannot perform, thoughts we cannot think, inquiries we cannot engage in. Why is this so? Because of limits on the capacity of our memory. Our argument in this essay moves us beyond Plato's notion of writing as an invention (and a questionable one at that) for recording the results of a living intelligence. As we consider the implications of this argument, new questions arise that provoke inquiry. And we find ourselves in a new arena for research.

17

The Ideal Orator and Literary Critic as Technical Communicators: An Emerging Revolution in English Departments

Merrill D. Whitburn

The needs of society have often stimulated an interest in rhetoric.[1] In ancient Greece, the establishment of democracy, especially democratic lawcourts with large juries, helped make rhetoric the heart of education. In medieval Italy, the considerable demand for excellence in diplomatic and legal correspondence promoted the rhetorical art of letter-writing. In the neoclassical period, opportunities for speech in the pulpits of France and before the parliament of Britain led to important rhetorical contributions.[2] Now, in our own times, the information revolution could well move rhetoric to the heart of education again.

Over fifty percent of the nation's work force is now concerned primarily with managing the flow of information.[3] Three kinds of tasks are assuming primary importance: acquiring information, making it usable for a specific audience, and transmitting it. Business, industry, and government are desperately searching for ways to improve the performance of such tasks. Among their approaches, these institutions are cooperating with education to support library science, computer science, and telecommunications toward the end of improving our methods of carrying out the first and third tasks, acquiring and transmitting information. For historical reasons, however, these institutions have cooperated very little with education to support the profession, variously called technical communication or professional rhetoric, designed to improve our methods of carrying out the second task, making information usable for a specific audience. Consequently, the need for education and research in technical communication or professional rhetoric has reached a critical stage.

A single example can suggest the dimensions of the crisis. A team of seven of us from Rensselaer Polytechnic Institute recently completed a survey of empirical research in graphics in this century. We were staggered by the amounts of time and money that were devoted to efforts like measuring reactions to kinds of typefaces as a means of making universal legibility recommendations. Most of the research was caught on the horns of a dilemma. If a simple enough communication situation were contrived for the methodology to be valid, the results were not applicable to actual communication situations. If, on the other hand, the research engaged an actual communication situation, the methodology proved inadequate. Furthermore, because concrete communication situations—with their varying subjects, media, audiences, and creators—differed so substantially from one another, it proved impossible to generalize results. Lastly, in not one instance did the research do anything other than confirm what was already known by the unaided reason. It is becoming increasingly clear that too many men and women participating in the information revolution are suffering from a failure of nerve. They seem incapable of making any decision without running some kind of empirical research to confirm it. The fruitlessness of so much of this research raises serious questions about the negative impact of misapplied empirical research on productivity. The waste in money and human energy has been extraordinary.

As this example demonstrates, the profession of technical communication or professional rhetoric faces critical methodological and theoretical problems. In this article, I intend to show that the beginnings of a model for addressing these problems can be found in classical rhetorical theory; I use Quintilian as my example because of his recognition that only the broadest range of approaches will be successful in addressing rhetorical problems and because of his belief that education is instrumental in developing these approaches. Unfortunately, at least in the field of technical communication, this model was abandoned after a split between the sciences and the humanities, originating in the rise of science in the late seventeenth century and the triumph of romanticism in the late eighteenth century. This split promoted a specialization that left technical communication largely to the proponents of scientific method. As a result, as I shall show in exploring an example of current practice, the use of content outlines in industrial writing, these proponents have made the mistake of favoring the use of those approaches that they believe have proved most fruitful in science. I conclude by suggesting how modern literary theory, with its breadth reminiscent of Quintilian, can improve our approaches to technical communication and why English departments should increase their participation in the information revolution. The reaffirmation of human capability, of human judgment, in solving the problems of communication is an underlying manifesto throughout the article.

Quintilian's Ideal Orator

The beginnings of a model for addressing our current problems in technical communication can be found in classical antiquity in the work of Quintilian. In his *Institutio Oratoria,* Quintilian describes the ideal orator as "a good man, skilled in speaking."[4] The ideal orator's virtue and eloquence result from a combination of natural gifts and education: "Since then the orator is a good man, and such goodness cannot be conceived as existing apart from virtue, virtue, despite the fact that it is in part derived from certain natural impulses, will require to be perfected by instruction. The orator must above all things devote his attention to the formulation of moral character and must acquire a complete knowledge of all that is just and honorable. For without this knowledge no one can be either a good man or skilled in speaking" (p. 125). For Quintilian, the ideal orator embodies the best values of his culture.

The knowledge of the orator should extend to everything worth knowing: "It is no hack-advocate, no hireling pleader . . . that I am seeking to form, but rather a man who to extraordinary natural gifts has added a thorough mastery of all the fairest branches of knowledge." (p. 121). One of these branches is philosophy; another, history; yet another, statesmanship. As Quintilian describes the requisite knowledge of the orator, we come to understand that nothing but the broadest education will suffice. Quintilian stresses, however, that the orator's knowledge must be not only broad, but deep. To avoid being merely a mouthpiece, Quintilian's orator must acquire a detailed knowledge of a subject before he can become an advisor or advocate in a particular case.

Quintilian's ideal orator, then, is no specialist; all knowledge is his province. And this knowledge should be put to use: "I desire that he, whose character I am seeking to mould, should be a 'wise man' in the Roman sense, that is, one who reveals himself as a true statesman, not in the discussions of the study, but in the actual practice and experience of life" (p. 126). Quintilian regrets the existing division between philosophy and statesmanship, between contemplation and action, and wishes that the philosopher and orator were one: "But inasmuch as the study of philosophy has been deserted by those who have turned to the pursuit of eloquence, and since philosophy no longer moves in its true sphere of action and in the broad daylight of the forum, . . . all that is essential for an orator, and yet is not taught by the professors of eloquence, must undoubtedly be sought from those persons in whose possession it has remained. . . . But how much greater and fairer would such subjects appear if those who taught them were also those who could give them most eloquent expression!" (p. 126). The ideal orator accumulates the wisdom of his age and applies it to human affairs. He bridges theory and practice.[5]

Although many theories of rhetoric flourished in classical antiquity, Quintilian's ideal orator represents the broad tradition of rhetorical excellence. That tradition disappeared in the Middle Ages only to reappear in the person of the Renaissance humanist. The humanists were bound by a faith in the universality of humanity and a desire to explore that universality together through a republic of letters. Humans, the nodal points of all creation, could ascend to the spiritual, to order and peace, or fall to the animal, to chaos and disorder. The road to the former was paved with absolutes. Absolutes existed not just because they were in the Bible but also because they were recognized by the collective wisdom of mankind. To discover this collective wisdom, humanists studied the letters of Greece and Rome. The broad aim of learning was virtue, and the practical aim was the active Christian life, especially public life. The last great exemplar of Renaissance humanism, John Milton, emphasized the necessity of testing our virtue, of uniting contemplation and action: "I cannot praise a fugitive and cloistered virtue, unexercised and unbreathed, that never sallies out and sees her adversary, but slinks out of the race where that immortal garland is to be run for, not without dust and heat."[6]

The Triumph of Specialization

While Milton was still alive, in the late seventeenth century, the scientific revolution ushered in a trend toward specialization that has continued until the very recent past. The resulting division of labor led men and women to limit the scope of their efforts—the kinds of problems they addressed, the places they looked to solve these problems, and the human faculties they used as resources. To better understand the significance of this shift, I shall explore the complex of ideas that was central to neoclassicism in the late seventeenth and early eighteenth centuries. This complex can then be used as a basis for comparing the ideas that gave rise to science during the same time period and those that comprised romanticism, a reaction to neoclassicism and science in the late eighteenth and early nineteenth centuries.

Alexander Pope's "An Essay on Criticism" contains a remarkable and well-known passage that embodies many of the ideas that were central to neoclassicism in the late seventeenth and early eighteenth centuries. Note the emphasis on tradition.

> First follow Nature, and your judgment frame
> By her just standard, which is still the same:
> Unerring NATURE, still divinely bright,
> One clear, unchang'd and universal light,
> Life, force, and beauty, must to all impart
> At once the source, and end, and test of Art.
> . . . .
> Those RULES of old discover'd, not devis'd,
> Are Nature still, but Nature methodiz'd;
> . . . .
> Learn hence for ancient rules a just esteem;
> To copy nature is to copy them.
>   [68–73, 88–89, 139–40][7]

According to Pope, then, we should focus on what has been uniform or standard down through history. We discover this uniformity by relying on the rules of the ancients. While Pope's vision was more complex than the extremes to which others often took similar sets of ideas—he did, after all, speak elsewhere of a grace beyond the reach of art—his emphasis on tradition was typical of a strong neoclassicism prevalent in his age.

At the heart of that neoclassicism is the assumption that reason is the same in all humanity.[8] The goal of writers is to understand how this uniform reason structures attitudes and activities and to pose the resulting universal as an ethical ideal. Writers grasp this intelligible order only after protracted study and experience of what throughout all time have been the attitudes and activities common to humanity. They reject as without value the original, individual, idiosyncratic, or exceptional— including all abstruse knowledge beyond the grasp of the majority. Change, then, is a negative force, and all changes in attitudes and activities since the earliest humans must have been changes for the worse; history is a story of multiplying error and increasing departure from uniformity and simplicity. In their efforts to move people toward the universal ethical ideal, neoclassical writers used the methods, skills, and crafts of their forebears, those who had a more perfect vision of what is best and most representative in people. A genre was often assumed to have attained its ideal form at birth, and the oldest examples of a genre were the standards of excellence.

While neoclassical ideas were influencing the humanities, a parallel and sometimes overlapping cluster of ideas was exerting force in science.[9] Among these ideas—emerging in various combinations—was a tendency to focus on "what is" or "what was" if it existed as an artifact that could be treated as "what is." Scientists did not explore "what ought to be." Like the neoclassicists, scientists assumed the world to be uniform and ordered, and those explanations of the world were most favored that could be considered universal or general and that could be characterized as simple, intelligible, economical, and harmonious. Scientists also resembled the neoclassicists in their efforts to free themselves from the imperfections, varieties, and distractions of actual experience. Rather than focus on the individual, idiosyncratic, or exceptional, they analyzed phenomena into the abstractions of matter and motion, which enabled the application of mathematics, one of the cornerstones of scientific method.

While the neoclassicists, like the classical rhetoricians and Renaissance humanists, were concerned with human nature, scientists considered the world external to humans primary and real and humans themselves mere effects of this world, creatures whose perceptions were misled by the vagaries of sense and mind and whose conclusions could be dismissed as opinion, illusion, or impressionism. Humans, to the greatest extent possible, were eliminated from the research process, and scientific instrumentation became critical, partially to minimize human error. Given this skepticism about human capability, thinkers rejected the all-inclusive or holistic philosophical systems of Aristotle and the Scholastics as fraught with error, preferring to dissect nature into parts and obtain certain knowledge about these parts. They assumed that the investigation of other aspects of nature would do no more than place such certain knowledge in a larger setting.

The differences between Quintilian and the followers of Galileo and Newton—at least until recent revolutions in scientific thinking—could hardly be more striking. To be sure, the early scientific apologists were interested in rhetoric. As Richard Foster Jones writes of these apologists, "We may say without exaggeration that their program called for stylistic reform as loudly as for reformation in philosophy."[10] The goal was a plain, objective, denotative style. As science progressed, however, its adherents sought to isolate research from questions of virtue; scientific research was supposed to be valueless. This research, furthermore, focused on specialized sectors of nature; scientists did not take all knowledge as their province. Although they assumed that the truths they uncovered would ultimately prove useful in gaining power over nature, they were, as scientists, not interested in putting their knowledge to use in the practical affairs of the state. Like the philosophers whom Quintilian criticized for withdrawing from practical affairs to the porches, gymnasia, and schools, the scientists—called natural philosophers, it should be remembered—kept to their laboratories and emphasized contemplation over action; they were concerned with discovery, a determination of what is, a search for truth much more than with purpose, a determination of what ought to be, a search for the good. Lastly, unlike Quintilian's ideal orator, their province tended not to include particular cases; their primary goal was to uncover general laws. As we shall see, these ideas profoundly affected research and education in English departments in the twentieth century.

Also affecting English departments was a reaction to neoclassicism and science called "romanticism." The various sets of ideas associated with the term "romanticism" so influenced the humanities and diverged so sharply from science that they helped promote the oft-noted two-culture split. In 1759, in "Conjectures on Original Composition," Edward Young attacked the reliance on tradition found in Pope and other neoclassicists and sang the praises of originality.[11] Among the ideas that emerged from the work of Young and others was the belief that poetry did not result from the protracted use of reason to study what had been common to all humanity. On the contrary, only concrete, particular things exist; generalities are abstractions of experience that have no counterpart in reality. Poets explore only what is most certain to them—their own consciousness and experience. They distrust universals and focus on their own individuality, that which most differentiates them from others. Their poetry must capture their natural selves, the free play of their unconsciously evolving personalities, that part of them that is most spontaneous, unpremeditated, untouched by reflection and design, liberated from convention.

The glorification of the natural self is part of the romantic's preference for nature over art, which also manifests itself in a concern for the primitive, landscape, and other natural objects before the structures of civilization. Poets attempt to capture in literature the overflow of their powerful feelings, and when they turn their attention to the external world, they render things as they are modified by their own personalities. They divide the world into concrete and transcendental with ultimate value placed on the latter; they often attempt to grasp the unimaginable or nonrational. For many, poetry has the character of soliloquy; poets themselves are their own audiences. In their noble quest, they might reject or defy social convention, law, or religion; they might step beyond the pale of morality.[12]

Differences between Quintilian and the various adherents of romanticism are also striking, then. To the extent that the romantic poet divides the world into concrete and transcendental, with ultimate value placed on the latter, the highest aspiration of humans will not be the preservation of the values of their culture. Far from embodying cultural ideals, poets are perceived as above social mores. They may even violate them. With poets as their own audiences, rhetoric and eloquence are unfashionable; poetry that has the goal of producing effects on others is disqualified as literature. Since poets focus on what is spontaneous, unpremeditated, untouched by reflection, they reject protracted study designed to make all knowledge their province. Nor do they wish to put their accomplishments to use in the institutions that govern society; the preference for the natural over the structures of civilization is too great. Like Quintilian, however, they do emphasize the importance of the particular.

Not all of the men and women in a historical period shared the ideas that I have described as characteristic of neoclassicism, early science, or romanticism. Indeed, no single individual may have subscribed to all of the ideas I have included in each set. But these ideas were prevalent in their times and had a significant influence on modern rhetoric and research and education in English departments.

The Particular Case: The Content Outline in Industry

As with Quintilian's ideal orator, the ultimate goal of technical communicators is performing well in particular cases. They represent a particular corporation in shaping a particular kind of information about a particular product for particular customers. And while technical communicators may lack the stature of the ideal orator, their prestige is growing rapidly. Writing in information industries, which tends to be called information or communication rather than rhetoric, has increasingly become part of the product instead of support for the product. For instance, computer corporations like IBM have begun to advertise their programming products by highlighting their easy-to-use instructions. Furthermore, as some technical communicators have developed information about programming products, they have changed the products to better meet the needs of users. They have assumed more important roles in product design.[13] Indeed, William L. Benzon predicts that the technical communicator and product designer (programmer) will eventually become one person; the differences between writing and programming will dissolve.[14] Writing in computer industries, then, may increasingly become a process of exploration without an entirely preconceived end.

As writing in computer industries has increased in importance, corporations are conducting extensive research toward the end of improving writing performance. This research has tended to fall into a pattern rooted in the ideas of early science and neoclassicism. One of the most highly regarded practices resulting from research in technical communication can serve as a suggestive example. This practice is to outline the content of a successful manual and use that outline—call it a "content outline"—as a guide to developing similar manuals in the future.

IBM is one of the information industries that use the content outline as an aid to writers. In a publications guideline, "Designing Task-Oriented Libraries for Programming Products," the corporation identifies a set of nine tasks that customers perform in using any of its programming products.[15] These include: "evaluation," "planning," "installation," "resource definition," "customization," "operation," "application programming," "end use," and "program service." The information necessary to carry out each of the nine tasks may become a manual, or sometimes information about related tasks is packaged together.

To assist its writers in developing a manual, the corporation provides a guide to the information necessary to enable customers to complete a task. For instance, in the case of evaluation (which refers to the customer's decision to purchase a program), the corporation provides 1) a list of the subtasks necessary to carry out the task of evaluation, 2) a proposed content outline for evaluation manuals, and 3) outlines of two purportedly successful evaluation manuals that exemplify the content outline. Writers are to use the list and outlines to generate manuals for new programming products. IBM, then, has developed a fairly elaborate writing aid to promote quality in its publications.

In technical communication articles and textbooks, content outlines may be highlighted more than any other aid to writers. An article by

Robert Hays in the first 1982 issue of *Technical Communication* is typical. The article, "Model Outlines Can Make Routine Writing Easier," is placed on a special section, "Organizing Written Material." Hays indicates that two questions concern the professional beginning a writing task: "'How do I plan this writing?' and 'how can I start?'"[16] He recommends content outlines to reduce the planning of reports to a routine, and he includes content outlines for eleven different kinds of reports. The extent to which content outlines are promoted in articles and books about technical communication is a measure of their acceptance and use throughout the field.

The approaches used in the development of content outlines have roots in a range of the ideas characteristic of early science and neoclassicism. When writers focus on past manuals as a source of content outlines, they take artifacts and treat them as "what is." They emphasize the use of reason to discover an intelligible, simple, uniform, harmonious, and economical order by inferring propositions from families of phenomena (manuals) and rendering them general by induction. Rather than focus on the individual, then, they abstract—after protracted study and experience—universals as guides to excellence. Like the neoclassicists obsessed with regress in the world, they turn to older examples as models. Like the scientists concerned with human frailty, they use instruments—content outlines—to extend human capability and limit human error. Lastly, in line with the tendency in early science to study only a part of nature, they focus on only part of the past communication situation (the work) and on only one facet of that part (its organization or content outline).

Most of the research by publication groups in industry tends to be rooted in the same idea. Typically, as is the case with the extremely popular development of readability formulas, communicators analyze some small excellence in a communication situation (a paragraph), derive a formula to test for this excellence in all future discourse (the formula often yielding numbers to proclaim success or failure), and design a computer program to insure that the frailties of human beings are eliminated from the test procedure.[17] Since science has been so profoundly influential in this century, often providing the basis for technological advances, it is not unexpected that publication groups in industry would use scientific approaches to solve their problems with discourse. At least as responsible for the dominance of these approaches, however, are English departments, which have remained aloof from industry and not provided alternatives.

The Fragmented English Department: Content Outlines in Rhetoric and Composition

Although the very early history of English departments reflected a healthy pluralism, the seeds of specialization sown by science were already in evidence. Shortly after the formation of the Modern Language Association, James Morgan Hart, in 1884–85, called on English to focus on literature and dispense with logic: "No disciplined mind of the present day can look upon logic and literature as having anything in common."[18] In 1886, James M. Garnet urged that rhetoric also be abandoned: "I am almost inclined to agree . . . that it should be excluded from the course of literature. . . . Any extensive study of Rhetoric in college seems to me productive of very little fruit."[19] As literature increasingly became the focus of English departments and other interests were frustrated, however, a wide range of innovators who believed that promoting the understanding of literary texts was not the only way that English could help human beings called for new academic units. To mention just two examples, in 1904 Joseph Pulitzer presented the first public argument for a College of Journalism.[20] In 1914 Charles H. Woolbert made his powerful argument that speech should secede from English.[21]

The result has been excessive specialization, fragmentation into smaller and smaller groups that have more reason to seek a common ground than to build isolated compartments. When people survey the scattered fragments of reading, business communication, rhetoric, literature, technical communication, speech, mass communication (radio and television), journalism, and composition, they might well remember John Donne's words: " 'Tis all in pieces, all coherence gone:/All just supply, and Relation."[22] Even within English departments, such groups as business communication, technical communication, and rhetoric and composition have their own journals and conferences and tend to isolate themselves from one another.

One of the largest groups of Quintilian's descendants, specialists in rhetoric and composition, have focused on student writing. Aware that most students were weak in writing, reading, speaking, listening, and thinking and convinced that the field of English should concern itself with literacy as well as literature, they have largely been absorbed in the problems of developing programs to meet basic communication needs in freshman English. For many years—years when I was both student and teacher—these freshman English programs were rooted in ideas characteristic of romanticism. Although students read essays and literary works as models, they tried to be original rather than build on tradition. Using their own experience as their primary resource, they tried to capture with appropriate feeling what was most concrete about their lives, often through an in-class essay that limited premeditation and promoted spontaneity. They rarely, if ever, considered audiences beyond themselves; their goal was to capture their subjects authentically, portraying things as they were transformed by their personalities.

Over the past decade, however, a movement stressing the composing process has emerged. Teachers and scholars have increasingly concerned themselves with invention or, to use a synonym also gaining currency, with heuristics. Many of their techniques of invention (or heuristic devices)—for instance, Burke's Pentad and Larson's lists of questions—are conceptual frameworks derived from an inductive review of examples of past discourse or an acceptance of the inductive reviews of others.[23] They are as closely related to the ideas underlying neoclassicism and early science as industry's content outlines. In fact—and this is symptomatic—despite an almost total absence of knowledge about writing in industry, rhetoric and composition scholars focusing on the writing process include at least two leaders who recommend the same kind of content outline promoted by IBM: Kenneth Bruffee and Frank J. D'Angelo.

Bruffee writes: "The conclusion I think I have been led to is this: that a writer's difficulty getting started has to do with his difficulty knowing and understanding the structure of the utterance he is setting out to make—not what he wants to say . . . but how he wants to say it. Once we know, however vaguely, the order or form of our discourse, we can begin that discourse, but not before . . . this hypothesis came to mind during a recent re-reading of Noam Chomsky's *Syntactic Structures.*"[24] Similarly, D'Angelo claims that the methods of development, a major writing aid in the nineteenth century, remain equally central in the twentieth, though they are buried "in textbooks as patterns of organization." These patterns serve as paradigms that "constitute a kind of deep structure of the essay" (a clear allusion to Chomsky's linguistics) and are most effective as a starting point in generating discourse: "Since one of the biggest failings of students is an inability to follow a logical plan of development in their writing, it makes sense to start with forms and structure first."[25] It is important to note that both Bruffee and D'Angelo find support for their ideas in Chomsky, who mainstreams Descartes to our age. Elsewhere Michael Halloran and I have shown Descartes' centrality to the cluster of ideas that gave rise to scientific method.[26]

Literary Theory: A Resource for Modern Rhetoric

In the twentieth century, most scholars in English departments have made the literary text the heart of education and research, carving out literary criticism as their niche in the world and systematically excluding other endeavors. On the national level, although the MLA has made impressive advances in broadening our view of the profession, its editorial advisors so favor the literary critics that their articles alone— apart from the yearly presidential address—appear in the pages of *PMLA*. On the local level, most executive committees in English departments, composed largely of specialists in literature, continue to stand firm against the development of degree programs in rhetoric, composition, and technical communication. Literature is often perceived as having value in itself; its experiences are treasured as highlights in private life.

Like the the philosophers whom Quintilian criticized, literary scholars in English departments fail to bridge contemplation in the study and action in the affairs of human society. They do not participate significantly in such major institutions that shape our civilization as business, industry, and government. Furthermore, those literary scholars aware of the opportunities of the information revolution generally insist that such participation would be a serious mistake. They reject such activity as "vocational," not really suggesting, however, what they include in that term to make it pejorative. They believe in promoting virtue in the affairs of human society, but they prefer to do so by assuming the stance of rebel—of Socratic gadfly—toward the rest of academic and public and professional life. Whether intentionally or not, they make a range of contributions to rhetoric. They develop the faculties of students, all of whom practice rhetoric. They promote good reading, which, in turn, promotes good writing. They help to convey cultural values, which a writer or speaker must know to communicate with an audience. And they assign literary talks and essays, which give students practice in speaking and writing.

While literary critics will acknowledge contributions like these, many have difficulty understanding how literary theory can contribute to rhetorical theory. They are skeptical about the value of poetics in solving rhetorical problems in information industries. When I have suggested such a possibility, the reply has frequently been: "How?" At first glance, many literary critics in this century have been as profoundly influenced by the ideas underlying neoclassicism and early science as technical communicators in industry and specialists in rhetoric and composition. As early as 1924, T. S. Eliot treats works of art as artifacts that should be studied as "what is." In "Tradition and the Individual Talent," he writes: "What is to be insisted upon is that the poet must develop or procure the consciousness of the past and that he should continue to develop this consciousness throughout his career." The reason is obvious: "If we approach a poet . . . we shall often find that not only the best, but the most individual parts of his work may be those in which the dead poets, his ancestors, assert their immortality most vigorously." A man should "write not merely with his own generation in his bones, but a feeling that the whole of the literature of Europe from Homer and within it the whole of the literature of his own country has a simultaneous existence and composes a simultaneous order."[27]

This concept flowered in the new criticism, which focused on the work of art itself, its parts and their mutual relations, in isolation from other factors that also shaped it like the writer, audience, and contemporary world. A look at a few of the characteristic ideas in one of the masterpieces of the new criticism, Wellek and Warren's *Theory of Literature,* can suggest the extent to which it conforms to ideas underlying neoclassicism and early science.[28] The work certainly encourages literary critics to focus on "what is" rather than "what ought to be": "The study of literature should . . . concentrate on the actual works of art themselves" (p. 140). Critics should examine literature in terms of conceptual frameworks derivable from an inductive review of the works: "There must be . . . some common elements or factors which would approximate two or more given works of art and thus would open the door to a transition from the analysis of one individual work of art to a type such as Greek tragedy and hence to tragedy in general, to literature in general, and finally to some all-inclusive structure common to all arts" (p. 151). One result of such analysis is a theory of genres, which "classifies literature and literary history . . . by specifically literary types of organization and structure" (p. 235). Because of its emphasis on the work of art itself, *Theory of Literature* minimizes the human being—either as creator or audience—as a force in criticism. The good writer works within a generic tradition: "The good writer partly conforms to the genre as it exists, partly stretches it. By and large, great writers are not the inventors of genres" (p. 245). Thus although the theory of genres is more sophisticated than content outlines, both are rooted in similar ideas.

Modern descendants of Eliot, Wellek, and Warren comprise a movement called structuralism; many of them are overt about their close relationship to the ideas of science. Robert Scholes provides a useful definition of this movement: "At the heart of the idea of structuralism is the idea of system: a complete, self-regulating entity that adapts to new conditions by transforming its features while retaining its systematic structure." In relating structuralism to science, Scholes writes, "By . . . seeking to define the principles of structuration that operate not only through individual works but through the relationships among works over the whole field of literature, structuralism has tried—and is trying—to establish for literary studies a basis that is as scientific as possible."[29] Another prominent literary specialist, Northrop Frye, limits criticism to what evolved into the structuralist approach: "If criticism exists, it must be an examination of literature in terms of a conceptual framework derivable from an inductive survey of the literary field." He also ties this approach to science: "The word 'inductive' suggests some sort of scientific procedure. . . . The presence of science in any subject changes its character from the casual to the causal, from the random and intuitive to the systematic, as well as safeguarding the integrity of that subject from external invasions."[30] As Bruffee and D'Angelo were influenced by the scientific ideas underlying Chomsky, so structuralist tendencies in modern literary criticism stem from the achievements of scholars such as Saussure, Jakobson, and Trubetzkoy, linguists who perceived themselves as participating in a broader scientific movement.[31]

Given this situation, our initial impulse might be to conclude that literary theory has no new perspective to bring to rhetorical theory. The masterpieces of literary theory in this century, however, often have a breadth not usually shared by work in industry and work on the writing process in rhetoric and composition, a breadth that begins to approach that recommended by Quintilian. A return to Wellek and Warren's *Theory of Literature* reveals that many of the ideas underlying romanticism, although they emerged in stark opposition to the ideas underlying neoclassicism and early science, are brought into creative tension with them in a coherent whole. Furthermore, unlike either early science or romanticism, *Theory of Literature* emphasizes the importance of an understanding of part-whole relationships.

According the Wellek and Warren, the good critic focuses not just on the general or universal but also on the concrete or particular: "Each work of literature is both general and particular" (p. 7). Reason will not always prove adequate: "The subject matter of his study is irrational or at least contains strongly unrational elements" (p. 3). In addition to rationality, the critic considers "the unconscious" (p. 75); "feeling, intuition, sensation" (p. 78); and various kinds of "imagery" (p. 191). Although Wellek and Warren question the reliability of human judgment in some passages, their attitude is fundamentally ambivalent; note the tentative trust in judgment in this passage: "It will always be possible to determine which point of view grasps the subject most thoroughly and deeply. A hierarchy of viewpoints, a criticism of the grasp of norms, is implied in the concept of the adequacy of interpretation" (p. 157). Unlike the scientific tendency to focus on a part of nature, *Theory of Literature* always emphasizes holism: "Sound and meter . . . must be studied as elements of the totality of a work of art, not in isolation from meaning" (p. 176). Finally, far from the scientific preference for simple explanations, Wellek and Warren stress multivalence, comprehensiveness, richness: "The maturity of a work of art is its inclusiveness, its awareness of complexity" (p. 257). Although I do not subscribe to the new criticism, I do subscribe to the belief that an adequate theory of poetics or rhetoric must include many of the ideas characteristic of neoclassicism, early science, *and* romanticism, and it must explore part-whole relationships.

Science, contemplation, and discovery have so captured the imagination of civilization that they have dominated virtually all realms of activity. The academic discipline of English has not escaped this domination. Although English and the other humanities might have been expected to concern themselves with human action (Who else should be concerned with the direction of human affairs but the humanists?), they have not been active in most of our major institutions. Notwithstanding the frequent claims of English to serve as an alternative to science, its primary activity in this century has been the contemplation of works of literature, the discovery of truths about them. Because the efforts of English scholars have been so directed to contemplation, they have shared a number of approaches to the world with early science. Fortunately, however, they have preserved a range of romantic approaches and an emphasis on part-whole relationships not shared by early science. I shall now explore how several of the ideas embodied in modern literary theory are among those that can be fruitful in exploring the limitations of content outlines as an aid to writing in industry.

The Possibilities and Limitations of Content Outlines

In the absence of efforts by humanists to engage the problems of action in our institutions, social scientists have taken the methodologies of contemplation, the ideas underlying neoclassicism and early science, and are applying them to human affairs. Nobody would deny the success of these methodologies in activities such as sampling as a means of predicting election outcomes. As was evident in our research on graphics at RPI, however, the application of the methodologies of contemplation to modern rhetoric has been less successful. People have used their understanding of past communication situations as sufficient guides for action in new situations. They have committed what, in my reading, is one of the most prevalent mistakes in modern thinking: they have identified *what was* and then used it as a standard for *what ought to be*; they have made description prescription. This is precisely the problem with the way content outlines have too often been used in industry.

I do not intend to suggest that content outlines cannot be potentially useful. To indicate just one advantage, the use of the content outline as a writing aid is supported by studies in cognition—for instance, recent schema theory. According to Sprague, a "schema is essentially the cognitive context or framework which each individual learner has when he or she enters a new instructional experience. The scope and nature of the learner's schema determines what new knowledge is learned and how it is incorporated or accommodated into the present cognitive framework or schema. Schema can . . . be characterized as a cognitive table of contents embedded in the mind which is cross-referenced for easy use."[32] It emphasizes the pattern of something rather than the something itself. The consistent use of a content outline to organize manuals would insure that this outline is incorporated well into schemas of audiences, enabling these audiences to find, understand, and remember new information more easily.

But the content outline is an expression of confidence in the past. The organization of prior work serves as a guide for present work. As was evident in my review of neoclassicism, this practice tends to thrive when times are perceived as either stable or getting worse and when forebears become standards of excellence. This hardly characterizes the computer industry, which is still experiencing a rate of progressive change that can best be described as revolutionary. The changes in the communication situation confronting the technical communicator have been extraordinary, and a review of but a few of these changes can serve as a caution against unqualified enthusiasm for content outlines as aids to writers.

Publication units in the information industry are attracting even more talented and better educated writers, and in some cases it may not make sense to have them imitate the organization of their less proficient predecessors. Product change has been dramatic in the computer industry; different products have different structures, and these structures affect the structures of information about them. Lastly, the instructions for the use of computers are increasingly on-line. That is, instead of having manuals next to their terminals, computer users are increasingly educated by small amounts of information independently called up on a terminal screen when needed. Long content outlines developed from complete hard copy manuals, then, may not be very fruitful for generating short sets of on-line information. This handful of changes is symptomatic of other innovations too numerous to note here, all of which make tradition a potentially unreliable or inapplicable guide.

Besides being often unreliable and sometimes inapplicable, content outlines also have the tendency to absorb too great a share of the communicator's attention. As the modern philosophers of science have taught us, our instruments affect our observation. Content outlines throw organization into high relief but leave other aspects of communication in the shadows. As a result, writers in industry often focus on organization and word and sentence counts when other concerns should take precedence. The communication situation as a whole should dictate the major concerns of the writer, not prescriptions about some part of that situation. Writers should engage their communication situations with a set of approaches comprehensive enough to suggest all the inherent possibilities for creation.

Technical communicators, influenced as they have been by the ideas of early science, have tended to ignore or limit approaches that have roots in the ideas of romanticism. One of these ideas is an emphasis on the concrete, and one of the major modern ways of capturing the concrete is through the use of the visual, of graphics. In the computer industry, one goal of manuals is to help users carry out such tasks as setting up computer hardware, objects like consoles, screens, and printers. Since many people understand and remember visual information more easily than verbal information, photographs and drawings to direct attention to visible parts may be the most important aspect of the manuals. The importance of capturing concrete realities graphically cannot be overestimated. But development of graphics in information industries has been slow. I attribute at least part of the problem to an overemphasis on such traditional and "scientific" writing aids as content outlines and readability formulas.

Another idea characteristic of romanticism and usually ignored in technical communication is the importance of ethos or persona in writing. Most modern technical communicators have continued to uphold the old scientific standard of the plain, objective, denotative style. Their focus on techniques like content outlines and readability formulas has diverted their attention from a reappraisal of the total communication situation they now confront. What a few innovative computer industries are discovering, however, is that their audiences too often either ignore or rush through documents without interest, awareness, or understanding. The pursuit of impersonality in technical discourse seems not to have worked. Writers have strained against the obligation to write impersonal prose, and readers have been bored by it. What is needed are rhetorical approaches to shape a persona that makes vivid appeals to the senses and subtle appeals to the emotions. Some computer corporations have made a few experiments in this direction; manuals that seek to engage audiences through a more vivid persona range from the relatively moderate *Fortran Programming: A Spiral Approach* and *The Applesoft Tutorial* to the rather extraordinary *Getting Started with TRS-80 Basic* and *A Fortran Coloring Book*.[33] Although limited in their success, these manuals signal substantial changes in the nature of industrial discourse.

Clearly, writers need to avoid approaching communication situations with too narrow a set of rhetorical approaches in mind. Modern technical communicators have been too dominated by approaches stimulated by the ideas underlying neoclassicism and early science. For instance, an emphasis on reason has constrained them from allowing their full selves to engage the communication situation—remembered and current perceptions, imaginative constructs, and feelings as well as ideas. An emphasis on abstracting universals from past works has constrained them from perceiving their current communication situations in all their concreteness and determining whether the universals are still applicable. An emphasis on this or that approach—for example, the content outline—has constrained them from an appreciation of the whole of a communication situation and the extent to which an understanding of the whole can affect the nature of a part. The ideal technical communicator embodies the complete set of rhetorical approaches (the whole of human knowledge and experience), grasps the whole of a concrete communication situation, and through an interrelationship between the two is free to use judgment to create an ideal coherence. The best modern literary theory, combining as it does many of the ideas underlying neoclassicism, early science, and romanticism in a coherent and creative tension, offers a rich source of knowledge that begins to approach the requisite breadth and can be extremely fruitful for the practice of modern rhetoric. The ultimate ideals are the Renaissance humanist and Quintilian's ideal orator, who embody the collective wisdom of humanity and apply it effectively to human affairs.

One result of using Quintilian's approach is a liberation of human judgment. The scientific revolution gave a needed shock to our confidence in human capability that persists to this moment. Few people, I suspect, harbor any illusions about the frailty of human beings; life in this century has certainly been generous with its reminders. But the diminishment of human capability has gone too far. Everywhere, men and women are striving to substitute inferior instruments—pathetic little methodologies—for a superior instrument, an astute, informed, wise human being. With the advent of the information revolution, a communication revolution that focuses in large part on the human being, all that belongs to our personality is valuable—what we sense, what we imagine, what we feel, what we think. At periodic intervals in the history of creativity, men and women have had a break free of harmful constraints. In the eighteenth century Samuel Johnson liberated drama from the constraint of the unities.[34] In our century Wayne Booth liberated the novel from the constraint of a set of supposedly universal norms.[35] Now, we need to liberate judgment from the constraint of inadequate technique. Another way of saying this is that we need to broaden technique until it becomes the kind of wisdom Quintilian advocates. To do so requires dramatic changes in our postsecondary educational system.

The Implications for English Departments and Universities

When we consider the state of many English departments today, we, like Willy Loman in *Death of a Salesman,* could well cry, "the woods are burning."[36] Preserving the focus on literature in English departments has brought severe problems, among them, loss of faculty lines through attrition, limited employment opportunities for students, lower student enrollments, and students of lesser quality. These developments confront us, however, at the very moment when society needs strong English departments more than ever. With the advent of the information revolution, information industries are turning to English for help in educating our age through technical communication about one of civilization's great accomplishments, computer science, which compares in its magnitude to the invention of the printing press. Pioneers such as Thomas Connolly and Roger Grice of IBM and William Bulloch and Lionel Howard of Bell Laboratories are encouraging English to assume a greater role in the area of technical communication; they are promoting education and research that represents a convergence of the humanities and science and technology.

Whether English departments will respond is still an open question. While literary scholars have been broad in their theories, they have not been broad in their view of their own profession. Influenced by the trend toward specialization promoted by the rise of science, they have favored the contemplation and understanding of literature over action and creativity in society. Through the years, since the institution of the Modern Language Association, they have ignored and even disparaged a range of educators in areas such as speech, rhetoric, and journalism who wanted to move from a concern for the private life alone to a concern for the public and professional life as well. Although literary scholars have allowed these educators token development, they have tended to dismiss their aspirations as vocationalism, a term once again in currency.

In response to this charge, an increasing number of scholars are identifying with the ideal orator of classical antiquity. The concept of the ideal orator was a rejection of the idea that liberal and vocational education, that contemplation and action could be separated. The ideal orator moved easily from the study to the forum; his contemplation was enriched by practical experience, and his work as a man of affairs gained authority from his contemplation. By moving into the professional world beyond the university, scholars believe they can help eliminate the split between humanistic and scientific-technical-industrial culture, which has become institutionalized in a way that grants immense power and resources to technologists but leaves humanists little but the power to protest the ill-considered use of these resources.[37] They believe that the difficult struggle to maintain what is best about humanity, nature, and civilization—and to make improvements where possible—can only succeed through deep involvement in the fabric of American society. Only through greater participation can English make its perceptions sharp, its criticisms trenchant, its influence felt.

Rhetoric and composition scholars may wish to join technical communication scholars in promoting education and research to assist those major institutions which are participating in the information revolution. A few notable leaders such as Edward P. J. Corbett and Lee Odell have already turned their attention to writing in business, industry, and government. Others, with their growing interest in "Writing across the Curriculum," are exploring the ways that writing is shaped by concrete environments, the ways, for instance, that writing in a physics course can differ substantially from writing in a history course. It is not much of a leap to begin exploring the ways that writing in a freshman English class can differ substantially from writing in an industrial environment. In a freshman English class students may be able to rely on memories to write about their own experiences, but in an information industry, employees may need to synthesize knowledge from rhetoric, computer science, literary criticism, linguistics, psychology, speech, communication as a social science, organization management, graphics, and publications production. It is not much of a further leap to realize that it hardly makes sense to teach students to write without a consideration of the factors that will have a bearing on their writing after they graduate. An acceptance of this belief will transform freshman English, eliminate the unfortunate divisions between rhetoric and composition, technical communication, and business communication, and promote interdisciplinary education and research.

Such steps as these carry implications for the structure of postsecondary education, however. If education and research increasingly require interdisciplinary solutions, the walls that exist between departments must be eliminated—or, at least, larger doorways created. Current departmental structures may prove obsolete, perhaps to be replaced or supplemented by interdisciplinary problem teams. What Arthur O. Lovejoy wrote on historiography in 1948 is especially true of English's confronting the communication problems of the information society. According to Lovejoy, the divisions of intellectual history

> are in part temporarily convenient isolations of certain objects from their contexts, to facilitate more minute scrutiny; and in part they are fortuitous, results of accidents in the history of education institutions or of the idiosyncratic limitations of the intellectual interests of influential scholars. And in the present phase of the development of, at least, several of these nominally distinct disciplines the lines of division are breaking down. They are breaking down because questions originally raised within the traditional limits of one or another of these subjects prove incapable of adequate and accurate answer without going beyond those limits. Ideas are commodities which enter into interstate commerce.[38]

English faculties, recognizing the need for synthesis, could become leaders both in and beyond universities. They have the extraordinary opportunity to move the humanities to the heart of American life, to be as much at the center of learning and society as the orator in classical antiquity.

18
A Bibliography of Works by Edward P. J. Corbett

Sara Garnes and Charles Zarobila

Aristotle understood the importance of what he called the *ethos,* or character, displayed by the orator. True, he did teach that both logical argument and emotional arousal were means to "persuasion," the end of the rhetorical art. Nevertheless, the trustworthy character of the orator, he felt, was as persuasive as the means of reason and emotion, if not more so. This ethical appeal, so important for suasory discourse and, by implication, for an expanded definition of rhetoric as the "art of effective communication," is present everywhere in the writings of Edward P. J. Corbett. His extensive knowledge—together with the ability to organize and state that knowledge clearly—inspires his readers' confidence, and his benevolent tone wins their favor. He is an erudite and amiable orator in the agorae of books and journals.

Edward P. J. Corbett was born October 19, 1919, in Jamestown, North Dakota, where his father worked for the Northern Pacific Railroad Company. After several moves, his family settled in Milwaukee, Wisconsin, where he attended school from fourth grade through high school. He received a rigorous high school education studying Latin and Greek at the Marquette University High School and graduated in 1938. He received his undergraduate education at Venard College in Clarks Summit, Pennsylvania, which he attended from 1938 to 1942. From 1943 to 1946 he served in the Pacific as a radar technician in the United States Marine Air Corps. Returning from the service, he enrolled at the University of Chicago where he received an M.A. degree in English language and literature in 1948.

Equipped with his degree, he began a teaching career that would take him to two universities. His first position was at Creighton University where he taught from 1948 to 1950, and again from 1953 to 1966. Having discovered on his own the value of Hugh Blair's *Lectures on Rhetoric and Belles Lettres* and Aristotle's *Rhetoric* in teaching his students at Creighton, he took his Ph.D. course work in English at Loyola University of Chicago from 1950 to 1953. From 1953 to 1956 he directed freshman English at Creighton and received the Ph.D. degree from Loyola in 1956.

His second affiliation has been with Ohio State University where he served as director of freshman English and vice-chairman of the Department of English from 1966 to 1970. During his years at Ohio State, he has directed numerous master's theses and doctoral dissertations, including those of two of the editors of this volume. Also, he has served in a range of capacities, in various offices and boards at the local, state, and national level.

One of the most important positions Professor Corbett has held, however, is the editorship of probably the most influential journal in the field of college composition, *College Composition and Communication,* a position he held from February 1974 to December 1979. After he relinquished the editorship, he was honored by the Ohio Council of Teachers of English Language Arts (OCTELA) when it published a volume consisting of articles which had appeared in *College Composition and Communication* during his tenure as editor. Although Professor Corbett's own writings do not appear in the volume, it is appropriate to cite this tribute to him here: *Composition and Its Teaching: Articles from "College Composition and Communication" During the Editorship of Edward P. J. Corbett,* edited by Richard C. Gebhardt, with forewords by William F. Irmscher and Richard L. Larson, published at Findlay, Ohio, by OCTELA in 1979.

Professor Corbett has been the recipient of many honors and awards. Perhaps the one that most appropriately symbolizes his contribution to the students he has influenced and continues to influence through his teaching and writing is the Edward P.J. Corbett Annual Award, established in 1979, given each year for the best article to appear in OCTELA's *English Language Arts Bulletin.*

The following bibliography is a tribute in itself to Professor Corbett's scholarship and constitutes the best evidence of his contribution to the study of rhetoric and composition. The fact that it is destined to be outdated even before it is published is witness to his productivity as well.

Books

"Hugh Blair: A Study of His Rhetorical Theory." Diss. Loyola 1956.

Classical Rhetoric for the Modern Student. New York: Oxford Univ. Press, 1965. 2nd ed., 1971. 3rd ed., forthcoming.

The Little English Handbook: Choices and Conventions. New York: Wiley, 1973. 2nd ed., 1977. 3rd ed., 1980.

With James B. Bell. *The Little English Handbook for Canadians.* Toronto: Wiley Canada, 1977. 2nd ed., 1981.

The Little Rhetoric. New York: Wiley, 1977.

The Little Rhetoric and Handbook. New York: Wiley, 1977.

The Little Rhetoric and Handbook. 2nd ed. Glenview, Ill.: Scott, Foresman, 1982.

The Little Rhetoric and Handbook with Readings. Glenview, Ill.: Scott, Foresman, 1983.

Books Edited

With Gary Tate. *Teaching Freshman Composition.* New York: Oxford Univ. Press, 1967.

With James L. Golden. *The Rhetoric of Blair, Campbell, and Whately.* New York: Holt, Rinehart and Winston, 1968. 2nd ed., 1980.

General ed. "Foreword" and "General Instructions for a Research Paper." In each vol. of The Charles E. Merrill Literary Casebook Series. 21 vols. Columbus, Ohio: Merrill, 1968–71.

Rhetorical Analyses of Literary Works. New York: Oxford Univ. Press, 1969.

With Gary Tate. *Teaching High School Composition.* New York: Oxford Univ. Press, 1970.

With Virginia M. Burke. *The New Century Composition-Rhetoric.* Based on the American classic by Fred Newton Scott and Joseph Villiers Denney. New York: Appleton-Century-Crofts, 1971.

Contributing ed. *Using Facts.* [Pamphlet] The University Independent Study Course in Effective Writing. Ed. Walker Gibson. Waltham, Mass.: Xerox, 1973.

The Essay: Subjects and Stances. Prentice-Hall English Literature Series. Ed. Maynard Mack. Englewood Cliffs, N.J.: Prentice-Hall, 1974.

With Gary Tate. *The Writing Teacher's Sourcebook.* New York: Oxford Univ. Press, 1981.

Contributions to Books

"A Method of Analyzing Prose Style with a Demonstration Analysis of Swift's *A Modest Proposal.*" In *Reflections on High School English: NDEA Institute Lectures 1965.* Ed. Gary Tate. Tulsa, Okla.: Univ. of Tulsa, 1966, pp. 106–24.

Rpt. in *Teaching Freshman Composition*. Ed. Gary Tate and Edward P. J. Corbett. New York: Oxford Univ. Press, 1967, pp. 294–312.

Rpt. in *Contemporary Essays on Style: Rhetoric, Linguistics, and Criticism*. Ed. Glen A. Love and Michael Payne. Glenview, Ill.: Scott, Foresman, 1969, pp. 81–98.

Rpt. in *Jonathan Swift: A Modest Proposal*. Ed. Charles Beaumont. The Charles E. Merrill Literary Casebook Series. Ed. Edward P. J. Corbett. Columbus, Ohio: Merrill, 1969, pp. 73–93.

Rpt. in *Teaching High School Composition*. Ed. Gary Tate and Edward P. J. Corbett. New York: Oxford Univ. Press, 1970, pp. 312–30.

Rpt. in *The Writing Teacher's Sourcebook*. Ed. Gary Tate and Edward P. J. Corbett. New York: Oxford Univ. Press, 1981, pp. 333–52.

"A New Look at Old Rhetoric." In *Rhetoric: Theories for Application*. Papers Presented at the 1965 Convention of the National Council of Teachers of English. Ed. Robert M. Gorrell. Champaign, Ill.: NCTE, 1967, pp. 16–22.

"A Composition Course Based Upon Literature." In *Teaching High School Composition*. Ed. Gary Tate and Edward P. J. Corbett. New York: Oxford Univ. Press, 1970, pp. 195–204.

"Rhetoric in Search of a Past, Present, and Future." In *The Prospect of Rhetoric*. Ed. Lloyd F. Bitzer and Edwin Black. Englewood Cliffs, N.J.: Prentice-Hall, 1971, pp. 167–78.

"Rhetoric, Whether Goest Thou?" In *A Symposium in Rhetoric*. Ed. J. Dean Bishop, Turner S. Kobler, and William E. Tanner. Denton, Tex.: Texas Woman's Univ., 1975, pp. 44–57.

Rpt. in *Rhetoric and Change*. Ed. William E. Tanner and J. Dean Bishop. Mesquite, Tex.: Ide House, 1982, pp. 15–30.

"Approaches to the Study of Style." In *Teaching Composition: 10 Bibliographical Essays*. Ed. Gary Tate. Fort Worth, Tex.: Texas Christian Univ. Press, 1976, pp. 73–109.

"Ventures in Style." In *Reinventing the Rhetorical Tradition*. Ed. Aviva Freedman and Ian Pringle. Conway, Ark.: Published for the Canadian Council of Teachers of English by L&S Books, Univ. of Central Arkansas, 1980, pp. 79–87.

"A Rhetorician Looks at Technical Communication." In *Technical Communication: Perspectives for the Eighties*. NASA Conference Publication 2203, Part I. Proceedings of the Technical Communication Sessions at the 32nd Annual Meeting of the Conference on College Composition and Communication, Dallas. 26–28 Mar. 1981. Comp. J. C. Mathes and Thomas E. Pinelli. Washington, D.C.: NASA, 1981, pp. 213–18.

"The Status of Writing in Our Society." In *Writing: The Nature, Development, and Teaching of Written Communication.* 2 vols. Ed. Marcia Farr Whiteman. Hillsdale, N.J.: Lawrence Erlbaum, 1981, I, 47–52.

"A Literal View of Literacy." In *Literacy as a Human Problem.* Ed. James C. Raymond. University, Ala.: Univ. of Alabama Press, 1982, pp. 137–53.

"Literature and Composition: Allies or Rivals in the Classroom?" In *Literature and Composition: Bridging the Gap.* Ed. Winifred B. Horner. Chicago, Ill.: Univ. of Chicago Press, forthcoming.

Articles

"Hugh Blair's Three (?) Critical Dissertations." *Notes and Queries,* NS 1 (Nov. 1954), 478–80.

"The Collegiate Muse: Gone Feminine." *America,* 1 Dec. 1956, pp. 265–66.

"Education at the Crossroads." *Benedictine Review,* 12 (Summer 1957), 5–10.

"*Gone with the Wind* Revisited." *America,* 24 Aug. 1957, pp. 524–26.

"Modern American Usage." *Nebraska English Counselor,* 3 (Apr. 1958), 3–9.

"Hugh Blair as an Analyzer of English Prose Style." *College Composition and Communication,* 9 (May 1958), 98–103.

"A Romp with Pop." *The Nation,* 17 Jan. 1959, pp. 51–53.

"The Sagging Pulpit." *Homiletic and Pastoral Review,* 59 (June 1959), 821–26.

"America's Sainte-Beuve." *Commonweal,* 13 May 1960, pp. 173–75.

"Raise High the Barriers, Censors." *America,* 7 Jan. 1961, pp. 441–43.

   Rpt. in *J. D. Salinger and the Critics.* Ed. William F. Belcher and James W. Lee. Belmont, Calif.: Wadsworth, 1962, pp. 54–59.

   Rpt. in *Ideas and Issues: Readings for Analysis and Evaluation.* Ed. Marvin Laser, Robert S. Cathcart, and Fred H. Marcus. New York: Ronald, 1963, pp. 274–81.

   Rpt. in *if you really want to know: a "Catcher" casebook.* Ed. Malcolm M. Marsden. Chicago: Scott, Foresman, 1963, pp. 68–73.

   Rpt. in *Salinger's "Catcher in the Rye": Clamor vs. Criticism.* Ed. Harold P. Simonson and Philip E. Hager. Boston: Heath, 1963, pp. 5–9.

   Rpt. in *Studies in J. D. Salinger: Reviews, Essays, and Critiques of "The Catcher in the Rye" and Other Fiction.* Ed. Marvin Laser and Norman Freeman. New York: Odyssey, 1963, pp. 134–41.

"Do It Yourself." *College English,* 22 (Apr. 1961), 507–8.

"A View from the Pews." *Pastoral Life,* 9 (July–Aug. 1961), 3–7.

"Professors, Old and New." *America,* 16 Sept. 1961, pp. 734–36.

"What Hath Webster Wrought." *America,* 20 Oct. 1962, pp. 929–31.

"The Usefulness of Classical Rhetoric." *College Composition and Communication,* 14 (Oct. 1963), 162–64.

"Rhetoric and Teachers of English." *Quarterly Journal of Speech*, 51 (Dec. 1965), 375–81.

"What Is Being Revived?" *College Composition and Communication*, 18 (Oct. 1967), 166–72.

"The Relevance of Rhetoric to Composition." *Kentucky English Bulletin*, 17 (Winter 1967–68), 3–12.

"The Rhetoric of the Open Hand and the Rhetoric of the Closed Fist." *College Composition and Communication*, 20 (Dec. 1969), 288–96.

   Rpt. in *Readings in Speech*, 2nd ed. Ed. Haig A. Bosmajian. New York: Harper and Row, 1971, pp. 14–26.

   Rpt. in *Contemporary Rhetoric: A Reader's Coursebook*. Ed. Douglas Ehninger. Glenview, Ill.: Scott, Foresman, 1972, pp. 202–10.

   Rpt. in *Coming to Terms with Language: An Anthology*. Ed. Raymond D. Liedlich. New York: Wiley, 1973, pp. 148–62.

"A Perspective on the Prospects." *Ohio English Bulletin*, 11 (December 1970), 2–4.

"The Theory and Practice of Imitation in Classical Rhetoric." *College Composition and Communication*, 22 (Oct. 1971), 243–50.

   Rpt. in *Rhetoric and Composition*. Ed. Richard L. Graves. New York: Hayden, 1976, pp. 303–12.

"Rhetoric, the Enabling Discipline." *Ohio English Bulletin*, 13 (May 1972), 2–10.

"The Rhetoric of Protest." *Rhetoric Society Newsletter*, 4, No. 2 (March 1974), 4.

"Improvement in Reading Skills." *Rhetoric Society Newsletter*, 5, No. 4 (Fall 1975), 9–10.

"If I Speak with Forked Tongue . . . " *North Dakota English*, 1 (Winter 1976), 3–14.

   Rpt. as "Public Doublespeak: If I Speak With Forked Tongue . . . " [Shortened version] *English Journal*, 65 (Apr. 1976), 16–17.

"Came the Revolution and Then . . . " *Iowa English Bulletin Yearbook*, 23 (1977), 6–7.

"Is Composition Decomposing?" *Minnesota English Journal*, 13 (Fall 1977), 26–47.

"My Work in Rhetoric." *fforum*, 1 (Winter 1980), 27–28, 55.

   Rpt. in *fforum: A Primer of Theory and Practice*. Ed. Patricia L. Stock. Montclair, N.J.: Boynton/Cook, 1983.

"Some Rhetorical Lessons from John Henry Newman." *College Composition and Communication*, 31 (Dec. 1980), 402–12.

"John Locke's Contributions to Rhetoric." *College Composition and Communication*, 32 (Dec. 1981), 423–33.

Rpt. in *The Rhetorical Tradition and Modern Writing.* Ed. James J. Murphy. New York: MLA, 1982, pp. 73–84.

"A Comparison of John Locke and John Henry Newman on the Rhetoric of Assent." *Rhetoric Review* 1 (Sept. 1982), 40–49.

Reviews

Rev. of *The Poorhouse Fair,* by John Updike. *America,* 31 Jan. 1959, p. 530.

Rev. of *London in Dickens' Day,* ed. Jacob Korg. *College Composition and Communication,* 12 (May 1961), 125.

Rev. of *Preface to Critical Reading,* 4th ed., by Richard D. Altick. *College Composition and Communication,* 12 (May 1961), 124.

Rev. of *Reading and Word Study: For Students of English as a Second Language,* by Kenneth Croft. *College Composition and Communication,* 12 (May 1961), 121.

Rev. of *Our Living Language,* by Kellogg W. Hunt and Paul Stoakes. *College Composition and Communication,* 12 (Dec. 1961), 251.

Rev. of *Science and Society,* by Thomas D. Clareson. *College Composition and Communication,* 12 (Dec. 1961), 255.

Rev. of *Shakespeare's Julius Caesar,* ed. Julian Markels; *Two Modern American Tragedies,* ed. John D. Hurrell; *Extrasensory Perception,* ed. Fabian Gudas; *The Hungarian Revolt,* ed. Richard Lettis and William E. Morris. *College Composition and Communication,* 12 (Dec. 1961), 258.

Rev. of *The Letters and Diaries of John Henry Newman,* Vol. XI, ed. Charles Stephen Dessain. *Pastoral Life,* 10 (May–June 1962), 56–57.

Rev. of *Newman, the Pillar of the Cloud,* by Meriol Trevor. *Pastoral Life,* 10 (November–December 1962), 54.

Rev. of *St. Thomas More: Selected Letters,* ed. Elisabeth Frances Roger. *Pastoral Life,* 11 (Jan. 1963), 52–53.

Rev. of *Newman at St. Mary's: A Selection of the Plain and Parochial Sermons,* ed. Lawrence F. Barmann, S.J. *Pastoral Life,* 11 (Feb. 1963), 55.

Rev. of *Newman, Light in Winter,* by Meriol Trevor. *Pastoral Life,* 11 (June 1963), 59–60.

Rev. of *The Letters and Diaries of John Henry Newman,* Vol. XII, ed. Charles Stephen Dessain. *Pastoral Life,* 11 (Sept. 1963), 56–57.

Rev. of *The Tenants of Moonbloom,* by Edward Lewis Wallant. *America,* 14 Sept. 1963, pp. 265–66.

Rev. of *Modern Prose Style,* by Bonamy Dobrée. *College English* 26 (December 1964), 247.

Rev. of *Giles Goat-Boy,* by John Barth. *America,* 17 Sept. 1966, p. 706.

Rev. of *The Birds Fall Down,* by Rebecca West. *America,* 29 Oct. 1966, p. 522–23.

Rev. of *The Man Who Knew Kennedy,* by Vance Bourjaily. *America,* 25 Feb. 1967, p. 289.

Rev. of *The Soldier's Art,* by Anthony Powell. *America,* 29 Apr. 1967, pp. 657–58.

Rev. of *F. Scott Fitzgerald: The Last Laocoön,* by Robert Sklar. *America,* 29 July 1967, pp. 117–18.

Revs. of *Tough, Sweet & Stuffy: An Essay on Modern American Prose Styles,* by Walker Gibson; *The Five Clocks,* by Martin Joos; *The Problem of Style,* ed. J. V. Cunningham. *Quarterly Journal of Speech,* 53 (Oct. 1967), 290–91.

Rev. of *North Toward Home,* by Willie Morris. *America,* 9 Dec. 1967, p. 720.

Rev. of *No Place for an Angel,* by Elizabeth Spencer. *America,* 16 Dec. 1967, pp. 747–48.

Rev. of *Making It,* by Norman Podhoretz. *America,* 3 Feb. 1968, pp. 161–62.

Rev. of *J. F. Powers,* by John V. Hagopian. *America,* 20 Apr. 1968, pp. 548–49.

Revs. of *William Faulkner: New Orleans Sketches,* ed. Carvel Collins; *Lion in the Garden: Interviews with William Faulkner, 1926–1962,* ed. James B. Meriwether and Michael Millgate. *America,* 28 Sept. 1968, pp. 261–63.

Rev. of *The Rise of Modern Prose Style,* by Robert Adolph. *Quarterly Journal of Speech,* 54 (Dec. 1968), 420–21.

Rev. of *The Department,* by Gerald Warner Brace. *America,* 4 Jan. 1969, p. 26.

Rev. of *The Sleep of Reason,* by C. P. Snow. *America,* 8 Feb. 1969, p. 173.

Rev. of *Biography: The Craft and the Calling,* by Catherine Drinker Bowen. *America,* 22 Mar. 1969, p. 341.

Rev. of *Bullet Park,* by John Cheever. *America,* 24 May 1969, p. 630.

Rev. of *The Four-Gated City,* by Doris Lessing. *America,* 13 Sept. 1969, p. 171.

Rev. of *Intensive Care,* by Janet Frame. *America,* 23 May 1970, p. 565–66.

Rev. of *Last Things,* by C. P. Snow. *America,* 22 Aug. 1970, p. 100.

Rev. of *The Castaways,* by Jamie Lee Cooper. *America,* 26 Sept. 1970, p. 209.

Rev. of *Islands in the Stream,* by Ernest Hemingway. *America,* 7 Nov. 1970, pp. 382–84.

Rev. of *A Theory of Discourse: The Aims of Discourse,* by James L. Kinneavy. *Freshman English News,* 1 (Mar. 1972), 12.

Rev. of *The Anatomy of College English,* by Thomas W. Wilcox. *Freshman English News,* 2 (Fall 1973), 14–15.

Revs. of *Aristotle: The Classical Heritage of Rhetoric,* ed. Keith V. Erickson; *Aristotle's Rhetoric: Five Centuries of Philological Research,* comp. by Keith V. Erickson. *Quarterly Journal of Speech,* 61 (Dec. 1975), 479–81.

Rev. of *Poetics, Rhetoric, and Logic: Studies in the Basic Disciplines of Criticism,* by Wilbur Samuel Howell. *Style,* 10 (Spring 1976), 209–11.

Rev. of *The Rhetoric of Renaissance Poetry,* ed. Thomas O. Sloan and Raymond B. Waddington. *Philosophy & Rhetoric,* 9 (Spring 1976), 127–29.

Rev. of *Classical Rhetoric and Its Christian and Secular Tradition from Ancient to Modern Times,* by George A. Kennedy. *Rhetoric Society Quarterly,* 10 (Spring 1980), 95–97.

Rev. of *A New Classical Rhetoric,* by Robert L. Kindrick, Larry R. Olpin, and Frank M. Patterson. *College Composition and Communication,* 32 (Feb. 1981), 86–87.

Microfiche

"A New Look at Old Rhetoric." In *Rhetoric: Theories for Application.* Papers Presented at the 1965 Convention of the National Council of Teachers of English. Ed. Robert M. Gorrell. Champaign, Ill.: NCTE, 1967, pp. 16–22. ERIC ED 017 504.

"The Relevance of Rhetoric to Composition." *Kentucky English Bulletin,* 17 (Winter 1967–68), 3–12. ERIC ED 019 276.

"What Is Being Revived?" *College Composition and Communication,* 18 (Oct. 1967), 166–72. ERIC ED 019 302.

Rhetoric: Olden New. [Nov. 1971] ERIC ED 085 747.

"Rhetoric, Whether Goest Thou?" In *A Symposium in Rhetoric.* Ed. J. Dean Bishop, Turner S. Kobler, and William E. Tanner. Denton, Tex.: Texas Woman's Univ., 1975, pp. 44–57. ERIC ED 108 231.

"Introduction," In *A Symposium in Rhetoric.* Ed. William E. Tanner, J. Dean Bishop, and Turner S. Kobler. Denton, Tex.: Federation of North Texas Area Universities, 1976, pp. 1–2. ERIC ED 157 097.

Miscellanea

"Statement from the Chairman." *Rhetoric Society Newsletter,* 2 (Summer 1972), 2–3.

"A Note from the Chairman." *Rhetoric Society Newsletter,* 3, No. 3 (May 1973), 1–2.

[Letter to Prof. Gordon F. Hostettler.] *Rhetoric Society Newsletter,* 4, No. 1 (Nov. 1973), 2.

With Richard L. Johannesen, comps. "The Rhetoric of Social Protest and Confrontation." [Bibliography] *Rhetoric Society Newsletter,* 4, No. 2 (Mar. 1974), 5–9.

"Introduction." In *A Symposium in Rhetoric.* Ed. William E. Tanner, J. Dean Bishop, and Turner S. Kobler. Denton, Tex.: Federation of North Texas Area Universities, 1976, pp. 1–2.

"Editor's Farewell." *College Composition and Communication,* 30 (Dec. 1979), 349–50.

With Sara Garnes. Interview by Jeanne Paul. "Learning Basic Writing Skills in College." *American Educator,* 4 (Spring 1980), 14–16.

Notes

Chapter 1. The Revival of Rhetoric in America

1. The *Port Royal Art of Speaking,* which came into use in the eighteenth century, took a classical rather than a Ramistic approach, and was followed by "classical" rhetorics by John Lawson, Joseph Priestley, and others.
2. Warren Guthrie, "The Development of Rhetorical Theory in America, 1635–1850," *Speech Monographs,* 14 (1947), 45.
3. The Boylston chair is the subject of a dissertation (Paul E. Ried, "The Philosophy of American Rhetoric as it Developed in the Boylston Chair of Rhetoric and Oratory at Harvard University," Ohio State Univ., 1959) and several articles. See, for example, Ronald F. Reid, "The Boylston Professorship of Rhetoric and Oratory, 1806–1904: A Case Study in Changing Concepts of Rhetoric and Pedagogy," *Quarterly Journal of Speech,* 45 (1959), 239–57.
4. We should note, however, that by the time Adams' lectures were published, Blair's essentially anticlassical approach had a firm hold in American colleges. Indeed, Kitzhaber says that these lectures, as well as Witherspoon's "Lectures on Moral Philosophy and Eloquence" had no perceptible influence on later American rhetorical theory. See Albert Kitzhaber, "Rhetoric in American Colleges, 1850–1900," (Diss. Univ. of Washington 1953), p. 90.
5. Michael Halloran, "Rhetoric in the American College Curriculum: The Decline of Public Discourse," *PrelText,* 3 (1982), 257.
6. William Riley Parker's "Where Do English Departments Come From?" *College English,* 28 (1967), 339–51, traces the development of English departments in America.
7. The man who succeeded Child as Boylston Professor was Adams Sherman Hill, who for thirty years presided over the demise of rhetoric at Harvard. For a discussion of Child's influence and of the alternative model developed by Fred Newton Scott at Michigan, see Donald C. Stewart, "Two Model Teachers and the Harvardization of English Departments," *The Rhetorical Tradition and Modern Writing,* ed. James J. Murphy (New York: Modern Language Association, 1982), pp. 118–29.
8. Two such style-based texts were Alexander Jamieson's *Grammar of Rhetorical and Polite Literature* (1820) and Samuel Newman's *A Practical System of Rhetoric* (1827).

9. For a discussion of Bain's influence, see Andrea Lunsford, "Alexander Bain's Contributions to Discourse Theory," *College English*, 44 (Mar. 1982), 290–301.
10. Richard Grant White, "The Public School Failure," *North American Review* (Dec. 1880), 537; Adams Sherman Hill, *Our English* (1890), p. 12; C. C. Thach, "The Essentials of English Composition to be Taught in Secondary Schools," *Journal of Proceedings and Addresses, National Education Association* (1898), 94.
11. Fred Newton Scott, "What the West Wants in Preparatory English," *School Review*, 17 (1909), 13–14.
12. Donald Stewart reviews the events of this period in "Some Facts Worth Knowing About the Origins of Freshman Composition," *CEA Critic* (May 1982), 2–11.
13. See Donald K. Smith, "Origin and Development of Departments of Speech," in *History of Speech Education in America*, ed. by Karl R. Wallace (New York: Appleton-Century-Crofts, 1954), 453–56.
14. See, for instance, the attitude reflected by James M. O'Neill in "Public Speaking and English," *Public Speaking Review*, 3 (1914), 132–40.
15. It is intriguing to note that Baldwin gave no credence to the speech movement at any time; he is firmly embedded in the older poetic-rhetorical tradition that developed in nineteenth-century English departments. In a statement on rhetoric in 1913, he drew no strong line between rhetoric and composition, and he seems to have had little trouble in adding Alexander Bain to his list of illustrious rhetoricians. He also subsumed modern Bainian additions to rhetoric under generally classical ideas. "For rhetoric is so old," Baldwin concludes, "that it made its educational survey early along permanent lines of human nature." ("Rhetoric" in *A Cyclopedia of Education*, Vol. 5, ed. Paul Monroe [New York: Macmillan, 1913], pp. 178–79.)
16. Cornell, even after Winans' departure in 1920, was the most important innovational department. In 1923 Cornell offered their first course in classical rhetoric, which Smith calls "a marked innovation." (Smith, in *History of Speech Education in America*, p. 457.)
17. I. A. Richards, *The Philosophy of Rhetoric* (New York: Oxford University Press, 1936), p. 3.
18. We would like to express our appreciation to John Gerber, who supplied us with very helpful information about the communications movement of the 1940s, and to Lynn Troyka, who gave us a copy of the first CCCC program for 1949 and referred us to Nancy K. Bird's "The Conference on College Composition and Communication: A Historical Study of its Continuing Education and Professionalization Activities, 1949–1975" (Diss. Virginia Polytechnic Institute 1977).
19. Kenneth Burke, *Counter-Statement* (Los Altos, Calif.: Hermes Press, 1953), p. 265.
20. A noted exception, of course, is Walter Ong, who came to rhetoric through Renaissance studies at St. Louis University and Harvard.
21. See, for instance, Weaver's *The Ethics of Rhetoric* (Chicago: Henry Regnery, 1953), and Duhamel's essay "The Function of Rhetoric in Effective Expression" (1949) reprinted in *The Province of Rhetoric*, ed. Joseph Schwartz and John Rycenga (New York: Ronald Press, 1965), pp. 36–48.
22. Richard E. Hughes and P. Albert Duhamel, *Rhetoric: Principles and Usage* (Englewood Cliffs, N.J.: Prentice-Hall, 1962), p. v.
23. Edward P. J. Corbett, "Preface to the First Edition" in *Classical Rhetoric for the Modern Student*, 2nd ed. (New York: Oxford Univ. Press, 1972), p. xi.
24. The most obvious and heartening evidences of this new sense of respect and cooperation were found at the Wingspread Conference and the National Confer-

ence on Rhetoric in 1970, which brought together scholars in speech, communications, philosophy, English, and sociology. As Corbett said to the Wingspread conferees: "Rhetoric is the common interest that has drawn us together. Perhaps the Humanities is the only other aegis under which one could imagine a convention of scholars from so many different departments." See "Rhetoric in Search of a Past, Present, and Future," in *The Prospect of Rhetoric*, ed. Lloyd F. Bitzer and Edwin Black (Englewood Cliffs, N.J.: Prentice-Hall, 1971).

25. Michael C. Leff, "In Search of Ariadne's Thread: A Review of the Recent Literature on Rhetorical Theory," *Central States Speech Journal*, 29 (Summer 1978), 90.
26. Ibid., p. 90.
27. In "Paradigms and Problems: Needed Research in Rhetorical Invention" (in *Research on Composing: Points of Departure*, ed. Charles Cooper and Lee Odell (Urbana, Ill.: NCTE, 1978), pp. 29–47), Richard Young, in summarizing what he sees as the dominant paradigm in composition studies, notes that "researchers have been primarily concerned with problems of application, most notably with pedagogical practice, rather than problems of theory" (p. 31).
28. There were a few exceptions to this situation. One of the most notable of those was the University of Iowa, which began offering graduate degrees in composition and rhetoric in the late 1960s. Rensselaer Polytechnic Institute announced a new program in communication and rhetoric in 1969, and the University of Southern California announced its doctoral program in literature, linguistics, and rhetoric in 1972.
29. See, for example, James J. Murphy, "Rhetorical History as a Guide to the Salvation of American Reading and Writing: A Plea for Curricular Change" and James Kinneavy, "Restoring the Humanities: The Return of Rhetoric from Exile" in *The Rhetorical Tradition and Modern Writing*, ed. James J. Murphy (New York: Modern Language Association, 1982), pp. 3–12 and 19–28, respectively.
30. For a discussion of some of these programs, see Janice M. Lauer, "Doctoral Programs in Rhetoric," *Rhetoric Society Quarterly*, 10 (Fall 1980), 190–94.

Chapter 2. Plato Revisited: A Theory of Discourse for All Seasons

1. James L. Golden, Goodwin Berquist, and William Coleman, *The Rhetoric of Western Thought* (Dubuque, Iowa: Kendall/Hunt Publishing Co., 1976). Also see 2nd ed., 1978.
2. In the development of these claims, the author is deeply indebted to his colleagues—Goodwin Berquist, William Brown, Josina Makau, and John Makay—for their helpful criticism and advice.
3. Cicero, *De Optimo*, vi, 17.
4. Max Harold Fisch and Thomas G. Bergin, trans., *The Autobiography of Giambattista Vico* (Ithaca: Cornell Univ. Press, 1944), p. 139.
5. Cicero, *Orator*, iii, 10.
6. Ibid., xix, 62.
7. Kenneth Burke, *Grammar of Motives and Rhetoric of Motives* (Cleveland: World Publishing Co., 1962), p. 253.
8. Pierre Lévêque has observed, "His [Plato's] influence was so profound, so enduring and so varied that . . . all the philosophers of the western world have only been able to add footnotes to his work." *The Greek Adventure* (Cleveland: World Publishing Co., 1968), p. 357; and Bertrand Russell asserted, "Plato and Aristotle were the most influential of all philosophers, ancient, medieval, or modern; and of the two, it was Plato who had the greater effect upon subsequent ages." *A History of Western Philosophy* (New York: Simon and Schuster, 1945), p. 104.

9. *The Autobiography of Giambattista Vico,* p. 199.
10. This point of view was expressed to the author by Dr. Robert Scott who made a lecture visit to Ohio State University.
11. Edith Hamilton and Huntington Cairns, eds., *Timaeus,* in *The Collected Dialogues of Plato* (New York: Bollingen Foundation, 1961), p. 1198. Unless otherwise specified all references to Plato's dialogues will be taken from this source.
12. *Sophist,* p. 1007.
13. *Euthyphro,* In Irwin Edman, ed., *The Works of Plato* (New York: Random House, Modern Library, 1928), p. 37.
14. After the author completed the original draft of his essay, the following insightful article appeared in print—James Hikins, "Plato's Rhetorical Theory: Old Perspectives on the Epistemology of the New Rhetoric," *Central States Speech Journal,* 32 (Fall 1981), 160–76. A principal thesis of this study is that Plato "developed a theory of discourse whose paradigmatic form was intrapersonal." The point of view being developed here, while recognizing the intrapersonal factor in Plato's theory, puts its primary emphasis on the interpersonal dimensions.
15. *Theaetetus,* in Edman, *Works of Plato,* p. 546. Subsequent references to this dialogue will be taken from this source.
16. See *Statesman,* pp. 1075–76. (It is interesting here to observe that, according to tradition, Demosthenes found much in Plato's teachings that assisted him in developing his orations. Cicero noted in the *Brutus,* "It is reported that Demosthenes read Plato diligently, even that he was his pupil—and this too is apparent from the character and sublimity of his vocabulary; in fact he himself is authority for the statement in one of his letters." XXXI, 121. Expressing a similar view, Plutarch observed, "Hermippus says that he met with certain memoirs without any author's name, in which it was written that Demosthenes was a scholar to Plato, and learnt much of his eloquence from him." *Lives* [New York: Random House, Modern Library, n.d.], p. 1025.)
17. *Phaedrus,* in Lane Cooper, ed., *Plato* (London: Oxford Univ. Press, 1938), p. 47. Subsequent references to this dialogue will be taken from this source. In buttressing the view set forth in the *Phaedrus,* Quintilian makes the following compelling observation: "Plato in his *Sophist* in addition to public and forensic oratory introduces a third kind which he styles προσομιλητική—which I will permit myself to translate by "conversational.' This is distinct from forensic oratory and is adapted for private discussions, and we may regard it as identical with dialectic." *Institutio Oratoria,* III, iv, 10.
18. The brilliant speech by Agathon in the *Symposium* is a typical example.
19. See the following essay dealing with Plato's method: Philip De Lacy, "Plato and the Method of the Arts," in Leitpold Wallach, ed., *The Classical Tradition* (Ithaca: Cornell Univ. Press, 1966), pp. 123–32.
20. Cicero, *de Oratore,* I, x, 47 and *Orator,* iii, 10; *On the Sublime,* pp, 165–69; W. Rhys Roberts, trans., *Demetrius on Style* (Cambridge: Cambridge Univ. Press, 1965), pp. 325, 415, 417; and *Institutio Oratoria,* V, vii, 28.
21. *Institutio Oratoria,* II, xv, 27.
22. C. E. M. Joad, *Guide to Philosophy* (New York: Random House, 1936), p. 277.
23. B. Jowett, trans., Plato's *The Republic* (New York: Random House, Modern Library, n.d.), pp. 360–64. All subsequent references to this dialogue will be taken from this source, which will be cited as *Republic.*
24. *Language as Symbolic Action* (Berkeley: Univ. of California Press, 1966), p. 373.
25. Ibid.
26. *Meno,* pp. 364, 370.
27. *Phaedo,* p. 73.

28. Kenneth Burke, *Language as Symbolic Action* (Berkeley: Univ. of California Press, 1973), p. 476. The following statement from Hikins is also instructive: Seen from Plato's perspective, "rhetoric serves to search for truths or probabilities yet to be discovered." "Plato's Rhetorical Theory: Old Perspectives on the Epistemology of the New Rhetoric," 171.
29. *Critias*, p. 1214.
30. *Republic*, p. 217.
31. Ibid., p. 206.
32. *Charmides*, p. 111.
33. *Cratylus*, p. 429.
34. *Meno*, p. 363.
35. *Philebus*, p. 1105.
36. *Laches*, p. 140.
37. *Republic*, p. 249.
38. *Laws*, p. 1496.
39. *Thaetetus*, p. 515.
40. *Republic*, p. 142.
41. *Laws*, p. 1508.
42. Ibid., p. 1256.
43. *Statesman*, p. 1082.
44. *Phaedrus*, in Lane Cooper, ed., *Plato* (London: Oxford Univ. Press, 1938), pp. 31–32. All subsequent references to this dialogue will be taken from this source.
45. *Meno*, p. 380; *Phaedo*, p. 144; *Republic*, pp. 99, 116, 140, 262, 347; and *Protagoras*, in Edman, *Works of Plato*, p. 255. All subsequent references to the latter dialogue will be taken from this source.
46. *Republic*, p. 148.
47. *Gorgias*, in Cooper, *Plato*, p. 154. All subsequent references to this dialogue will be taken from this source.
48. *Laches*, p. 132.
49. *Sophist*, pp. 976, 978, 1017; *Statesman*, pp. 1060, 1069; *Theaetetus*, pp. 494, 498; and *Laws*, p. 1464.
50. *Gorgias*, pp. 196–97.
51. *Laws*, p. 1319; *Philebus*, p. 1121; *Republic*, p. 157.
52. Teilhard de Chardin, *The Phenomenon of Man* (New York: Harper, Colophon Books, 1955), p. 264.
53. *Republic*, p. 344.
54. *Phaedrus*, pp. 26–42.
55. Ernesto Grassi, *Rhetoric as Philosophy: The Humanist Tradition* (University Park: Pennsylvania State Univ. Press, 1980), pp. 30–32.
56. Ibid. The author is indebted to Grassi for his thoughtful analysis.
57. *Statesman*, p. 1075.
58. *Laws*, pp. 1308, 1441.
59. *Phaedo*, p. 66; *Gorgias*, pp. 112, 194, 199–205.
60. *Gorgias*, p. 179.
61. Grassi, p. 32.
62. *Phaedrus*, p. 60.
63. *Statesman*, p. 1080.
64. *Republic*, p. 344.
65. *Phaedrus*, p. 59.
66. *Sophist*, p. 993. For a further discussion of this point, see Burke. *Grammar of Motives and Rhetoric of Motives*, pp. 119, 230.
67. *Republic*, p. 74.

68. *Parmenides,* 924–25.
69. *Sophist,* p. 977.
70. *Republic,* p. 136. Another interesting point on age is Plato's opinion that prime of life for women ranges from twenty to forty, and for men twenty-five to fifty-five. These ages are tied in with the begetting of children. Ibid. p. 184.
71. Ibid., p. 176. The author is aware of the fact that women normally were not a part of the typical rhetorical situations in the ancient period. Yet what Plato says on sex differences and similarities is of importance to the modern student of rhetoric.
72. *Phaedrus,* pp. 31–32.
73. *Republic,* p. 174. Here Plato says, "the physician and the carpenter have different natures."
74. Ibid., p. 151.
75. *Menexenus,* p. 188.
76. *Phaedrus,* pp. 60–61.
77. *Statesman,* p. 1055.
78. *Laws,* p. 1313.
79. *Cratylus,* pp. 457–58. Also see *Laws* for similar comments on voice control and bodily activity. *Laws,* p. 1386.
80. *Republic,* p. 282.
81. *Sophist,* p. 998.
82. *Republic,* pp. 237, 281.
83. George Kennedy, *The Art of Persuasion in Greece* (Princeton: Princeton Univ. Press, 1963), p. 75.
84. *Gorgias,* p. 115. Also see *Phaedrus,* pp. 54, 68.
85. *Phaedrus,* p. 53.
86. De Lacy, "Plato and the Method of the Arts," p. 123.
87. Ibid., p. 123. Also see *Sophist,* p. 1006, and *Phaedrus,* p. 54. It is interesting to note that Plato's discussion of analysis and synthesis, of dividing and combining, is similar to Chaim Perelman's treatment of associative and dissociative techniques.
88. *Statesman,* pp. 1043–44.
89. *Gorgias,* p. 115.
90. *Sophist,* p. 973.
91. See *Phaedo,* p. 73; and *Theaetetus,* pp. 515–16.
92. Michel Meyer, "Dialectic and Questioning: Socrates and Plato," *American Philosophical Quarterly,* 17 (Oct. 1980), 283. The author is deeply indebted to Mr. Meyer for forwarding to him a copy of this extremely perceptive essay. Its influence has been present throughout this paper.
93. See Meyer's analysis.
94. *Apology,* in Edman, *Works of Plato,* p. 76.
95. *Meno,* p. 363.
96. Ibid.
97. *Theaetetus,* p. 492.
98. Ibid., pp. 501–2.
99. Meyer, "Dialectic and Questioning: Socrates and Plato," 281.
100. Ibid., 289.
101. Hamilton and Cairns, *Collected Dialogues of Plato,* p. 526.
102. For interesting insights on writing, see the *Phaedrus,* pp. 66–67. Plato's own methods of criticism are observable in his frequent comments on the speaking practices of the Sophists, and in his analyses of the oratory and writings of Pericles and Isocrates. Some of these evaluations may be found in the *Phaedrus,* pp. 58, 70–71; and in the *Gorgias,* pp. 192–93.

Chapter 3. On Distinctions between Classical and Modern Rhetoric

1. Daniel Fogarty, S.J., *Roots for a New Rhetoric* (New York: Russell and Russell, 1959), p. 130.
2. We are thinking particularly of Otis M. Walter, "On Views of Rhetoric, Whether Conservative or Progressive," *Quarterly Journal of Speech,* 49 (Dec. 1963), 367–82; rpt. in *Contemporary Theories of Rhetoric,* ed. Richard Johannesen (New York: Harper and Row, 1971), pp. 18–38; Richard Ohmann, "In Lieu of a New Rhetoric," *College English,* 26 (Oct. 1964), 17–22; rpt. in Johannesen, pp. 63–71; Wayne E. Brockriede, "Toward a Contemporary Aristotelian Theory of Rhetoric," *Quarterly Journal of Speech,* 52 (Feb. 1966), 33–40; rpt. in Johannesen, pp. 39–49; Herbert W. Simons, "Toward a New Rhetoric," *Pennsylvania Speech Annual,* 24 (Sept. 1967), 7–20; rpt. in Johannesen, pp. 50–62; Douglas Ehninger, "On Rhetoric and Rhetorics," *Western Speech,* 31 (1967), 242–49, and "On Systems of Rhetoric," *Philosophy and Rhetoric,* 1 (Summer 1968), 131–44; rpt. in *Contemporary Rhetoric,* ed. Douglas Ehninger (Glenview, Ill.: Scott, Foresman and Co., 1972), pp. 49–58; Howard Martin and Kenneth Andersen, *Speech Communication: Analyses and Readings* (Boston: Allyn and Bacon, 1968); Richard Young, Alton Becker, and Kenneth Pike, *Rhetoric: Discovery and Change* (New York: Harcourt, Brace, and World, 1970); S. Michael Halloran, "On the End of Rhetoric, Classical and Modern," *College English,* 36 (Feb. 1975), 621–31, and "Tradition and Theory in Rhetoric," *Quarterly Journal of Speech,* 62 (Oct. 1976), 234–41; Robert L. Scott, "A Synoptic View of Systems of Western Rhetoric," *Quarterly Journal of Speech,* 61 (Dec. 1975), 439–47, and its companion piece of the same title by Douglas Ehninger, 448–53; Richard Young, "Paradigms and Problems: Needed Research in Rhetorical Invention," in *Research on Composing,* ed. Charles Cooper and Lee Odell (Urbana, Ill.: NCTE, 1978), pp. 28–48; Frank Zappen, "Carl R. Rogers and Political Rhetoric," *Pre-Text,* 1 (Spring–Fall 1980), 95–113; and Paul Bator, "Aristotelian and Rogerian Rhetoric," *College Composition and Communication,* 31 (Dec. 1980), 427–32.
3. See, for example, Ehninger, "A Synoptic View of Systems of Western Rhetoric," p. 452; Young, Becker, and Pike, *Rhetoric: Discovery and Change,* p. 6; Halloran, "Tradition and Theory in Rhetoric," 236; and Zappen, "Carl R. Rogers and Political Rhetoric," 98.
4. These definitions stem primarily from Kenneth Burke's profound efforts to articulate a contemporary rhetoric, though Burke in no way upholds or sets forth the problematic distinctions we have previously detailed. For a discussion of man as communal, see Young, Becker, and Pike's *Rhetoric: Discovery and Change,* pp. 7–9, and the articles on dialogic communication listed in note 9.
5. Halloran, "On the End of Rhetoric, Classical and Modern," 624.
6. *Rhetoric: Discovery and Change,* p. 6. This notion is reiterated by Paul Bator in "Aristotelian and Rogerian Rhetoric."
7. Douglas Ehninger, "George Campbell and the Revolution in Inventional Theory," *Southern Speech Journal,* 15 (May 1950), 274.
8. See, for example, Robert L. Scott, "Dialogue and Rhetoric," in *Rhetoric and Communication,* ed. J. Blankenship and H. G. Stelzner (Urbana: Univ. of Illinois Press, 1976), p. 101; David B. Strother, "Communication and Human Response: A Heuristic View," also in the Blankenship and Stelzner volume; and Paul Bator, "Aristotelian and Rogerian Rhetoric," previously cited in note 2. *Rhetoric: Discovery and Change* also perpetuates this view.
9. Richard L. Johannesen, "The Emerging Concept of Communication as Dialogue," *Quarterly Journal of Speech,* 57 (1971), 373–82; John Stewart, "Foun-

dations of Dialogic Communication," *Quarterly Journal of Speech,* 64 (1978), 183–201; John Poulakos, "The Components of Dialogue," *Western Speech,* 38 (1974), 199–212; Floyd Matson and Ashley Montagu, eds., *The Human Dialogue* (New York: Macmillan, Free Press, 1967); Frank Keller and Charles Brown, "An Interpersonal Ethic for Communication," *Journal of Communication,* 16 (1968), 73–81.

10. *Rhetoric: Discovery and Change,* pp. 8–9.

11. Ehninger, "On Systems of Rhetoric," in *Contemporary Rhetoric,* p. 53.

12. I. A. Richards, *The Philosophy of Rhetoric* (New York: Oxford Univ. Press, 1936), p. 24.

13. Wilbur Samuel Howell, *Eighteenth-Century British Logic and Rhetoric* (Princeton, N.J.: Princeton Univ. Press, 1971), pp. 441–42.

14. See note 2 for full citations.

15. Ohmann, "In Lieu of a New Rhetoric," rpt. in *Contemporary Theories of Rhetoric,* p. 64.

16. They do so often in reference to Aristotle's condemnation, early in Book I, of *pathos* in the hands of the technographers. Yet Aristotle by no means denies that *pathos* is part of the rhetorical art. He is rather questioning the misuse of *pathos* by these technographers. See William Grimaldi, *Aristotle, Rhetoric I: A Commentary* (Bronx, N.Y.: Fordham Univ. Press, 1980), p. 7.

17. As we were completing this essay, we were fortunate to receive a copy of an article by Floyd D. Anderson, "The Classical Conception of Communication as Dialogue." Professor Anderson makes a very persuasive argument in his essay for all of classical rhetoric as sharing what we argue is an Aristotelian view of communication. We are indebted to Professor Anderson for sharing his insights with us.

18. William M. A. Grimaldi, *Studies in the Philosophy of Aristotle's Rhetoric* (Wiesbaden: Frans Steiner Verlag, 1972), p. 18. Subsequent references will be cited in the text as *Studies.*

19. Christopher Lyle Johnstone, "An Aristotelian Trilogy: Ethics, Rhetoric, Politics, and the Search for Moral Truth," *Philosophy and Rhetoric,* 13 (Winter 1980), 1–24. Subsequent references will be cited in the text.

20. The failure to read the *Rhetoric* in light of Aristotle's other works is further exacerbated by difficulties in translation. In "The Greekless Reader and Aristotle's *Rhetoric,*" Thomas M. Conley demonstrates that Lane Cooper's popular translation is seriously flawed in a number of places. In particular, Conley argues that where Aristotle discusses the importance of getting the "judge into the right frame of mind," the Greek does not "express the one-way view of persuasion" ususally inferred. *Quarterly Journal of Speech,* 65 (1979), 75.

21. Lawrence W. Rosenfield, "Rhetorical Criticism and an Aristotelian Notion of Process," *Quarterly Journal of Speech,* 33 (Mar. 1966), 1–16. Subsequent references will be cited in the text.

22. Douglas Ehninger notes, for example, in his discussion of "Campbell, Blair, and Whately Revisited," *Southern Speech Journal,* 28 (Spring 1963), 169–82, that in classical rhetorical theory the *pisteis* "were viewed as autonomous. Each was considered as complete in itself, and as entirely capable of effecting conviction without the aid of the others" (172).

23. Grimaldi, *Aristotle, Rhetoric I: A Commentary.* Subsequent references will be cited in the text and notes as *Commentary.*

24. The heart of Grimaldi's analysis reveals that the Greek word for *pisteis* is used by Aristotle to indicate both *logos, pathos,* and *ethos* (the *entechnic pisteis*) and *enthymeme*

and *paradeigma* (the *apodeictic pisteis*). See especially the Appendix, "The Role of the *Pisteis* in Aristotle's Methodology," *Commentary*, pp. 349–56.

25. See Aristotle, *The "Art" of Rhetoric*, trans. John Henry Freese (Cambridge: Harvard Univ. Press, Loeb Classical Library, 1926), 1355a 27–28, 1395b 31–1396a 4, 1402a 33–34.

26. We are indebted to Michael Halloran for pointing out that the oratory of fourth-century B.C. Athens reveals much about contemporary cultural turmoil.

27. Lloyd Bitzer, "Aristotle's Enthymeme Revisited," *Quarterly Journal of Speech*, 45 (Dec. 1959), 408.

28. Grimaldi makes essentially the same point: "As soon as it is understood that rhetoric for Aristotle is an activity which engages the whole person in an effort to communicate meaning by way of language a major obstacle toward understanding the *Rhetoric* is removed" (*Studies*, p. 53).

29. Richard Hughes, "The Contemporaneity of Classical Rhetoric," *College Composition and Communication*, 16 (1965), 158–59.

30. Kenneth Burke, *A Rhetoric of Motives* (1950; rpt. Berkeley: Univ. of California Press, 1969). p. 46.

31. Ibid., p. 43.

32. In "Rhetoric in the American College Curriculum: The Decline of Public Discourse" *Pre/Text*, 3 (1982), 245–69, Michael Halloran traces the move from oral discourse to written discourse in American colleges and draws a number of provocative and insightful conclusions about the results of that move.

33. Grimaldi provides an illuminating discussion of the relationship of *techne* to *dynamis* in *Commentary*, pp. 5–6.

34. Among the articles we have read which draw distinctions between classical and modern rhetoric, Michael Halloran's works cited in note 2 deal substantively with this epistemological difference.

35. Michael Polanyi, *Personal Knowledge: Towards a Post-Critical Philosophy* (Chicago: Univ. of Chicago Press, 1962), p. 3.

36. Otis Walter has recently argued that the opening sentence of the *Rhetoric* be interpreted as "Rhetoric must follow the lead of an informed, searching and brilliant intellect" and that this sentence is the most significant in the *Rhetoric* because it "carries Aristotle's revolutionary intent, because it suggests his concern for knowing, [and] because it contains the ethical case for knowledge." Such an interpretation fits well with, and indeed supports, our view of Aristotle's concept of rhetoric and its relationship to knowledge and human action. See "The Most Important Sentence in Aristotle's Rhetoric," *Rhetoric Society Quarterly*, 12 (1982), 18–20.

37. In "An Adequate Epistemology for Composition: Classical and Modern Perspectives," also in this volume, John Gage presents a persuasive discussion of how the concept of the enthymeme has been reduced to sterile formulae in modern texts, and he goes on to show how a fuller understanding of Aristotle's enthymeme can provide the kind of theoretical framework we are calling for here.

Chapter 4. The Evolution of the Analytic *Topoi*: A Speculative Inquiry

1. Richard Young, "Invention: A Topographical Survey," in *Teaching Composition: 10 Bibliographical Essays*, ed. Gary Tate (Fort Worth: Texas Christian Univ. Press, 1976), p. 3.

2. Ibid.

3. Ibid., p. 4.

4. Frank J. D'Angelo, "An Ontological Basis for a Modern Theory of the Composing Process," *Quarterly Journal of Speech*, 64 (Feb. 1978), 79. The connections I am making in this paper are generally true for Western thought only.
5. Heinz Werner, *Developmental Processes: Heinz Werner's Selected Writings*, Vol. 1, ed. Sybil Barten and Margery B. Franklin (New York: International Universities Press, 1978), pp. 86, 111–12.
6. Eric Havelock, *Preface to Plato* (Cambridge: Harvard Univ. Press, 1963), pp. 198–99.
7. Julian Jaynes, *The Origin of Consciousness in the Breakdown of the Bicameral Mind* (Boston: Houghton Mifflin Co., 1977), p. 69. Some of Jaynes' ideas have been widely criticized, but his conclusions about Iliadic man seem to be supported by Havelock.
8. Havelock, *Preface to Plato*, pp. 216–20.
9. Ibid., p. 264.
10. Ibid., pp. 295–97.
11. Walter J. Ong, S.J., *The Presence of the Word* (New Haven and London: Yale Univ. Press, 1967), pp. 82–83.
12. Ibid., p. 85.
13. Havelock, *Preface to Plato*, p. 296.
14. Jaynes, *The Origin of Consciousness*, p. 279.
15. Robert E. Ornstein, *The Psychology of Consciousness* (New York: Viking Press, 1972), p. 67.
16. G. E. R. Lloyd, *Polarity and Analogy: Two Types of Argumentation in Early Greek Thought* (Cambridge: At the Univ. Press, 1966), p. 6.
17. Mario Untersteiner, *The Sophists*, trans. Kathleen Freeman (Oxford: Basil Blackwell, 1954), p. 29.
18. Lloyd, *Polarity and Analogy*, p. 23.
19. Ibid., p. 16.
20. Ibid.
21. Ibid., p. 125.
22. Ibid., pp. 126–48.
23. Ibid., p. 127.
24. Ibid., pp. 148–58.
25. Ibid., p. 162.
26. Ibid., p. 305.
27. Ibid., pp. 403–14.
28. Ong, *The Presence of the Word*, p. 85.
29. Friedrich Solmsen, "The Aristotelian Tradition in Ancient Rhetoric," *American Journal of Philology*, 62 (1941), 40.
30. I am listing them in tabular form for ease of reference, based on the notes, in *The Rhetoric of Aristotle*, trans., Lane Cooper (New York: Appleton-Century-Crofts, 1932), pp. 159–72.
31. William Grimaldi, S.J., "The Aristotelian Topics," *Traditio*, 14 (1958), 1.
32. Donovan J. Ochs, "Aristotle's Concept of the Formal Topics," *Speech Monographs*, 36 (Nov. 1969), 420.
33. Ibid., p. 424.
34. See especially Cicero's *Topica* in *De Inventione, De Optimo Genere Oratorum, Topica*, trans. H. M. Hubbell (Cambridge: Harvard Univ. Press, Loeb Classical Library, 1949).
35. Sister Miriam Joseph, *Shakespeare's Use of the Arts of Language* (New York and London: Hafner Publishing Co., 1966), pp. 35–36.

36. Ibid., p. 36.
37. J. Donald Ragsdale, "Invention in English 'Stylistic' Rhetorics: 1600–1800," *Quarterly Journal of Speech* (Apr. 1965), 164.
38. S. M. Halloran, "Tradition and Theory in Rhetoric," *Quarterly Journal of Speech,* 62 (Oct. 1976), 239.
39. Theodore Hunt, *The Principles of Written Discourse,* 2nd ed. (New York: A. C. Armstrong and Son, 1884), pp. 95–120.
40. James de Mille, *The Elements of Rhetoric* (New York: Harper & Brothers, 1878), pp. 102–203; David J. Hill, *The Science of Rhetoric* (New York: Sheldon and Co., 1877), pp. 202–43 passim.
41. John F. Wilson and Carroll C. Arnold, *Public Speaking as a Liberal Art,* 3rd ed. (Boston: Allyn and Bacon, 1974), p. 79.
42. Otto Bird, "Tradition of the Logical Topics: Aristotle to Ockham," *Journal of the History of Ideas,* 23 (July 1962), 311–12.
43. William F. Nelson, "Topoi: Evidence of Human Conceptual Behavior," *Philosophy and Rhetoric,* 2 (Winter 1969), 9.
44. Ibid., pp. 9–10.
45. Frank J. D'Angelo, "Notes Toward a Semantic Theory of Rhetoric Within a Case Grammar Framework," *College Composition and Communication,* 27 (Dec. 1976), 259–62.
46. W. Ross Winterowd, "The Grammar of Coherence," *Contemporary Rhetoric* (New York: Harcourt Brace Jovanovich, 1975), pp. 225–26.
47. Kenneth Pike, "Language as Particle, Wave, and Field," *Texas Quarterly,* 2 (1959), 37–54.
48. Richard Young, Alton Becker, and Kenneth Pike, *Rhetoric: Discovery and Change* (New York: Harcourt, Brace, and World, 1970), p. 27.
49. Frank J. D'Angelo, *A Conceptual Theory of Rhetoric* (Cambridge, Mass.: Winthrop Publishers, 1975).
50. Frank J. D'Angelo, "An Ontological Basis for a Modern Theory of the Composing Process," *Quarterly Journal of Speech,* 64 (Feb. 1978), 79–85.
51. D'Angelo, *A Conceptual Theory of Rhetoric,* pp. 42–47.
52. Frank J. D'Angelo, "Paradigms as Structural Counterparts of *Topoi,*" in *Linguistics, Stylistics, and the Teaching of Composition,* ed. Donald McQuade (Akron, Ohio: L & S Books, 1979), pp. 41–51; "*Topoi,* Paradigms, and Psychological Schemata," in *Proceedings of the Inaugural Conference of the University of Maryland Junior Writing Program,* 17 March 1980, ed. Michael Marcuse and Susan Kleimann (College Park: Univ. of Maryland, 1981), pp. 12–16.

Chapter 5. Translating Theory into Practice in Teaching Composition: A Historical View and a Contemporary View

1. Kathleen Freeman, *Ancilla to the Pre-Socratic Philosophers: A Complete Translation of the Fragments in Diels' Fragmente der Vorsokratiker* (Cambridge, Mass.: Harvard Univ. Press, 1956), p. 13; J. B. Bury, *The Ancient Greek Historians* (New York: Dover Publications, 1958), p. 5.
2. Bury, *The Ancient Greek Historians,* p. 15.
3. Ernst Cassirer, *An Essay on Man* (New Haven: Yale Univ. Press, 1944), pp. 111–17.
4. Plato, *Phaedrus,* trans. W. C. Helmbold and W. G. Rabinowitz (Indianapolis: Bobbs Merrill Co., 1956), 271D–272B.

5. But cf. D. Levi, "Il concetto de *kairos* e la filosofia di Platone," *Rendiconti della Reale Accademia Nazionale dei Lincei, Classe di scienzia morali,* Ser. 5, 33 (1924), 93–118.

6. *On Literary Composition,* trans. W. Rhys Roberts (London: Macmillan and Co., 1910), pp. 12, 84.

7. Isocrates, *Isocrates II,* trans. George Norlin, "On the Peace" (Cambridge: Harvard Univ. Press, Loeb Classical Library, 1968), Sec. 8.

8. Isocrates, "Antidosis," Sec. 271, same edition as cited in note 7.

9. See Ben Jonson, "Timber, or Discoveries," *Ben Jonson,* ed. C. H. Herford, Percy and Evelyn Simpson (Oxford: At the Clarendon Press, 1947), VIII, pp. 637–41.

10. See Donald Lemen Clark, *Rhetoric in Greco-Roman Education* (New York: Columbia Univ. Press, 1957), pp. 177–211.

11. Isocrates is also usually given credit for providing the political basis of humanism, which he equated to the intellectual and the cultural. See Isocrates, *Isocrates I,* trans. George Norlin, "Panegyricus" (Cambridge: Harvard Univ. Press, Loeb Classical Library, 1968), Sec. 51: "The man who shares our paideia is a Greek in a higher sense than he who only shares our blood."

12. Werner Jaeger, *Aristotle: Fundamentals of the History of His Development* (Oxford: Oxford Univ. Press, 1948); Ingemar During, *Aristoteles: Darstellung und Interpretation seines Denkens* (Heidelberg: Karl Winter, 1966); François Nuyens, *L'Evolution de la psychologie d'Aristote,* trans. from Dutch, no trans. given (Paris: Librairie Philosophique J. Vrin, 1948).

13. Anton-Hermann Chroust, *Aristotle: New Light on His Life and on Some of His Lost Works, Vol. II: Observations on Some of Aristotle's Lost Works* (Notre Dame, Ind.: Univ. of Notre Dame Press, 1973), pp. 29–42.

14. See René Antoine Gauthier, O.P., and Jean Yves Jolif, O.P., *Aristote: L'Ethique a'Nicomaque* (Louvain: Publications Universitaires de Louvain, 1959), II, 466–67.

15. I do not mean to imply that the inductive method of Plato is a necessary corollary of a *theoria,* nor that the deductive method of Aristotle is a corollary of a modified *theoria.*

16. See Martin Heidegger, *Being and Time,* trans. John Macquarrie and Edward Robinson (New York: Harper & Row, 1962), pp. 148–60, for his basic presentation of the notion of interpretation (pages are from the seventh German edition, glossed in the English translation).

17. See Heidegger, *Being and Time,* pp. 157–58, 232–34, 290–91, 311–13, 327–33.

18. Hans-Georg Gadamer, *Truth and Method,* trans. Barden J. Cumming (New York: Seabury Press, 1979), pp. 241–74.

19. See the introductory section to Kenneth Burke, *A Grammar of Motives* (Berkeley: Univ. of California Press, 1969).

20. Rudolf Bultmann, "New Testament and Mythology," In Hans Werner Bartsch, ed., *Kerygma and Myth: A Theological Debate,* trans. Reginald H. Fuller (London: S.P.C.K., 1953), pp. 1–45.

21. See Rudolf Bultmann, *The History of the Synoptic Tradition,* trans. John Marsh (New York: Harper & Row, 1968), p. 4.

22. See Roy Turner, ed., *Ethnomethodology: Selected Readings* (Baltimore, Md.: Penquin Books, 1975).

23. See the largest section in Turner, *Ethnomethodology,* pp. 21–194.

24. See Jean-Paul Sartre, *The Critique of Dialectical Reason, Vol. 1: The Theory of Practical Ensembles,* trans. Alan Sheridan-Smith, ed. Jonathan Ree (London: NJB, 1976), pp. 79–94; Jurgen Habermas, *Theory and Practice,* trans. John Viertel

(Boston: Beacon Press, 1973); Pierre Bourdieu, *Outline of a Theory of Practice*, trans. Richard Nice, ed. Jack Coody, in Cambridge Studies in Social Anthropology, 16 (London: Cambridge University Press, 1977); J. Bernstein, *Praxis and Action: Contemporary Philosophies of Human Activity* (Philadelphia: Univ. of Pennsylvania Press, 1971).

25. Lloyd F. Bitzer, "The Rhetorical Situation," *Philosophy and Rhetoric*, 1 (1968), 1–14.

26. See Richard Vatz, "The Myth of the Rhetorical Situation," *Philosophy and Rhetoric*, 6 (1972), 154–61.

27. Ernesto Grassi, *Rhetoric as Philosophy: The Humanist Tradition*, trans. John Michael Krois and Azizeh Azodi (University Park: Pennsylvania State Univ. Press, 1980); Samuel Ijselling, *Rhetoric and Philosophy in Conflict: An Historic Survey*, trans. Paul Dunphy (The Hague: M. Nijhoff, 1976).

28. See Kurt Baier, *The Moral Point of View: A Rational Basis of Ethics* (Ithaca, N.Y.: Cornell Univ. Press, 1958).

29. Chaim Perelman and L. Olbrechts-Tyteca, *The New Rhetoric: A Treatise on Argumentation*, trans. John Wilkinson and Purcell Weaver (Notre Dame, Ind.: Univ. of Notre Dame Press, 1969).

30. Heidegger, *Being and Time*, pp. 157–59; and "The Question Concerning Technology," trans. William Lovitt, in *Martin Heidegger: Basic Writings*, ed. David Farrell Krell (New York: Harper & Row, 1977), pp. 283–317.

31. Frederich Pollock, "Empirical Research into Public Opinion," trans. Thomas Hall, In *Critical Sociology*, ed. Paul Connerton (New York: Penguin Books, 1976), pp. 225–36.

32. Theodore W. Adorno, "Sociology and Empirical Research," trans. Graham Bartram, in Connerton, *Critical Sociology*, pp. 237–57.

33. Max Horkheimer, "Traditional and Critical Theory," trans. M. J. O. O'Connell, in Connerton, *Critical Sociology*, pp. 206–24.

34. Hugh Mehan, "The Imposition of Reality," in Hugh Mehan and Houston Woods, eds., *The Reality of Ethnomethodology* (New York: John Wiley & Sons, 1975), p. 54.

Chapter 6. Rational Appeal and the Ethics of Advocacy

1. Advocacy in the Greek rhetorical tradition centers on every man's being his own advocate. But with the introduction of ghost-written speeches and with professional advocacy in Roman legal traditions we have a narrow or restricted sense of advocacy. Deception, on the other hand, at least in the tradition of logical fallacies, moves from the restricted sense of deliberate deception as in Aristotle's treatment of fallacies to their psychological treatment beginning with Francis Bacon and John Locke. To treat fallacies as mental mistakes extends deception to self-deception and mistakenly induced confusion. Of course, rhetors can be held ethically responsible for intellectual mistakes even though not deliberate or intentionally manipulative.

2. Aristotle, *Rhetoric*, 1355B. All quotations from Aristotle's *Rhetoric* and *On Sophistical Refutations* are from *Basic Works of Aristotle*, Richard McKeon, ed. (New York: Random House, 1941).

3. Aristotle, *Rhetoric*, 1355A.

4. "A Revision of the Concept of Ethical Appeal," *Philosophy and Rhetoric*, 12 (Winter 1979), 41–58.

5. "Licit and Illicit in Rhetorical Appeals," *Western Journal of Speech Communication*, 22 (Fall 1978), 222–30.

6. Ibid., 230.
7. Plato, *Phaedrus* 269–74.
8. Aristotle, *Rhetoric,* 1354A.
8. Ibid., 1356A.
10. Ibid.
11. Ibid., 1354A.
12. Ibid.
13. Ibid.
14. Ibid., 1355A.
15. Ibid., 1354B.
16. Aristotle, *On Sophistical Refutations,* 165B.
17. Ibid., 168A.
18. C. L. Hamlin, *Fallacies* (London: Methuen, 1970), p. 17.
19. Aristotle, *Rhetoric,* 1401A.
20. Ibid., 1402A.
21. Ibid.
22. Lane Cooper, *The Rhetoric of Aristotle* (New York: Appleton-Century-Crofts, 1932), p. 177. Edward Meredith Cope, *The Rhetoric of Aristotle with Commentary,* vols. I, II, and III, John Edwin Sandys, ed. (New York: Arno Press, 1973), 321.
23. Hamlin, *Fallacies,* p. 94.
24. "Lying and Communication," an unpublished paper delivered at the Conference of College Composition and Communication, Apr. 1979.
25. Augustine, "Lying," *Treatise on Various Subjects,* ed. R. J. Defarri, Fathers of the Church (New York: Catholic Univ. of America Press, 1952), Vol. 14, ch. 14. Thomas Aquinas, *Summa Theologica,* 2.2 question 110 art. 2, 4.
26. Sissela Bok, *Lying: Moral Choice in Public and Private Life* (New York: Knopf, Vintage, 1979).
27. H. P. Grice, "Logics and Conversation," *The Logic of Grammar,* Donald Davidson and Gilbert Harman, eds. (Encino, Calif.: Dickenson, 1975), pp. 64–75.
28. "Rules, Conventions, Constraints, and Rhetorical Actions," *Rhetoric Society Quarterly,* 9 (Winter 1979), 28–35. I tried to outline in this article the range of constraints that are not dependent upon rules or conventions of speech acts and the degree to which speech act theory is not adequate to the study of constraints in rhetorical situations. I wish to emphasize that although speech act theory is important in analyzing what it is to lie, a wider sociological frame is necessary for a careful analysis of what it is to lie.
29. J. L. Austin, *How to Do Things With Words* (Cambridge: Harvard Univ. Press, 1962).
30. John Searle, *Speech Acts* (Cambridge: Cambridge Univ. Press, 1969), pp. 57–64.
31. Hugo Grotius, *On the Laws of War and Peace* (New York: Bobbs-Merrill, 1925), bk. 3, chap. 1.
32. Henry Sidgwick, *The Method of Ethics,* 7th ed. (Chicago: Univ. of Chicago Press, 1970), p. 315.
33. *Official Rules of Card Games,* 61st ed. (Cincinnati: United States Playing Card Co., 1968).

Chapter 7. Ethos and the Aims of Rhetoric

1. For other views on the status of ethos see George E. Yoos, "A Revision of the Concept of Ethical Appeal," *Philosophy and Rhetoric,* 12 (Winter 1979), 41–58. Yoos traces his interpretation of how ethos has "become a morally neutral term in

contemporary studies" (p. 41). See also Christopher Lyle Johnstone, "An Aristotelian Trilogy: Ethics, Rhetoric, Politics, and the Search for Moral Truth," *Philosophy and Rhetoric,* 13 (Winter 1980), 1–24.

2. Plato, *Gorgias,* trans. Walter Hamilton (Middlesex: Penguin Books, 1975), p. x. All other references to Plato's *Gorgias* are cited parenthetically. The remainder of Plato's commentary on rhetoric is in *Phaedrus.* References in this discussion to *Phaedrus* refer to the following edition. *Phaedrus,* trans. W. C. Helmbold and W. G. Rabinowitz (Indianapolis: Bobbs-Merrill Educational Publishing, 1978).

3. See also *Gorgias*: "The good orator, being also a man of expert knowledge, will have these ends in view in any speech or action by which he seeks to influence the souls of men. . . . his attention will be wholly concentrated on bringing righteousness and moderation and every other virtue to birth in the souls of his fellow citizens" (pp. 112–13).

4. See Plato, *The Republic,* trans. H. D. Lee (Middlesex: Penguin Books, 1973), "The Philosopher Ruler" and "The Immortality of the Soul and the Rewards of Goodness," pp. 231–78 and 387–93.

5. *Republic,* trans. H. D. Lee, p. 251. Plato's description of the philosopher- orator in the *Gorgias* is based on his overall definition of the role of the statesman which he articulates most fully in the *Republic.* He points out that "anyone who is to be a really good man" must have "truthfulness" as a "first requisite."

6. Aristotle, *Rhetoric,* Trans. Ingram Bywater (New York: Random House, Modern Library, 1959), p. 24. All other references to the *Rhetoric* are to this edition and are cited parenthetically.

7. George Yoos observes that Aristotle's presentation of ethos "lays a foundation for dissimulation" in the portrayal of character. See Yoos, "Revision of the Concept of Ethical Appeal," p. 45. I would argue that "confused aims" about ethos have resulted from the failure of later rhetoricians, particularly of Cicero, to incorporate Aristotle's notion of the Good.

8. See Aristotle, *The Nicomachean Ethics,* trans. David Ross, (Oxford: Oxford Univ. Press, 1980), Book One, "The Good for Man," p. 1–29.

9. Aristotle's discussion of the "mean" and moral "virtue" in Book II of *The Nicomachean Ethics,* trans. David Ross, outlines his theory that virtue is a quality of aiming at the "intermediate". This is a very different notion from those usually associated with ethos: the "convenient" or the "expedient".

10. Quintilian, *Institutio Oratoria,* trans. H. E. Butler (Cambridge: Harvard Univ. Press, Loeb Classical Library, 1960), I, 18. Other references to Quintilian are to this text and are cited parenthetically. Like Cicero, Quintilian held that the orator should be a person of broad intellectual competence; however, Quintilian's intention to educate the moral statesman reflects a certain nostalgia for a return to a sociocultural climate in which rhetoric had a greater impact than it had in the early Empire.

11. Cicero, *De Oratore,* trans. H. Rackham (Cambridge: Harvard Univ. Press, Loeb Classical Library, 1968), Books I–II. See I, vii–viii. Other references to Cicero are to this edition and are cited parenthetically.

12. This view of the history of rhetorical thought is thematic rather than schematic and attempts to view the evolution of the discipline as a whole, as a process emanating from a single source—classical rhetoric. For differing views of the tradition see Douglas Ehninger, "On Systems of Rhetoric" and Wayne E. Brockriede, "Dimensions of the Concept of Rhetoric," reprinted in *Contemporary Theories of Rhetoric: Selected Readings,* ed. Richard L. Johannesen (New York: Harper & Row, 1971), pp. 327–39 and 311–26.

13. Ars praedicandi flourished between 1200 and 1600 A.D. Over three hundred manuals on preaching from this period are still available to us. These texts are Ciceronian in framework but ethical in orientation. Ars dictaminus, a popular rhetorical art between 800 and 1250, incorporates Ciceronian stipulations about format. Alberic of Monte Cassino (1081) and Laurence of Aquilegia (1300) were major contributors to the theory of writing letters. For an extensive discussion of the development of these arts see James J. Murphy, *Rhetoric In the Middle Ages: A History of Rhetorical Theory from Saint Augustine to the Renaissance* (Berkeley: Univ. of California Press, 1974).

14. Anonymous, *The Principles of Letter-Writing* in *Three Medieval Rhetorical Arts,* ed. James J. Murphy (Berkeley: Univ. of California Press, 1971), pp. 1–26.

15. For an extensive discussion of the development of the rhetorical arts in the postclassical period see James J. Murphy, *Rhetoric in the Middle Ages: A History of Rhetorical Theory from Saint Augustine to the Renaissance* (Berkeley: Univ. of California Press, 1974).

16. Augustine, *On Christian Doctrine,* trans. D. W. Robertson, Jr. (Indianapolis: Bobbs-Merrill Educational Publishing, 1978), p. 118. Augustine's discussion of oratory is in Book Four, pp. 116–69. Other references to Augustine's work are to this edition and will be cited parenthetically.

17. George Campbell, *The Philosophy of Rhetoric,* ed. Lloyd E. Bitzer (Carbondale: Southern Illinois Univ. Press, 1963), p. 1. Other references cited parenthetically.

18. See Campbell, *The Philosophy of Rhetoric,* ch. IX, pp. 96–98.

19. See Joseph Priestley, *A Course of Lectures On Oratory and Criticism,* ed. Vincent M. Bevilacqua and Richard Murphy (Carbondale: Southern Illinois Univ. Press, 1965). Priestley discusses "sympathy" in Lecture XV on forms of address to gain belief. He explains that "the principle of sympathy" propagates conviction: "We are, in all cases, more disposed to give assent to any proposition, if we perceive that the person who contends for it is really in earnest and believes it himself" (p. 109). Similarly, Day discusses "sympathy" as a "law" of communication by which "emotion is communicated directly from one person to another." See Henry Day, *Elements of the Art of Rhetoric* (New York: A. S. Barnes & Burn, 1866), p. 145. Although faculty psychology appears to us now a terribly limited framework for explaining the relationship between cognition, response, and expression, its adaptation by influential rhetoricians of the eighteenth and nineteenth centuries as a philosophical matrix is yet another example of the consistency with which rhetoricians have traditionally related rhetorical theory to views of the nature of human understanding.

20. Hugh Blair, *Lectures on Rhetoric and Belles Lettres,* ed. Harold F. Harding (Carbondale: Southern Illinois Univ. Press, 1965), p. 100. All other references to Blair are to this text and will be cited parenthetically.

21. Richard Whately, *Elements of Rhetoric,* ed. Douglas Ehninger (Carbondale: Southern Illinois Univ. Press, 1963). Whately discussed sympathy and ethos in Part II, Chapter 1, under "the art of influencing the Will." Like Campbell and Blair, Whately sees ethos as a means to move the passions. See pp. 173–88.

22. Edward T. Channing, *Lectures Read to the Seniors in Harvard College,* ed. Dorothy I. Anderson and Waldo W. Braden (Cabondale: Southern Illinois Univ. Press, 1968), p. 23. Channing argues that although the nature of society has changed since the classical period, the need for oratory is even greater: "the orator himself is but one of the multitude, deliberating with them upon common interests, which are well understood and valued by all" (p. 17). Hereafter cited parenthetically.

23. Franz Theremin, *Eloquence A Virtue: An Outline of A Systematic Rhetoric,* trans. William T. Shedd, (Philadelphia: Smith, 1859). References will be made to the 1859 edition. Shedd describes Theremin's rhetoric as "organic" because Theremin refuses to separate invention, form, and content from a consideration of ethical intention. Shedd's preface to the work is a lengthy defense of the philosophical approach to rhetoric and a critique of the skills-oriented texts of the period. All references to Day's *Elements* will be made to the 1866 edition and will be cited parenthetically. Day's contribution to rhetoric lies mainly in his restoration of invention to rhetorical education at a time when stylistic technique was overemphasized. Day also innovated by treating expository writing as a mode equally important to the mode of persuasion, previously the single subject of rhetoric texts; Matthew Boyd Hope, *The Princeton Textbook in Rhetoric* (Princeton, N.J.: John T. Robinson, 1859). All other references are to this edition and will be cited parenthetically. Hope recommends that his text replace Whately's *Elements of Rhetoric* and be used in conjunction with Day's and Theremin's works, thus advising that the rhetorical curriculum could take on a more functional and pragmatic direction. Hope wanted his students to have a text that would instruct them in everyday communication.

24. Notable exceptions to this view are texts that reject the Aristotelian framework in part or altogether and present writing as a process of self-discovery or self-expression. See Ken Macrorie *Telling Writing,* 3rd ed. (Rochelle Park, N.J.: Hayden Book Company, 1981); Peter Elbow, *Writing With Power* (New York: Oxford University Press, 1981); William E. Coles, Jr., *Composing II: Writing As A Self-Creating Process* (Rochelle Park, N.J.: Hayden Book Company, 1981); Ann E. Berthoff, *Forming, Thinking, Writing: The Composing Imagination (Rochelle Park, N.J.: Hayden Book Company, 1978).*

25. Even a cursory review of current texts in composition reveals the frequency with which these terms give labels to the speaker's persuasive appeal. Representative examples include Glenn Leggett, C. Davic Mead, and William Charvat, *Prentice-Hall Handbook for Writers* (Englewood Cliffs, N.J.: Prentice-Hall, 1978). pp. 159–61; H. Ramsey Fowler, *The Little, Brown Handbook* (Boston: Little, Brown, 1980), pp. 88–89, 14–15; Frank D'Angelo, *Process and Thought in Composition* (Cambridge: Winthrop Publishers, 1980), pp. 20–21.

26. Maxine C. Hairston, *Successful Writing: A Rhetoric for Advanced Composition* (New York: W. W. Norton, 1981), p. 51. See also pp. 50–55.

27. Winston Weathers and Otis Winchester, *The New Strategy of Style* (New York: McGraw-Hill Book Company, 1978), p. 144.

28. An influential proponent of a neo-Aristotelian approach to rhetoric and ethos has been James Kinneavy, whose text *A Theory of Discourse* articulates a theory of rhetoric as competence in the forms of referential, persuasive, literary, and expressive prose. See *A Theory of Discourse* (Englewood Cliffs, N.J.: Prentice-Hall, 1971).

29. Richard M. Weaver, "Language is Sermonic" in *Language Is Sermonic: Richard M. Weaver on the Nature of Rhetoric,* eds. Richard L. Johannesen, Rennard Strickland, and Ralph T. Eubanks (Baton Rouge: Louisiana State Univ. Press, 1970), p. 54. All other references cited parenthetically.

30. Wayne Booth, *Modern Dogma and the Rhetoric of Assent* (Notre Dame: Univ. of Notre Dame Press, 1974), p. xiii. All other references cited parenthetically.

31. For samples of efforts to redirect contemporary rhetorical theory and education toward philosophical aims see John Warnock, "New Rhetoric and the Grammar of Pedagogy," *Freshman English News,* 5, No. 2 (Fall 1976), 1–21; Richard L.

Johannesen, "Some Pedagogical Implications of Richard M. Weaver's Views on Rhetoric," *College Composition and Communication,* 29, No. 3 (Oct. 1978), 272–79; Allen Ramsey, "Rhetoric and the Ethics of 'Seeming'," *Rhetoric Society Quarterly,* 11, No. 2, (Spring 1981), 85–96; David V. Harrington, "The Ethics of Invention," *Rhetoric Society Quarterly,* 10, No. 4 (Fall 1980), 254–60; Walter R. Fisher, "Rationality and the Logic of Good Reasons," *Philosophy and Rhetoric,* 13, No. 2 (Spring 1980), 121–29.

Chapter 8. The Continuing Relevance of Plato's *Phaedrus*

1. John H. Mackin, *Classical Rhetoric for Modern Discourse* (New York: Macmillan, Free Press, 1969), p. vi. For reasons which are not clear to me, Mackin does not indicate that he has quoted Plato, *Gorgias,* trans. Walter Hamilton (New York: Penguin Books, 1960), pp. 114–15 verbatim.
2. For discussion of these points, as well as other issues regarding the *Phaedrus,* I have drawn upon Oscar L. Brownstein, "Plato's *Phaedrus*: Dialectic as the Genuine Art of Speaking," *Quarterly Journal of Speech,* 51, No. 4 (1965), 392–98; G. J. De Vries, *A Commentary on the Phaedrus of Plato* (Amsterdam: Adolf M. Hakkert, 1969); George Grote, *Plato, and the Other Companions of Sokrates* (London: J. Murray, 1888; rpt. New York: Lenox Hill, 1973), III; William H. Thompson, note on p. 44, William Archer Butler, *Lectures on the History of Ancient Philosophy,* ed. Thompson (Cambridge: Cambridge Univ. Press for Macmillan and Co., 1856), II; Alfred E. Taylor, *Plato: The Man and His Work* (London: Methuen and Co., 1926); Werner Jaeger, "Plato's *Phaedrus*; Philosophy and Rhetoric," in *Paideia: The Ideals of Greek Culture,* trans. Gilbert Highet (Oxford: Blackwell, 1947), III, pp. 182–96; Mackin, *Classical Rhetoric for Modern Discourse*; Claude A. Thompson, "Rhetorical Madness: An Ideal in the *Phaedrus,*" *Quaterly Journal of Speech,* 55, No. 4 (1969), 358–63; Richard Weaver, "The *Phaedrus* and the Nature of Rhetoric," in *The Ethics of Rhetoric* (Chicago: Henry Regnery Co., 1953), pp. 311–29; Plato, *Phaedrus,* trans. Reginald Hackforth (London: Cambridge Univ. Press, 1972); E. B. Black, "Plato's View of Rhetoric," *Quarterly Journal of Speech,* 44, No. 4 (1958), 361–74; and Malcolm Brown and James Coulter, "The Middle Speech of Plato's *Phaedrus,*" *Journal of the History of Philosophy,* 9, No. 4 (1971), 404–23.
3. De Vries, in his *Commentary,* offers an extensive record of the scholarship on this point as well as on many other issues concerning the *Phaedrus*: its authenticity, textual history, characters, dramatic date, date of composition, representation of Lysias, references to Isocrates and response from him, and evaluation of writing.
4. See note by Thompson in Butler, *Lectures on the History of Ancient Philosophy,* II, p. 44; Grote, *Plato,* I, p. 263; Taylor, *Plato: The Man and His Work,* pp. 299, 300.
5. Taylor, *Plato: The Man and His Work,* p. 300.
6. Jaeger, "Plato's *Phaedrus*: Philosophy and Rhetoric," p. 186. Some extremely sophisticated and provocative modern explanations of the relationship between the treatment of love and rhetoric in the *Phaedrus* are provided by Black, Brownstein, and Brown and Coulter. The latter say that "the affinity of *eros* and rhetoric, and therefore the singular fitness of love as a subject for rhetoric, rests above all on the fact . . . that in Plato's view the rhetorician, like the philosopher, is also a lover. A discourse on love will therefore not only point up the skill of the rhetorician; it is also an appropriate means for revealing the very essence of his activity" (p. 418).
7. Thompson, "Rhetorical Madness," p. 358.

8. Plato, *Phaedrus,* trans. Hackforth, p. 9.
9. Ibid.
10. For amplification of this point, see Grote, *Plato,* III, p. 28; Donald C. Bryant, "The Most Significant Passage (for the Moment) in Plato's *Phaedrus,*" *Rhetoric Society Quarterly,* 11, No. 1 (1981), 10.
11. Thomas Conley, "*Phaedrus* 259e ff," *Rhetoric Society Quarterly,* 11, No. 1 (1981), 12.
12. Ibid., p. 14. Another who shares Conley's disenchantment with the *Phaedrus* is Richard Leo Enos, "The Most Significant Passage in Plato's *Phaedrus:* A Personal Nomination," *Rhetoric Society Quarterly,* 11, No. 1 (1981), 17. John Gage, in "A New Way into the *Phaedrus* and Composition: A Review," *Rhetoric Society Quarterly,* 11, No. 1 (1981), 29–34, also deals with the problem of the kind of knowledge Plato expected the rhetorician to have. His essay is a review of Ronna Burger's *Plato's Phaedrus: A Defense of the Philosophical Art of Writing* (University: Univ. of Alabama Press, 1980), which takes up the problem in still more detail.
13. Brownstein, "Plato's *Phaedrus:* Dialectic as the Genuine Art of Speaking," pp. 395–98.
14. Jaeger, "Plato's *Phaedrus:* Philosophy and Rhetoric, pp. 192–94. See Weaver, "The *Phaedrus,*" on this point, also.
15. Black, "Plato's View of Rhetoric," p. 374.
16. Plato, *Phaedrus,* trans. Hackforth, p. 128.
17. Fred N. Scott, "Rhetoric Rediviva," ed. Donald C. Stewart, *College Composition and Communication,* 31, No. 4 (1980), 415.
18. D. Gordon Rohman and Albert Wlecke, "Pre-Writing: The Construction and Application of Models for Concept Formation in Writing," Cooperative Research Project No. 2174, HEW (East Lansing: Michigan State Univ., 1964), 57–58, 124.
19. Albert R. Kitzhaber, "Rhetoric in American Colleges: 1850–1900" (Diss. Univ. of Washington 1953); and Robert J. Connors, "The Rise and Fall of the Modes of Discourse," *College Composition and Communication,* 32, No. 4 (1981), 444–55.
20. Michael Leff, "The Forms of Reality in Plato's *Phaedrus,*" *Rhetoric Society Quarterly,* 11, No. 1 (1981), 22.
21. Ibid., p. 22.
22. Ibid.
23. Winston Weathers, *The Broken Word* (New York: Gordon and Breach, 1981).
24. Ibid., p. 206.

Chapter 9. Issues in Rhetorical Invention

1. Janice Lauer, "Invention in Contemporary Rhetoric: Heuristic Procedures" (Diss. Univ. of Michigan, 1967).
2. Richard E. Young, "Paradigms and Problems: Needed Research," in *Research on Composing,* ed. Charles Cooper and Lee Odell (Urbana, Ill.: National Council of Teachers of English, 1978), pp. 29–47. John Warnock, "New Rhetoric and the Grammar of Pedagogy," *Freshman English News,* 5 (Fall 1976), 12–22; and James Berlin and Robert P. Inkster, "Current-Traditional Rhetoric: Paradigm and Practice," *Freshman English News,* 8 (Winter 1980), 1–4, 13–18.
3. I suggest some criteria for discriminating among exploratory models in "Toward a Metatheory of Heuristic Procedures," *College Composition and Communication,* 30 (Oct. 1979), 268–69.
4. Janice M. Lauer, "Heuristics and Composition," in *Contemporary Rhetoric: A Conceptual Background with Readings,* ed. Ross Winterowd (New York: Harcourt

Brace Jovanovich, 1975), pp. 97–102; and "Writing as Inquiry: Some Questions for Teachers," *College Composition and Communication,* 33 (Feb. 1982), 89–93.

5. In this essay I am concerned only with those texts that include treatments of invention; many texts do not yet do so.

6. James McCrimmon, *Writing with a Purpose,* 7th ed. (Boston: Houghton Mifflin, 1980), pp. 6–7.

7. Frank D'Angelo, *Process and Thought in Composition,* 2nd ed. (Cambridge, Mass.: Winthrop Press, 1980), pp. 6–19.

8. Edward P. J. Corbett, *Classical Rhetoric for the Modern Student,* 2nd ed. (New York: Oxford Univ. Press, 1971), pp. 46–47.

9. Richard E. Young, Alton Becker, and Kenneth Pike, *Rhetoric: Discovery and Change* (New York: Harcourt Brace Jovanovich, 1970), pp. 89–117.

10. Janice M. Lauer, Gene Montague, Andrea Lunsford, and Janet Emig, *Four Worlds of Writing* (New York: Harper & Row, 1981), pp. 21–24.

11. Linda Flower, *Problem-Solving Strategies for Writing* (New York: Harcourt Brace Jovanovich, 1981), p. 21.

12. James Corder, *Contemporary Writing: Process and Practice* (Glenview, Ill.: Scott, Foresman, 1979), pp. 8–24.

13. Ray Nadeau, "Classical Systems of *Stases* in Greek: Hermagoras to Hermogenes," *Greek, Roman and Byzantine Studies,* 2 (Jan. 1959), 51–71.

14. Wayne Thompson, "*Stasis* in Aristotle's *Rhetoric,*" *Quarterly Journal of Speech,* 58 (Apr. 1972), 134–41.

15. Cicero, *De Inventione,* trans. H. M. Hubbell (Cambridge: Harvard Univ. Press, Loeb Classical Library, 1949), I, viii, 10. All further references to this work appear in the text.

16. Harry Caplan, trans., *Rhetorica ad Herennium* (Cambridge: Harvard Univ. Press, Loeb Classical Library, 1954), p. 32.

17. *The Institutio oratoria of Quintilian,* trans. H. E. Butler (Cambridge: Harvard Univ. Press, Loeb Classical Library, 1920), III, vi, 5. All further references to this work appear in the text.

18. *Cicero on Oratory and Orators,* trans. or ed., J. S. Watson (Carbondale: Southern Illinois Univ. Press, 1970), II, xxv. All further references to this work appear in the text.

19. Caplan, trans., *Rhetorica ad Herennium,* p. 32.

20. Thomas Wilson, *Wilson's Arte of Rhetorique,* ed. George Mair (Oxford: Clarendon Press, 1909), pp. 86–87, 108.

21. Walter Ong, S.J. *Ramus: Method and the Decay of Dialogue* (Cambridge: Harvard Univ. Press, 1958), p. 288.

22. Ibid., pp. 291–92.

23. Isidore of Seville, "The Etymologies, II. 1–15: Concerning Rhetoric," trans. Dorothy V. Cerino, *Readings in Medieval Rhetoric,* ed. Joseph M. Miller, Michael H. Prosser, and Thomas W. Benson (Bloomington: Indiana Univ. Press, 1973), p. 84.

24. Alcuin, *The Rhetoric of Alcuin and Charlemagne,* ed. and trans. Wilbur Samuel Howell (Princeton, N.J.: Princeton Univ. Press, 1941), pp. 73–75.

25. Wilson, *Wilson's Arte of Rhetorique,* p. 88.

26. Richard Whately, *Elements of Rhetoric* in the *Rhetoric of Blair, Campbell, and Whately,* ed. James Golden and Edward P. J. Corbett (New York: Holt, Rinehart, and Winston), pp. 311–13, 298–99.

27. Corbett, *Classical Rhetoric for the Modern Student,* pp. 107–8.

28. Young, Becker, and Pike, *Rhetoric: Discovery and Change,* pp. 119–53.

29. William Irmscher, *The Holt Guide to English: A Contemporary Handbook of Rhetoric, Language, and Literature*, 3rd ed. (New York: Holt, Rinehart, and Winston, 1981), pp. 26–42.
30. Gregory and Elizabeth Cowan, *Writing* (New York: John Wiley and Sons, 1980), p. 3.
31. Plato, *Phaedrus* in *The Dialogues of Plato*, trans. Benjamin Jowett, reprinted in Great Books of the Western World, ed. Robert Maynard Hutchins (Chicago: Encyclopaedia Britannica, 1952), p. 140 (277).
32. Donald Bryant, "The Most Significant Passage (for the moment) in Plato's *Phaedrus*," *Rhetoric Society Quarterly*, XI (Winter 1981), 10.
33. George Kennedy, *Classical Rhetoric and Its Christian and Secular Heritage from Ancient to Modern Times* (Chapel Hill: Univ. of North Carolina Press, 1980), p. 64.
34. Richard Enos, "The Most Significant Passage in Plato's *Phaedrus*: A Personal Nomination," *Rhetoric Society Quarterly*, XI (Winter 1981), 17.
35. Thomas Conley, "Phaedrus 253e ff," *Rhetoric Society Quarterly*, XI (Winter 1981), 11–15.
36. Ronna Burger, *Plato's Phaedrus: A Defense of the Philosophical Art of Writing* (University: Univ. of Alabama Press, 1980).
37. William Grimaldi, *Aristotle, Rhetoric I: A Commentary* (New York: Fordham Univ. Press, 1980), p. 2.
38. Ibid., p. 1.
39. Edward Meredith Cope, ed., *The Rhetoric of Aristotle with a Commentary*, rev. ed. (New York: Arno Press, 1973), pp. 1–2.
40. Kennedy, *Classical Rhetoric and Its Christian and Secular Heritage*, p. 25.
41. Forbes Hill, "The *Rhetoric* of Aristotle," *A Synoptic History of Classical Rhetoric*, ed. James Murphy (New York: Random House, 1972), p. 72.
42. Richard Hughes, "The Contemporaneity of Classical Rhetoric," *College Composition and Communication*, 16 (1965), 157–59.
43. Richard Enos, "Words Shimmering on the Surface of the Water: A Reconsideration of Aristotle's Notion of Heuristics," Paper presented at the Conference on College Composition and Communication, San Francisco, Mar. 1982, p. 1.
44. Robert of Basevorn, *The Form of Preaching* (Forma praedicandi), trans. Leopold Krul in *Three Medieval Rhetorical Arts*, ed. James Murphy (Log Angeles: Univ. of California Press, 1971), p. 114–215.
45. Richard McKeon, "Rhetoric in the Middle Ages," in *The Province of Rhetoric*, ed. Joseph Schwartz and John Rycenga (New York: Ronald Press, 1965), pp. 181–83.
46. Wilson, *Wilson's Arte of Rhetorique*, p. 6.
47. Ong, *Ramus*, p. 275. For a list of Ramus' and Talon's works, see Ong, *Ramus and Talon Inventory* (Cambridge: Harvard Univ. Press, 1958).
48. Whately, *Elements of Rhetoric*, pp. 284, 296.
49. Hugh Blair, *Lectures on Rhetoric and Belles Lettres*, in *The Rhetoric of Blair, Campbell, and Whately*, ed. James Golden and Edward P. J. Corbett (New York: Holt, Rinehart and Winston, 1968), pp. 117–19.
50. Corbett, *Classical Rhetoric for the Modern Student*, pp. 108–10.
51. Irmscher, *The Holt Guide to English*, pp. 27, 48.
52. Young, Becker, and Pike, *Rhetoric: Discovery and Change*, pp. 119–35.
53. Corder, *Contemporary Writing*, p. 26.
54. W. Ross Winterowd, *The Contemporary Writer*, 2nd ed. (New York: Harcourt Brace Jovanovich, 1981), p. 57.

55. Lauer et al., *Four Worlds of Writing,* passim.
56. David Harrington et al., "A Critical Survey of Resources for Teaching Rhetorical Invention: A Review Essay," *College English,* 40 (Feb. 1979), 641–61. See also Richard Enos et al., "Heuristic Procedures and the Composing Process: A Selected Bibliography," *Rhetoric Society Quarterly,* Special Issue, No. 1 (1982), 47–54.
57. These responses were made to an unpublished questionnaire that I distributed to colleges and universities in 1980.
58. Grimaldi, *Aristotle, Rhetoric I: A Commentary,* p. 6.
59. Ibid.
60. Ibid., p. 31.
61. Hill, "The *Rhetoric* of Aristotle," p. 29.
62. Ibid., pp. 53–54.
63. Michael Polanyi, *Personal Knowledge: Toward a Post-critical Philosophy* (Chicago: Univ. of Chicago Press, 1958), passim.
64. Wilson, *Wilson's Arte of Rhetorique,* pp. 13–14.
65. Alcuin, *The Rhetoric of Alcuin and Charlemagne,* p. 115.
66. McKeon, "Rhetoric in the Middle Ages," pp. 188–89.
67. Ibid., p. 71.
68. William Grimaldi, *Studies in the Philosophy of Aristotle's Rhetoric,* in *Hermes Zeitschrift fur Klassische Philologie,* 25 (Wiesbaden: Franz Steiner Verlag, 1972), pp. 36–38, 123–35.

Chapter 10. Enthymemes, Examples, and Rhetorical Method

1. This and all subsequent quotations from the *Rhetoric* are from John Henry Freese's translation, *The "Art" of Rhetoric* (Cambridge: Harvard Univ. Press, Loeb Classical Library, 1926).
2. *The Rhetoric of Aristotle,* trans. Lane Cooper (1932; rpt. Englewood Cliffs, N.J.: Prentice-Hall, 1960), p. xxvi. Further references will be cited in the text.
3. Solomon Simonson, "A Definitive Note on the Enthymeme," *American Journal of Philology,* 66 (1945), 303–6.
4. Richard L. Lanigan, "Enthymeme: The Rhetorical Species of Aristotle's Syllogism," *Southern Speech Communication Journal,* 39 (Spring 1974), 207–22.
5. Arthur B. Miller and John D. Bee, "Enthymemes: Body and Soul," *Philosophy and Rhetoric,* 5 (Fall 1972), 201–14.
6. Alan Ross Anderson and Nuel D. Belnap, Jr., "Enthymemes," *Journal of Philosophy,* 58 (1961), 713–23.
7. Lloyd F. Bitzer, "Aristotle's Enthymeme Revisited," *Quarterly Journal of Speech,* 45 (Dec. 1959), 399–408.
8. Chaim Perelman and L. Olbrechts-Tyteca, *The New Rhetoric: A Treatise on Argumentation,* trans. John Wilkinson and Purcell Weaver (Notre Dame, Ind.: Univ. of Notre Dame Press, 1969). See especially pp. 63–110.
9. William M. A. Grimaldi, S.J., *Studies in the Philosophy of Aristotle's Rhetoric* (Wiesbaden: Franz Steiner, 1972), p. 82.
10. William M. A. Grimaldi, S.J., *Aristotle, Rhetoric I: A Commentary* (Bronx: Fordham Univ. Press, 1980), p. 22. Grimaldi is quoting Wallace's essay, "The Fundamentals of Rhetoric," in *The Prospect of Rhetoric,* eds. Lloyd F. Bitzer and Edwin Black (Englewood Cliffs, N.J.: Prentice-Hall, 1971), p. 15.
11. William L. Benoit's very useful "partial bibliography of works on the enthymeme and on the example" reflects the proportion of interest these two terms have

generated among scholars: Benoit lists twenty-two works on the enthymeme and four on the example. "The Most Significant Passage in Aristotle's *Rhetoric*," *Rhetoric Society Quarterly*, 12 (Winter 1982), 7–9.

12. Desiderius Erasmus, *On Copia of Words and Ideas*, trans. Donald B. King and H. David Rix (Milwaukee: Marquette Univ. Press, 1963), p. 67.

13. Sigmund Freud, *New Introductory Lectures on Psycho-Analysis*, trans. W. V. H. Sprott (New York: W. W. Norton, 1939), reprinted in Great Books of the Western World, ed. Robert Maynard Hutchins (Chicago: Encyclopaedia Britannica, 1952), vol. 54, p. 875.

14. Perelman and Olbrechts-Tyteca, *The New Rhetoric*, p. 1, emphasis original.

15. Wayne C. Booth, *Modern Dogma and the Rhetoric of Assent* (Notre Dame, Ind.: Univ. of Notre Dame Press, 1974). Booth's reservations about Aristotle's *Rhetoric* appear on p. 144, n. 3: "the rhetoric of assent is not by any means Aristotelian . . . Aristotle is much too interested in being scientific . . . he seems to say 'Oh, yes, indeed, there are many other forms of proof besides the apodictic proof that scientific demonstration affords, and I will deign to give you a book about them; but isn't it, after all, a pity that it cannot all be done with greater rigor.' "

16. Edward P. J. Corbett, "Some Rhetorical Lessons from John Henry Newman," *College Composition and Communication*, 31 (Dec. 1980), 409 and "John Locke's Contribution to Rhetoric," *CCC*, 32 (Dec. 1981), 432.

17. Edward P. J. Corbett, *Classical Rhetoric for the Modern Student*, 2nd ed. (New York: Oxford Univ. Press, 1971), see especially pp. 72–83.

18. Corbett, "Some Rhetorical Lessons from John Henry Newman," p. 411.

19. *The Nichomachean Ethics*, trans. H. Rackham (Cambridge: Harvard Univ. Press, Loeb Classical Library, 1934), p. 9.

Chapter 11. An Adequate Epistemology for Composition: Classical and Modern Perspectives

1. G. B. Kerferd, *The Sophistic Movement* (Cambridge: Cambridge Univ. Press, 1981), p. 78. For a discussion of Gorgias' relativism, see pp. 93 ff.

2. Ibid., p. 62.

3. See, for example, the discussion by Donald Lemen Clark, *Rhetoric in Greco-Roman Education* (New York: Columbia Univ. Press, 1957), pp. 38–40.

4. William M. A. Grimaldi, S.J., *Studies in the Philosophy of Aristotle's Rhetoric* (Wiesbaden: Franz Steiner Verlag, 1972), p. 18.

5. As had Gorgias; see Kerferd, *The Sophistic Movement*, p. 82. On Aristotle's view of knowledge, see Grimaldi, *Studies in the Philosophy of Aristotle's Rhetoric*, p. 22.

6. Aristotle, *The "Art" of Rhetoric* (I, ii, 13), trans. John Henry Freese (Cambridge: Harvard Univ. Press, Loeb Classical Library, 1926), p. 23. Hereafter cited as *Rhetoric*. This doctrine is associated with the sophist Protagoras; see Kerferd, *The Sophistic Movement*, p. 84.

7. Grimaldi, *Studies in the Philosophy of Aristotle's Rhetoric*, p. 23.

8. Richard McKeon, "Aristotle's Conception of Language and the Arts of Language," *Critics and Criticism: Ancient and Modern*, ed. R. S. Crane (Chicago: Univ. of Chicago Press, 1952), p. 179.

9. *Rhetoric* (II, xxiv, 11), p. 335.

10. This idea is related to Kenneth Burke's "sociology of knowledge." See especially *The Rhetoric of Motives* (1950; rpt. Berkeley: Univ. of California Press, 1969), pp. 197–203 et passim. Burke says, for instance, "A man is necessarily talking error unless his words can claim membership in a collective body of thought." Quoted

by Wayne C. Booth, *Modern Dogma and the Rhetoric of Assent* (Chicago: Univ. of Chicago Press, 1974), p. 86. See Booth's own discussion of "a kind of social test for truth," pp. 101–39. et passim.

11. See Ronna Burger, *Plato's Phaedrus: A Defense of a Philosophical Art of Writing* (University: Univ. of Alabama Press, 1980), especially pp. 70–89.

12. James H. McBurney, "The Place of the Enthymeme in Rhetorical Theory," rpt. in *Aristotle: The Classical Heritage of Rhetoric,* ed. Keith V. Erickson (Metuchen, N.J.: Scarecrow Press, 1974), pp. 128, 122.

13. In addressing the whole person, the enthymeme is not only an element of *logos,* but must embody decisions in the realms of *ethos* and *pathos.* Ethical and emotional arguments will necessarily be based on enthymemes and be persuasive insofar as they connect with shared ethical and emotional assumptions. See Grimaldi, *Studies in the Philosophy of Aristotle's Rhetoric,* pp. 53–67, and McBurney, "The Place of the Enthymeme in Rhetorical Theory," pp. 127–30.

14. Thus Aristotle discusses the unsaid parts of a narrative and of a metaphor in the same way in which he discusses the unsaid parts of an enthymeme, as that which is supplied by the hearer. In this sense, features of arrangement and of style can also be said to be determined enthymematically. *Rhetoric* (III, xvi, 1–3), pp. 443–45; and (III, 4, 1–5), pp. 367–69.

15. See McBurney, "The Place of the Enthymeme in Rhetorical Theory," pp. 132–36.

16. *The Institutio Oratoria of Quintilian* (I, x, 38; II, xx, 7), trans. H. E. Butler (Cambridge: Harvard Univ. Press, Loeb Classical Library, 1920), pp. 179–353. Hereafter cited as *Institutio.*

17. Wayne N. Thompson, *"Stasis* in Aristotle's *Rhetoric,"* rpt. in *Aristotle: The Classical Heritage of Rhetoric,* ed. Keith V. Erickson (Metuchen, N.J.: Scarecrow Press, 1974), pp. 267–77.

18. *Rhetoric* (II, xxii, 4–5), p. 291.

19. Grimaldi, *Studies in the Philosophy of Aristotle's Rhetoric,* p. 118.

20. *Institutio* (III, xi, 21–23), p. 533.

21. I have purposefully paraphrased Kenneth Burke's "Proposition: The hypertrophy of the psychology of information is accompanied by the corresponding atrophy of the psychology of form." *Counter-Statement* (1931; rpt. Chicago: Univ. of Chicago Press), p. 33. Like Burke's "psychology of information," technique is viewed from the writer's perspective, and, like Burke's "psychology of form," inquiry is viewed from the reader's.

22. Aldo Scaglione, *The Classical Theory of Composition from its Origins to the Present: A Historical Survey* (Chapel Hill: Univ. of North Carolina Press, 1972), p. 14. As Richard McKeon has shown, subsequent developments in the history of rhetoric have employed Aristotelian categories only as they were seen through the uses to which Roman rhetoricians adapted them, devoid of Aristotle's larger philosophical context. "Rhetoric in the Middle Ages," *Critics and Criticism,* especially p. 263.

23. Cicero, *De Oratore* (I, xxxii, 146), trans. E. W. Sutton (Cambridge: Harvard Univ. Press, Loeb Classical Library, 1942), p. 101.

24. Frank J. D'Angelo, *A Conceptual Theory of Rhetoric* (Cambridge, Mass: Winthrop Publishers, 1975), p. 2.

25. Gilbert Ryle, *The Concept of Mind* (1949; rpt. New York: Barnes &Noble Books, 1977), pp. 30–31.

26. Polanyi even argues that only those who already know *how* to perform an action

prescribed by a maxim or defined by a pattern will be able to understand the maxim or pattern. See *Personal Knowledge: Toward a Post-Critical Philosophy* (Chicago: Univ. of Chicago Press, 1962), p. 31.

27. W. Ross Winterowd, *The Contemporary Writer: A Practical Rhetoric*, 2nd ed. (New York: Harcourt Brace Jovanovich, 1981), p. 20.

28. Maxine Hairson, *A Contemporary Rhetoric*, 3rd ed. (Boston: Houghton Mifflin Company, 1982), p. 73.

29. Fred R. Pfister and Joanne F. Petrick, "A Heuristic Model for Creating a Writer's Audience," *College Composition and Communication*, 30 (May 1980), 213–14.

30. Walter J. Ong, S.J., "The Writer's Audience is Always a Fiction," *PMLA*, 90 (Jan. 1975), 9–21.

31. Richard Young makes a similar point about any invention exercise which does not begin with "problematic data." "Invention: A Topographical Survey," *Teaching Composition: Ten Bibliographical Essays*, ed. Gary Tate (Fort Worth: Texas Christian Univ. Press, 1976), p. 40.

32. Richard E. Young, Alton L. Becker, Kenneth L. Pike, *Rhetoric: Discovery and Change* (New York: Harcourt, Brace & World, 1970), p. 274.

33. Richard M. Coe, *Form and Substance: An Advanced Rhetoric* (New York: John Wiley & Sons, 1981), pp. 337, 342–43.

34. *Institutio* (XII, xxx, 12). See Samuel Ijsseling, *Rhetoric and Philosophy in Conflict: An Historical Survey* (The Hague: Martinus Nijhoff, 1976), p. 39.

35. For example, Cleanth Brooks and Robert Penn Warren, *Modern Rhetoric*, 4th ed. (New York: Harcourt Brace Jovanovich, 1979), p. 371.

36. Hairston, *A Contemporary Rhetoric*, pp. 332, 334–35.

37. *Rhetoric* (III, xiii, 1–3), p. 425.

38. William J. Brandt et al., *The Craft of Writing* (Englewood Cliffs, N.J.: Prentice-Hall, 1969), p. 23.

39. For further discussion, see my "On the Difference Between Invention and Pre-Writing," *Freshman English News* (Fall 1981), 4–14. See also Young's "Invention: A Topographical Survey," with attention to the role that audience plays in the systems of invention he surveys.

40. Young writes, "if heuristic procedures are to be more than aids for retrieving information, they must be embedded in a process of inquiry which begins with a problem and ends with a tested solution." "Invention: A Topographical Survey," p. 27. He does not include as a possible criterion for measuring the adequacy of heuristic procedures, however, the distinction between problems posed by the writer and problems posed by the writer's audience.

41. It is one's presence in such a situation that leads to what Wayne Booth has called "the rhetorical stance." "The Rhetorical Stance," *Now Don't Try to Reason With Me: Essays and Ironies for a Credulous Age* (Chicago: Univ. of Chicago Press, 1970), pp. 25–34. See also A. M. Tibbetts, "Rhetorical Stance Revisited," *Composition and its Teaching: Articles from "College Composition and Communication" During the Editorship of Edward P. J. Corbett,* ed. Richard C. Gebhardt (Ohio Council of Teachers of English Language Arts, 1979), 67–71. Rather than the sense of commitment that comes from finding oneself in a situation that needs resolving, the term has been used in composition textbooks to stand for the kinds of "adjustments," in tone and technique, that one makes for different audiences. See, for example, Winterowd, *The Contemporary Writer.* pp. 219–20.

42. I have deliberately phrased these "confidences" to resemble the "scientismist," "irrationalist," and "motivist" dogmas analyzed by Wayne Booth as chiefly responsible for the crises in contemporary rhetoric. That crisis consists of a lack of

faith in reason to resolve conflict, and takes many eristic, as well as brutal, forms. The present essay has its origins, in part, from Booth's "view of rhetoric as the whole art of discovering and sharing warrantable assertions." *Modern Dogma and the Rhetoric of Assent,* p. 11.

Chapter 12. Symmetrical Form and the Rhetoric of the Sentence

1. George Kennedy, *The Art of Persuasion in Greece* (Princeton, N.J.: Princeton Univ. Press, 1963), pp. 65–66.
2. *The Institutio Oratoria of Quintilian,* Vol. III., trans. H. E. Butler (Cambridge: Harvard Univ. Press, Loeb Classical Library, 1921), p. 489.
3. Kennedy, *The Art of Persuasion in Greece,* p. 66.
4. Kenneth Burke, *Counter-Statement* (Los Altos, Calif.: Hermes Publications, 1953), p. 46.
5. Ibid., p. 140.
6. Susanne K. Langer, *Mind: An Essay on Human Feeling,* Vol. I (Baltimore: Johns Hopkins Univ. Press, 1967), p. 125.
7. The direction which the field of psycholinguistics has taken supports Kenneth Burke's contention that psychology has replaced metaphysics as a foundation of aesthetic theory. See *Counter-Statement,* p. ix.
8. Fred Attneave, "Symmetry, Information, and Memory for Patterns," *American Journal of Psychology,* 68 (1955), 209–22.
9. Ibid., p. 209.
10. Ibid., p. 220.
11. I have not included in this outline such essential cues to parallelism as "both . . . and," "not only . . . but also," and so forth. Most teachers of composition already recognize, I believe, their significance.
12. In *Artful Balance: The Parallel Structure of Style,* Mary P. Hiatt encourages a broader view of parallelism: "let us no longer insist on 'parallel ideas,' whatever they may be. Let us not jump too hastily at 'faulty' parallelism. Let us become aware of the rhetorical patterns of repetition that add emphasis to parallelism. Let us, in other words, encourage more flexibility in our approach to parallelism and indulge in less didacticism" (New York: Teachers College Press, 1975), p. 9.

Chapter 13. Figures of Speech in the Rhetoric of Science and Technology

1. Carollyn James, "The Gravity of the Situation," *Science 81,* 2 (Dec. 1981), 90.
2. Michael J. Reddy, "The Conduit Metaphor—a Case of Frame Conflict in Our Language about Language," in Andrew Ortony, ed., *Metaphor and Thought* (Cambridge: Cambridge Univ. Press, 1977), pp. 284–321; Robert R. Hoffman, "Metaphor in Science," in Richard P. Honeck and Robert R. Hoffman, eds., *Cognition and Figurative Language* (Hillsdale, N.J.: Lawrence Erlbaum Associates, Publishers, 1980), pp., 393–423.
3. Aristotle, *The Rhetoric and the Poetics of Aristotle,* trans. W. Rhys Roberts and Ingram Bywater (New York: Random House, Modern Library, 1954), p. 166.
4. Quoted in R. F. Jones, *The Seventeenth Century: Studies in the History of English Thought from Bacon to Pope* (Stanford: Stanford Univ. Press, 1951), p. 76.
5. Thomas Sprat, *History of the Royal Society,* ed. Jackson I. Cope and Harold Whitmore Jones (St. Louis: Washington Univ. Press, 1959), p. 112.
6. James Stephens, "Rhetorical Problems in Renaissance Science," *Philosophy and Rhetoric,* 8 (1975), 213–29.

7. Our rough division of the figures into schemes and tropes we take from Edward P. J. Corbett, *Classical Rhetoric for the Modern Student* (New York: Oxford Univ. Press, 1965), pp. 425–48. Corbett defines both classes of figures as deviations from a norm: schemes deviate from "the ordinary pattern or arrangement of words," tropes from "the ordinary and principal signification of a word" (p. 427).

8. Joseph N. Ulman, Jr., and Jay R. Gould, *Technical Reporting* 3rd ed. (New York: Holt, Rinehart, and Winston, 1972), p. 135.

9. Donald H. Menzel, Howard Mumford Jones, and Lyle G. Boyd, *Writing a Technical Paper* (New York: McGraw-Hill Book Company, 1961), pp. 71–72.

10. Waldon Willis, *Better Report Writing* (New York: Reinhold Publishing Company, 1965), p. 156.

11. W. Earl Britton, "What Is Technical Writing?" in W. Keats Sparrow and Donald H. Cunningham, *The Practical Craft: Readings for Business and Technical Writers* (Boston: Houghton Mifflin Company, 1978), pp. 10–11.

12. Paul de Man, "The Epistemology of Metaphor," in Sheldon Sacks, ed., *On Metaphor* (Chicago: Univ. of Chicago Press, 1979), p. 11.

13. James L. Kinneavy, *A Theory of Discourse* (Englewood Cliffs, N.J.: Prentice-Hall, 1971), p. 177.

14. John M. Neale and Robert M. Liebert, *Science and Behavior: An Introduction to Methods of Research* (Englewood Cliffs, N.J.: Prentice-Hall, 1973), p. 2.

15. The story of their discovery, and of subsequent work in the field of molecular biology, is told in Horace Freeland Judson, *The Eighth Day of Creation: The Makers of the Revolution in Biology* (New York: Simon and Schuster, 1979); see also Gunther S. Stent, ed., Norton Critical Edition of *The Double Helix* (New York: W. W. Norton & Company, 1980). For a rhetorical analysis of Watson and Crick's early work, see S. Michael Halloran, "The Birth of Molecular Biology: An Essay in the Rhetorical Criticism of Scientific Discourse," *Quarterly Journal of Speech*, in press.

16. Graham Chedd, "Genetic Gibberish in the Code of Life," *Science 81*, 2 (Nov. 1981), 50.

17. John Pfeiffer and the Editors of *Life*, *The Cell* (New York: Time Incorporated, 1964), p. 68.

18. Walter Gilbert, "Why Genes in Pieces?" *Nature*, 271 (9 Feb. 1978), 501.

19. For example: Francis Crick, "Split Genes and RNA Splicing," *Science*, 204 (20 Apr. 1979), 264–71; Karen E. Mercola and Martin J. Cline, "The Potentials of Inserting New Genetic Information," *New England Journal of Medicine*, 303 (Nov. 27, 1980), 1297–1300; Pierre Chambon, "Split Genes," *Scientific American*, 244 (May 1981), 60–71.

20. J. D. Watson and F. H. C. Crick, "Genetical Implications of the Structure of Deoxyribonucleic Acid," *Nature*, May 30, 1953, pp. 964–67; Watson and Crick, "The Structure of DNA," *Cold Spring Harbor Symposia on Quantitative Biology*, 18 (1953), 123–31. Both papers are reprinted in Stent's Norton Critical Edition of *The Double Helix*; the quoted passages appear on pp. 244 and 267.

21. Gunther S. Stent, "Cellular Communication," *Scientific American*, 227 (Sept. 1972), 43.

22. George Lakoff and Mark Johnson, *Metaphors We Live By* (Chicago: Univ. of Chicago Press, 1980).

23. The story of this episode is told in Judson, *The Eighth Day of Creation*, pp. 318–21.

24. Watson and Crick, "The Structure of DNA," in Stent, Norton edn. of *The Double Helix*, p. 270; Pfeiffer et al., *The Cell*, p. 72; Chedd, "Genetic Gibberish in the Code of Life," p. 53.

25. Hoffman, "Metaphor in Science," p. 405.
26. Richard A. Lanham, *Style: An Anti-Textbook* (New Haven: Yale Univ. Press, 1972), pp. 44–68. Lanham is concerned with the transparent style only as something to be discarded in favor of its opposite, the opaque style. Our own brief for a more abundant use of figures in scientific and technical writing amounts to something similar, though we would be inclined to qualify some of his enthusiasm for stylistic opacity.
27. Philip Rubens, "Testing the Readability of Written Materials," unpublished manuscript, Rensselaer Polytechnic Institute.
28. Kenneth Burke, *Counter-Statement* (1931; rpt. Berkeley: Univ. of California Press, 1968), p. 31.
29. This interpretation of Cicero's theory of style is developed in S. Michael Halloran and Merrill D. Whitburn, "Ciceronian Rhetoric and the Rise of Science: the Plain Style Reconsidered," in James J. Murphy, ed., *The Rhetorical Tradition and Modern Writing* (New York: Modern Language Association, 1982), pp. 58–72.
30. Northrop Frye, *Anatomy of Criticism* (1957; rpt. Princeton: Princeton Univ. Press, 1973), p. 247.
31. This revision of Genesis 1:24–25 was done by Lenora Vesio, in a rhetorical theory course which I taught at the Bell Laboratories facility in Murray Hill, N.J. I gave the class the list of figures of speech in Corbett's *Classical Rhetoric for the Modern Student* (pp. 428–47), and asked them to find examples and/or comment on their usefulness in technical documents of the kind they worked with as writers and editors. They found examples of every one, with the exception of irony. (S.M.H.)
32. John H. Mitchell, "It's a Craft Course: Indoctrinate, Don't Educate," *Technical Writing Teacher,* 4 (Fall 1976), 2–6. Professor Mitchell is a past president of the Association of Teachers of Technical Writing.
33. Cicero, *De Oratore* I and II, trans. E. W. Sutton and H. Rackham (1942; rpt. Cambridge: Harvard Univ. Press, Loeb Classical Library, 1959), pp. 208–11, bk. II, ch. iv.

Chapter 14. Classical Rhetoric and the Basic Writer

1. For a fuller profile of the hopes, dreams, and learning characteristics of the Basic Writers I am discussing, see: Lynn Quitman Troyka, "Perspectives on Legacies and Literacy in the 1980s," *College Composition and Communication,* 33 (Oct. 1982), 252–62.
2. See especially, Frank Smith, *Comprehension and Learning* (New York: Holt, Rinehart & Winston, 1975); *Understanding Reading,* 2nd ed. (New York: Holt, Rinehart & Winston, 1978); "Demonstrations, Engagement, and Sensitivity: A Revised Approach to Language Learning," *Language Arts,* 58 (Jan. 1981), 103–12.
3. Smith, "Demonstrations," pp. 109, 111–12.
4. (New York: Oxford Univ. Press, 1971).
5. (New York: Harcourt Brace Jovanovich, 1975), pp. 265–66.
6. All student work used with permission. Some names changed at the students' request.
7. (New York: Oxford Univ. Press, 1977).
8. *College English,* 40 (Sept. 1979), 38–46.
9. Lynn Quitman Troyka, "Cognitive or Learning Styles and Their Implications for the Composition Classroom," *Proceedings of the City University Conference on Errors and Expectations* (New York: CUNY, 1979); also Troyka, "Legacies and Literacy."
10. Smith, *Comprehension and Learning,* p. 12.
11. Smith, "Demonstrations," p. 109.
12. I am indebted to Lawrence Klein, dean of instruction at City College of San

Francisco, formerly a Basic Writing teacher at St. Louis Community College at Meramec, for making this point strongly in conversations and correspondence with me concerning our mutual interest in classical rhetoric for Basic Writers.

13. *Language as a Way of Knowing* (Toronto: Ontario Institute for Studies in Education, 1977), p. 1.

14. In *Teaching the Linguistically Diverse* (New York State English Council, 1979). See also Edward Anderson, "The Use of Black Folk Tradition in The Teaching of Composition," *Teaching English in the Two-Year College*, 8 (Spring 1982), 221–26.

15. (Boston: Houghton Mifflin, 1977).

16. *Errors and Expectations*, p. 257.

17. Ibid. p. 272.

18. *Basic Writing*, 2 (Fall/Winter 1978), 2–12.

19. Why did Stella write "Too bad he's from Ohio?" She told me that if Corbett lived in New York (where she is a student) she would have been able to thank him in person. My suggestion that she write to him was not accepted; she felt more comfortable talking than writing, she said.

20. Other sources for effective "demonstrations" are discussed in these by Lynn Quitman Troyka: "Legacies and Literacy"; "The Effect of Simulation-Games on Expository Prose Competence" (Diss. New York Univ. 1973) and (with J. Nudelman) *Taking Action* (Englewood Cliffs: Prentice-Hall, 1975); and "The Writer as Conscious Reader" in *Building Bridges Between Reading and Writing*, Marilyn Sternglass and Douglas Butturff, eds. (Conway, Ark.: Language & Style Books, forthcoming).

Chapter 15. Classifying Discourse: Limitations and Alternatives

1. Edward P. J. Corbett, *Classical Rhetoric for the Modern Student*, 2nd ed. (New York: Oxford Univ. Press, 1971).

2. *College Composition and Communication* (hereafter *CCC*), 32 (1981), 444–55.

3. See also Frank D'Angelo, "Nineteenth-Century Forms/Modes of Discourse: A Critical Inquiry," *CCC*, in press.

4. George Bramer, "Like It Is: Discourse Analysis for a New Generation," *CCC*, 21 (1970), 347–55.

5. *CCC*, 22 (1971), 147–55.

6. James Kinneavy, *A Theory of Discourse* (Englewood Cliffs, N.J.: Prentice-Hall, 1971). Kinneavy's taxonomy was originally published in his article "The Basic Aims of Discourse," *CCC*, 20 (1969), 297–304.

7. Frank D'Angelo, *A Conceptual Theory of Rhetoric* (Cambridge, Mass.: Winthrop Publishers, 1975).

8. James Britton, *The Development of Writing Abilities (11–18)* (London: Macmillan Education, 1975), pp. 4–5.

9. James Moffett, *Teaching the Universe of Discourse* (Boston: Houghton Mifflin, 1968). Moffett's system is also available in brief form in "I, You, and It," *CCC*, 16 (1965), 243–48.

10. See especially their essays "The Cognition of Discovery: Defining a Rhetorical Problem," *CCC*, 31 (1980), 21–32, and "A Cognitive Process Theory of Writing," *CCC*, 32 (1981), 365–87.

Chapter 16. Why Write? A Reconsideration

1. Plato, *Euthyphro, Apology, Crito, Phaedo, Phaedrus*, trans. Harold North Fowler (1914; rpt. Cambridge: Harvard Univ. Press, Loeb Classical Library, 1971), 274E–275B.

2. Marshall McLuhan discussed the effect technological change has had on the production of speech and writing in *The Gutenburg Galaxy* (Toronto: Univ. of Toronto Press, 1962), and later argued for the vast changes electronic media seem likely to make in the ways we think about the world in *Understanding Media: The Extensions of Man* (Toronto: McGraw-Hill, 1964) and other works. Jeanne Halpern reported on one of these changes in "Effects of Dictation/Word Processing Systems on Teaching Writing" (paper presented at College Composition and Communication Conference, San Francisco, March 1982), documenting how a number of major companies are composing correspondence using dictation without review. A more general argument about the far-reaching effects of media innovations can be found in Dan Lacy's "Print, Television, Computers, and English," *ADE Bulletin*, No. 72 (Summer 1982), 34–38. For discussions of various implications of electronic technology for writing and the printed word, see *The Future of the Printed Word*, Philip Hills, ed. (Westport, Conn.: Greenwood Press, 1980).

3. For a general review, see Edward P. J. Corbett, "The Status of Writing in Our Society" (paper presented at the NIE Conference on Writing, Los Alamitos, California, June 1977).

4. See D. Gordon Rohman, "Pre-Writing: The Stage of Discovery in the Writing Process" *College Composition and Communication*, 16 (May 1965) 106–12; Ira Progoff, *At a Journal Workshop: The Basic Text and Guide for Using the Intensive Journal Process* (New York: Dialogue House Library, 1975); Janet Emig, "Writing as a Mode of Learning," *College Composition and Communication*, 28 (May 1977), 122–28; Barrett J. Mandel, "Losing One's Mind: Learning to Write and Edit," *College Composition and Communication*, 29 (Dec. 1978), 362–68.

5. James Britton, Tony Burgess, Nancy Martin, Alex McLeod, and Harold Rosen, *The Development of Writing Abilities (11–18)* (London: Macmillan Education, 1975); and James Britton, "Shaping at the Point of Utterance," *Reinventing the Rhetorical Tradition*, Aviva Freedman and Ian Pringle, eds. (Conway, Ark.: L & S Books for the Canadian Council of Teachers of English, 1980), pp. 61–65.

6. David R. Olsen, "From Utterance to Text: The Bias of Language in Speech and Writing," *Harvard Educational Review*, 47 (Aug. 1977), 257–81.

7. Walter J. Ong, S.J., *Rhetoric, Romance, and Technology: Studies in the Interaction of Expression and Culture* (Ithaca: Cornell Univ. Press, 1971), p. 2.

8. "Short-term memory," "working memory," and "active memory" are technical terms that refer to the same phenomena. In *Cognitive Psychology and Its Implications* (San Francisco: W. H. Freeman, 1980), John Anderson explains current theories of memory in psychology and distinguishes the terms in this way: "Short-term memory connotes the transient character of memory. . . . working memory conveys the fact that information is being held for use by mental procedures. . . . active memory implies the fact that the units of this memory are in a special active store" (p. 168).

9. George A. Miller, "The Magical Number Seven, Plus or Minus Two: Some Limits on Our Capacity for Processing Information," *Psychological Review*, 63 (1956), 81–97. More recent work has suggested the number is actually lower, if we insist on totally correct responses; the most current comprehensive statement about short-term memory capacity is offered by Frank N. Demster, "Memory Span: Sources of Individual and Developmental Differences," *Psychological Bulletin*, 89 (1981), 63–100.

10. This example is adapted from G. H. Bower and F. Springston, "Pauses as Recoding Points in Letter Series," *Journal of Experimental Psychology*, 83 (1970), 421–30.

11. Herbert A. Simon, "How Big is a Chunk?" *Science*, 183 (1974), 482–88; rpt. in Simon, *Models of Thought* (New Haven: Yale University Press, 1979), pp. 50–61.

12. D. F. Danserau and L. W. Gregg in "An Information Processing Analysis of Mental Multiplication" (*Psychonomic Science,* 6 [1966], 71–72) argue that units of information in multiplication problems can be figured using a step analysis.
13. For an illustration see Bruce Schlechter's, "The Fine Art of Calculating," *Discover* (Oct. 1981), pp. 34–38.
14. Quoted in L. S. Vygotsky, *Thought and Language,* ed. and trans. by Eugenia Hanfmann and Gertrude Vakar (Cambridge: MIT Press, 1962), pp. 143–44.
15. There are differences, of course, in the ways we remember events and stories, on the one hand, and math sums, on the other, differences of precision of information primarily. The math sums will be remembered exactly, while the details of a remembered event or the exact wording of a tale may vary. But they are similar in ease of retrieval from long-term memory and in the minimal short-term processing they require. See Michael M. Nagler, *Spontaneity and Tradition: A Study in the Oral Art of Homer* (Berkeley: Univ. of California Press, 1974) for a discussion of formulas and themes in oral composing; Albert B. Lord, *The Singer of Tales,* Harvard Studies in Comparative Literature, 24 (Cambridge: Harvard Univ. Press, 1964), for a discussion of the oral composing process; G. H. Bower, J. B. Black, and T. J. Turner, "Scripts in Memory For Text," *Cognitive Psychology,* 11 (1979), 177–220, for a model of research into scripts and what people remember from reading; Ulric Neisser, *Memory Observed: Remembering in Natural Contexts* (San Francisco: W. H. Freeman, 1982), pp. 239–324, for an introduction to research into long-term, or permanent, memory.
16. C. Linde and W. Labov, "Spatial Networks as a Site for the Study of Language and Thought," *Language,* 51 (1975), 924–39.
17. Ibid., p. 927.
18. The spatial memory pattern used corresponds very closely to Simonides' strategy for identifying the victims after the collapse of a building. See Frances A. Yates' *The Art of Memory* (Chicago: Univ. of Chicago Press, 1966) for a discussion of techniques used by this classical mnemonist.
19. Lord, *The Singer of Tales,* pp. 130–32, and Erich Auerbach, *Mimesis: The Representation of Reality in Western Literature,* trans. by Willard R. Trask (Princeton: Princeton Univ. Press, 1953), pp. 3–23.
20. For example, see John D. Gould, "Experiments on Composing Letters: Some Facts, Some Myths, and Some Observations," in *Cognitive Processes in Writing,* Lee W. Gregg and Erwin R. Steinberg, eds. (Hillsdale, N.J.: Erlbaum, 1980), pp. 97–127.
21. John D. Gould, "How Experts Dictate," *Journal of Experimental Psychology: Human Perception and Performance,* 4 (1978), 655.
22. Carl Bereiter, "Development in Writing," in *Cognitive Processes in Writing,* Lee W. Gregg and Erwin R. Steinberg, eds. (Hillsdale, N.J.: Erlbaum, 1980), pp. 87–88.
23. Britton et al., *The Development of Writing Abilities,* p. 35.
24. Quoted in A. R. Luria, *The Working Brain: An Introduction to Neuropsychology* (London: Penguin Books, 1973), p. 31.
25. For example, Janet Emig, "Hand, Eye, Brain: Some 'Basics' in the Writing Process," in *Research on Composing: Points of Departure,* Charles R. Cooper and Lee Odell, eds. (Urbana, Ill.: National Council of the Teachers of English, 1978), p. 62; Nancy Sommers, "Revision Strategies of Student Writers and Experienced Adult Writers," *College Composition and Communication,* 31 (Dec. 1980), 381; Marilyn S. Sternglass, "Creating the Memory of Unheard Sentences," in *Reinventing the Rhetorical Tradition,* Aviva Freedman and Ian Pringle, eds. (Conway, Ark.: L & S Books for the Canadian Council of Teachers of English, 1980), p. 117.

26. Carl Klaus, "Public Opinion and Professional Belief," *College Composition and Communication,* 27 (Dec. 1976), 338.

Chapter 17. The Ideal Orator and Literary Critic as Technical Communicators: An Emerging Revolution in English Departments

1. I am indebted to many of my graduate students for research materials, especially Ellen O'Bryan, David Brenner, Nancy Betz, and Elizabeth Nash.
2. For these and other examples, see George A. Kennedy, *Classical Rhetoric and Its Christian and Secular Tradition from Ancient to Modern Times* (Chapel Hill: Univ. of North Carolina Press, 1980).
3. Marc V. Porat, "The Information Economy" (Diss. Stanford Univ. 1976), p. 1. For an excellent yet brief description of the information society, see Daniel Bell, "The Social Framework of the Information Society," in *The Computer Age: A Twenty-Year View,* ed. Michael L. Dertouzos and Joel Moses (Cambridge: MIT Press, 1979), pp. 163–211.
4. Quintilian, *Institutio Oratoria,* trans. H. E. Butler, in *Readings in Classical Rhetoric,* ed. Thomas W. Benson and Michael H. Prosser (Bloomington: Indiana Univ. Press, 1972), p. 118. Future references to this work will be cited by page number in the text.
5. For my thinking on classical rhetoric and Quintilian, I am especially indebted to Arthur M. Eastman's classes; Edward P. J. Corbett, *Classical Rhetoric for the Modern Student,* 2nd ed. (New York: Oxford Univ. Press, 1971); and S. M. Halloran, "On the End of Rhetoric, Classical and Modern," *College English,* 36 (1975), 1–11.
6. "Areopagitica," in *John Milton: Complete Poems and Major Prose,* ed. Merritt Y. Hughes (New York: Odyssey Press, 1957), p. 728.
7. *A Collection of English Poems: 1660–1800,* ed. Ronald S. Crane (New York: Harper & Row, 1932), pp. 387–89.
8. For elaborations of the ideas in this paragraph, see Arthur O. Lovejoy "The Parallel of Deism and Classicism," in *Essays in the History of Ideas* (1948; rpt. New York: G. P. Putnam's Sons, 1960), pp. 78–98; and Walter Jackson Bate, *From Classic to Romantic: Premises of Taste in Eighteenth-Century England* (1946; rpt. New York: Harper & Row, 1961).
9. In part, the ideas in this paragraph summarize the notion of scientific method found in William Wotton, *Reflections Upon Ancient and Modern Learning* (1964; rpt. Hildsheim: George Ohms, 1968). Wotton's ideas are amplified and confirmed as representative by Edwin Arthur Burtt, *The Metaphysical Foundations of Modern Physical Science* (1924; rpt. New York: Doubleday, Anchor, 1954); Basil Willey, *The Seventeenth-Century Background: Studies in the Thought of the Age in Relation to Poetry and Religion* (1934; rpt. New York: Doubleday, Anchor, 1953); and A. R. Hall, *The Scientific Revolution 1500–1800: The Formation of the Modern Scientific Attitude,* 2nd edition (1962; rpt. Boston: Beacon, 1966).
10. "Science and English Prose Style in the Third Quarter of the Seventeenth Century," in *The Seventeenth Century: Studies in the History of English Thought and Literature from Bacon to Pope* (Stanford: Stanford Univ. Press, 1951), p. 88.
11. In *Eighteenth-Century English Literature,* ed. Geoffrey Tillotson (New York: Harcourt, Brace & World, 1969), pp. 871–89.
12. For extended discussions of the ideas in the last two paragraphs, see Bate, *From Classic to Romantic.* Also, see David Perkins, "General Introduction," *English Romantic Writers* (New York: Harcourt, Brace & World, 1967), pp. 1–24; and Arthur O. Lovejoy, "On the Discrimination of Romanticisms," in *Essays in the History of Ideas.*

13. Robert A. Ward, "The Marriage of Information and Computer Function to Produce Friendly Computer Programs," in *Proceedings of the 29th International Technical Communication Conference* (Boston: Society for Technical Communication, 1982), pp. C99–C101.

14. "The Computer and Technical Communication," *Journal of Technical Writing and Communication,* 11 (1981), 103–14.

15. (Poughkeepsie, N.Y.: IBM, 1980).

16. *Technical Communication,* 29 (1982), p. 4.

17. For a severe criticism of readability formulas, see S. Michael Halloran and Merrill D. Whitburn, "Ciceronian Rhetoric and the Rise of Science: The Plain Style Reconsidered," in *The Rhetorical Tradition and Modern Writing,* ed. James J. Murphy (New York: Modern Language Association, 1982).

18. "The College Course in English Literature, how it may be Improved," *PMLA,* 1 (1884–85), 66.

19. "The Course in English and its Value as a Discipline," *PMLA,* 2 (1886), 66.

20. "The College of Journalism," *North American Review,* 178 (1904), 641–80.

21. "The Organization of Departments of Speech Science in Universities," *Quarterly Journal of Public Speaking,* 2 (1916), 64–77.

22. *Donne: Poetical Works,* ed. Sir Herbert Grierson (London: Oxford Univ. Press, 1933), p. 214.

23. For articles on these developments, see, for instance, Richard E. Young, "Paradigms and Problems: Needed Research in Rhetorical Invention," in *Research on Composing: Points of Departure,* ed. Charles R. Cooper and Lee Odell (Urbana, Ill.: NCTE, 1978), pp. 29–47; and James Kinney, "Classifying Heuristics," *College Composition and Communication,* 30 (1979), 351–56.

24. "Getting Started," *Language and Style,* 13 (1980), 52.

25. "Paradigms as Structural Counterparts of Topoi," *Language and Style,* 13 (1980), 41, 43, 50.

26. "Ciceronian Rhetoric."

27. In *Criticism in America: Its Function and Status* (New York: Harcourt, Brace, 1924), pp. 218, 213–14.

28. René Wellek and Austin Warren, *Theory of Literature* (New York: Harcourt, Brace, 1942). Future references to this work will be cited by page number in the text.

29. *Structuralism in Literature: An Introduction* (New Haven: Yale Univ. Press, 1974), p. 10.

30. *Anatomy of Criticism: Four Essays* (Princeton: Princeton Univ. Press, 1957), p. 7.

31. Scholes, *Structuralism in Literature,* p. 6.

32. Gregory A. Sprague, "Cognitive Psychology and Instructional Development: Adopting a Cognitive Perspective for Instructional Design Programs in Higher Education," *Education Technology,* 21 (1981), 28.

33. Charles B. Kreitzberg and Ben Shneiderman, *Fortran Programming: A Spiral Approach* (New York: Harcourt Brace Jovanovich, 1975); Caryl Richardson, *The Applesoft Tutorial* (Cupertino, Calif.: Apple Computer, 1980); George Stewart, *Getting Started with TRS-80 Basic* (Fort Worth, Tex.: Radio Shack, 1980); and Roger E. Kaufman, *A Fortran Coloring Book* (Cambridge: MIT Press, 1978). I thank Brenda Rubens for bringing these manuals to my attention.

34. *Eighteenth-Century English Literature,* ed. Geoffrey Tillotson, pp. 1072–73.

35. Wayne C. Booth, *The Rhetoric of Fiction* (Chicago: Univ. of Chicago Press, 1961).

36. Arthur Miller, *Death of a Salesman* (New York: Viking, 1949), p. 107.

37. Thanks to Philip Rubens for this idea.

38. "The Historiography of Ideas," in *Essays in the History of Ideas,* pp. 2–3.